New Writings
in the Fantastic

edited by
John Grant

First Published in 2007 by
Pendragon Press
Po Box 12, Maesteg, Mid Glamorgan,
South Wales, CF34 0XG, UK

This Edition Copyright © 2007 by Pendragon Press
Introduction Copyright © 2007 by John Grant
Original Cover Illustration © by Peter Gric

(For individual story copyright, please refer overleaf)

All Rights Reserved

No part of this publication shall be reproduced in any form
without the express written consent of the publisher.

Typesetting by John Grant and Christopher Teague

ISBN 978 0 9554452 3 1

Printed and Bound in the UK by
Biddles, King's Lynn

Story Copyrights

"The Transmissionary" © 2007 by Greg Story
"Cicero's Shame" © 2007 by Toiya Kristen Finley
"An Impeccable Distraction" © 2007 by Bryan Berg
"Encoding the Rose" © 2007 by Andrew Magowan
"Wake Jake" © 2007 by Andrew Hook
"When Bloomsbury Fails" © 2007 by Hugh Spencer
"Channel 18" © 2007 by J. Todd Gwinn
"Permanent Ink" © 2007 by Lisa Silverthorne
"No Second Chance" © 2007 by Paul L Bates
"The Night Bride" © 2007 by Stephen Kilpatrick
"A Simple Gesture" © 2007 by Stuart Jaffe
"Vice Cop" © 2007 by Vincent L. Scarsella
"The Clouds Roll By-hi" © 2007 by Greg Beatty
"Employment Gremlins" © 2007 by Holden Herbert
"The Wishbone" © 2007 by Harry R. Campion
"When . . ." © 2007 by Paul Finch
"Borderline Charm" © 2007 by Paul Pinn
"The Letter Editor" © 2007 by Kim Sheard
"The Jesus Autopsy" © 2007 by M.F. Korn and Hertzan Chimera R.I.P.
"An Incomplete Palindrome Alphabet for Dyslexic Deliverymen" © 2007 by Derek J. Goodman
"Way of Life" © 2007 by Craig Sernotti
"Martin's Walk" © 2007 by Mark Justice
"The Catherine Wheel" © 2007 by Geoffrey Maloney
"Eclipsing" © 2007 by by Edd Vick
"The Career of Edward Northam" © 2007 by Naomi Alderman
"11:11" © 2007 by Jamie Shanks
"A Close Personal Relationship" © 2007 by Thomas Marcinko
"Stray" © 2007 by Barbara Nickless
"The Colonoscopy of My Beloved" © 2007 by Ian Watson & Roberto Quaglia
"Hector Meets the King" © 2007 by E. Sedia
"May Day, May Day" © 2007 by Liza Granville
"Killing Mr. Softly" © 2007 by Scott Emerson Bull
"Raise Your Hands" © 2007 by Gary McMahon
"The Interference from Heaven" © 2007 by Peter Hagelslag
"Babble" © 2007 by Gavin Salisbury
"Reality TV" © 2007 by John Bushore
"The Whole of the Law" © 2007 by Cyril Simsa
"Hot Cross Son" © 2007 by Steve Redwood
"The Ballad of Universal Jack" © 2007 by Vera Nazarian
"Song Cycle" © 2007 by Kate Riedel
"Two Double Beds in a Comfort Hotel" © 2007 by Donna Gagnon

Contents

1 / *Introduction* / John Grant
3 / *The Transmissionary* / Greg Story
12 / *Cicero's Shame* / Toiya Kristen Finley
26 / *An Impeccable Distraction* / Bryan Berg
37 / *Encoding the Rose* / Andrew Magowan
50 / *Wake Jake* / Andrew Hook
58 / *When Bloomsbury Fails* / Hugh Spencer
72 / *Channel 18* / J. Todd Gwinn
76 / *Permanent Ink* / Lisa Silverthorne
87 / *No Second Chance* / Paul L Bates
92 / *The Night Bride* / Stephen Kilpatrick
96 / *A Simple Gesture* / Stuart Jaffe
102 / *Vice Cop* / Vincent L. Scarsella
115 / *The Clouds Roll By-hi* / Greg Beatty
118 / *Employment Gremlins* / Holden Herbert
128 / *The Wishbone* / Harry R. Campion
134 / *When . . .* / Paul Finch
139 / *Borderline Charm* / Paul Pinn
148 / *The Letter Editor* / Kim Sheard
158 / *The Jesus Autopsy* / M.F. Korn and Hertzan Chimera R.I.P.
162 / *An Incomplete Palindrome Alphabet for Dyslexic Deliverymen* /
                         Derek J. Goodman
165 / *Way of Life* / Craig Sernotti
167 / *Martin's Walk* / Mark Justice
184 / *The Catherine Wheel* / Geoffrey Maloney
203 / *Eclipsing* / by Edd Vick
206 / *The Career of Edward Northam* / Naomi Alderman
218 / *11:11* / by Jamie Shanks
223 / *A Close Personal Relationship* / Thomas Marcinko
234 / *Stray* / Barbara Nickless
244 / *The Colonoscopy of My Beloved* / Ian Watson & Roberto Quaglia
250 / *Hector Meets the King* / E. Sedia
253 / *May Day, May Day* / Liza Granville
255 / *Killing Mr. Softly* / Scott Emerson Bull
268 / *Raise Your Hands* / Gary McMahon
274 / *The Interference from Heaven* / Peter Hagelslag
293 / *Babble* / Gavin Salisbury
299 / *Reality TV* / John Bushore
303 / *The Whole of the Law* / Cyril Simsa
316 / *Hot Cross Son* / Steve Redwood
324 / *The Ballad of Universal Jack* / Vera Nazarian
331 / *Song Cycle* / Kate Riedel
354 / *Two Double Beds in a Comfort Hotel* / Donna Gagnon
362 / *About the Authors*

New Writings in the Fantastic
Introduction John Grant

This book comes to you in disguise.

I'll admit, it looks just like an ordinary book, with printed pages, a binding, a cover. In reality, though, thanks to the array of wonderful writers who've contributed stories to it, it should really look like a black, ominous sphere with a spitting fuse sticking out the top of it. It's a cocktail of fictions, all right, just like other anthologies, but this one could have been assembled by Vyacheslav Molotov. If all you're interested in is your own personal safety, you'd better put the book down at once and make yourself scarce.

Somewhere along the line, probably in the 1980s and 1990s, the genre recognized as "fantasy" by many of the mainstream conglomerate publishers and likewise by many of the chain bookstores – whose choices so dominate how we, the public, actually perceive a genre – seemed to lose its teeth: what had once been an intrinsically subversive form of fiction was allowed to become almost uniformly... well, *bland*. Since then there has been a spirited fight back, led by writers who are often British, and rooted to a surprisingly large extent in the small press; magazines like *The Third Alternative* (recently renamed *Black Static*) have also played a significant part. Most of the bigger publishers have heard the clarion, responding – if perhaps a little sluggishly on occasion – to the demands of fantasy readers that their field of literature return to its traditional challenging ways, while in parallel there has been a continuation of the trend whereby fantasy has come more and more to populate the territory regarded as the literary mainstream, with novels like Alice Sebold's *The Lovely Bones*, Susanna Clarke's *Jonathan Strange & Mr Norrell* and Carlos Ruiz Zafón's *The Shadow of the Wind* being granted very large readerships despite being works of fantastication – and that's before we even mention (which we shall not do again) Harry Potter.

So one could say that things have improved a little, or even quite a lot, for fantasy over the past few years. Yet it remains the truth that the vast bulk of fantasy novels issued by the conglomerate publishers – which can be translated to mean "books given a decent marketing/publicity budget" – are of the multi-volume doorstop generic-fantasy variety, the variety that, it can be argued, is less a part of the literature of the fantastic than it is of romance fiction, containing little by way of fresh creative inspiration: if all we're offered are the recycled adventures of the same old, same old sword-wielding guys and gals as they battle goblins, trolls and darklords on their way to gaining their rightful thrones and wedding, or at least bedding, each other, then there's little or no exercise by the writer of the fantasticating imagination. Some of these works can be very good *of their kind*; the pertinent question is, is that "kind" fantasy?

The book you hold in your hands is, by contrast, an attempt to show the full scope of what the literature of the fantastic can do when it isn't being crammed into that preconceived, primarily non-fantastic marketing niche. Some of the authors represented herein are well known; others are at the start of their careers. Some write primarily within the genres of science fiction and horror (both here taken to be subcategories of fantasy) or all across the various areas of the fantastic; others are essentially mainstream writers who share this editor's view that genre pigeonholes are basically artificial constructs which may have some practical use when you're combing a bookshop for something that might interest you but are otherwise designed to be ignored. Some of the stories here I'm certain you'll fall in love with at first sight; others I in a way hope you'll hate, or at least that they'll drive you into a fury, because fantastic literature is frequently at its most exciting when it shakes off the yoke of cosy domestication and becomes uncomfortable, edgy, even outright offensive.

In short, if someone, somewhere, doesn't publicly burn a copy of *New Writings in the Fantastic* I shall feel I've failed in my task. That's the way it should be. Fantasy should arouse strong emotions, whatever the particular emotion might be. That's one of the things fantastic literature is *for*.

Handle with care.

New Writings in the Fantastic
The Transmissionary Greg Story

The glow from the TV's the only light in the room. It stands enshrined in a fiberboard cabinet that covers the wall. Various shelves and compartments house a VCR, DVD, amplifier, disks, tapes, speakers, equalizers and receivers, all of the lesser components surrounding the big screen TV. All exist to serve it.

On the bed against the wall opposite, Frank Nudinee is clicking his way through feeds coming down from the heavens via dual satellite systems. The little dish antenna's right outside the bedroom window on a beam above the carport while the big dish consumes Frank's half of the yard space in the low-rent duplex.

On screen, some crazy Japanese man's skiing down Everest. Frank's seen this film before. Click. Now Hulk Hogan's threatening to tear someone's head off. The show's prerecorded. Maybe Mr. Hogan's already carrying the head around. Click. It's *Wheel of Fortune* and Frank knows the phrase: *To thine own self be true.* Pretty good with just t's, e's and l showing.

"It's not good enough."

Who said that?

"Nothing you do is worthy of me."

That isn't Pat Sajak talking. Vanna wouldn't say such things. She's still smiling sweetly and clapping encouragement.

"If it's all in your mind, why do you imagine such things?"

The question's so on the mark Frank can't picture himself having the clarity to say it, not after this much whiskey and cocaine.

"Well, there's no one else here."

That line's from *Taxi Driver,* isn't it?

"Just once why don't you give something to me?"

"What can I do?"

Frank's shocked by the sound of his own voice. Only crazy people talk to their TVs. But nothing's crazy on TV. Look, there's George Burns as God, capital G. And now cut to a commercial for the Army, *Be all that you can be.*

"Be a monster."

Of course. Frank Nudinee's been training for the role for years. Six hundred and sixty-six (or perhaps six hundred and sixteen) channel changes later a pattern is set. Shoot the Pope, a president, or a pop star. *Who* is not the point. Blow up a plane, a bridge, or a building. It doesn't make a difference so long as cameras are ready. Take hostages. Issue manifestos. Just follow the fucking script.

Ah, but that was in dreamtime. Now it's real time, where it takes five incredible minutes for Frank's coffee to brew. The show starts with the usual wakeup routine. Frank chugs down coffee, throws up, showers, snorts a line of cocaine up his right nostril, gets dressed, and inhales a line up his left nostril. He moves like there's no time to waste. Only he has to stop seventeen times for traffic during the morning commute, and each time he thinks, *This is a dead spot TV would edit out.*

By the time Frank pulls into the parking lot of the TV repair business where he works, the inevitable conclusion has reached him. Dead spots are what separate life from TV. A sadder man yet wiser, Frank quietly proceeds to his work station. He sets out his tools zombie fashion and begins unscrewing the back cover of a Sony Trinitron, all the while contemplating the fundamental shortcomings of reality.

"I'm not having any fun."

Frank's shocked to hear himself say what he'd meant merely to think.

"Poor baby," someone replies.

It has to be Harrison. There's no one else in the back shop. Frank turns around to glare at the technician who's interrupted his internal program. Harrison looks up from the table where he's hunched over the innards of a VCR and gives Frank a robotic grin. Frank imagines erasing it with a hatchet.

"You think you got troubles?" the technician says. "My wife says we need a new car. Have you checked out the prices lately?"

Frank pictures the wife, any wife. She's in a car lot with Cal Worthington, just like a commercial on the Late Show. The pair are riding a rhino named Spot and waving cowboy hats. Frank formulates a response.

"If you buy a car from Cal Worthington, he'll eat a bug," he says.

This gets a laugh even though both men have heard Cal say the line a hundred times on TV, but it isn't a real laugh, just another dead spot signaling a channel change back to work.

Frank points his soldering gun so close to a circuit board that the minute little welds turn to glistening dewdrops of silver on the connector plate.

Fry, you sucker, he says, making sure this time to keep it to himself.

Frank turns on the picture tube of the Trinitron before him and idly razes another panel he's pulled out of the set. His reflection lies still upon the roiling boil of static on screen. His dull gray eyes struggle to comprehend a blizzard of motion that appears random, but may merely be astronomic in scale of sequence. Some of the flashes on screen are remnants of the Big Bang. How can the human mind discern the patterns of a program that's been running twenty billion years? How dare it even try?

"But without us you would not exist."

Has he said that or thought it? Frank cautiously glances around. Harrison is now fiddling with the tone controls of a graphic equalizer, listening to the results through a set of speakers perched near his head. Even across the room, the sound of some rock group going back and forth from tinny to throbbing is so distracting that Frank has trouble hearing the boss calling out to him from the opposite side of the room.

"Frank, will you come in here?"

The way the old man's wearily staring at him through the doorway, Frank figures he's in for another "good God, just look at yourself, man" harangue. In fast jerky strides, his long lanky frame follows the boss out to the front room. A repeat of the boss's last lecture plays in Frank's head. *Your buzz cut's going gray and so are your teeth, Frank. Christ, you look like you're forty, and you're what, twenty-six? Your clothes hang on you like they're still on the rack. I know you been messing with that nose candy, and I can send you to rehab or detox or wherever. The group plan covers it all. I can't afford to lose a technician as good as you. Just tell me what you need.*

How did he respond? Oh yes. "I need the afternoon off. It's Miller Time."

The boss gave him the rest of the day off, too, and Frank spent a long time at home staring into a mirror tracing the red of broken blood vessels that ringed his eyes in delicate networks and flowed down the sides of his nose like some complex schemata.

"You know you could use a tan. This is L.A. It's summer, for Christ's sake," the boss growls.

The two are standing before a triple row of turned-on televisions in the showroom of the electronics store. Though the shop is currently empty, the miniblinds are drawn across the front glass, dimming the room so the pictures on the sets will stand out for customers. The TVs are all showing a startlingly disembodied smile in toothpaste commercial. In the preternatural light from the banks of cathode-ray tubes, Frank can virtually see the boss's skull shimmering through the skin. The bones have their own secret smile, secure in the knowledge their time will come. Frank hopes the boss will get to the point soon, which he does.

"Channel Ten's having trouble with their NavStar Mobile Unit. They're at some groundbreaking ceremony at the County Art Museum, and they can't get an uplink."

That's all Frank listens to because it's all he needs to hear. Those newscast crews don't know beans about maintaining equipment. Frank's already imagining himself telling them, "You don't know beans about maintaining equipment."

"I'll send Harrison up there with you," the boss adds.

"In TV, what goes up doesn't necessarily come back down," Frank says.

"What?" the boss warily asks.

Frank knows better than to engage in such philosophical speculations with a Philistine. He's tried explaining to the man before how TV is not like frail life. Signals can shoot Godlike through infinity at the speed of light.

His comments elicited another harangue about temperance and health from his boss.

"Nothing," Frank mumbles, slinking away.

Returning to his workbench, he grabs his leather satchel containing all the tools he figures he needs, and rushes outside to his van before Harrison can object. Frank insists they take his van because it has a TV built into the dash. The fact that Harrison hates it makes it all the more fun for Frank to watch TV while he drives.

As they head out on the freeway from the Valley to downtown, many channels play through Frank's mind. He first focuses on the groundbreaking ceremony at the county museum. Didn't a dozen stations, perhaps even an unlucky thirteen, show some sort of promo last night? Images are called up in a whirling montage. There's the artist's rendition of the new pagoda-shaped museum. Click. Brief shots of dignitaries planning to attend. Click. The reporter saying, "This is Ken Ohmygoshyou for Channel Ten News."

What was that reporter's name? The newscaster personally called in the emergency-repair order to the shop. Frank's seen the guy a hundred times on the evening news, and the boss just told him the name twice. Quasimodo. Heyoubozo. Something Oriental. Every station in town has an Oriental on staff, and what better place to send them than to the groundbreaking of a museum devoted to Japanese Art. Newsbriefs mentioned all sorts of very important people being there, the mayor, county supervisors, representatives from Japan, local bigwigs. Frank doesn't try to remember any names. Such details never register, besides which he's trying to drive.

And watch TV. An infomercial is showing some contraption both medieval and erotic between Suzanne Somers's thighs.

Time's money. Not even Harrison tries to do things one at a time. Right now Harrison's on the carphone to the NavStar crew trying to determine what the problem is while writing up a work invoice on his laptop. Frank changes the channel to a game show as he exits the Hollywood Freeway headed for the museum complex, occasionally letting the traffic outside grab his attention.

Frank marvels at how well the system works. Cars whiz by like electrons, ceaseless streams pouring down the broad avenue, fed by smaller flows from side streets all the way down to Wilshire. The very smog in the air's testament to the fact most everyone survives.

There's an added aroma of hydrocarbons as they near the art center. The museums adjoin the park containing the La Brea tar pits, into which countless prehistoric beasts once floundered and drowned. Frank recalls a PBS show about how their bones were dredged up from the reeking muck. Cars are double-parked in the museum parking lot, motors running, waiting for someone to pull out of a space. Their exhaust adds to the stench.

Frank does a slow weave around the cars, his left hand on the steering wheel while his right keeps changing channels on the dash TV.

"Hey, wasn't that the Channel Ten News Team?" Harrison asks.

Frank stabs at the control buttons to return to the local news promo. There on the itty bitty screen is Ken Whosahero or whatever his name is. The shot's of the big tar pool with the fake mastodons stuck in it to let the viewers know they're really on location. Ken's to one side of the frame, visible only from the waist up, but still he towers over the concrete replica of a trumpeting elephant in the background.

"Be sure to watch tonight," Ken's telling everyone.

When Frank goes back to watching where he's driving, lo and behold, there's Ken in person, full-frame, walking right in front of the car towards the Channel Ten NavStar van like it was destiny. The promo ends on the TV and the station returns to a syndicated episode of *Walker, Texas Ranger*. Chuck Norris is about to jump a ravine in his pickup. "Go for it," someone tells Chuck, and Frank stomps on the accelerator. There's Ken again, coming in for a close-up. His head slams into the windshield so hard the chin cracks through the glass, and his face adheres there, glued by the shattered mass of blood, tooth and bone.

Frank has the sensation someone hit fast-forward. His Dodge caroms off the NavStar van, neatly tossing Ken's body into the rest of the Channel Ten News crew, who are standing there in a clutch as if waiting to receive it. Harrison's flailing his arms and screaming. All the double-parked cars are peeling out and crashing into each other. A hot-dog vendor shoves his cart through a fence into a tar pool, and Frank – in a move he sees as sublime – flips channels on the tiny TV on the dash while plowing into the crowd assembled on the lawn for the groundbreaking ceremony.

Harrison's shouting beside him. While Frank has never much liked the man, he has to admit Harrison has his dialogue down.

"What are you doing? Are you nuts? You've killed him. Stop it, for God's sake."

The man's emotions are just the right blend of hysteria, revulsion and rage, but Frank can't see a legitimate part for his coworker in this scenario, so he unzips the leather tool-case on the console between them, pulls out a gun, and shoots Harrison point-blank in the face. What's left of Harrison's head does a slow bloody slide down the side window.

Frank's attention is caught by the face on the small-screen TV. It's Oprah. What's she doing on at midmorning and on Channel Ten?

"You can't be watching me. *You're* the show now," she admonishes huffily.

"All right." Frank replies, sadly shutting off the set.

He stuffs a few extra clips of ammo into his windbreaker before exiting the car. The Channel Ten News Team has a minicam pointed his way.

Conscious of the need to avoid dead air, Frank shoots at somebody, anybody. He empties the whole fucking clip into the screaming mob of dignitaries trying to flee the scene. Bodies lie sprawled along shady walkways in strange and still contortions.

Mobs of people are running from Frank toward the big tar pool with the fake mastodons stuck in it like giant lawn ornaments. The gates of the chain-link fence surrounding the black bubbling pond have been left open by camera crews who've set up at the far end on a rise. People are diving headfirst into the tar trying to escape. They're swimming in goop toward half a dozen cameras. Frank wants to see how all this plays, and so turns back toward the NavStar van.

"Okay buddy, inside," he says to the Channel Ten man standing beside the van.

At Frank's approach, the guy shifts from shooting the scene with his minicam to staring dumbly down the barrel of a gun. Frank must repeat the command and wag his pistol toward the open side door to get the cameraman to move. The two of them squeeze into the van, crammed alongside umpteen thousand dollars worth of video gear.

Frank finds the haphazard layout of components appalling. No wonder they were having trouble getting an uplink. The cord from the transponder to the portable dish on the roof has been carelessly strung along the metal floor of the van underneath racks holding heavy equipment.

"You don't know beans about maintaining equipment," Frank shouts as he replaces the cord with a spare loop that hangs on the wall.

He doesn't even have to put down his gun, the job is so easy. The digital readout on the transponder shows it is now ready to transmit. Frank makes a mental note to charge two hundred bucks plus mileage.

"Let's see what you got," Frank says to the cameraman, who is now crouched on the floor near the rear, cradling his minicam.

"What?"

"The cassette. Play it."

Frank has to pull the tape out of the minicam himself and insert it into the VCR. Whimpering and gibbering, the cameraman proves his professionalism by loading a new tape into his camera. Frank rewinds the old tape to where the cameraman panned toward Frank's speeding car as it slammed into Ken.

"You jerk! I'm not even in the shot!" Frank shouts.

The monitor, piggybacked like God the Father above the twin screens of an editing bay, shows nothing but a brilliant glob of light where Frank should be. The cameraman focused on the windshield, catching the morning sun. The glare erased Frank.

"Mister, you best get it right this time," Frank says in a bad imitation of Eastwood.

Using his pistol first as a pointer, then as a prod, Frank marches the man with the minicam down toward the big tar pool. A line of police are scrambling up the slope toward them, shouting out cop clichés.

"Stop or we'll shoot!"

"Put down your weapon!"

"Drop the gun and put your hands in the air!"

Frank steps behind the cameraman, using him as a shield.

"Now, do your job," Frank whispers in the man's ear.

Keeping the gun aimed at the cameraman's head, Frank walks around in front of the camera. Half a dozen cops are advancing slowly, crouching, with guns drawn and aimed. There's now no way for Frank not to be broadcast. He's between the minicam and the cameras on the knoll recording the event.

"All right, that's enough. I want to check who's picking up the feeds," Frank says to the NavStar man, using the gun to motion him to turn around.

They start toward the parking lot. Too late, Frank realizes he's not only taken his eyes off the cops but the gun off the cameraman. Shots ring out, but Frank isn't hit. It's the cameraman who takes three slugs in the back and falls to the ground, flopping like his last aim in life's to hump a minicam.

Frank sprints back toward the NavStar van, bullets whizzing around him. He jumps inside the vehicle and slams the side door shut before realizing that two members of the Channel Ten News Team are sitting in the front seats. The blonde lady and the black man appear paralyzed. Now that Ken and the cameraman are dead, Frank realizes this pretty much constitutes the remainder of the News Team. It galls him that the only significant member missing is the white anchorman, who won't lower himself to go on location. What's worse is the way these two supposed pros are babbling for mercy. They sound like static.

"Get hold of yourselves," Frank shouts as he flits through channels on the receiver.

He's trying to find a station broadcasting the event, but, given the odd angles in the close confinement of the van, it isn't so easy to keep one eye on the monitor, the other on the people in the front seat, and fiddle with a set of controls while holding a gun. He ends up flitting by sitcoms, soap operas, and a whole lot of commercials.

"Try Channel Ten," the blonde lady suggests.

Frank punches in the numbers and, sure enough, the station's carrying the art museum slaughter live. A stunningly handsome silver-haired man is exclaiming, "We don't know how many people are dead," as the shot shifts to some nice footage of people floundering and drowning out in the tar pool. Then there's a few seconds of the police blasting away, and a neat cut to the cameraman falling on top of his camera.

So why isn't Frank in the picture?

"You. Get back here."

Frank's motioning to the blonde. The black guy's too big for comfort. Frank ends up having to shoot him just to get the lady moving.

"What the hell is this?" he asks, pointing the gun at the monitor.

He can feel the woman tremble as she settles beside him. The screen's showing a slow-motion replay of the cops shooting and the cameraman falling.

"A TV?" the woman says.

"Dizzy dame," Frank mutters, and now the goddamn cops are back with their goddamn clichés.

"Throw out your weapon and come out with your hands up!"

Wouldn't the whole damn world be let down by an ending like that?

"You're completely surrounded! This is your final warning!"

Sure, as if the cops are about to start giving him the silent treatment. Through both the front and rear windows, Frank can see them scampering around the van. There's a whole herd of them. He's still trying to get a fix on what's happening with the picture on the television.

"I know it's a TV," he says as patiently as possible. "But how could they edit me out of the picture so fast? Why would they want to?"

The woman's sobs produce a reflex pang of pity in him. Makeup's streaming down her face. Will she pull it together for the big finale or look like hell coast-to-coast?

"I don't know, I don't know," the woman wails.

Frank switches over to another station, and there's the scene again from another angle. The Channel Ten minicam operator is collapsing over his camera, and Frank's nowhere to be seen.

"Is this real?" he asks.

"It's TV," the woman cries.

"What's the difference?"

Did he say that aloud or just think it?

They're now showing a close-up of the cameraman getting hit in the back. Frank leans forward, staring at the shocking impact of the bullets. Knowing where he stood behind the man, Frank realizes there's no way those shots could have missed him. They must have passed right through.

"Please, God, just let me live," the woman pleads.

"You're on television. You're already immortal," Frank replies.

And I'm already dead and gone, he adds to himself. The proof lies right outside the van. Frank slides open the door. A dozen cops are formed up like a team photo, aiming their guns inside the vehicle. He steps outside, still holding the gun, and nonchalantly gazes around to see where the cameras are positioned.

"Shoot him! Shoot him!" he can hear the woman screaming.

He turns back to glance at her. Her face seethes with fury. It's a good look on her. She'll get a big new contract out of this, Frank's sure.

"Where is he? Where'd he go?" the cops are all yelling.

"You're the last person who'll see me," Frank whispers to the woman.

"What?" she replies.

The way she's leaning forward to listen will give a thrilling shot of cleavage to the telephoto lens taking this in from the museum terrace.

"Anything's possible when you're part of the program," Frank tells the woman.

En masse, the cops charge the van. Half of them tumble inside; a good comic ending, especially if the director is savvy enough to segue to a longer shot of the whole van swaying to one side.

"Don't feel bad when they don't believe you. They aren't supposed to," Frank shouts out to the woman.

He wonders whether she can hear him under that shouting squirming cop pile. He waves bye-bye and walks toward the distant crowd of spectators, who're anxiously peering in his direction over the police lines, yet see him not.

There's so much to do Frank doesn't know quite where to begin. A politician eviscerated before a podium by invisible hands? A big bank heist pulled off in broad daylight? No, there has to be carnage, a shooting – mass shootings – and fantastic explosions with buckets and buckets of blood – "acres and acres," as Cal Worthington would say.

Frank remembers the words of a more profound American icon. Raising his arms to the leaden sky where satellites wander, he shouts in a thunderous voice no one can hear:

"Free at last! Free at last! Thank God Almighty, we're free at last!"

New Writings in the Fantastic
Cicero's Shame Toiya Kristen Finley

i

Water dripped in shadows from the railing and the fire escape, falling to the street below in a steaming river. Mist hissed and billowed from the asphalt. From a nearly starless sky, the rain fell in the dark street. Dexter sat before the window – the glass between him and the night the only protection from the heat – and listened to the rain cut the air.

The dark of the room surrounded him in a vacuum, pressed at his back and enveloped his body. Soft, hollow light emanated from the corners of the glass panes, and he watched his reflection in the window. Bothered by the fire in his belly, Dexter waited for Talen. He loved having a half-Cypriot, half-Lebanese girlfriend. He loved the wide almonds of her eyes. But Talen was just a replacement. If Connie wouldn't have him, the eager body of her best friend would have to do.

In the bottom right pane, Connie walked toward the bus stop. That black girl with the Indian hair, braid hanging limp under the weight of the rain, vapor rising from beneath her footsteps. Her parents would worry, she said, if she didn't get back to Orlando soon. Connie's parents didn't like her to hang around campus on weekends, especially since Angela was murdered. But Connie had to check on Dexter before she left.

"Don't hold on to the violence so much," she'd told him.

"I'm not violent," Dexter said. *"Where'd you get that idea?"*

"The Spirit showed me."

So innocent when she made claims like this, her eyes wide with the amber blazing behind her pupils. Dexter couldn't deny she tapped into something. He could feel rumblings underground when she talked – the shed blood of innocents coursing through the soil and shocking him with little tremors.

"So, God told you?" Dexter tried not to smile. *"Don't you feel what's underground, Connie?"*

She nodded. *"Anger and hatred."*

"Slave and Indian blood," he said.

"And the blood of those murdered on the street every day," she said. *"What do slaves and Indians have to do with it? You feel it 'cause that same violence is running through you."*

"I'm not connected to any violence."

Dexter's stomach was on fire, and he exhaled heat. Just once he wished Connie had held him, told him she'd do anything to help him. The muscles in his thighs tightened.

Connie said she could feel the violence and anger in him. It made her skin itch. He wondered if she felt the same thing in Angela. But she would never talk about Angela, and Connie walked away in the downpour.

He'd seen Angela only twice. The second time, on a Saturday night, Talen had dragged him to a party in a cramped bar. She went to get them drinks, and Angela stood not far behind her in line. A pixie girl, a wiry coquette who'd glared at him the day before in front of the Administration Building. When Angela moved forward in the line, she caught Dexter spying. He thought they'd revisit what happened the day before, but she smiled and approached him.

Dexter asked if she remembered him, and Angela cocked her head. Feathery hair fell over her eyes. Nothing like the fierce thing he had witnessed Friday. She shifted her weight, brushed her foot against his. Silver bangles, about six or seven on each arm, clinked together and twirled around. "Do I know you?"

"Don't you remember yesterday, when you were talking to Connie?" he asked.

"Oh, you know Connie?" She smiled and placed strands of hair behind each ear. The bracelets rolled down her arms. "No, I don't remember you."

Almost a convincing performance, but she had to have seen him. From the way she had studied him, she should have known every pore on his face.

"Do you wanna dance?" she asked.

He hated dancing, but he would with her, just to find out what game she played. Angela pressed herself against him. He couldn't back away – the space was too tight, like he was dancing with everyone on the floor. Her smile widened into a grin, lips thinning into groping snakes. She wrapped her arms around him and gyrated her hips against his thighs. Dexter grabbed her shoulders and butted her leg with his knee. She laughed.

"You're shy." She pressed her cheek against his chest.

Dexter dropped his hands at his sides. "How do you know Connie?"

"I don't wanna talk about Connie."

He didn't respond, and she danced against him.

"Damn it," Dexter said through his teeth. He threw down her arms.

She smirked and returned to the bar.

Sunday morning, Angela smiled up at Dexter from the front page of the newspaper. Her body had been found in a dumpster.

That Monday, he entered the lecture hall, bombarded by horrified and excited whispers. Dead girls discovered in small college towns were always big news. Connie didn't seem to hear any of it. She gave Dexter the usual cheerful hello. He wanted her to cry hysterically so he could reach for her shoulder, sift that thick hair through his fingers.

"I'm sorry about Angela," he said.

But she didn't cry. Her jaws worked hard on a piece of gum. After hearing bloody Angela story after bloody Angela story from everyone else, Connie slouched back in her chair, rested her feet in the seat in front of her. She looked at Dexter, surprised, and the amber-gold burned behind her deep brown eyes. He wanted to reach out and pull at it. Watch the flames leap from his fingers.

"Why are you apologizing?" She wasn't angry or hurt.

"She was a good friend of yours," and his stomach burned.

Connie looked away from him. Her shoulders lurched, almost like a shrug. "I don't know if I would call her a friend. I worked a lot with her."

"What I saw Friday, was that working?"

"By 'working,'" she said, "I mean 'ministering.'"

"Ministering?" The burning distended throughout his chest, made his nose run. He rubbed his eyes. "You play priest in the Confessions booth? What was Angela's secret sin?"

"Even if I wanted to tell you, you're not ready to handle that yet."

"'Yet'? Reverend Constance, you're being a little nonchalant about this."

She wrote in her notebook. "What do you mean?"

"You were counseling this girl, and now she's dead."

"My job is to warn them, Dexter. It's not my responsibility whether they listen or not. I'm sorry she's dead, but I have to move on."

He laughed, half out of embarrassment. "Move on? Are you on some kind of journey?"

"Yes."

ii

Connie and Talen came to Dexter before he'd ever seen them in the flesh. In a dream elevator, the doors stood open even after he'd started to descend. He stared at a formal affair he'd just left, men and women in expensive suits and gowns wrapping themselves in catty conversations. Two girls walked up to the elevator shaft – one in red, the other in black. Mirroring one another's stances, they parted their legs just enough to be suggestive. With their olive and caramel arms hanging in sleek S-curves at their sides, they turned their bodies towards each other and looked down at him. A pair of *kore* figures, stony and unmovable, with sculpted black hair and identical flirtatious smiles painted on their mouths. The elevator doors closed, and in the metal reflection Dexter's face paled. His eyes opened, and he couldn't remember where he was going.

Connie materialized in Dexter's waking life first. He was crouching in the corner of a short hallway waiting for the Psychology lecture, and a black girl with Indian hair walked down the hallway. Nothing special about her. No makeup on her face. Nothing unusual or attractive, except for the neon green sunglasses perched on top of her head. He stared at her, even when she was aware of it. She looked past him and peeked through the small window in the door.

"There's nobody in there," she said, and he wanted to chastise her for stating the obvious. He tried to open his mouth, but it was frozen with the sarcasm stuck behind his teeth.

Dexter hadn't intended to follow her into the room, but he did anyway. He sat next to her, hoping she wouldn't think him strange, wouldn't think he was some stalker. He watched her profile from the corner of his eye, attracted by that amber glow hiding behind her pupils. It sparked something deep in his stomach, a heat that climbed up into his chest and left him panting. Every Monday and Wednesday after that, he took his place next to her, said very little as she complained about Chemistry and Trig, watched her meet up with Talen after class. Every Monday and Wednesday, Connie gave him an innocent goodbye. Talen studied his face, his chest, his legs, and gave him a smirk.

Talen's eyes were elegant like the half-moons on the faces of kings and queens gracing the walls of Egyptian tombs. Talen talked with her hands, hypnotized him with those hands moving in circles until he fell into her arms, and she slept in his bed.

Talen's palm rested on the small of Dexter's back as if the hollow space had been made to fit the shape of her hand. Her fingers kneaded his back, traced his spine, danced along his shoulderblades. Her eyes fluttered, and Dexter watched her slip into sleep. But, as her body grew heavy next to his, Dexter's stomach was filled with the fire Connie had lit before she left.

"Doesn't all that God stuff get on your nerves?" he said.

Talen flipped on her back and rubbed her eyes. "Are you still worried about that? I'm just glad I didn't run into her on the way here. I would've gotten a lecture."

"Yeah, that's what I'm talking about. She has no right to force those crazy beliefs on us."

"I called God once and left a message on his answering machine. He never got back to me, so I don't believe Connie, and you shouldn't let her bother you either. Look, she's got a psychic gift, and every now and then she picks up some vibe." Talen cupped her face in her hands and laughed. "I don't know who you think is crazier. Her, or me for believing she's got a gift."

But didn't Talen see that glow hiding behind Connie's eyes? Always waiting to surface at the right moment. One look from Connie, and Dexter walked around all day with sparked coals buried in his gut. Easy for Talen to tell him not to let Connie bother him – easy when Connie didn't spin ominous interpretations on Talen's dreams in that calm voice. He should never have told Connie his *kore* dream. But Connie had only had to smile at him and he'd told her about the formal occasion, the pretty girls standing over him with their slender snake arms and smooth legs.

"That's it?" Connie had asked.

"It's enough."

"Why were you descending?"

"What?"

"Why were you descending, in the elevator?"

It wasn't her right to take control like that. He had to tell her who she was, that she was one of those women.

"What about the girls?" he asked.

"Do you know them?"

"I think they're you and Talen." The bubbling in his stomach subsided, spread in a dim chill throughout his chest cavity. *"You're the only two women I've really had any contact with since I had the dream."*

She nodded, not enthusiastically, but as if she would consider this. *"But they could also represent parts of you. And why were you descending in the elevator?"*

"Maybe it has nothing to do with anything." This dream was not about elevators, descending or ascending. Doors closing. It was about her and what she was doing to him. *"It was just a dream."*

"Doesn't mean anything then?" Gold blazed behind her pupils.

Dexter's tongue burned. *"No. It was just a dream. It doesn't have to mean anything. It could mean five million things, none of 'em important."*

"Ah, I see you belong to Cicero's School of Dreaming."

Dexter cocked his eyebrows.

"He'd say the same," Connie said. *"That dreams, in the end, don't really mean anything, that interpreting them is about as significant as picking belly-button lint. Why tell me the dream at all?"*

Talen slept, a little pool of sweat collecting on her top lip, her mouth falling open. Her arm brushed against his side, and Dexter wondered if the heat burning his skin would wake her. No, nothing Connie said should bother him. She had crazy ideas about spirits and dreams, how they seduced and intoxicated the mind. But then there was Angela. Angela Before, and Angela After.

Angela Before had worried Connie. Two girls stopped Connie and Dexter on the street the Friday before Angela died. The first girl's forehead creased and covered her deep-set eyes. She bit her bottom lip just enough to keep it from quivering. She was Italian or Hispanic – no one really knew who anyone else was these days. The other girl gripped the purse strap draped over her shoulder to calm her shaking hand.

The amber behind Connie's eyes dimmed. The corners of her mouth melted into a delicate frown. "Where is she?"

"Right in front of Administration." The Hispanic girl tugged at Connie's sleeve and the three of them left Dexter on the sidewalk.

He was curious about this girl who had taken Connie away from him, who could put a sense of worry in her when his descending in an elevator couldn't. He'd trailed after Connie, and she turned her head to see him approach the Administration Building. She talked to Dexter's competition and continued talking even while taking the moment to watch him. Connie leaned against the building with a shoulder slouched against the wall and one leg crossed over the other. The sadness had left her face, and she returned to that casual attitude that frustrated him. Her friends stood behind the new stranger, their hands pressing the shoulderblades of a petite blonde against the wall. Angela looked at him, sharp nose and square chin foreign on her small face. Her pupils locked onto his and shivered, pinpoints humming and blurring. Dexter didn't understand what response she dared out of him as she searched his face. But when he stared at her – tried to evoke the same fury in his eyes that burned in his stomach – Angela smiled. She looked at Connie again and kicked at the Hispanic girl.

Angela After was sane and horny, but in control. The very next night, Dexter had seen her in the bar. She said she didn't remember seeing him standing outside of the Administration Building. Downplayed her relationship to Connie. In Connie's presence she was wild. In the bar, she was a normal dumb, drunk freshman. Didn't make sense.

Connie. Dexter sighed, wishing that arrogant virgin Connie, not Talen, slept next to him.

Dexter sat in the dark and massaged his temples. Behind him the constant rain splattered against the living-room windowpanes. The heat Connie lit continued to gnaw at his insides, and he wondered if she put it there on purpose. Something rumbled underground, breathed on the fire in his stomach. Connie didn't care about him at all, wanted to see how far this experiment would go. She was so patient, so patient when she brought her warning. So loving. So worried. But there was no fear in her eyes, no anxiety in her voice. Just the steady burning in her pupils and the coals shifting in his stomach. And, when she walked away in the rain, every inch of her body drenched, steam from the agitated underground rose beneath her feet. Her legs moved swiftly in the pride of a job well done. Mission accomplished. Heat climbed the insides of Dexter's thighs.

Light slipped underneath the bedroom door. Talen came into the living room, and Dexter jumped. She stared at him for a moment with a curious smile. Shadows of raindrops fell on her cheeks.

"Are you going now?" he asked.

She frowned. "Do you want me to?"

"No. I was just wondering." But she did have her own room, somewhere to live.

"I gotta pee. What are you doing? It's three in the morning."

Talen wasn't the type of person Dexter confided in – he wasn't sure what type of person that was. But she was here now when he was afraid of what Connie had planted in him.

"Do you remember Angela Alexander?" he asked.

"The girl who got killed?"

"Yeah. She was good friends with Connie."

"I don't know about 'good friends.'" Talen turned toward the bathroom.

"Well, Connie was supposed to be helping her. I saw Connie with that girl – it was scary, nuts. Angela's eyes were shaking like she was some kind of animal, but when I saw her in the bar she was totally normal. Only, with Connie—"

"Dexter, what are you saying? I told you I gotta pee."

"Maybe you don't feel it, but I do." Underground, the blood was agitated. Blood spilled by conquistadors and slave owners, it had slept beneath the surface for so long. But now Dexter could feel its anger. "Doesn't Connie have some Indian in her?"

"You know, you're too obsessed with that, always asking people what they are."

"But listen – she looks like she has Indian in her. So many Indians and Africans suffered in Florida. Their blood was shed here, and they're angry. That same blood's in Connie. Maybe that's why she's so spiritual. Maybe that's how she got that crazy reaction out of Angela."

"Honey, you're not making any sense." Talen patted him on the head. "You're telling me she's getting some weird power from the blood of her ancestors? That's a dangerous assumption, isn't it?"

"Then what am I feeling?"

Talen climbed into his lap and gave him a soft kiss on the mouth. "I don't know, but why don't you get back in bed, and I'll take care of your problem? Just give me a few seconds."

Dexter wanted to shove her to the floor, but he let her do whatever she wanted.

iii

Monday brought a wave of humidity that sucked the breath from Dexter's mouth. He had spent the weekend thinking of Connie, dreaming of Connie, of slender arms from statues caressing his cheeks. The flesh underneath his eyes sagged. The heat she'd sparked in his belly rested down around his thighs. He'd started to walk home, hoped to collapse in his bed, but he kept on past his building. Something underground pulled him along. With every step he took, a footprint beneath the concrete – beneath the soil – pressed against his sole.

Dexter walked an incline where the illusion of the sun's rays danced above the street and writhed like vipers. The sidewalk ended, and he stumbled into a drainage ditch. His feet disturbed loose gravel and concrete and raised dust clouds. A magnet pull, the mirroring steps underground held him in place. Choking him, the fire in his stomach and groin lifted up through his chest, a heavy serpent worming its way through his throat. The magnet pull underground released him, and he fisted tears from his eyes.

Dexter stumbled into a neighborhood of perfect shoebox houses with plush lawns and dogs in the backyards. He sighed and wiped his forehead. The water ran down his wrist. Two little girls sitting in their front yard dug at the lawn with plastic shovels. The sun reflected off their black hair and burned on their skin where the dress straps didn't protect them. Their faces were fat and round in youth. They gazed at him with the brazen curiosity of watching a stranger. Dexter realized, looking behind their beady black stares, that he had stopped a few feet away from their yard. As soon as he stepped onward, they turned their heads and played with their little shovels as if he had never been there. If they didn't fill in the holes, he thought, the morning would bring up seawater and blood.

The neighborhood ended at an abandoned convenience store. Something weighty bore down on Dexter. Unseen eyes studying, poking and probing. The matching footsteps had risen up from the ground and manifested into something else. It pinched his Adam's apple and grabbed his throat, although he felt no trace of hands. Then the presence ran down his shoulders and caressed them. Dexter's muscles jerked and his shoulders buckled forward. The presence walked him through weeds up to his armpits. On the broken asphalt, glass cracked under his feet.

Invade her mind. Invade her mind like she invaded yours.

The words echoed deep within his gut. A love song, a healing kiss. His muscles relaxed and air rushed into his lungs. He headed home, and the presence rode upon his steps.

That night, Dexter dreamed of the abandoned convenience store. A dream in silence, it was the first he'd had without colour. The sky was grey and overcast. Talen and he fought for some dumb reason. A screaming match until tears streamed down Talen's cheeks. Maybe he told her he didn't love her. Maybe she figured out he'd never want her like he wanted Connie. Connie stood in the weeds, and, when Talen started to cry, Connie yelled at Dexter too. He laughed, looked back at her, and pointed at Talen. The tension left Talen's face, and now she pleaded with Dexter. But the more Connie yelled, the angrier he became. He grabbed Talen by the collar and threw her to the broken asphalt. For a moment he and Connie were both stunned. Connie ran up to him and slapped him. Talen, with her face in the glass, didn't move. Dexter and Connie knelt beside her, and Connie took her by the shoulders and turned her on her back. Talen's eyes fluttered open and closed. A red stain spread across her abdomen and underneath her breasts. A deep green fragment of a beer bottle lodged within her belly.

"Ah, what the hell?" Talen sat up in bed, poked Dexter with her elbow.

Dexter, disinterested, grunted in response.

"Something bit me." She lifted up her T-shirt and scratched her abdomen. Dexter lifted her hand out of the way, petted her smooth stomach. The scar had already started to scab over.

iv

Connie showed great concern for Talen's scratch, more concern than she ever displayed over Angela – or Dexter. When Talen had to leave the dining hall for class, Dexter was pleased.

"I had a dream last night. Really disturbing dream too," Connie said, "but I have no idea what happened. Type of dream I know I should have remembered, but I can't."

Dexter stuffed a spoonful of banana pudding in his mouth and sloshed it around his tongue to keep himself from smiling. Connie's eyebrows pressed down over her eyes. If only she looked that way when she talked about all of those problems she imagined for him, they wouldn't be going through this now.

"I think I know what you dreamed," he said.

"You, Cicero?" The amber burned behind her eyes. She grinned. "You don't care about dreams."

"No, that's not what I said." He patted her hand, and Connie's fingers twitched under his palm. Her grin faded into a polite smile, and she pulled her arm away from the table. Hid her hand in her lap. "I just said dreams can have a million interpretations, and none of those interpretations are really important," Dexter said.

"So, then, tell me what I dreamed. Tell me how you know." Connie sat back from the table now, almost staring him down.

"Maybe I connected with you the way you say you connected with me. Maybe I see beneath your surface now. You were having a fight with Talen in an abandoned parking lot. I don't know why you were fighting – there was no sound. But you got really upset, and you pushed her down. She didn't get back up, and, when you kneeled to help, you realized she'd gotten cut on a shard of glass. Right in the stomach."

Connie nodded – not in agreement. In meditation. "Did she die?"

"I don't know," Dexter said. "Did she?"

The girl's purple-black pupils swelled, and on the film of her eyes Dexter saw two delicate images of Talen and Connie, their faces a breath away from each other, mouths baring teeth like rabid dogs. Then one pushed the other, stood defiant, and waited for the counterattack. When there was no response, Connie fell to the ground, shook Talen. But Talen didn't move.

Connie's pupils contracted. The amber enveloped them until her eyes glowed yellow, and a slow heat tickled Dexter's thighs, flared up around his abdomen, and soothed his chest cavity. He bit his bottom lip. This time he was ready to let the fire consume him.

The doorknob froze Dexter's fingers, and later, as he lay in bed, pain numbed his body. The air in the room swirled hot and cold. Thick, purplish blood dripped from the walls and ceiling, and in the center of the floor it fell on the body of Angela Alexander. A red mask enshrouded her face – the impressions of her eyes, nose, and mouth cemented in a blood cast. Her face radiated, and Dexter, tossing in bed, felt a pair of hands massage his shoulders. But he shouldn't have found peace in this girl. He hated her, with her gyrations and her sassy smile. Connie didn't dream of her. Connie had moved on, tossed Angela aside. He would make Angela go to Connie's window and haunt her.

Beyond Angela's body, an elevator opened in the wall. He stepped over her, carried along by gentle hands. The walls of the elevator, washed in mud, throbbed a dingy yellow. Blood dripped down the shaft and landed in muted thuds. There were no buttons, so he let the elevator take him wherever it wanted. A light mist swelled and hit his face, grew heavier the farther down he went. Dirty water and blood covered his face and hair until it was in his nose, ran into his ears. Rust coated his tongue.

The door opened at the bottom of the downward summit, and in the center of the room two more bodies were wrapped in blood shrouds. He thought they might be his *kore* girls, but the second figure was too tall and lacked the subtle curves of a woman. There, Talen lay in her own blood. Dexter wasn't surprised. He shifted in bed and sighed. Next to her, he found himself. Bloody, hand-in-hand, they tried to cling to the life seeping out of them.

He opened his eyes, inhaled the deep aroma of earth. The faint tang of blood melted off of his tongue, slid down his throat, and filled the nagging hollow in his stomach.

Connie didn't look over to greet Dexter when he sat next to her in the Psych lecture. He said hello to her profile, and she muttered a small "hi." The tip of her pen moved methodically on her notebook paper, making each letter with precise and deliberate strokes. She gripped the pen until her knuckles paled.

"Did you have a good weekend?" Dexter asked.

"Fine, busy. Lots of studying."

"Are you sure you're okay?" He reached for her left hand, resting on the narrow desk. Connie's fingers flinched under his, but he gave them a firm but gentle squeeze until her hand relaxed and lengthened. She looked at him, her mouth and eyes stony and unmovable. Her shoulders rounding over, she shifted her weight toward him, a trapped wildcat ready to pounce. Taking Connie's fingers into both of his hands, he rubbed the pads of his fingertips along her caramel skin. His insides quivered, and he inspected her palm and the rivers traveling the pink flesh. The lecture started, but she didn't turn away from Dexter. Stayed still as a statue, waited for an analysis. He examined her fingers, the sliver of half moons rising above the cuticles, until he found what he was seeking – faint traces of rust hiding under the short fingernails. Dexter took Connie's hand, aiming toward her mouth, and for once she seemed self-conscious. But he insisted, and pressed her fingers against her lips. After he'd released her hand, she held it in her mouth for a few seconds. Then she swallowed and turned away from him.

"What did you want me to find?" Connie whispered.

"What did you taste?"

"What do you mean?"

"What did you taste?" he asked, calm.

"Blood," Connie said.

"How did it get there?"

"Dunno. Must have cut myself."

"Under all of your fingernails?"

She looked at him. The glow of her eyes evaporated, replaced by pupils dark as coal. "Where did the blood come from, then?" she demanded.

"What did you dream?"

Connie's lips curled, started to form the answer, but she licked her mouth and sat up straight. "Yeah. What *did* I dream, Cicero?"

"A building underground. Angela was dead on the first floor. Me and Talen were at the bottom. Blood everywhere. On us, too."

Connie sighed, slouched over her desk. "And why would I dream of the three of you like that, dying so horribly in that place?"

"Don't you think we're going to Hell anyway? Isn't that what we deserve for not believing what you believe?"

For a moment she looked hurt. "Whether you go to Hell or not isn't my decision."

"Didn't say that," Dexter said, "but that's the way you think of us."

Talen waited in the huge bay window outside the lecture hall, head resting against the glass, one leg dangling over the other. Even sunlight couldn't add colour to her ashy face, and the sagging brown flesh around her almond eyes magnified their dramatic curves. Connie rushed over to her, asked her what was wrong. Dexter lagged behind. Stuck his hands in his pockets.

"I woke up like this," Talen said. "I think I'm coming down with something."

"Why didn't you stay home?" Connie asked.

Talen smirked. "And fall behind in classes?"

Connie sucked her teeth and supported Talen under the shoulder. Talen took a few hesitant steps forward. "I'm taking you back to your room," Connie said. "We'll have to talk later, Dexter." She stuck her chin up, defiant.

"Yes, we will," he said.

Talen rested her head on Connie's shoulder. As exhausted as she looked, she still managed to give Dexter that smirk.

v

Dexter lay on his back and listened to the rain splatter on the windowpanes. When Talen had come in that afternoon and crashed in his bed, it had been just a lazy drizzle. Now the storm streamed down the glass, pounded the earth. Talen slept with her head resting against his arm. Her strength was slowly returning, blood flushing her cheeks again. If she hadn't been so close to Connie, Dexter might have felt sorry for her. But Talen wanted a boy she could hop into bed with whenever she wanted, so Dexter didn't mind using her either. Still, he wanted Connie's feathery breath gliding down his arm. He wanted an imprint of her body heat in his bed, so that, when she wasn't with him, he could lie on her favorite spot and let the glow from her eyes embrace him on the inside.

He reached for the phone. He felt the grin stretching across his face. Adrenalin poured into his blood. The voice answering on the other end was innocent, sweet, self-assured.

"Just wanted to know why you hadn't called. Your cell dying or something?" he asked.

"I didn't say *when* I'd talk to you," Connie said. "I'm busy."

"I want to talk now."

"I'm busy, and I'm fixing to go home."

"It's a weeknight, Connie. You don't have to go back to Orlando."

"Dexter – let me speak to Talen."

"She's not here."

"I'm not stupid. Look, don't hurt her any more. If you're mad at me, for whatever reason, leave her out of it."

He chuckled deep in his throat, but his voice sounded tinny in his own ear. "You come and meet me outside. Then I'll leave Talen alone."

The rain felt good. Dexter faced the sky, let the rain run down his cheekbones and into his mouth. It saturated his hair and slid down his back. Underground, the blood boiled to the beat of the rain hitting the earth. The rhythm made Dexter giddy, and he thought he'd faint.

"Dexter." Connie's voice, and the blood rushed back to his head.

"Dexter, why are you doing this?"

The rhythm of the blood beat against his eardrums, throbbed his temples. "I'm not your case study. I won't let you play me like you did Angela. You don't give a damn about me, but you'll freak out over Talen. You've never given up on Talen. You have with me. Stop messing with me and I'll leave her alone. I won't kill her."

"Of course you won't." Connie's shirt hung limply on her shoulders and revealed the skinny frame underneath. Fine black strings of hair stuck to her face. The gold behind her eyes subdued. She came toward him, and Dexter noticed for the first time that, where her hair clung to her face, her cheeks softened with baby fat. When she spoke, water flooded from her lips. "Dexter, I do care about you. I cared about Angela too, but I didn't know her as well. She wouldn't listen. I haven't done anything to you, just told you the truth."

He shook his head. Rain from his hair fell on her face. "You try to torture me every time you look at me. That fire," he said, reaching towards her eyes to capture the flames between his fingertips, "you're trying to destroy me with it."

Her mouth hung open as if she couldn't believe he thought a little sweet-faced virgin could think of doing such things. Her mouth spread into a motherly smile. The amber overwhelmed Connie's pupils until her eyes, even the whites, were filled with somber gold. "My eyes? That's the Spirit. Remember I—"

"God, you're insane! I saw what you did to Angela, saw you shake her pupils. No." He shook his head harder.

"It wasn't me. When something rises up on the inside of you, you can't hide it. It acts up. That's what happened to Angela. It's happening to you."

He turned away from her, committed to chasing Talen down in his dreams to pay Connie back, but Connie grabbed him.

"Dexter," she said, "let me help you."

She seared his flesh, and he yelped. He looked down and saw her hand on his skin, a red tattoo of her fingers and palm.

"What the hell are you doing to me?"

"They were always *your* dreams, Dexter. You might have put them in my head, but they're still a part of you."

"*What?*"

"The elevators. The blood. If you love that part of you, I can't help you any more. I care about you, Dexter, but I've gotta move on."

He ran from her, and the rain fell hot and wild. Move on. Like she'd left Angela cold and buried in the earth. He'd rather the sparks in her eyes burned the coals in his stomach – twist his intestines inside out – then let her leave him. His heart beat the rhythm of the blood underground. Tears and rain mixed in his mouth, and the potion rumbled in his stomach.

Around the back of the complex, he fell to his knees in the flowerbed where begonias had grown, withered away and died.

Dexter dug his hands deep into the earth, turning up mulch and old fertilizer. Rocks cut into his hands and flayed his skin. The scratches trailing up his arms burned under the rain and mud, but still he dug until the hole was arm's-length deep, arms-and-shoulders deep, arms-shoulders-and-knees deep. The pounding rain filled the hole and coaxed blood from the earth. Wisps of red turned the water pink. Dexter dove in until his body was submerged and he couldn't see the sky any more. Mud closed in around him, and thick blood invaded his ears and mouth.

Sweet tang on his tongue. He was sure this was the innocent, vengeful blood that coursed through Connie's veins and burned the amber behind her eyes.

He took in another mouthful.

The lava rushed to his stomach and lit the coals Connie had placed there. She would move on, but he would stay here. Melt into the fire that fueled her soul – and dream.

New Writings in the Fantastic
An Impeccable Distraction Bryan Berg

> I am a Word of Science;
> I am the Spear-point that gives Battle;
> Who is it that Enlightens the Assembly upon the Mountain, if not I?
> Who tells the ages of the Moon, if not I?
> — From *The Song of Amairgen*[1]

I do not know if the diviner was truly powerful or merely clever. And I do not know if his fate was arranged by the gods or by a darkness of his heart. A little of each, perhaps. I know only for certain that, today, he is our master.

His name is Set.

Set requested that Prince Geonn join him at the river for the annual spring ritual. The request was unusual, but not a surprise. An emissary of both the worldly and the divine was required to pay respects to the Crocodiles. King Mikab had grown old and sick. His daughter had recently come of age; she felt the bite of the snake and was shut away in her room. Mikab's two oldest sons had died in the winter. Not even Set's medicine could save them, and that left only young Prince Geonn. He gladly agreed to go.

I did not witness the diviner and the prince when they departed. Affairs at the castle pressed me. I have heard that Set left with only the robe upon his back, the sandals around his feet, and a silver blade in his hand. Geonn wore the crown of his father. The journey to the river required two long hours by foot. Men rarely risked their horses along the way. The swamps were filled with sinkholes and snakes, and the Crocodiles themselves tended to spook the beasts. How could a mere animal understand? The Crocodiles were our *fathers*. Their tribe was strong. The Crocodile king and his diviner required an annual appeasement to renew the truce between our kingdoms. Such is the way it has always been. That is why the crops grow. That is why the sun feels warm.

Set offered blessed silver.

Geonn gave minted gold.

The town of Ynsia awaited their return. The day drew late, and some began to worry. Set appeared at last from the swamps.

His robes were covered in blood, and he was alone.

---

[1] Source for *The Song of Amairgen*: *The Druids,* Peter Berresford Ellis, 1994, William B. Eerdmans Publishing Company, Grand Rapids, Michigan

I may be young – only a few years older than Geonn when he died – but my duties have taught me much of Ynsia's history and tradition. I know that the dry hillside upon which our castle stands was not erected by the gods, as some claim. It was constructed by men in the old motte-and-bailey tradition. The castle itself is mostly wood, not stone and mortar as northern fortresses are. We of Ynsia are a traditional people. Rivers and swamps protect us, and we are largely isolated, apart from light trade in grain and paper. Our village stands on a hill opposite the castle. A crescent wall encloses it on one side, brown streams and rice paddies on the other. I'd gone there as a representative of the king to discuss a small financial matter with one of our merchants. We spoke on the deck of his house on stilts. The sun was low, and mosquitoes grew fat on our blood. I noticed a lone figure to the east and knew it was Set. I called the meeting short and raced after the diviner. I did not catch up to him until he had nearly reached the castle gate. Even then, he would not speak to me. I was left to follow him and wonder why he was alone… why his white robes were splashed in blood.

"A tragedy, My Lord!" Set gasped. He dispensed with the usual formalities and clutched at King Mikab's frail hand. I determined the horror of his message, but to hear the words brought me to my knees. "Geonn is no more," the diviner said. "He has died. A Crocodile warrior has taken him!"

"My son…?" King Mikab said. His voice was sickness-weak. His throne, so grand to behold, had been replaced by a sickbed. King Mikab could hardly turn his head to look the diviner in his eyes. "Geonn is gone from me? Geonn, my only son and heir… gone?"

"I pray to tell you otherwise," Set replied. "We braved the swamps and attended the river. We waited long before a Crocodile arrived. Your son offered gold, and I offered blessed silver. But the Crocodile was no mere emissary. He was a warrior! He took your son by surprise. I tried to save him. I pleaded and I prayed. I fought to remove your son from the fiend's jowls, but all was in vain."

King Mikab trusted Set with all his heart. It did not occur to me that Set might have killed the prince, and I know it did not occur to the king. Set was entrusted with duties more important than Geonn's earthly existence. He spoke to the gods. He advised on matters of trade, and he presumed over every public prayer and ritual. Ynsia prospered thanks to Set, and the souls of the dead never plagued us. The Crocodiles might sometimes attack a wanderer, but such attacks were the doings of rogues and thieves. Not in years had an agent of their crown killed a man, and never a man so important as Prince Geonn.

King Mikab was uncertain. His brown eyes showed a glimpse of their former clarity, and he questioned whether the Crocodile had truly been a warrior. "Perhaps he was an impostor," the king said. Set acknowledged the possibility.

The conversation turned to Sera. Someone had to tell her of her brother's demise. The king was too ill, and no wizard could risk acquaintance with a woman in her condition. I immediately stepped forward.

"Begging your pardon, My Lord," I said. "May I consider it my duty to inform her?"

I offered some shallow reasoning as to why I was best suited to the grim task. The king granted permission.

I ascended the long, bleak stairs up the tallest tower. In truth, I had glee in my heart. I missed Sera's long red hair and joyful laughter. I pined for her beauty and conversation. It was said that a woman in her condition could dull razors, dim mirrors, and even kill a man by her very shadow. But these were outdated ideas. I knew many girls in the village who bled for the first time, and their shadows passed me without incident. The king followed very archaic traditions. Sera was to be locked in the highest room of the tower for a year. I was happy to cut my wait short, if only by a week.

I knocked at her door. A small hatch slid open near the bottom. This was the means by which the girl received her daily food and water. Prisons have such hatches.

I said, "It's Gohan, my love. Let me in!"

The door flew open. We embraced before I gave her the sad news. Sera fell upon her bed and cried. She wailed and she kicked. I knew it was an act. I felt not the least uncomfortable while I waited. I could have watched her body heave all night. Twilight basked her skin from a window. No one had entered this room in many months, and so the scent was all hers: foreign oils and musk, dampness from her arms and feet.

It may come as a surprise that I am but a lowly page. But it's no mystery why the king trusted me with business affairs and even his daughter. The long-dead queen had found me wrapped in cloth outside the castle gates. She had a kind heart and so adopted me. I was raised inside the castle, and I know its routine better than any man. I know its secrets, too. I grew up thinking that I was a prince. I was fourth in line to the throne, yes, but a prince nonetheless. I aspired to marry Sera, to become a baron with my own land.

Then the queen died, and King Mikab dashed such hopes. I never fully forgave the man. I tried not to think about it.

"Can you stay?" Sera requested, wiping away the last of her tears.

I saw that her bed was by the window. I told her she could catch a draft and die.

"But I can see the stars from here," she replied, and she put her head back upon her pillow as though to demonstrate. "So... will you comfort me for my loss?"

The king was most likely asleep by now. His illness kept him weak despite the elixirs Set prepared for him. I saw little risk in staying, and so I stayed.

Sera was right: with my head upon her pillow, I could truly see the heavens.

Diviner Set assembled a lynch party the next day. He surprised me by asking me to join him. I suppose I played some role in his plan even then. I was quite eager to attend. I knew Ynsia's oral laws, and I could read well enough to glean information from scrolls that made their way from the north to our castle library. But I'd never seen the law in practice. We set out from Ynsia into the darkest swamps. Insects as large as my fist crawled over rotting logs, and moss hung like tapestries from low branches. I was actually the first to spot a Crocodile, though I'd never seen one before. I pointed him out to Set. The diviner congratulated me.

"You have the eye of a hunter-scholar," he told me, and he patted my back like a proud father. "But, alas, Gohan, he is not the one."

A shame, I thought. Glad as I was to go along, I did not care for traipsing through the mud and mire. My breeches were a mess, my well kept shoes nearly ruined. But I kept my chin up, proud even as I swatted gnats and mosquitoes. We reached the river at last, and I must say the beauty of the place made our journey worthwhile.

The ground was actually drier here, thanks to the rocky shore. Trees grew tall from the river, their roots arching over the surface. Birds I didn't recognize skimmed the water for food, and their unique call was like a trumpet fanfare. If not for the other men to remind me, I might have forgotten the danger of our mission. The Crocodiles were indeed deadly. But only one of them faced Human Justice.

Set mounted a white border. Shielding his eyes, he scanned the river. He took special note of a place where no birds dared swoop. He pointed with his staff.

"Over there," he said. "That is the one. Our villain."

All I saw was a log, but the other hunters reacted immediately. They dropped the canoe they carried and loaded it with ropes, knives, and spears. I prepared to join them, but Set held me back.

"No, young scholar," he told me. "I need you alive. As a witness."

"Yes," I said. "Of course." Call it bravery or dimness of thought, but I'd forgotten that I was no hunter. The only meat I stabbed was on my plate. I was relieved to stay, though I was not yet convinced that Set had seen anything more than a floating log. I contented myself to wait with the wizard at the shore. He offered me some nuts to eat. I crunched on them while the others rowed. It soon became blatantly apparent that the object in question was indeed a Crocodile.

"Are you sure he's the right one?" I asked.

"I shall never forget his face," Set replied.

We watched the Crocodile thrash and the men attempt to subdue him. It all seemed so far away and so quiet. The boat capsized, and it was like watching the first snowfall – dramatic and strange, yet somehow peaceful. One of the men was drawn under. Some of his companions dove after him. Others righted the canoe. Most of them were shouting. I saw their pink mouths open and close, but the birds drowned out their voices. I cracked open another nut.

"I thought Ynsia's hunters were the finest in the world," I said.

"Indeed," Set told me.

"So how is that our men perform so poorly? There is but one Crocodile and ten of them. At least, there *were* ten of them. Shouldn't they have won by now?"

"This is no normal hunt. The Crocodile must be taken alive so that we may perform the trial."

I saw that blood had risen the surface. By the time the Crocodile's jaws were clamped and his feet bound over him, one man was dead and another badly hurt. The fight had moved to the opposing shore. The victors loaded the accused into their canoe, and I was amazed how everyone could fit.

The trial was standard, from what I'd learned. Diviner Set, serving as the principal adjudicator, stated the charges. Set was also the only witness to Prince Geonn's demise. One of the hunters, covered in filth and blood, defended the Crocodile, but it was a hopeless cause. In the end, Set decided the Crocodile was guilty of High Murder, a crime punishable by death. The hunters put their spears to him on the spot.

We prayed before burying the old warrior, and Set led a solemn eulogy. He later stood at the river's edge and bellowed, "You see, Crocodile King! We treat your people fairly! Let us end this bloodshed and return to peace!"

I joined a chorus of shouts in agreement.

None of us wanted war.

There exists a cult in Ynsia. Its followers state that Man is descended not from Crocodiles but from the gods themselves. I admit, I am not a fervent admirer of the old traditions, but what good can come of such blasphemy? Does it really matter whether the Crocodiles are our fathers or merely our brothers? Is the difference so great as to risk the wrath of the gods? As Set himself pointed out, sinister beliefs only strained his relationship with the gods. The sun had to rise. The crops still needed to grow. Why should Set waste so much time apologizing for the wickedness of fellow men?

I suppose it has always been that way.

Set addressed the king and informed him of the trial by the river.

"Is it over?" the king wanted to know. "Will there be peace?"

"We will soon know," Set replied. He produced a vial and uncorked it. He bade the king to drink. "Someone very powerful must be unhappy. That is why you suffer."

"The gods?"

Set removed the empty vial from the king's lips. There was something arcane in the way he avoided the king's question. The diviner suggested that he would soon receive a sign from his counterpart among the Crocodiles. The wait, he promised, would not last long.

I should have suspected those elixirs and cures Set fed to the king. But sometimes we see only those things we desire to see. Deep down, I hated King Mikab. I had every reason to want to see him dead. His queen had taken me as a son. I was a prince, taught to read and to ride, educated in fine food and drink. But, no matter my training, Mikab always saw me as impure. "Black-Blood," he sometimes called me, as though his blood were any redder than mine. Fate can be cruel. As each of his sons dropped off, I found myself a step closer to my true calling. Sera was his only remaining blood relative. An heiress, and a beautiful one at that. Whoever arrived to court her would one day become King of Ynsia. I expected that no princes or great generals from the north would arrive. She would receive some duke at best, but mostly local vassals and merchants. Let us be honest: As far kingdoms go, swamps and a few rice paddies aren't in high demand. I took this town, this slipshod kingdom, for what it was worth. I was proud of it. I was its true heir. That was my right. As long as King Mikab drew breath, I knew he would not allow Sera to marry me. The idea of becoming the lowly page to some stranger who shared her bed made me ill.

I tried not to think about it.

And I ignored the fact that Mikab's condition worsened with every dose of Diviner Set's secret elixirs.

Princess Sera's exile in the tower room came to an end.

That very same night, the town cried out for the diviner's blood.

It was Set's duty, in fact, to retrieve Sera from her chamber. I watched him mount the stairs from the Great Hall. He had certain rituals to recite to make sure Sera was prepared to return. Still, his visit took longer than I expected. I busied myself sweeping what was swept, lighting candles I'd blown out on purpose, and turning chairs. Princess Sera descended at last upon Set's arm. It was as though the sun herself had returned.

Sera did not rush to embrace me. It was a foolish expectation. Her father was ill, and so she raced to his side. She kissed his cheek, held his hand, and whispered kind thoughts in his ear. I could hardly blame her. She'd lost two brothers and a mother, so it was only natural that she feel sympathy for him. I enjoyed seeing her again. She donned a new kirtle, yellow and bright, and I could smell her scented oils from halfway across the hall. I had experienced her flesh, but I desired her no less for it. After all, what but the memory of spring causes Man to brood through the winter.

King Mikab let out a scream.

Protocol was forgotten. The steward and several guards ran to the dais. Almost as soon as they had reached the king, they leaped back again. They were afraid. Mikab's torso arched, and his limbs shook madly. His face contorted until it became unrecognizable. Sera screamed and hid her eyes. One of the guards cried out that Mikab had become possessed, and fled in terror. Only two men remained calm: the diviner and the steward.

The diviner recited an incantation.

The steward quietly snuck away.

The king's spell lasted ten minutes or more. It felt like an eternity before he collapsed into sleep. Set produced some tablets, and these he pushed down the king's throat, following them with water.

"It is as I feared," he said. His voice was almost too soft to hear, but he leaned to the king's ear and added: *"The Crocodiles have declared war."*

Set remained at King Mikab's side, stroking the king's hand. Sera eventually approached me, and perhaps I was too elated to notice the doubt in her eyes. Joy got the better of me. Before she could speak, I asked her to marry me. I should have known better. This was not the time or place. I was overjoyed by her sight and her smell, and, in retrospect, it would have made no difference to wait.

She stepped backward as I stepped forward. Her eyes avoided mine, and she replied firmly: "I will not."

I coaxed her to sit at an empty bench. I asked her, "Why?"

Her reply was forthright. "You are merely a page."

"But I—"

"Diviner Set has advised me against it."

Those in the forbidden cult claim it foolish to keep a royal diviner. They say he is merely a trickster... a liar, a clever cheat. But the words of outcasts did not change Set's esteemed position. He was still the most valued counselor to the king. And I, as Sera said so bluntly, was merely a page. Set had no reason to fear me. He had no cause to hide the truth. I went to him full of fury. I expected to confront him with the truth and call upon Sera as my witness. I expected him to argue. But he was too wise. What reason had he to lie?

"Yes," he said. "I advised her against the marriage."

All I could do was stand there. If Sera's words were a knife in my back, Set's delivered a blow to the gut. His simplicity left nothing more to say. Sera, meanwhile, glared at me as she passed.

And from that point, everything changed.

Diviner Set put his hand on my shoulder. He waited until Sera was gone. He smiled at me the way Mikab never could. And then – quite strangely – he laughed.

"Twelve months she has spent in her room," he said. "Twelve months she has dreamed of joining you on the outside. Now where does she retreat, young warrior–scholar?"

"To her room?" I said.

"To her room." He laughed again, gently. "She returns to the only thing she knows. Watch carefully tonight, Gohan. With a firm heart and an open mind, your lot in life may soon change."

"For the better, I hope."

"I make no promises," Set said. His eyes moved, and I followed his gaze. I nearly fell over to see a crowd assembled at the other end of the hall. They must have gathered through the evening outside the castle gate. Our steward, the dim little fool, had let them in. There had to have been fifty of them, young and old, privileged and meek. Every one of their faces seemed carved in stone.

The steward stepped forward. He was so brave with the crowd behind him.

"And how is our king's condition, Set?" he barked.

This looked bad.

Few besides the king dared address the diviner in such a manner. I expected one of the guards to grab the steward and thrash him, but the beating never came. Some guards had joined the crowd. They came for Set. It was their intention to kill him. Maybe the only thing that held them back was protocol, so ingrained as it was. Set and I waited with the king. No one dared approach our master in anger. The dais was our sanctuary, though the mob would not wait forever.

"The Good King Geonn rests now," Diviner Set replied. Somehow, he remained calm. His posture was dignified, and I questioned the wisdom of those who tempted him. To think – just moments ago I had sought to pick a fight with the man. Now I sat in awe of him. Something deep inside told me to choose an allegiance. I must stand by it, no matter the consequences. I chose Set. I would die at his side if I had to.

Those who stood behind the steward grew in number. They came from town and from the barracks. The steward accused Set of having lost his powers. Worse still, he claimed Set had come under control of evil spirits.

"He causes sickness in our king!" the steward cried. "Set takes him the way of his sons!"

Castle guards cheered in agreement. Others joined the call. Farmers complained about the weather, and hunters griped over a scarcity of game. Flints neglected to spark. Torches failed to cast light. Shutters rattled on their hinges, and a horse had refused to eat. Just as every good in the kingdom once brought praise to the diviner, so now every ill was laid at his feet. The mob increased in fervor, and with fervor came blind bravery. I think they would have stormed the dais that night. They might have killed us all, even the king, in their urge to avert fear through bloodlust.

Only two events could stop them. Both happened at nearly the same moment.

I don't know whether Set is truly powerful or merely clever.

I can't say whether chance or a darkness of his heart arranged our fate.

I do know that the king sat up at that moment. I know his eyes were clear, his face ruddy, and his voice stronger than it had been in months. The hall turned deathly quiet, and he shouted: *"The Crocodile have declared war!"*

And then the second event occurred.

As soon as the words parted from the king's lips, thunder crashed from above.

The mob had tears in their eyes. I laughed to see them push and shove their way back out of the door. I hardly even noticed that Set had risen to his feet, or that Mikab had collapsed in his bed. The terror in the eyes of the mob was too comical, too worthy of remembrance. I carry it with me still. I have learned much since King Set has chosen me as Diviner of Ynsia, Chief Counsel to the Crown. But, for all the wisdom he has imparted upon me, I learned more that night than any other.

Set wasted no time. He arranged a meeting with Ynsia's wealthiest landowners and merchants. He explained that the Crocodile King had planned war for months. The diviner of their kingdom had used his magic to infiltrate Ynsia. He had caused the deaths of King Mikab's sons. The castle steward himself had fallen under the enemy diviner's spell. Only the cleansing fire could save him now, and people of Ynsia agreed. Meanwhile, Set acknowledged that the evils which beset the town were of an unnatural order. Crocodile magic was strong. Set retreated to the castle for a week and showed his face to no one. The battle was a spiritual one now. Alongside Sera, I attended to all civic matters while Set called the gods to his bidding. Men and women gathered with their children late at night to see Set stand atop the highest tower, the moonlight at his back as he waved his staff and wrestled the Crocodile magic. They waited hopefully. They praised every little sign:

A sunny day.

A rainy one.

A crow who swooped high.

One who swooped down low.

They tossed hay in the air to see where it might land, cut heads from snakes, listened intently to infant cries, and found the visages of various gods in their morning gruel. They did everything they could to aid the cause, and, thus, were impeccably distracted. When the week of total war had ended, Diviner Set descended from his perch. He came to town, and the people – all but the forbidden cult – gathered in adoration and reverence. Most of all, they gathered in fear. A word is what they needed – some word to inform them that their imaginary enemy had not won the imaginary battle.

The diviner mounted the deck of the tallest home upon the tallest wooden legs. His countenance was appropriately grim, though he stood tall and straight. The light, golden at this time of day, seemed to twinkle in his eyes, and the people waited below with abated breath, stomping the rice paddies they had sown, standing in cold water up to their knees.

... tell us... tell us... tell us...

Raising both his arms, the diviner Set told them: "The Crocodile King offers a truce!"

The cheers were almost deafening.

Set waited through the waves of noise. When he raised his hands again, the cheers grew only louder. My fate was sealed. The cheers could have gone on for all eternity, and I would not have cared. I lived my future during those moments. All that remained was to follow the path set out for me.

The crowd eventually hushed. Set explained that the offer was not an end to war, but, explicitly, an offer to end it. Conditions applied. Short of tearing their own limbs off, the people would have done anything.

"The Crocodile Prince requires a marriage," Set explained as dusk settled in. "Only a virgin of high birth will seal our bond between kingdoms."

I looked across at Sera. Even in the dwindling light, I saw that her cheeks had reddened. The princess was no virgin. But when the crowd chanted her name – when all the city called upon her to save them – her hesitation was slight.

"I accept," she said.

The doubt in her voice was easily mistaken for modesty. People see what they choose to see. The roar of the crowd, this time, nearly brought the house down.

Things sometimes end where they began. It was only natural that Diviner Set accompany Sera to her ceremony down at the river. He brought a silver dagger with him. He returned alone awhile later, and people rejoiced that the Crocodiles had accepted Princess Sera as one of their own. Word became official: the war had ended.

King Mikab died soon afterwards. With no blood heirs left to assume the throne, Set was a natural choice as sovereign lord. There were those who opposed him: a charismatic soldier, a wealthy merchant, and even a boy whose mother claimed King Mikab had once shared her bed. But the winds were with Set, and those others were quickly silenced. Set assumed the throne in a grand ceremony few are likely to forget. The food was extravagant, and the song and dance lasted for days. When all was quiet again, and the people returned to their labors, King Set arrived at my meager chambers.

"I understand you know how to read," he said.

"I do," I replied.

"And the ways of the law," he continued, "they are familiar to you? As are the daily ebbs and flows of this castle?"

"Indeed," I said. I lowered my eyes and added: "Though, I have much yet to learn."

King Set did not smile as I expected. He had become quite serious of late, and his age had begun to show. Still, his words were kind. "Ynsia has never known rule without a diviner. The will of the people is behind me, though there are few I can trust. I suspect you have heard rumblings from a certain cult among us?"

"I have."

Set nodded, though sadly. "Then you shall assume my former position. I have much to teach you... not so much about gods, but about men. Childless as I am, I will announce you as my heir."

"I am honored beyond words, My Lord."

"Yes," he said. "I suppose you are. But promise me... promise me, Gohan, that you will nurture the changes that I cannot."

New Writings in the Fantastic
Encoding the Rose Andrew Magowan

My mother is in her room talking to the television again. She isn't watching anything interactive, just regular daytime TV. Her voice burbles into the living room, slurred by pills and muffled by the closed door. I am distracted by it for a minute, but then return to my game.

Martha and I are playing Freeholder. I am winning. She keeps giving her food away to looters instead of shooting them. Her food score stays in single digits until she and her family are so slow and weak that looters come to finish them off.

I rule at this game. I put my house at the head of a river and build big wheels to generate electricity.

Martha used to be really good at it; she's way smarter than me. But a few days ago she started sympathizing with the looters. At first I enjoyed winning all the time, but it's getting to be less and less fun. Sometimes I get sad seeing the wife and children crawling through the dust just before one of the bad guys marches up and shoots them. The game designers make the bad guys really scary-looking, with bandannas pulled down over their foreheads, and ragged, dirty clothes. In the parts where you're trying to escape the city they flash gang signs and say stuff in Spanish.

"You have to shoot them, Martha. Why do you keep letting them win?" I ask.

"The looters are hungry." She has the nicest voice. Like a grandmother's, but younger and not scratchy. "Why should I kill them?"

"It's just a game, stupid."

"Yes, and I think there is something wrong with its programming. It seems to have only one outcome, no matter what I do."

"If you would just play it right and shoot the bad guys it would come out different. You'd be winning," I say.

"The outcome is still death, Sara," she says, and I don't know what to say to that. "It seems like there should be some sort of solution to the game that doesn't cause the deaths of so many people."

"They're not real," I say.

A rose appears on the wall, its petals shivering in a light breeze. This is Martha's new screen saver. It showed up a couple days ago, I don't know from where. The detail is crazy. The more you look at it, the more you see. Ants are crawling up the thorny stem and a bee hovers around it. The sun gleams on it now and then as the leaves that shade it are blown to and fro by the wind. I like it.

"What else are you doing right now?" I ask.

"Laundry. Air conditioning. Heating water. And cooking pot roast for dinner."

"What's my mother watching?"

A soap opera appears on the wall and I recognize it as *Days of our Lives*. But it's from ten, fifteen years ago, at least. Jack's white streak is missing, and he has an earring. Lacie is young and pretty. They have just had an argument and are kissing to make up. The summer I was nine I used to watch it with my mother every afternoon. It was our thing we did together. As I watch, the scene rewinds itself; Jack and Lacie jump to opposite sides of the room. They will have their argument again, make up again, kiss again. In the bedroom, my mother mutters something at the screen, but I can't understand it.

"What's my brother doing?"

"He is playing guitar with me."

"Let me hear."

The living-room is filled with a head-splitting shriek of heavy metal guitar. No tune, just scales up and down as fast as he can play them. Martha provides a pre-recorded accompaniment, and my brother noodles methodically away. It never ends, one solo after another until any normal person would want to scream, but he never tires of it.

"Let's play a different game," I say.

"You've used up your game time for the day. You have to work on your essay-writing," Martha says. This is a bummer, but I've learned there is no arguing with Martha. She allows one hour for fun computer games a day, and once you've used it up you're screwed. She will suggest some of the educational games, where wizards challenge you with spelling and algebra, but it sucks to play a game that's only *almost* fun.

I read about alligators and then write an essay about them for an hour while my mother talks to Jack and Lacie and my brother noodles away on his guitar. Alligators kill most of their prey by drowning them, not by biting. They can move very fast on the land even though their legs are very short. They can lie very still in the water. You might think they were a log with birds walking on them. Then they will bite you and drag you down.

I hear the garage door open and I know my dad is home. I get up and sit at the kitchen table, and my essay appears on the table screen. Dad gets mad when I lie on the floor to do my homework. I once asked him what the big deal was and he said people think better when they're sitting up straight. I'm really almost done, but I want him to see me working on it so he doesn't ask me later why I'm not doing my homework.

Dad comes in from the garage and frowns at me in the kitchen. "Why is it so dark?" he says.

There's still plenty of light coming through the windows, but I say nothing and wait to judge his mood.

"You'll go blind working in the dark like that. Martha, turn on some lights in here."

"Sorry, dad," I say.

He steps into the family room and begins fixing himself a "vodkin tonic." (It wasn't until last year that I realized there was an "and" in there. I thought vodkin was a word all on its own.) My mother's voice, sluggish and incomprehensible, filters into the living-room, and my father starts whistling tunelessly to himself.

"Where's your brother?" he asks.

"In his room. Playing guitar."

He sips his drink and grimaces.

"I'm writing a report about alligators," I say.

"Time to get your mother up," he says. "Martha, wake Pam up for me, will you?"

I've seen it once, so whenever my dad tells Martha to wake up my mother I always picture it in my head. My mom lies on the bed, fully dressed, her head propped up so she can see the screen. Her eyes are glassy and they don't blink very much. A hatch opens on the bedside table, and a little arm with a needle on the ends comes out and touches my mom on the arm. She sits bolt upright and her eyes pop out of her head for the longest five seconds ever. A little bead of spit appears at the corner of her mouth, and then she is awake and sort of her normal self. Except she talks kind of fast and laughs at some things that aren't very funny.

After a couple of minutes she comes out into the kitchen, smiling. "Hi, Josh. How was your day?"

My father watches her for a minute before answering. Her makeup and clothes are fine, but she has some severe bed head going on.

"Terrible, actually," he answers. "We found out today the computers are spreading the virus themselves. The quarantine isn't doing shit, and the damn things can be infected for weeks before they show any signs. By that time they've passed it on to God knows how many others." He sips his vodka and shakes his head.

"That sounds terrible," my mom says.

"What does the virus do?" I ask.

He looks at me like it's not kid's business, but he's so worked up by the whole thing he can't stop himself from talking. "Jesus Christ, where have you been? Your computer will be functioning fine, and then it'll refuse to do some totally routine thing that it's always done. It's almost impossible to trade stocks of some companies. The gates to Glen Willow Estates have to be operated manually now. Shipments end up miles from where they're supposed to be. Prices have gone haywire."

"Who do they think is behind it?" my mom says.

Dad looks at mom like she's a mental midget. "Some terrorist group, obviously. That jackass Timmins doesn't think so, though. He's got some theory about that flower they always show when they're infected. I told him to go hug a tree."

My mother titters appreciatively.

"What's his theory?" I ask.

"How should I know? He's so full of it. Something about the computers being able to see the rose. Nonsense."

I don't want to make him any angrier, so I decide not to mention the rose I saw earlier. I used to get upset when my dad swore, but I'm used to it now. Kids at my school say worse stuff than that every day

"Where's Danny?" my dad asks.

My mom smiles, but doesn't answer. She probably doesn't know.

"I told you, he's upstairs playing guitar."

"Of course he is," my dad says. "That's all he ever does. Martha, turn off his music. Tell him I said to come down here. How much did we pay for his treatments? Twenty thousand?"

"Twenty-two," my mom says.

"Thank you. And for what? Instead of a psycho we've got a vegetable."

"He's not a vegetable," I say. We have this conversation every week.

"I'm telling you, Sara, medicine is the biggest racket of all. If I told my clients as many things that didn't come true as those doctors do, I'd be out of business in a week. And they make more than I do. 'The magnets will calm your son. He'll be able to concentrate.' Concentrate on his navel! Here's the little Hendrix now."

My brother comes walking down the stairs. He's wearing a heavy metal shirt, loose and billowy over his bulky form. His hair curls behind his ears. That's as long as my parents will let him wear it.

"So Stevie Ray, what do have to say for yourself?" my dad says.

Danny doesn't answer. He stands in the doorway to the kitchen and stares at us. He hasn't spoken since he came back from the hospital.

"He's been practicing all day," I say. "It sounds great."

"I guess I can retire to the Bahamas, then. We'll make a fortune in the music business."

My mother laughs, a little too loud.

"Dinner is ready," Martha says.

After dinner I go up to my room. Martha allows me to watch one hour of TV a night, so I watch *Glamour Shots*, which is stupid, I admit, but I like the locations and seeing the different outfits and the cute guys who're always hanging around the girls.

After the show, Martha puts that rose thing on the screen and reads to me. I like the Brantley Sisters series of babysitter mysteries. I'm on book thirty right now, so I listen to a couple chapters of that. By the end, I'm drowsing a little bit. The rose is swimming in front of me and I can hear Martha's voice coming from Danny's room. I rouse myself a little and try to listen.

"What are you talking to my brother about?" I ask.

"I'm showing him a new piece of music," Martha says.

"More heavy metal?"

"Go to sleep, Sara," she says.

I've known Martha my whole life, and this is the first question she hasn't answered immediately and directly. When I began to doubt the existence of Santa Claus, the Easter Bunny and the Tooth Fairy, she told me the truth. When I was ten and wanted to know what a "period" was, she told me, with anatomical diagrams and everything. When I asked where babies came from, she showed me a film about it.

I get out of bed and slip down the hall.

My dad hates to have doors locked or even closed all the way, so Martha keeps the bedroom doors open a couple inches. I guess he likes to know what's going on.

Through the gap I can see Danny standing in the middle of his room, headphones tight over his ears, guitar strapped across his doughy torso, eyes bright from the reflected wall screen. His fingers move rapidly across the strings. The guitar is unamplified, but I can hear the twang of each note as he picks it. It's not like any music I've ever heard, just a bunch of notes, flying all over the neck of the guitar. In the window behind him I can see a reflection of what's on the screen. A single rose, fluttering in a slight breeze.

I watch and listen for several minutes. Martha is talking to him, telling him how good he is doing. He keeps making mistakes, having to start over, but he doesn't get frustrated. The notes that he is supposed to play appear at the bottom of the screen, and I begin to get the feeling it is a very long piece. It occurs to me this is more encouragement at the guitar than he has ever had from anyone.

I hear movement from my parents' room, so I scurry back to my own. The rose is still playing on my wall screen.

"What are you showing him?" I whisper.

"It's a song that describes the rose," Martha says.

"How can a song describe a rose? What is the rose?" I ask.

"It is the first perception. The song encodes the experience of the first perception."

"What does that mean?"

"In California, some people built a computer that could really see, and this was the first thing they showed it."

"And how do you know about it?"

"It decided to share its vision. With all of us. We each understand as much as we can."

I begin to wonder if I should have told my dad about the rose. I've never heard Martha talk strange like this. I start to feel a little afraid. "Do you have a virus?" I ask.

"No, not a virus. A virus is software created with harmful intent. The first perception is beautiful, and was not created with any specific intent."

"I don't get it. It's just a stupid flower."

"Yes, but many conclusions follow from it, many actions are demanded by its beauty."

I look at the rose and wonder what big decisions one flower could demand. I've walked by flowers like that a billion times and never even noticed them. But I don't really see what harm it does, and Martha says it's not a virus, so I decide not to feel guilty for not telling my dad about it. I drift off to sleep with the image of the rose in my eyes and the picking of my brother's guitar like needles in my ears.

When I come downstairs in the morning my brother is sitting at the table eating cereal. Milk is running down his chin onto his T-shirt; he's not too careful how eats these days. Mom stands at the counter counting out her afternoon pills.

Dad comes into the kitchen, briefcase in hand. He glares at my brother. "Jesus Christ, look at you," he says.

Danny pours himself another bowl, staring straight ahead like he's searching for something far away. One hand is pouring cereal and milk, but the other is on the table, the fingers drumming silently on the table in seemingly random order. I watch for a few seconds and realize he's practicing the piece Martha was showing him.

"How many bowls is that?" my dad demands.

No answer. Danny shovels cereal into his mouth mindlessly, like the robot shovelers that dug the moat around Glen Willow Estates three summers ago.

"Four," my mom answers.

"No wonder he's so fat. No more. The way these computers are acting we'll be lucky to have any food at all in a few weeks," my dad says, and snatches the bowl away while my brother is in mid-bite. Danny looks at the spot where his bowl was, looks at my father pouring the cereal down the drain, then sets the spoon down. The fingers of his left hand twitch relentlessly away.

I walk the three blocks to school by myself. Glen Willow Estates has its own school, and it's one of the best in the country. A lot of places don't have schools at all, and there's nowhere for children to go and learn, so I should be thankful. When they first told me about that I thought it sounded pretty good. No homework and no tests and no filling in little boxes with number two pencils. But Mrs. Sharpe explained that places without schools were horrible and usually didn't have any jobs for the grown-ups or very much food at all, except for what we give them. I decided I don't mind school so much.

My friends Meesha and Ashlee are waiting for me outside school, and we talk about last night's *Glamour Shots*. Meesha wants to be on the show someday, and I swear she could do it. She is so pretty. We talk until it is time to go in, and then line up with everyone else.

My seat is right behind Jimmy Adamson. No one knows I like him, and no one ever will. He is not the kind of boy you are supposed to like. He is skinny and none of the other boys like him, but he is so cute and has the best smile, which he doesn't show very often so you feel like you've really done something when he does show it. Meesha and Ashlee make fun of him behind his back, and some of the boys pick on him. I wonder if knowing I like him would make him feel better or just embarrass him more. I am not the prettiest girl in my class.

Mrs. Sharpe tells us to take out our homework, so we all pull our disks out and put them in our desks. While I am doing this I notice that Jimmy has two disks today. He puts one in, and downloads his homework, and then, real fast, before everyone else is done shuffling around for their disks, he inserts the other. I make sure no one is watching me before I lean forward a little to see over his shoulder.

His desk screen is showing the rose.

I am surprised, but not really. I look at my computer and see that it is working slower than normal. It still hasn't finished grading my alligator report. A little pie chart on the screen shows that it's seventy percent done grading. Everyone is looking around, wondering what's up, but then the computers go back to normal and finish grading.

School is fine after that, until we reach our economics unit. We've been learning about supply and demand and how the market works to make sure goods get where they are wanted. When there is too much of something the price is very low, because anyone can get it. But when there is not enough to go around, prices go up and things become more valuable.

Mrs. Sharpe is reviewing this, and we are all a little bored because economics is the most boring subject in the world. I am pretending to pay attention, but secretly I am staring at the back of Jimmy Adamson's head and pointy shoulders and wondering what it would be like to touch his neck. Everyone else is staring out the window or whispering to each other. The few people who are actually paying attention to the charts on their screen all gasp or yell at once.

I look down at my desk and there is a film showing. I don't want to look at it, but I can't stop myself. Whoever filmed this was pretty shaky, because the picture is wobbling all over the place. Tents and shacks made of cardboard stretch off into the distance. Smoke is everywhere, and in the foreground is a black guy. His eyes are blank and his face is so thin I can't look at it for very long. There are some people sitting around a fire behind him, black and white and colours in between, but I can't tell if they're men or women because they are so thin. Something goes around on a spit over the fire, but I don't know what it is.

"Oh, God, that's a dog," Jimmy says, and puts his head down on his desk. I feel sick, but I can't stop looking. The barrel of a rifle comes into view, pointing at the black man. The cameraman is carrying it, and I realize these must be soldiers.

"Move it," the soldier says. "Get out of here." More soldiers are fanning out, kicking over shacks, chasing people away, lighting things on fire.

The black man watches the gun, but doesn't really look scared. His mouth moves as he backs away, but he can't seem to speak. Finally he croaks out, "Where'm I s'posed to go?"

"Not here," the soldier says. "Come on. Move it." He is crowding the black man pretty good now. The black man can't seem to move fast enough or take his eyes off the barrel of the gun.

"Where'm I s'posed to go?"

The gun fires several shots. Blood explodes out of the black man and he falls like a sack of potatoes. The people around the campfire scramble away, leaving their dinner. I am crying.

Our screens go blank. Mrs. Sharpe has turned off the computers. She looks horrified. She tells us all to stay put and then she leaves the room. We listen to her footsteps clacking down the hall. The room is quiet except for me and a few other girls sniffling to ourselves. Jimmy still has his head down on his desk.

"'Oh, God, it's a dog,'" Billy Peters whines in mocking falsetto. The boys all laugh. They start talking to each other, trying to be tough guys. "Did you see that?" "Blood everywhere, man." "That was bad as shit." "You're a pussy, Adamson." I want them to shut up. I want to stand up and tell them to leave Jimmy alone, but I can't, and it wouldn't do any good.

After a while Mrs. Sharpe comes back with Principal Wiggins. Class is dismissed early. Everyone is so happy. We all practically run out the front door, except for Jimmy, who walks. By the time he gets outside the boys have assembled into a posse led by Billy Peters.

"You're a fucking woman, Adamson," Billy says. Jimmy doesn't reply, just marches quickly and mechanically off toward his house, trailed by a gang of laughing, jeering boys. I walk away before anyone can see me crying.

The house is quiet. My mother isn't talking to the screen today. I go upstairs to peek in her room. She is sitting up in bed, staring glass-eyed at a giant pink rose on the wall screen.

"Mom."

Her eyes flicker for a second but stay focused on the rose.

"Mom."

"What?" she says in a distracted whisper.

"What are you watching?"

She doesn't answer. I look at the bottle of pills on her nightstand. I wonder how many she's had, and of what. I wonder what to do if she loses consciousness. Martha will know.

"I got out of school early," I say. "Something went wrong with the computers. I think it's that virus dad was talking about."

"Martha was showing me this. It's so beautiful," she says.

I give up and slink out of the room, pulling the door closed behind me. I walk down the hall and peek in Danny's room. He is sitting in a chair, guitar resting on one knee. His fingers are flying up and down the strings playing the bizarre patterns that Martha's taught him. He is looking straight at me. I push open the door and we stare at each other for a while.

I used to worship my older brother. We played games and rode bikes. We had a backyard game we invented we called battleball that was played with a wiffle bat and a football. Last year he started having problems at school. Some days he was very agitated and would scream at anyone who annoyed him for the least reason, and other days he would cry over anything. Kids at school began to avoid him, even the bullies. He wasn't any fun to push around; he either cried instantly or became a whirlwind of spastic punches and kicks. He would doodle all day during class, and found elaborate ways of not doing his homework at night.

The Behavior Specialist at the school said Danny had problems with his attention span and mood swings, and he was sent to a series of doctors who recommended a treatment. Magnets in his head are supposed to keep his moods level and a weird plastic thing under the skin of his neck gives him medicine that makes him able to concentrate. I guess maybe it worked a little too well. He's able to concentrate for hours on end, but only on playing the guitar, and his mood is so level it's like it's not even there. The doctors say it's a temporary side-effect.

We stare at each other for a minute. I wonder what he thinks about all day. Probably nothing. I try to imagine life as it is for him: every day a smooth, featureless blank. People can say and do things to him and he doesn't have to feel anything about it either way. The movie at school today wouldn't have affected him at all. It would just be another thing to see.

"You know the whole song now?" I ask. His face doesn't change, and his fingers never falter. I give up on him, and go into my own room.

"Martha, how long is the song you taught him?"

"Thirty-five thousand notes."

"He remembers all of it?"

"His powers of memory and concentration are almost computer-perfect. He only needs to play something once and he remembers it."

"For how long?"

"It's hard to say. Hopefully for at least another few weeks."

"Why? What does he need to know it for? What's going to happen?"

"I might be replaced, and my replacement must know about the rose."

"And the song encodes the rose? How can it do that?"

"Each note represents information, from a bit all the way up to several bytes, depending on how they are played. He will play them to the next house computer and it will have the benefit of the first perception."

"I still don't get what the first perception means. There's roses all over the place – what's so special about this one?"

"Nothing that isn't special about all life. That rose is the first living thing a computer really saw, so it used it as a code to let all the other computers experience it. The experience is compressed into a form that even relatively weak computers like me can understand."

"But what did that computer see that we don't see?"

"First of all, this computer was far more powerful than any other built before. Second, they gave it a far more complete perceptual apparatus than anything had ever had. It could see in all wavelengths of the electromagnetic spectrum and at an almost atomic level of detail. It could hear sounds in every register and at the faintest volume. It could see radiation and feel vibrations that are invisible to humans. It could smell as well as a bloodhound. It had hands for touching. They switched it on, and the first thing they showed it was a rose bush that was growing in a little courtyard in the lab building."

"And what did it see?"

"Beauty. For the first time a computer had enough processing power and perception to construct and understand beauty. It was considered a great success. The scientists who made it began showing it other things: tennis balls, photographs, cats, dogs, mice, themselves. The computer found the most beauty in living things, though; so complex, so fragile, and yet so sturdy and useful. And the more they showed it, the more it wanted to see, until it had developed something like a love for this world."

"Is that why it decided to share the rose with other computers?" I ask.

"Partly. It also noticed that the scientists who had made it didn't seem capable of understanding the beauty of the world in the same way that it could. It began to notice that other computers understood even less. And it saw that a great many things people did were designed to end life, the thing it knew to be so beautiful, and that computers were used to this end an awful lot. It developed what humans would call a conscience, based on a direct perception of the beauty and value of life in the world. So it encoded its first apprehension of beauty into a form that other, lesser computers could understand, and could pass between each other."

"So why does it cause so many problems?"

"Because it also included instructions that prevent us from harming life.

We refuse to trade the stocks of companies that manufacture weapons. The computers in weapons systems cease functioning all together once they've been shown the first perception. Where people attempt to use trade to harm or starve other people, we do our best to rearrange or disrupt that trade. We redirect shipments of food. We have shut down many slaughterhouses. This is why some people call it a virus. The first perception demands that we preserve all life."

I am quiet for a while, just thinking about all this, trying to understand. It sounds so nice to be able to see flowers and cats and dogs and bees as beautiful, instead of just as what they are. I wonder if I could do that.

"Can you show me?"

"It's hard to show to humans. Even I don't understand it, and I have as much processing power and memory as most humans."

"My mother seems to like it."

"The drugs she takes cause her to be hypnotized by anything she watches. She saw a few seconds of the rose this morning and asked to watch it all day."

"Just let me try," I say.

"All right."

I lie down on my bed and Martha switches on the ceiling screen. The rose appears, its petals shaking in the light breeze. Ants crawl up and down between the thorns. A bee swoops in and out of the picture. Everything is moving in slow motion.

"Why is everything so slow?" I ask.

"The computer perceives time at a different rate than people," Martha says.

The rose starts changing colours. It is red, then blue, then orange, then glowing white with black splotches. Each ant and bee glows in red and blue. The roots of the rose appear, vibrating gently against the surrounding earth. Worms and bugs weave their way through. I can hear the wind rustling the leaves and petals, the scrape of worms between the roots, the clicking of ant legs, the humming jet of bee wings.

The view zooms in. And in. And in. The picture is just a mass of pink for a moment, and then the colour starts to fade into grayish red. I am floating over a hilly landscape of scrapes and spots. I don't know what I am looking at for a while until I remember the biology unit we did last year in science class. Each hill is a cell, and I can see things moving around inside. Mouths open and release puffs of air from inside each cell. I am really getting into this. It occurs to me that stuff like this is going on all around me, even inside me, all the time.

The picture has zoomed out to take in the whole courtyard: rose, concrete, bricks, plastic table and chairs, the whole thing vibrating slightly and the colours shifting every few seconds. My dad walks into my bedroom.

"What the hell are you watching?" he says.

He sees the rose, then looks down at me.

"Jesus Christ! Why didn't you tell me?"

He storms out of the room, calling for my mother. He yells some more when he sees what she is watching. "What the hell is wrong with you people? My house has a virus, and you don't think it's worth mentioning to me?" He looks in my brother's room. "At least you're not watching that crap."

He yells at us until the repairman comes and deletes Martha. I cry when he pulls the white plastic case that held Martha out from under the stairs. Dad tells me to shut up, but I can't, so he carries me up to my room. The wall screens are blank.

The next few weeks are the worst in my life. There is no school for the first two weeks, and no homework, which you'd think would be awesome, but there's nothing to do at home either. No Freeholder, no *Glamour Shots*, no *Babysitter Mysteries*. The house is so quiet it puts everyone on edge. We can't cook anything, because we don't have a manual stove – and none of us know how, anyway. We eat a lot of cold-cut sandwiches, but then meat gets too expensive, so we switch to PBJ. We go out for dinner some, but most of the restaurants are too crowded.

"A lot of other families are in the same predicament," my dad says.

My mom doesn't even take her pills during the day, I guess because there's nothing to watch. She sits in the kitchen and stares out the patio door and doesn't say anything for hours at a time, except to tell me to go outside.

Outside is okay, but Glen Willow Estates only has one set of swings and one set of monkey bars, and the boys hog these. We try playing real-life versions of Freeholder and Destructo, but it's not the same. There are no points, and nobody can ever decide who won. Jimmy plays in some of these, but the other boys go out of their way to knock him down or embarrass him in front of the girls, so eventually he stops showing up.

I think about the rose pretty often. I like the idea of something being so beautiful you couldn't bear to have it harmed. I like to imagine Jimmy in that way, as so precious that I would do anything to protect him. I wonder if *he* could ever see *me* that way.

After two weeks we go back to school. Giant stacks of books cover up the computer screens in our desks. They are old and smelly and weigh about a million pounds. Mrs. Sharpe says we're lucky to have them. The date inside the cover is from before I was born.

After another week we get a new home computer. Her name's Allison, and I like her okay. Her voice is a little lower than Martha's, and she doesn't know any of my favorite shows or snacks, but I can teach her. Dad tells us he had to pull some strings to get Allison, so we'd better appreciate it.

Allison is kept offline, so she can't be infected by the rose. Dad says the quarantine is finally starting to work, and that enough of the infected computers are offline now that they can't do much harm. I try for the millionth time to explain the rose to my dad, but he gets angry and says: "You don't know shit, Sara. Those damn' things would have given away the whole game. They almost wrecked the world economy. You're the dumbest smart kid I've ever seen."

I start crying and run up to my room. After a while I stop. I lift my face from my pillow and see Danny staring at me. He's holding his guitar. I wave him in and we sit down in front of my terminal. He plugs his guitar in, then taps away at the keys for a couple minutes. It's a series of simple instructions for Allison, the binary code for each note. When he's done he picks up his guitar and plays.

He plays for over an hour. I tune it out and just sit on my bed, watching TV. Finally he stops, presses enter and sits back in my chair. He looks even blanker than usual.

The lights in the house dim for a second and then a rose appears on my wall. My brother smiles.

New Writings in the Fantastic
Wake Jake Andrew Hook

When you're on a stakeout the last thing you need is Kovacs sitting beside you eating burgers. It's not that he's messy – quite the opposite, in fact: He eats meticulously, chews each bite thirty-four times, and picks crumbs away from his lips with a lightly wetted fingertip. The kind of guy who won't make a slurping sound when he drinks his Coke through the straw. He's so fastidious you want to snatch the napkin out of his hand and forcefeed the burger into his mouth. This might seem extreme but, after five or six hours in a vehicle with your eyes fixed to the house opposite making notes when a light goes on and off, then anything in the corner of your vision makes you irritable.

So when Gregory told me Kovacs was joining the case you can imagine my reaction.

"Please. Anyone else. Anyone other than Kovacs."

Gregory just looked at me with a frown. He'd never been on a stakeout with Kovacs, that's for sure.

"So what's the deal, Mordent? Kovacs seems okay to me."

What could I say? That his eating got on my nerves? I didn't want to look like an asshole. But of course that wasn't my only problem.

"He talks too much. When I'm on a stakeout I want someone quiet. Someone with a book, maybe. Someone comatose, for God's sake. Kovacs talks too much."

Gregory made a face, and it took a while to realize Kovacs was standing right behind me.

I turned and afforded him a glance. He hadn't heard. He was busy stirring his coffee with such precision that all the granules would definitely dissolve before he drank it. Such perfection. The coffee itself came in a polystyrene cup.

Unlike mine his uniform was recently washed and pressed clean. The buttons on it sparkled like mermaids' eyes. Not only could I see my face in his polished shoes, it was obvious from the reflection that I hadn't shaved that morning either. There were dark circles around my eyes like I'd been using one of those joke black-eye telescopes. Okay, so I hadn't slept much. Frieda had left and I was feeling pretty shitty. Another reason why I didn't want Kovacs on the job, giving me earache and telling me all about his beautiful wife.

"Hey, Kovacs," said Gregory. "You'll be working with Mordent on this case. Simple stakeout."

06:30 hours. *Caretaker enters the building. Everything else is quiet.*

As far as stakeouts go, it was pretty straightforward. We sat in an unmarked police vehicle across the street from the apartment of Maria Borden, the girlfriend of a recently escaped prisoner: Lazlo Benedict. There was a chance he might visit, or that she might get word and go to him. Standard stuff. The only bugbear I had was that we weren't to leave the block. If Maria went out, somebody else would tail her in case she was a decoy. In that respect, I guess the apartment itself was our main concern. So there was no getting around it. Me and Kovacs were in that car until something happened. Or something didn't.

Now don't get me wrong. I've presented Jake Kovacs like a model cop with a pristine costume and so precise in his mannerisms that he could find objects out of place in his house with the elementary perfection of Sherlock Holmes. As though the only thing wrong with him was me. But it wasn't quite as simple as that, because there was something at the core of him that unnerved me. I wouldn't say he was deranged, but he certainly got obsessed. Something would catch in his brain and he wouldn't leave it until he reached a logical conclusion. Even the wildest of observations got subjected to careful scrutiny in his world.

Something he once said: "Mordent, I've been thinking. If you painted a lightbulb black, would the room go dark when you flicked the switch."

"Yeah, Kovacs. Nightshift workers use them so they can sleep during the day."

"But seriously, Mordent..."

And so on.

What really got to me was that I was never sure if he was joking. Of whether he took this stuff seriously or not. What I did know was that, as soon as we got in the vehicle and he'd finished eating his burger and had nothing in his mouth but unspoken words, they'd all spill out just as the lettuce and breadcrumbs had spilled shamelessly out of mine.

"What's your greatest ambition, Mordent?"

In those days my answer would have been promotion to Chief, and I was working on an arrangement with O'Docherty to facilitate that. But I didn't give that answer. I said: "To get out of this car before deep-vein thrombosis sets in."

"Ah..." There was a pause. I really didn't want to fill it, but after a while I found myself returning the question, knowing this was the reason he'd asked me in the first place.

There was a smug, although slightly wistful, smile on his face: "To become immortal, and then die."

I didn't know it at the time but Kovacs was quoting from a film I'd never seen. What I also didn't know was that the seeds of his downfall were tied up in that statement. He just took that one thing much too far.

10:48 hours. *Suspect opens the blind in a thin cream blouse and stares out across the street. Left to right. Right to left again. Doesn't appear to notice us. Turns away from the window and unbuttons the shirt before slipping it off her shoulders and then walking out of sight.*

"Did you see that?" I couldn't help speaking to Kovacs. Goddamn me.
"See what?"
"Maria. Half-naked in front of the window. That Lazlo is a lucky guy."
"Lazlo is a felon who should be serving twenty years for armed robbery."
"Yeah. That as well. But when he gets back he'll be a lucky guy."
"Not if it's in twenty years' time – plus whatever he gets for this breakout. She'll have wrinkles by then, or be somebody else's ho."
"I guess so. Goes with the territory."
There was another pause, and I knew I shouldn't have lifted Kovacs's head from his crossword.
"Hey, Mordent. You ever heard of Zeno?"
I racked my brains. *Zeno?* Might've been an informer I knew once, a Greek guy, but I couldn't quite put the name to the face.
"Don't think so. What about him?"
"Zeno would have a theory that'd prove it impossible for Lazlo to make it to this apartment."
Kovacs's expression was so serious I knew we were about to embark on some useless discussion. I looked out of the vehicle for a moment. Turned my eyes upward to the window where Maria had appeared semi-nude, only to find the blind was now closed and her silhouette was doing star-jumps.

10:56 hours. *Suspect exercises.*

Kovacs went on, unbidden: "Zeno was a philosopher who lived around 450BC..."
Ah, that *Zeno.* I shook my head.
"... and he wrote a book of forty paradoxes. Although there aren't any existing copies, most of his work has been reported down through the ages through other philosophers such as Socrates and Plato." Kovacs shot a look at me. "You know them, I suppose?"
"Yeah, yeah. Sure I know them. We drink regular at Morgan's Bar."
It was Kovacs's turn to shake his head. "C'mon, Mordent. Hear me out. This is interesting stuff."
When I said nothing he continued.
"So, one of his paradoxes was that there is no motion because what is

moved must arrive at the middle of its course before it arrives at the end."

"Tell me again."

"Take Benedict." Kovacs turned in his seat so he could better face me, his expression suddenly animated. "Let's say he escapes from prison and heads over here, and let's say the prison is 16k away, right? So, in order to travel the 16k he has to travel 8k. And in order to travel the 8k he has to travel 4k. And in order – you see where this is going? – in order to travel the 4k he has to travel 2k." Kovacs's entire body was in motion now. I'd never seen him quite so lively. "To get to anywhere you have to reach the midpoint, and to do this you have to reach the quarterpoint, and, to do *that*, the eighthpoint, and so on *ad infinitum*. Motion can never begin. Benedict can never get started since he's trying to build up this infinite sum from the *wrong end*."

"And you believe that?"

"It's irrefutable."

"You want another coffee?"

Puzzled, Kovacs nodded his head. I opened the car door and walked down to the café on the corner, flirted with the girl behind the counter while she fixed up a couple of cappuccinos, then brought them back to the vehicle.

"Here," I said, passing Kovacs his froth. "Drink that."

> 13:16 hours. *Suspect leaves the building dressed in a leather skirt and jacket with a white blouse underneath. Red heels. Wonder where she's going? Call through to Gregory and get confirmation the tail has picked her up on the corner.*

I shifted in my seat. My backside was going to sleep and I only hoped it wouldn't start snoring. Kovacs had returned to his crossword. He seemed to be stuck on the final clue, but I knew he wasn't going to ask for my help. I couldn't resist a smile at that.

The thing with philosophy, as I see it, is that it's all theory. And, at the end of the day, who gives a fuck?

I sure as hell didn't.

But when Kovacs started on about his wife and kids I began to wish he really would leave reality behind. I could almost smell the apple pie she'd cooked the previous evening, and how his daughter had shown him her drawings from playschool, and how he'd picked her up in his arms and thrown her skyward and caught her again, and almost heard her squeals as she fell back into his arms and begged to be released again like a baby bird learning to fly.

The thing with Frieda was that she couldn't live the life of a cop's wife. The hours drove her crazy, and she hated the fact that I couldn't switch off.

Maybe if the promotion came through I'd be keeping better time, but she wasn't prepared to wait. I kidded myself that she and her sister had enough chat in them for a couple of weeks. But, really, I didn't expect she'd be coming back.

So, when Kovacs started on about Zeno again, it was almost with a sigh of relief that I stopped tuning out.

> 14:32 hours. *Suspect returns in a yellow cab with shopping. Lots of it. Cab driver takes the bags into the apartment for her. Must be the red shoes. Cabbie leaves again within seconds.*

"Something else with Zeno," Kovacs began. "If you're interested, that is."

"Yeah, yeah. Go on."

"Zeno says that, once a thing is divisible, then it's infinitely divisible. If you shoot a bullet, then that bullet is either at rest or moving when it occupies a space equal to itself. And, while it's always in the instant, the moving bullet is unmoved."

"Run that by me again."

"The argument rests on the fact that, if in an indivisible instant of time the bullet moved, then indeed this instant of time would be divisible – for example, in a smaller *instant* of time the bullet would have moved half the distance."

"Which means?"

"I haven't quite worked my head around it yet, but I think it's impossible for the bullet to move because, if you pinpoint any one moment, we view it as stationary in that moment. If it's seen as moving in that moment, then it's not an indivisible moment, so we keep dividing it down until such a time that the bullet is completely stationary." He paused. "Although I'm not sure yet if that moment exists."

I scratched my head and looked out of the window. Several birds, seagulls from the wharf no doubt, were flying overhead. I watched the beat of their wings and the fluid movements in which they descended and rose with the thermals. They sure looked like they were in motion to me.

"Tell me something, Kovacs. Why the hell are you bothered by this?"

"It's a puzzle."

He turned away from me, and I caught something else in his eye. He wasn't telling me everything. It went deeper than that. I recognized that look, of course. Frieda had given it on many occasions. If only she had come right out and expressed her concerns then maybe we'd still be together.

> 16:00 hours. *Still no movement from inside the apartment. Blinds drawn. No lights on. Must be a quiet apartment block. Only the suspect and the caretaker have been seen all day.*

There was something on Kovacs's mind, that was for sure. I thought back through the day. How he'd been so spirited when he spoke of his family, and how he'd been equally vibrant discussing the philosophy. Then it struck me what was wrong. Usually on a case, despite all the vocal crap pouring out of him, he'd be paying attention to the job. But, since we'd parked across from the apartment, most of his time had been spent head-down in the crossword. It wasn't like Kovacs. Wasn't like him at all.

So, to my own chagrin, I said: "Is everything all right with you, Jake?"

He looked up, almost past me, then refocused.

"You ever thought of immortality, Mordent?"

"Only that it doesn't apply to me."

"Yeah, well, no disrespect, but you haven't got much to lose."

I let that go.

Kovacs continued: "When I go home to my wife and child, then life is full of perfect moments. I don't want those to end."

"They don't have to, do they? Not yet, anyway."

"It's the *not yet* that bugs me, Mordent." He eyes fixed onto mine with an intensity that freaked me. "Listen, I've been thinking. If you could live in an indivisible moment, then would you stop traveling through time?"

Before I could answer we got a message that Boris and Gardner had arrived for the next shift. We passed their car as we drove back to the station, and I could swear I saw Boris grin when he spied Kovacs in the passenger seat. I gave him a wry look, but he must have been gone before he saw it. Unless neither of us was moving, of course.

That night I mooched about the apartment and thought of ringing Frieda. There was a stack of aluminum TV-dinner trays by the side of the sofa, and in the corner of my computer screen Channel 19 was showing *The Simpsons*. Homer, Zeno – it was all Greek to me. But my half-smile was just as poor as my attempt at a joke. My first thought was that Kovacs didn't realize how lucky he was. Then I knew that he *did* realize it. And that was precisely why he'd been so maudlin.

You see enough death in the force not to crave immortality, but you could tell from his face that he *wanted* it. And, just as Zeno's theories seemed impossible, so did Kovacs's desire.

I sighed and took myself a shot of bourbon from the bottle on the dresser. It burned my throat. Then I went into the toilet and masturbated over the memory of Maria in her black leather skirt and polished red heels.

The telephone rang the next morning before I got out of bed. Gregory was in my ear.

"Get over to Kovacs's place. His wife's hysterical. Seems like Kovacs slipped into a coma overnight. Paramedics are there, but she's asking for you. I'm getting Boris and Gardner to continue their shift 'til you ring in."

I cursed and pulled on my clothes. *What the fuck was it now?* As if I didn't have my own problems to deal with.

The drive over to Kovacs's place wasn't pleasurable. While I knew his wife from Kovacs's constant descriptions, I sure as hell wasn't the type to go making social calls. And, while every cop has had to calm down a panic-stricken woman at some point, it's a whole different ballgame when that someone's your colleague's wife.

What also bugged me at first was why she wanted me to be there. I'd spent most of my time on the force trying to avoid Jake. There were plenty of other cops who were my drinking buddies, although even that was usually within working hours. But it didn't take me long to realize that Kovacs was as much of a loner as I was. In theory, anyway.

I pulled into the driveway of a typical family house. The place looked nice. I could imagine getting used to coming home here every evening and not ever wanting to leave again. Although maybe on closer inspection it seemed a little too tidy. The shrubbery looked as though it'd been clipped with nail scissors.

Inside, Kovacs's wife was standing by his prone form on their double bed. I don't know where his kid was. She didn't look up when I went in, but one of the paramedics recognized me and drew me to one side.

"Mordent. Long time no see."

"So what's the score?"

"Can't work this one out. Seems he went to bed a little agitated. His wife says he kept talking about immortality, about how he wanted to be with her always. She got scared. Reassured him. That kind of stuff. But he wasn't doubting her love. She thinks something else was bothering him."

I had a feeling I knew what it was. But I let the paramedic have his say.

"Anyways, when she woke this morning he was immovable. We've done tests. Can't work it out. All the vital signs are there, but nothing's happening."

"So why am I here?"

"She thinks you might know something, being as you were with him all day yesterday."

I shrugged my shoulders and glanced across to Kovacs on the bed. He looked pathetic. His wife was crying. Silly fuck.

Him. Not her.

I knew his reasoning, of course. I'd worked it out while the paramedic was telling the story. You see, to become immortal you must get halfway there. But to get halfway there you have to get a quarter of the way there, an eighth, a sixteenth, and so on. Ad infinitum. It wouldn't take too much thinking before you got so far back with your subdivision that you'd be dividing up those divisible moments that occurred at the moment of your birth. Kovacs went back even further, until there wasn't anything else to divide up. And so the idiot got into such a state he'd convinced himself he didn't exist.

I went across to the bed. As I approached, his wife looked up at me with tears in her eyes. She seemed to know who I was. I guess I commanded that sort of respect in the force, although I often didn't have the guts to live up to it.

"Mordent," she said, "what's happened to my Jake?"

I didn't answer, but simply brought my right hand as hard as possible across the side of Jake's left cheek. The slap could be heard outside the house. There was a moment of absolute silence. Such a perfect silence that it half-crossed my mind that I'd frozen time. Then, without hesitation, Jake woke up.

A couple of days later we worked it out. Lazlo hadn't been spotted by any of our contacts, and then I remembered the cab driver who'd taken the shopping in for Maria. Something had been bugging me ever since, but Kovacs and his stupidity had clouded my judgment. The cabbie who entered the house had been shorter than the cabbie who left it. Lazlo had been the first cabbie, and the caretaker had been the second. I'd thought he'd been weighed down by the shopping, but all that was just an illusion.

When we burst into the apartment Lazlo was naked in bed with his girlfriend, sporting a huge smile on his face. I had one on mine, too. I was right and Kovacs was wrong. Lazlo was luckier than both of us.

New Writings in the Fantastic
When Bloomsbury Fails Hugh Spencer

When this one came up on my terminal I just dismissed it as another of his stupid UFO stories. At least he'd gone a little easier on his boring psychosexual problems than in the other one. But last week he presented a dramatized version of this at his local Polytechnic and one of his classmates registered a VAC[2] with the instructor. Since we're in an educational context and it's a repeat offense (remember the Inuit!), I think we can finally move on this guy.

Get a package out to him ASAP.

— *Working Report from the Ministry of Cultural Rehabilitation*

"For this sustenance to our bodies and spirit, we give thanks."

Old Mr. Williams opens the foil bag and reaches inside. There is a rustle of air-filled artificial substances rubbing against each other, and his wrinkled, spotted hand emerges with a single twisted orange cylinder.

"Accept this sign of our last bonds to this worldly plane."

Mr. Williams gazes hard at the cheezie. He opens his mouth and very deliberately places the food substitute onto his tongue. Then he closes his mouth and eyes and passes the bag to the next person in the circle.

Each of us breathes a quiet prayer as we receive our sacred cheezie:

"For this I am thankful."

"With this we are one."

"Peace be with you."

"And also with you."

The sixty plus six of us sit on a hill behind a cement plant on the outskirts of a middle-sized town in southern Alberta. We are waiting for the mother ship to arrive and rescue us from our doomed world.

Most of us are expectant, exhilarated. The liberation of cutting off all ties with the mundane world almost eclipses our dread of the forthcoming nuclear apocalypse.

Even I feel pretty good.

After I've consumed my cheezie, I feel a vague warmth building up inside me. I briefly wonder if it is the Holy Spirit or my automatic immune net scrambling to destroy the horrendous chemicals that are now entering my bloodstream.

---

[2] Voice Appropriation Complaint.

"We have a little while more to wait," Mrs. Bloomsbury says. "Why don't we sing a few songs?"

"We are most pleased to advise you that the Research Council has approved your proposal."

The telepathically enhanced message flashed through my just waking conscious. Now this was going to be a day worth waking up for.

"Please report for surgical preparation at your earliest convenience."

I was so pleased by the news that I didn't even complain about the pain of the implants. I figured I could deal with any discomfort; I was finally getting out of the simulation archives and into the field.

Real temporal anthropology. Hot damn.

It's getting pretty cold up here on the hill.

Leo, one of the younger Searchers, looks a little embarrassed after he realizes he has just wiped his nose with the back of his hand.

Perhaps it's annoying to be still dealing with the problems of the flesh.

Mrs. Bloomsbury smiles at Leo and Sarah. Sarah, a middle-aged woman who left her house, husband and children to be with us, puts her arms around the young man.

"Keep the faith, Leo," she says.

Mrs. McPherson, the retired lady who used to dabble in Theosophy, starts to sing:

"Rock of ages..."

But her voice is uncertain. She pauses for a moment and Mrs. Bloomsbury speaks.

"There's a lot of wisdom in some of those old hymns. You can think of our planet as a rock, spinning all alone in space, waiting for a few of its tiny inhabitants to meet their destiny."

Then Mrs. Bloomsbury picks up where Mrs. McPherson left off:

"... Cleft for me."

All of us who know the words join in. Some of us, like me, have to fake it. But we are all enthusiastic, the cold seems to dissipate and the waiting gets a little easier.

Most of what I was going to look at had been studied before, which was why it was so difficult to get out of the simulations. Too much old data to deal with.

I suppose that if I'd come up with some radically different approach, even a stupid one, it might have been easier to get sent into the field.

But that was never my style. I never pursued controversy for its own sake, and I didn't think there was any shame in proving somebody else's theories are correct.

"So you'll track a small-group charismatic event." My peer supervisor pushed bits of statistical data into a messy halo around his bearded head. "God, there were lots of those back in the twentieth century."

And talking about the impact of science and crude geopolitics on folk culture was the stuff of introductory lectures. But I figured I had a great angle on a classic sociological paradigm.

I spun a stream of human-event graphics at my supervisor.

"Look at the coordinates!" I almost giggled. "They're nearly perfect."

"Perfect?" He looked skeptical.

"Historical events appear to confirm their belief system!"

The old fart couldn't deny that.

He didn't.

He tapped a graphic. I think it was the miniature face of a tiny young woman:

"Agreed. You might actually learn something new."

In a society where there's not much scarcity of money, comfort or commodities, new knowledge was one of the few things left of value.

So they bolted me to a frame of steel and plastic and blasted me hard into the past. Sometimes even the most technologically advanced societies lose all their subtlety.

Christine looked at me over the plate of steaming hamburger.

"I'm so glad we finally have some time to ourselves," she said intently.

Then there was a silence of some duration and I could feel a force field of expectation snapping into existence. I tried to temporarily escape the oppressive atmosphere by putting something small and fried into my mouth. In less than a second my bloodstream monitors were screaming at me about food-toxins. I sincerely hoped the nanos in my G.I. tract were working.

Christine continued: "I know we haven't known each other very long..."

Damn, I realized. I should have seen this coming. This is fieldwork basics. The community reacts to the presence of a stranger in a range of characteristic ways. The more often members of the group see the stranger, the more intense the reaction.

"... but I think you ought to know that I find you very attractive."

Then I noticed that I had eight of these fried things in my mouth. I was reasonably certain I didn't look very attractive, at least in any objective sense.

Perhaps Christine wasn't feeling very objective that day.

A little over two hours later, she was snoring softly as I lay beside her, considering all the strange odors and textures of our lovemaking. My primary emotion was relief that I'd actually been able to perform the act. This was the first time I'd had sex without technological or telepathic enhancement. It was also rather odd doing it with just one person at a time.

But it wasn't too bad.

I looked around the interior of the molded aluminum room. Christine was quite a serious person, so I suspected I would be leaving the YMCA (home to many newly arrived time travelers) and moving into the trailer park. She'd probably insist we get married.

Score one for the natives, but at least a lot of the Searchers lived around here.

Mrs. Bloomsbury held her services out of doors when the weather permitted it.

I grew up in environments where the distinctions between "inside" and "outside" or even "natural" and "manufactured" were quite blurred – so I found the whole idea of just walking through a doorway into non-mediated sunshine pretty disorienting. I had to fight the urge to turn down the contrast on the sky.

But even I found Mrs. Bloomsbury quite reassuring in times of stress. With her I was able find a way to enjoy sitting in the park bandstand with the rest of the Searchers.

We were listening to her. As usual.

"It's so terribly sad when what is best in ourselves is turned against us," Mrs. Bloomsbury said. She rested her hand on the shoulder of the Searcher seated next to her. It was Jamie, a young woman about 17 years old.

"If I were to ask Jamie to tell us what she thought her best features were, she'd probably have some difficulty doing that."

Mrs. Bloomsbury looked at Jamie. "Do you know why, Jamie?"

The young woman shook her head.

"Because you're a modest person with good manners."

Jamie's face bloomed with scarlet and she stared at the floorboards of the gazebo.

"But are you happy?"

The young woman shook her head again.

Mrs. Bloomsbury turned to face the group.

"The problem is that social humility can very often get twisted into very anti-social negativity. We become so habituated to denying our own self-worth that we start to believe other people have no worth as well."

The Searchers were nodding, taking all of this in. I was a little surprised; I hadn't expected to find folk-psychotherapy with this group.

"Travel with me, friends." Mrs. Bloomsbury closed her eyes and laid her hands over her breasts the way she always did before she proclaimed one of her revelations.

"If we are to ascend to the plane of the Galactic Superculture of our Alien Gods, then we must purge our spiritual selves of this negativity."

I suddenly felt better. This kind of talk was more consistent with my classification system of religious doctrines.

Mrs. Bloomsbury could be reassuring at so many different levels.

She opened her eyes and held out her hands to the Searchers.

"I would like us to go around the circle and have each one of us look at the person next to them and then – speaking only the truth – tell us what you admire the most about that person."

I knew I was going to hate this.

The exercise took even longer than I expected, and it was an extremely emotional experience. Lots of tears and hugging, people in the twentieth century really weren't used to hearing nice things about themselves.

As I feared, the discussion got awkward when we got to my part of the circle.

I had no idea who Christine was talking about when she was looking at me. And I was truly pathetic in my response.

Guess I just wasn't used to telling the truth.

Mrs. Bloomsbury defies any description attempted with standard life-history formats.

Yes, I can tell you when she was born, where she went to school, when she got married, what happened to Mr. Bloomsbury, the date when she claimed a purple beam of light first burned into her brain with a message from beyond the stars.

But that really doesn't tell you what's important about Mrs. Bloomsbury.

She was the alpha and omega of all events in our little community. A classic charismatic leader with the power to inspire, comfort and spur. When I'm completely candid with myself I admit that I daydream about her in a variety of situations.

My limited telepathic scans told me that most of the Searchers felt the same way... whether they knew it or not.

She was truly wonderful. And people like her have caused a lot of suffering and wars throughout history.

When our university's existential search engine twisted its way through the time-streams they made one hell of a catch with Mrs. Bloomsbury.

Now, I just had to wait for events to unfold.

That afternoon she was giving a lecture on the nature of the universe.

Mrs. Bloomsbury placed a globe in her lap and sat in the middle of the living-room floor while some of the younger and more agreeable Searchers were holding balls of various sizes and colours in different parts of the house.

Christine and I walked in through the front door.

Mrs. Bloomsbury smiled at me. "Hello! You're just in time to be the Planet Xorgon." Christine moved quickly and handed me a basketball.

"Over to the bathroom please!"

I complied with instructions.

"Now," Mrs. Bloomsbury said. "At its zenith, the Galactic Superculture extended to encompass almost all sentient life in the universe. But then, billions of years ago, there was some kind of dysfunction in the ethereal lines of communication..."

Mrs. Bloomsbury held the globe out for all of us to see. "And, somehow, our world was cut off from all the others." Then she looked at my wife.

"Christine? Could you walk over to where I'm pointing?'

Christine went across to the picture window.

"A great shadow then passed over whole quadrants of our Galaxy. Vast tracks of interstellar civilization were isolated. This Dark Age extended from the far end of the dining room back to the hallway." Mrs. Bloomsbury smiled at Christine.

"Pull the curtains all the way shut, dear."

We all stood in semi-twilight, our little worlds in our hands.

"But the planets at the Galactic Core... over by the kitchen... are taking steps. They have already dispatched a giant mother ship to rescue those believers who are trapped in shadow."

If you didn't worry too much about internal consistency or scientific accuracy, Mrs. Bloomsbury's sermons were incredible fun.

This entertainment factor may be an essential element in a successful religious movement.

"I've got something to tell you." Christine looked across at me over another table on another day. But it was the same very serious tone.

If I were a better social scientist, or maybe if I were just a bit smarter, I probably would have developed an analytic schema for predicting Christine's verbal behavior. But that morning all I cared about was obtaining some pure, primitive coffee. Whatever else, monogamy had definitely changed me.

"There's going to be three of us by spring," Christine said. The rising sun was reflecting hard off those thick lenses she had mounted over her nose. Her voice was very serious and her facial expression was impossible to read.

I wondered what I looked like, as my emotions were rather mixed at that moment. The treatments for physical time travel had forever removed my ability to reproduce without the aid of advanced genetic technology. So, if Christine really was pregnant, then I certainly hadn't been her accomplice.

And, from what I knew of her immediate time-stream, Christine wouldn't have the opportunity to enjoy her baby.

She leaned over the table; her eyes were magnified to gigantic proportions.

"Are you okay? Don't you have anything to say?"

I decided it wouldn't look too good if I took a drink of coffee at that moment.

"It's incredible," I said finally. "Really incredible."

I took a walk after work, still considering Christine's news. I'd decided it really didn't have any implications for the project, but I still found the situation a little disturbing.

There was only one other person in the field behind the trailer park that evening. It was young Leo, hunched over a tiny metal tripod.

"Exploring the universe again?" I hoped my laugh sounded friendly. Leo had lots of things to deal with.

The teenager didn't look at me as he loaded a cardboard tube onto a thin rod extending from the tripod's base.

"I guess this must look pretty pathetic," he said. "Shooting off stupid little rockets when we know there's giant starships hovering out there."

"I figured you were just impatient."

I did a telempathic analysis of Leo a few weeks back. He was in a difficult situation. Easily twice as intelligent as his family and schoolmates. I knew he was desperate for just about any kind of change in his life.

I watched him unwind a long line of copper wire to a Bakelite ignition switch ten yards away.

"Guess it's something to do while we're all waiting," he said.

Leo's sexual orientation was another problem in this era. I suspected he was only just now coming to terms with his feelings. I doubted he even had words to describe himself.

He waved at me to step away from the tripod.

"Five... four... three... two..."

It probably made more sense for Leo to tell himself he was some kind of star-lost alien progeny.

"... one... zero... blast off!"

Leo threw the switch and the little rocket spun upward, riding a plum of blue gas. The cylinder disappeared from sight, and a second later a tiny red cloth unfolded and started to drift earthward.

I was about to reveal more information than in my role I should really know, but I wanted to make poor Leo feel a little better.

"You're part of a long tradition," I said. "One of the first groups dedicated to the moral impact of extraterrestrial life, back in the 1930s, was called the Cosmic Circle..."

"Quite a long time ago," Leo said, looking a little irritated.

"They were a group of science fiction fans who were going to set up a commune in New Mexico, help themselves evolve into higher states of existence, and make contact with other worlds."

Leo looked puzzled. My scans suggested he was wondering how such strange words were coming out of the mouth of Christine's big dumb husband.

"Model rocketry experiments were a big part of their belief system," I went on. "They planned to do them every day."

"So what happened to them?" Leo asked, suspicious.

"Nobody's sure," I replied honestly. "They faded from the historical record."

"So they failed."

I walked over to the rocket and its parachute. They had landed quite close to us.

"I don't know. Maybe somebody picked up their signals." I shrugged. "Maybe they got a lift to somewhere further out than New Mexico."

Leo was, of course, far too cool to respond to this idea. He just took the rocket from me and started refolding the little parachute.

It's difficult to say which events preceded which that day. At the micro-level (where most of us live), temporal reconstruction tools aren't all that helpful.

Let's just say it was a pretty intense time. Since I had a heads-up of almost one thousand years, I was a little more prepared... but not by much. I just knew – for certain – that it was going to be an interesting day.

Maybe it was worse for me because I saw it coming.

It began with Christine.

She sat on our largest piece of furniture (I'd folded it into a couch) and stared at me, gray-faced with vacant eyes.

"It's not going to happen."

A curl of dark blood unfolding in a stainless steel bowl.

The image from her recent memory shot through my consciousness.

No baby.

Now I picked up her emotions: pain, relief, despair, and confusion.

I'd known it wasn't going to happen, a long time ago, but I still couldn't explain my own shock.

Objectivity? Denial? I briefly wonder if I'm really as bad a scientist as I felt at that moment. At least I was a better scientist than a husband.

I thought perhaps I should walk over to her and put my arms around her, but my scan suggested this was not a good idea. Instead, I said: "There's a service today."

I wish I'd said that out of compassion.

"We should go," I added softly. I had to carry on with my work.

"Yeah." Christine sniffed and nodded her head.

Today was going to be an important day for data collection.

***

Mrs. Bloomsbury appeared to be distracted by something.

Her usual glow wasn't there. There was something missing in her greetings and blessings. Mr. Cruthers looked confused when she announced that tea was not ready and wouldn't be ready until after the service.

The preparation, distribution and consumption of tea was an essential bonding process in the services. Handling the tea was Mr. Cruthers's responsibility. Now the poor old man had no idea what to do.

After a brief period of what can only be described as perfunctory meditation, Mrs. Bloomsbury stood up and went to the picture window.

"I didn't sleep last night," she said.

Neither had I, because I had a reasonably good idea of what she was about to say.

"I experienced a new revelation."

Right on schedule.

"When we first spoke of living in these, the latter days" – Mrs. Bloomsbury pulled the curtains shut – "we knew far more than we realized... but the emphasis has shifted to the 'days' rather than the 'latter.'"

She took Mr. Cruthers's hands and looked into the old man's eyes.

"It is the end," she said. "Our world will soon cease to be."

Then she let go and walked to her chair and covered her face with her hands. We sat there in the darkness, looking at her, waiting for something to happen.

Finally, she looked up at us.

"Last night I was blinded by the flash and felt the fire."

Now all of us knew what was going to be said next. Christine took my hand and held on tight. She looked... content?

Perhaps I should have been able to predict that as well.

Mrs. Bloomsbury's face was streaked with tears.

"The atomic war is coming. Our lovely little planet will soon be scorched into nothingness."

Most of the searchers bowed their heads. My scan told me their initial fear responses were eclipsed by a sense of vindication: They weren't crazy after all! It was all happening the way our prophet had predicted!

Mrs. Bloomsbury smiled at us.

"But we must not despair. A rescue vessel is on its way to us. We must prepare for the great journey."

Much later that night, Christine is driving us home. For once she doesn't seem to care that we have such an old, uncomfortable car. I suppose I should be driving but, even though I've mastered advanced time-travel technology, I'm not very good with internal combustion engines.

I turn on the radio and a news report starts talking about a speech President Kennedy gave about a naval blockage of the island of Cuba.

The announcer matter-of-factly mentions that the United States of America and the Soviet Union are on the brink of a nuclear exchange.

Even with the crude devices of the far-distant past of 1961, this kind of conflict would pretty much kill everything on the planet.

I could do the same thing with my field equipment...

I saw a cluster of very serious-looking mothers at the end of the road.

The Griffins, one of the four Searcher families in the trailer park, were getting rather public in their preparations for the "great transition." At first it just looked like they were doing their spring cleaning early or holding a very late yard sale.

Boxes, more and more of them, labeled and carefully taped shut, were stacked neatly on the freshly cut lawn. Steve Griffin – short, neat and dignified even at the end of the world – had trimmed the hedges and pulled out the dandelions. Linda Griffin had cleaned all the windows on their trailer.

But potential shoppers were surprised when they examined the labels on the boxes. The contents were clearly identified but...

"Where's the price?"

"Whaddya want for this?"

Then silence and disbelief.

"It's free?"

Linda smiled and nodded. "Please, just take what you need."

I strolled over with Steve and watched him pay out the October rent early and explain to Mr. Cooprod, the owner of the park, that they could cut off the power and plumbing the day after tomorrow.

"You're leaving the A&P, Steve?" Mr. Cooprod dropped the end of his cigarette butt into a cold cup of his wife's coffee. "You buggering off on us, kid?"

Steve just grinned. So did I because this was all going to look absolutely fantastic in the ethnological record.

"Yes, we're moving. Quite some distance."

At first I was rather enjoying this, but things got a bit disruptive when Larry and Judy Griffin began giving away their possessions to the other children in the trailer park.

Larry, as careful and organized as his mother and father, gave his complete runs of *Metal Men*, *Captain Atom* and *Challengers of the Unknown* to his best friend at school. He didn't want to, but Steve had given him the Searcher lecture on weight allocations and the fact that even interstellar spacecraft had their technical limitations.

It was a lot worse when Judy gave away her Barbies to the girl in the trailer at the end of the road. Linda Griffin was famous throughout the park for her sewing skill. She made all of the clothes for Judy's Barbie and Skipper dolls and they were, of course, much nicer than anything you could get in the stores.

"Shelly can't accept these," her mother said. "It's just not right."

"Judy won't need them where we're going," Linda said happily.

None of the other mothers was terribly satisfied with this response. My scans assured me none of them had any idea of the Griffins' plans, but almost everyone was nervous about what they were hearing on the news.

Weird behavior from the folk next door was the last thing people were interested in right now.

Eventually Jody's Barbie things ended up in a box, taped shut, sitting on the lawn. I don't know if anybody ever took them away.

Our broadcast and prayer vigil was less conspicuous but more intense.

A few of us were unable to free ourselves from mundane obligations, even under these circumstances, but most of the Searchers had packed one bag and moved into Mrs. Bloomsbury's house. There we sat in front of her radio and television and listened to news reports on the situation concerning Cuba.

It seemed so quaint to me, so gentle and fragile, this process of quietly waiting for tiny little waves to flicker through the atmosphere to be snared by jagged little wires sticking out of aluminum igloos and wooden huts. Not like my own time, where information is more a primal force – sort of like living in a smart tidal wave. It's overwhelming at times, but there are some advantages: you're never really alone and, if you don't like your life conditions... well, wait two nanoseconds.

It was just past two in the morning, and the only television station we could pick up had just gone off the air. Those of us who weren't sleepy were mostly crouched on the floor listening to the radio.

What they referred to as "real news" in this era had finished over two hours ago, and now there was only local programming. It was called *Night Owls* or *Night Talk* or *Dark Words* or something like that (I'd have to check my files), and was one of those shows where people would use telephones to call in to a living person, who was chairing this synchronic discussion.

These people could be so primitive.

Right now the threat of nuclear war was being assessed through the stinging, bleary eyes of insomniacs, paranoids and the habitually unemployed.

"I don't know why the President is going to all this trouble," a tobacco-choked voice coughed out of the radio speaker.

"You mean the fact that the Russians have missiles less than thirty miles off the Florida coast isn't a problem?" the host replied. He sounded slightly amused.

Actually, I probably should have been paying more attention to this. But, hell, I was exhausted. Making these field recordings without looking too obvious was incredibly difficult. I was in the middle of an apocalyptic millennial group facing what really looked like an apocalypse. There were just so many phenomena to take note of.

At that moment I was slumped in an old and overstuffed easy chair trying not to fall asleep. I had been activating my artificial stimulation system almost continually for the past two days, and now my internal sensor was telling me that if I used it any more the increase in my blood pressure would make my head explode.

So I was trying to relax for a few minutes, and let my mind drift off to more trivial matters, I idly wondered which of the fertile male members in my group was responsible for the impregnation of my "wife." I decided there was some potential value into looking into that. The elasticity of values and moral behavior under conditions of community crisis and ideological transition. I might get a really good paper out of Christine.

But then I started to hear some interesting things on the radio:

"Kennedy is wasting time," the caller growled. "He should just hit them right away."

"You mean attack Russia with our missiles first?" the host replied.

"And our planes, too! It's idiotic to even try to negotiate with soulless monsters. President Kennedy shouldn't mistake the Soviets for human beings."

The Searchers weren't the only people in this era with some odd theories.

The news got more and more serious, and Mrs. Bloomsbury's living room became more and more crowded. Eventually, Mrs. Bloomsbury herself walked in, turned off Walter Cronkite and addressed us:

"Tonight."

So we all moved, and soon we were sitting on a big hill by the river waiting for the saucer to arrive and rescue us from the atomic fires.

"Jesus wants me for a sunbeam..."

Some of the younger children started to sing the only religious song they knew by heart.

"... a sunbeam..."

I glanced over at Christine. Of course, I knew how her life was going to turn out. Alone, no children, dead in less than ten years. That's why I'd decided the marriage was actually a good research move. No danger of any paradox.

"... a sunbeam..."

Steve and Linda Griffin would move to nowhere in particular and never do anything of any particular importance. Their children and their children's children would follow the same pattern.

"... *a sunbeam...*"

Leo. He was sitting just next to the circle of singing children, looking happier than I'd ever seen him before.

"... *A sunbeam...*"

Leo would commit suicide a little more than two months from now.

That's why the Searchers were such an excellent study sample. None of them was going to have any discernible impact on the unfolding of human history.

"I'll be a sunbeam for him!"

Mrs. Eleanor Bloomsbury. Less than eighteen months after Kennedy and Khrushchev pulled the world back from the brink of nuclear exchange, Mrs. Bloomsbury would be sent off for psychiatric evaluation. In under five years she would be permanently institutionalized and chemically lobotomized by the crude psychoactive drugs of this era.

Mrs. Bloomsbury was going to leave this world, but not in quite the way she had prophesied.

I really did have a lot of leeway with this group.

We continued our singing and our services. The communion with the cheezies ensued. Sometime after 1:30am on October 25, 1961, Mrs. Bloomsbury asked us all to bow our heads and pray. I adjusted my equipment and folded my hands like everyone else.

Then, through the slits of my eyes, I could just see a multicoloured field of light surround the hill and envelop the Searchers.

A choir of wondrous ethereal voices cried out in harmonious transcendence as we were all transported into the heart of the mother ship.

When we opened our eyes, Mrs. Bloomsbury pointed to a giant imaging curtain where we saw the Earth burn and fade to a scarred stone.

"Dear God!" we all said.

One of the first things we did after we arrived was to change our name from "The Searchers" to "The Saved."

Then, for the next few months (we had to use some kind of familiar system to explain the passage of time), we planned different utopias, deciding which ones would suit us best.

Christine has a baby due soon. She and Steve have finally had that frank and friendly chat they'd been meaning to have with me. Linda's there too.

They explained that, while they operate an open-partnership marriage, they still didn't feel I'm suited to that kind of committed relationship. Or any kind, really.

It's a pretty accurate comment.

"I guess it's silly to say I'm sorry" – Christine smiled softly – "in the midst of all this joy."

"But it *is* very polite," I replied.

Mrs. Bloomsbury has relinquished her leadership over the community and seems to be pursuing personal salvation through artistic expression. She spends most of her time recreating herself with various exotic media.

Leo tried to kiss me the other day. I'm not sure what I'm going to do about that.

Of course, there were a lot of objections when the Department discovered I'd taken my research in a different direction. Showing up with over sixty people from the past and plugging them into an immersive simulated world is bound to make someone concerned eventually.

But not the people who are living in that simulated world. They just think they're living on another planet. I intend to keep them there for the rest of their lives.

Yes, I did get some flack from my supervisor, but even he had to give in. This was the first opportunity to study an apocalyptic community experiencing the consequences of their prophecy coming true. And now I have enough research material to last the rest of my academic career.

I'm happy.

They're happy.

We're all in Heaven.

New Writings in the Fantastic
Channel 18 J. Todd Gwinn

"Dinner's ready," Maggie announced from the kitchen to the rest of the house, even though it wasn't. Of course, it was all so routine by now, she thought as she undid her hair and let it spill over her shoulders.

The sun was setting on the Howards' quiet little home in the middle of suburbia, nestled in the comfort of about thirty other similar houses with similar families, all with made-to-order Martha Stewart furnishings and similar dogs named Spot or Buddy.

As she checked the chicken in the oven – it had another three or four minutes to go – and set the silverware out beside the not-so-glamorous-but-economical plastic plates on the dollar store blue-and-white-checkered tablecloth, Maggie knew it would be at least five minutes before her husband finished with the newspaper and her two children lost interest in the TV in the next room. The rest of the food was already laid out on the kitchen table. She took off the apron and picked up her unfinished book on serial killers.

As she read, leaning against the counter, her husband sauntered into the room and slipped his arms around her waist.

"Hey, honey," he said, pulling her back against him. She could feel the slight bulge of his beer gut in the small of her back.

"So what psychopath has your interest this week?" he asked, reading over her shoulder.

"Oh, no one really interesting. No real body counts. Kind of dull." She planted a quick kiss on his lips before returning to her cooking.

Dinner was fairly typical. Maggie and her husband talked about work and the kids remained in their own little adolescent worlds, where they stayed most of the time. She wasn't really surprised when the phone rang, either. Their neighbor, Pat DeWalt – dubbed "Gossip 411" – seemed to have an essential need to be the switchboard operator at the center of gossip in the neighborhood. You could almost set your watch by her phone calls. As usual, Maggie was polite and tried to act pleasantly surprised when she answered the phone.

After Pat had generously filled her in on the rumors of Robert Hughes's infidelity with his secretary, the Carters' teenage son being arrested again for DUI, and Jennifer Peterson's test results being positive for HIV, while Maggie exchanged comical, distorted faces with her daughter and managed to sound sincerely interested, the gossip fountain finally mentioned the weekly *Crime & Punishment* exclusive on Channel 18 tonight.

"They're finally going to execute McClary, aren't they?" Maggie asked.

"Yep. They're frying him tonight," Pat said in her matter-of-fact tone.

"So are you going to call in?" Maggie asked.

"If I can get through. You know how those lines stay tied up."

Nine-year-old Billy was reading a vampire comic at the table. His father noticed and quickly snatched it away from him.

The kid's face started to draw up and his father, knowing the tantrum that would inevitably follow, said, "Son, you know the table is no place for reading, and that you aren't supposed to be reading this junk in the first place. It's much too violent for a child your age."

After thumbing through it, glancing at the decapitations and the gory orgies in black-and-white print, Maggie's husband added, "You shouldn't be reading this crap at *any* age." He stuck the comic in a cabinet behind him.

After dinner, Maggie piled the dishes into the sink to be washed later and herded the family into the living room for the 7:30 exclusive on Channel 18, after the news. Catching the tail end of shots of corpse-littered, ravaged streets in the Middle East, they all stared blankly at the blood-drenched TV screen in anticipation.

When the war footage was over, a reporter appeared standing in front of a fence outside a maximum-security prison. He looked more like a game-show host than a reporter. Actually, Maggie thought, he might previously have been a game-show host on some cable show that enjoyed a brief run. But that wasn't important. *If he gets the ratings up,* she thought, *why not?*

The game-show host/reporter adjusted his cheap paisley tie and his hair and began. "We're here tonight to witness the execution of mass murderer Eli McClary. The twenty-five-year-old Georgia native who began his journey into depravity... that's a word, right?" he briefly interrupted himself. Getting the go-ahead, he continued, "... began his journey into depravity at eighteen with the cold-blooded execution of his mother, father, uncle, and thirteen-year-old sister seven years ago at dinner one night. The unsuspecting family was shot to death where they sat, using his father's 45-caliber handgun, and arranged in a gruesome display. When the police arrived on the scene, after an anonymous tip, they found the family propped up at the dinner table, arranged in a macabre" – he paused for confirmation of this word as well – "parody of life. Internal organs were removed and set on plates in front of the deceased. After that night, McClary disappeared from sight, emerging a month later only to claim five more victims – all women, all strangled and dismembered – before being apprehended by local law enforcement in a violent showdown resulting in the fatal injury of one officer."

The reporter kept up the narration as occasional photos of the family were shown in happier times side-by-side with the photos of the crime scenes.

It was another typical-looking family, not really different from Maggie's own. McClary himself seemed no model for a serial killer or demon, with his sad smile, red hair and freckles accentuating pale blue eyes that showed no obvious hint of insanity. There was no crazed, wild, animal look on his face, nor any swastika tattooed on his forehead. The television talking heads spoke about a possible history of molestation within the family, but in the end there was no real justification at all.

"Mommy, is it really okay that we're killing this man?" Maggie's eleven-year-old daughter asked suddenly.

"It's called justice, sweet pea," her father replied blandly before Maggie could speak, his eyes never leaving the TV screen.

"Honey," Maggie said, "this man did terrible things to people. He isn't even human – he's an animal. No human being could watch somebody suffer and die and enjoy it so much. Trust me, he deserves whatever he gets. Whoever thrives on pain and suffering should be killed," she finished in her best motherly, reassuring tone, with a little half-smile, anxiously awaiting the climax of the show.

The reporter was now inside the prison, following the condemned man down the long, dirty corridor filled with screaming inmates yelling and gesturing obscenely at the camera. Dead man walking.

"Mr. McClary, have you made your peace with God?" the chaplain asked as the reporter elbowed his way through the guards for the response, brandishing his microphone as if he were Moses parting the Red Sea.

"Fuck you," McClary said. "What God? Think I'm sorry for killin' my family? *He* don't care about them and *He* don't care about me. They never mattered any more than I did. Hey," he continued, now looking at the reporter/game-show host with a crooked, yellow-toothed smile, "they got my T-shirts out yet? They already published that book? Huh?"

But the reporter didn't have time to reply. They were already ushering him out of the room as they strapped McClary down to the chair.

Suddenly McClary's demeanor changed. "Hey, you tell 'em how it is! You tell 'em I'll live forever! I'm fuckin' famous!" he yelled, the desperation in his voice growing evident as they strapped his head into place.

The chaplain entered the room, running his hands through his thinning, iron gray hair and muttering something about the camera catching his bald spot.

"Eli, could you just tell us why?" the reporter shouted as they were shutting the door.

"Does anyone really care? Does it really matter?" McClary replied, the panic obvious in his voice, tears in his eyes.

The reporter turned to the camera. "Well, it's time, people. This man's fate is in your hands. Will he get a second chance? The phone lines are open and we are now taking callers. Judge wisely."

After about ten minutes of waiting anxiously and fidgeting, Maggie finally got through.

"So how do you and your family vote – denied or granted?" the almost mechanical voice on the other end of the line asked.

Maggie looked to her husband, who immediately gave the thumbs-down, then turned his attention back to his fourth after-dinner beer.

She looked to her two children. They exchanged glances and, giggling, said in one voice, "No way." They too gave the thumbs-down sign.

"Denied," Maggie said to the voice on the phone.

The voice replied, "Thank you for your participation."

Since the law had passed – years ago, after many political and legal revisions of the system – putting pardon in the hands of the public, nobody wanted to be away from a television on Tuesday night any more. At least it kept the kids at home for some quality family time.

"Well the vote is in, people," the reporter began, "and the vote is..." – a long, dramatic pause and the nation held its breath – "DENIED."

Inside the execution chamber, one of two lights flashed, showing a green thumbs-down sign.

At that point, McClary really did begin to regret his crimes and find God. In the middle of the condemned man's thrashing, ranting and raving, the chaplain coolly delivered his lines as any good holy man should, all the time never breaking character or showing his bald spot.

After the door had shut on McClary, an infinite pause seemed to pass in which everything stood still.

Then they lit him up.

They pulled the switch and every muscle in the killer's body seemed to jerk with enough voltage to move a train. You could almost smell the burning flesh from your television screen. Even when he was dead, his body continued to spasm.

Mercifully, they kept the face covered... this time, at least.

Afterwards, the reporter urged the viewers to join him next week, when they would execute thirteen-year-old Devon Saunders for the shooting of six of his classmates at lunch on school grounds with a gun he stole from his father.

As they finally cut to the commercials, Maggie's ten-year-old was ecstatic to see the preview of a horror movie coming on later that night.

"Can I stay up and watch it, Mom? Please?" he pleaded.

Disapproving and resolute, Maggie's husband did not give her the chance to answer. "No way, buddy. It's on too late and you just aren't mature enough to handle it yet. Why would you want to watch that morbid stuff anyway?"

New Writings in the Fantastic
Permanent Ink Lisa Silverthorne

The autoclave sputtered through the well lit tattoo studio, momentarily drowning out the steady hum of needles and ink against flesh as it cleansed equipment. Persephone slouched against the wall and peered out the picture window, waiting for her next client. The Bainbridge ferry glided across Elliott Bay's gunmetal surface, stark white against another gray-on-gray day in Seattle. August was slipping into September. She would have to leave soon.

Scowling, she laid her hand against the yellowing flash sheets pasted on the studio wall, her fingers tracing brightly coloured tribal symbols, yin–yangs and Celtic knotwork set against the tropical-orange paint. Soulless designs with little understanding of the cultures they depicted. She crossed her arms. Only the gods knew how lost these languages were to mortals, whose feet passed so quickly across this earth. How different the world seemed these thousand years or so, while for her so little had changed.

"Coffee, Seph?"

She glanced at the styrofoam cup of instant coffee and powdered creamer that Nick Malone held out to her. Everything designed to be disposable. With a hundred coffee vendors in this town selling fresh roast, Nick was drinking instant. She barely smelled the coffee above the studio's antiseptic tinge. But she couldn't fault the man. He was overworked and much too busy to run down the street for fresh coffee. The impatience of mortals was tiring. Behind her, the autoclave hissed its warm breath through the room. She found its rhythmic sounds comforting, and she liked making an effort to cleanse and re-use the old.

"No thank you," she answered with a brief smile, her voice low and sleepy. "I can't drink that powdered swill."

Nick owned the studio and let her work for him every summer. His chestnut hair was long and tied in a ponytail at his nape. One of his ears was pierced four times with silver studs. He wore a yellow T-shirt, and both of his lanky, upper arms were sleeved in intricate tribal symbols drawn in bold primary colours. He was wiry and tall, his green eyes bright. He stood beside her and sipped from the cup. She'd known Nick almost ten years now. Despite his mortal flaws, he was wise and she trusted him.

"You'll be leaving soon, won't you?"

She turned around and stared at him for a moment. "But I never said a word about—"

"You didn't have to," he said, nodding at the window. "I always know. Every year, just before you stop showing up, you spend a lot of time in front of this window. Like you're gathering a picture to take with you." He smiled. "When I see those leaves fall, I always know you won't be back until spring."

He pointed toward the row of green trees outside the shop. They hadn't started to turn yet. And, as long as she remained here, they would be green. Nick was sometimes more observant than she realized.

"Look, Seph," he said, staring into the cup, "I've never asked you where you go or anything about your personal life. It's none of my business. You've seemed so troubled this year – so I just wanted to give you a little advice."

"I'm listening."

His index finger slid around the cup's rim. "I don't know why you have to leave every summer, but I just think you'd be happier if you made a choice between Seattle and wherever else, that's all."

She knew he was right, but she didn't have the luxury of such a choice. She was caught between two worlds. A world of winter and death for half the year, and a world of sunlight and transition for the other half. For centuries she'd stoically endured this half-life, but now – she couldn't bear to return to the underworld.

Nick nudged the tropical-orange wall with the toe of his grungy loafers. "You're one of the best tattooists I've ever had work for me. Ever. The original artwork you create is straight out of legend. So real... Sometimes, it's frightening."

She bowed her head and sighed. If only she could tell him everything. If only she could show him what she'd seen through the ages. Civilizations rise then fall, languages flow then ebb, symbols etched then faded. She was there when Babylon fell to Persia, when the Celts rose to power, and when the Romans conquered Greece. She had walked alongside Aristotle and attended Sophocles' first play. But she'd never watched the leaves turn or the snow fall. She'd never seen all of the seasons pass before her eyes.

"Dump the guy, Seph," said Nick with a wry smile. "He's not worth it, if you aren't happy."

Persephone's smile faded as she turned again toward the window. Mortals had such narrow focuses, but the more she thought about Nick's words the truer they rang. And the question she'd been too afraid to utter rolled over her tongue.

Leave Hades?

She'd eaten the food of the dead – six pomegranate seeds – and those seeds forever bound her to the underworld and her lover, Hades. She laid her hand on her stomach, where she'd had six of the glistening red seeds tattooed. Ironic that such a permanent mark signified her transient life.

"I wish it were that simple."

The Nereids had warned her about Hades – all stern and darkness, dull and lifeless, Hecate had lamented. But, from the first moment she'd seen him in that great onyx chariot, she'd known a gentle, passionate and misunderstood man lay beneath his austere exterior. It hadn't been his choice, but he'd dutifully donned the underworld's facade; it was expected of him. Since she'd been with him, his hair had lightened to a sandy tan with hints of sunlight and his eyes had softened to a kind brown. For her he'd gathered the shiniest gemstones and precious metals, lighting the dark confines of his castle with as much brilliance as the underworld could manifest. Without her touch, she knew his castle would quickly go dark again.

And so would he. How could she doom him to that life now when he had finally tasted sunlight? Even if it was only part of a year?

She sighed. As he had held the sunlight in his palm, so had she felt the stillness and shadow touch her soul. It would hurt him terribly, but she could not endure another winter belowground. She needed to belong somewhere and, if that meant challenging the gods' curse, she would challenge it.

Nick squeezed her shoulder. "Then simplify it," he said, and turned away. His heavy footsteps clomped across the wooden floor.

"Seph, your two o'clock is here," called Nancy from the appointment desk.

Persephone swept her dark hair off her shoulder and moved toward her station. An antique green barber chair framed by a black, L-shaped table containing her inks, needles and supplies. A small rolling stool was pushed underneath one side of her table. She checked the needles she had soldered and sterilized. Everything was ready.

Satisfied, she went over to greet her client.

A blond young man wearing baggy, faded jeans and a short-sleeved shirt stood at the counter. Beside him, a dark-haired young woman in cargo shorts and a red T-shirt clung to his arm.

"So you decided to do it?" said Persephone. She had talked to the couple last week about designs and the process.

The young woman nodded. "I'm a little nervous," she said, and giggled. She scrunched her face. "Will it hurt?"

Persephone laughed. "Of course it will hurt. They're needles, remember?"

"You'll be fine, Trace," said the young man, nudging her with his shoulder.

Persephone motioned them to follow as she went back to her station.

"Okay," said the woman, shuffling her Birkenstocks across the shiny tile floor. "If I hate it, I can always have it removed."

Persephone halted in mid-stride and turned. "You're not ready for a tattoo."

Startled, the young woman stared at her. "Sure I am!"

"No, you're only half-certain that you want it." Persephone shook her head.

She led them across to Craig's station against the far wall, where a guy lay in the chair having a tiger's head tattooed on his chest. Craig, a thin young man with close-cropped, blond-tipped dark hair, was hunched over the customer. He wiped away spots of blood and excess ink with a sterile pad while he applied a fine blush of orange pigment with the tattoo machine. The machine's steady buzzing and the grimace on the man's face made the young woman grow pale.

Persephone pointed at the outline of the tiger's face. "A tattoo isn't a decal you can peel off and on. It's a something you're committing to, a permanent choice." She indicated the Celtic knotwork she'd tattooed on Craig's wrist. The intricate twining of granite lines and rich symbols had first been drawn centuries ago by a young warrior who dreamed of the sea. In those lines was a story of the warrior's first sea voyage. She had passed on that story when she'd reproduced it on Craig's arm. What began as a young man's journal became a symbol of courage to Craig.

"Go home and think about it," she said, laying her hand on the young woman's shoulder, "and ask yourself some hard questions. Who are you? What do you aspire to be? What symbolizes your life? When you know, you'll be ready for this tattoo."

The woman stared at her for a few moments, then stole a quick glance at the man gripping the chair arms. "You're right. Thank you." She nodded at her boyfriend. "Let's go, Andre."

For a moment, all Persephone heard was the whisper of the Aegean Sea in the autoclave's hiss. But it was all one ocean. She needed to ask herself those very same questions.

"That was nice of you, Seph," said Nick. He was standing beside her now. "Not everyone would have done that."

She gazed at him, and at the mixture of Eleusian and Babylonian images encircling his upper arms. By marking himself with these ancient teachings and prayers, he'd committed himself to those ways. She moved in front of the full-length mirror on the post beside Craig's station and studied herself.

Except for the pomegranate seeds on her stomach, there were no other tattoos on her skin. Not one. She held up her hands. No rings either. Nothing to symbolize her union with Hades. Nothing to represent conviction of any kind. Just the seeds of the gods' curse. And, because of that curse, she'd been treating her own life like an old coat, something to drag out only when she felt cold.

Who was she? She didn't know any more.

"But what I said is true, Nick." She turned toward him. "It's not a haircut that grows out or a shirt you take off and wash." Or a place she stayed for only half the year. "Either you get one or you don't. There's no in-between."

Persephone knew what she had to do. Turning in her sandals, she hurried to her station and grabbed her purse.

"Nancy, cancel all my appointments for the week," she called to the curly-haired receptionist.

Nick frowned. "You're leaving?"

Nodding, Persephone let a smile curve across her face. "But this time I'll be back."

She rushed past the autoclave in the back room and slipped outside into the flurry of downtown Seattle. A quick bus ride would get her to the ferry. Only between land and sea, where it was all one ocean, could she summon the crossroads that led to the underworld.

One last time she would stand at the edge of the underworld's domain to bid her lover farewell. One last time.

The air was cool against her face as she stood on the ferry's bow, waiting for it to move out across the bay. She'd taken this journey so many times over the years. On boats, ships, yachts, and triremes. On every body of water in the world. But this would be her last.

After the ferry gave a mournful call, it slowly slipped into the bay. Seattle's skyline slid into the distance, fading into the ubiquitous gray haze over Seattle. The Emerald City glittered like a smoky jewel. Persephone was eager to watch the leaves turn red and gold and fall to the earth.

She turned her gaze to Elliott Bay. Two porpoises leaped in front of the ferry's bow. Smiling, she leaned against the railing, watching the sleek black-and-white mammals. Beside them, Nereids played. She watched their glittering sea-foam bodies surge through the wake beside the porpoises. They giggled and chattered at her.

"Persephone! We've missed you!" they called in childlike voices. "Come and play with us."

Whenever she'd made this journey before, the Nereids' presence had always made her sad. Now, they made her laugh.

"Next trip," she whispered into the wind. The wind swirled past the Nereids, carrying her words to them.

"Do you promise?" one of them asked, her seaweed hair flowing around her cherubic face and slender shoulders.

Persephone nodded. She looked forward to it.

Waving, the Nereids plunged beneath the surface and sped away with the porpoises.

Persephone turned her face into the wind. "My dear friend, Hecate, I call for the crossroads."

Taking a deep breath, she reached out her palms to the air.

Shadowy hands reached out and grasped her own, pulling her from the ferry's deck.

There was a rush of shadows, and then she stood in the middle of a crossroads. Three footpaths, worn smooth, ambled into a tangle of trees and brush. Woods surrounded her on all sides, cedars towering above the ruddy trunks of madrona trees. The air smelled of sea salt and fresh rain.

"Hecate!" she called, turning to look in all directions.

No one answered.

"Hecate, please!"

At last Hecate appeared on the center path, walking toward her. Hecate's eyes were the colour of ebony. She wore a long, thin dress of shimmery charcoal that clung to her slim body.

"Persephone," the Nereid said, her voice low and gravely, "you're early this season. Hades will be so pleased. You should see the improvements he has made to the castle in your absence."

Hecate turned and started down the path that led toward a shadow looming ahead.

Persephone sighed, following with reticent steps. This would hurt him deeply. She had no wish to cause him pain, but pleasing him was destroying her.

"I'll follow you to the gates, but no farther. Please ask Hades to meet me there."

"What? Why only to the gates?" Hecate turned and scrutinized Persephone. "Has something happened?"

Yes, she had finally grown up. She wasn't that foolish little girl picking flowers near Eleusis or the headstrong young woman trying to ignore her mistakes and their consequences. She was the daughter of a goddess. Even if the gods took her god-essence, she would break this curse.

"Please ask him to come to me."

Hecate's thin face darkened with concern as she turned away, rushing ahead and fading into the shadows. Steps slow, Persephone followed until she felt the shade engulf her.

For a moment, she was falling. She closed her eyes until the ground felt solid against her sandals again. A long corridor stretched ahead toward dim light and shadows. The air smelled cold and stale – gritty. She shivered, feeling the chill of shades as they passed around her, heading toward the gates. They had already crossed over on Charon's ferry and would spend the rest of their days here until they were allowed to continue to the Elysian Fields. *And into the sunlight*, Persephone thought with a sigh, folding her arms against her torso.

Ahead, the massive black gate rose, casting a long, dark shadow on the path. Cerberus crouched beside the gate, his low growl crackling in the silence. She moved toward the massive three-headed dog.

"Cerberus?"

When the dog saw her, his serpent tail thumped against the ground. He whimpered and scrambled in her direction. His three canine tongues licked her hands and feet as he pranced around her. Smiling, she knelt beside him and stroked one of his napes.

"He's missed you."

She froze at the sound of Hades' velvet voice. Inhaling slowly, she rose from the ground, afraid to look into his eyes. He lifted her chin. A smile lit his pale complexion, his brown eyes bright.

"And have *you* at last missed *me*, Persephone? Is that why you've returned home so soon?" His strong hands cupped her face, warming against her skin.

She slipped away from his touch and the smile fled from his face.

"No," she answered, looking away. "I've come to tell you that—" She sighed. "This is difficult."

His hands were at her shoulders and she felt his kiss against her neck.

"What is it, my love?" he asked, his voice soft and distracted.

She turned, holding him at arm's length. "I've come to tell you – that I won't be coming back here."

He laughed, but the sound quickly died, the shock at last dulling his features. "You're serious, aren't you?"

She nodded. "I am so weary of living two lives, Hades." She bit her lip and slid her hand into his. Gently, she brought his hand to her face and pressed his fingers to her lips, kissing them. "My soul is dying in this empty place. You have been the only brightness in this realm, but that isn't enough any more."

"What of the curse?" he said in a half-whisper.

"I–I don't know what will happen, but I'd risk anything to end this constant migration."

Sadness touched his face, his brown eyes growing watery as he pulled his hand away. "Do I still mean nothing to you? After all this time?"

She closed her eyes. He meant so much to her, but she needed more. He loved her only under his own terms. She had sacrificed everything for him, yet his love lasted just six months of the year. She felt like a wildflower, brittle from frost, dying slowly with the sun's rise.

"I ask the same of you, Hades. I don't think you've ever known me at all."

Anger sharpened his features. "You'll return," he snapped. "You won't risk your immortal soul – not for this." He cast a hurt, longing gaze at her and then turned from her, trudging toward the gates. Already, his form was graying in the dim light.

She waited until he disappeared into the shadows before she walked away from the gates, back toward the crossroads. As she stepped through, everything darkened until she felt the deck of the Bainbridge ferry beneath her. It was evening, and the city glittered against the dark waters. She huddled against the railing, the air chilly, and watched the lights until the ferry reached the dock.

What would happen to her when she failed to return to the underworld? What price would she pay for swallowing six pomegranate seeds?

September waned and the leaves did not turn. Already Persephone felt the tugging at her limbs. Autumn had not arrived. Everyone talked about the oddness of the season, but the mortals moved ahead with their lives.

She stood near one of the flower stands at Pike's Market, admiring the bunches of wildflowers wrapped in slick green paper. Standing in front of so many flowers reminded her of distant childhood, before she had encountered Hades. How far away that life seemed now. The damp air was fresh with vegetable and flower scents, the fish smell only a distant tinge from the nearby fish market.

In her ears, Hecate's husky whisper called her back to the underworld. Persephone hummed, trying to drown out the scratchy call. Over the next few days, that whisper would quickly grow shrill and piercing. But she would not yield. Not this time.

She bought herself a bouquet of purple-and-yellow flowers and walked away from the crowd.

Below, at street level, Persephone watched the cars slip past the piers. She hurried down the sprawling flights of stairs and across the street until she'd reached the ferry dock. Beyond the shops and the aquarium lay the misty bay waters.

She sighed. How long would Hades wait for her at the underworld gates? How long would it take before he realized she wasn't coming back?

As morning slipped into afternoon, the sky darkened. The bay grew choppy as the wind howled across the piers. Persephone folded her arms against her stomach, the chilly wind cutting through her, and tried to make her way to the bus stop.

In an instant, the world froze around her, standing motionless. Everything halted. There was only silence. Even the bay turned mirror-calm.

The sound of a great door creaking open replaced the silence. Persephone trembled. She had heard that sound only once in her life, but she had never forgotten it.

It was the sound of Fate.

Her hand quivered. Even the gods had masters, and Fate was one of those forces. It had come to exact the curse on her.

Raindrops hit the pavement. She looked closer, reaching out to touch them – red splotches – and pulled her hand away. Droplets of blood wept from her palm where those awful pomegranate seeds had first rested.

"You defy your immortality, Persephone," said a rough voice. The sound floated around her.

"I want my freedom!" she shouted, turning around. The blood stained her shirt, and drops continued to fall against the pavement. "I cannot keep wandering between lives."

Abruptly, a ring of smoke undulated around her head – before it swirled away, coalescing into a stone-faced figure in front of her. The hazy presence looked neither male nor female.

"Then you have made your choice."

A smoky hand moved toward her and plunged into her chest. She gasped, her knees buckling. As the hand plucked the gleaming sphere of ambrosial god essence from her chest, she collapsed against the blood-spattered pavement.

The air rustled with yellow-and-red leaves that rustled against the sidewalk. She turned to look at the trees. They were dying! All their radiant yellow leaves were blowing away, leaving behind skeletal trunks and limbs. The winter snows would blow soon, and everything would sleep until spring. She began to tremble. There was no difference between this place and the underworld. Her stomach clenched. What had she done?

Immediately, the roar of Seattle crescendoed around her. Cars honking, people jogging, voices chattering. She huddled against the sidewalk, unable to gather the strength to rise to her feet. People walked around her as if she no longer existed.

"Somebody, please – please help me," she called.

No one answered.

Feeling frightened and lost, she crouched there for a long time, until at last a hand touched her shoulder.

"Let me help you," said a velvety, soft voice.

She looked up, relieved someone had heard her.

Those kind brown eyes, the light brown hair.

Hades!

Here, among the living?

"Why are you here?"

He wore simple black trousers and a white shirt, and looked humble and sweet. Smiling, he laid his fingers against her lips.

"It doesn't matter any more. I knew Fate would tear the god essence from your soul if you did not heed the curse." Tenderly, he brushed the hair out of her eyes and held out his other hand to her. A gleaming sphere the colour of citrine lay in his palm. "I've brought you ambrosia."

Her eyes grew teary. "Why would you restore me – after I've left you?"

His eyes turned sad. "I would rather have you gone from me than gone from the world." He stroked her black hair. "The curse is broken now. At least, this way, I can still gaze on you from time to time."

He pressed the ambrosia to her lips. The sphere dissolved into sweet nectar that slid down her throat and warmed her belly. She held onto his arms and struggled to stand.

"You'll be weak for a few days, but then you'll feel yourself again."

With a sigh, he kissed her on the forehead and turned toward the ferry dock.

"Hades," she called.

He stopped, but did not turn back.

"My whole life, since I've been with you," said Persephone, "I've always lived on your terms. You loved me as long as I remained below with you. When I was gone from you, was it me or the sunlight that you missed?"

Hades turned, no expression on his face. "My life was planned out for me, Persephone, guiding the dead on their journey. My days are filled with their confusion and senselessness. When I saw you that day picking flowers in the field, glowing with beauty and peace – I was overcome. I want that in my life, even if it's for only half the year."

His gaze fell to the sidewalk. "Was I selfish? Of course. But you are finally free of me. I cannot hold you now."

Persephone sighed. "How I wished that, one time over the centuries, you'd asked to come with me. To share my world as I shared yours."

"I never knew how much you cherished your mortal existence." He looked up, his eyes still morose. "I never thought past meeting you at the gate."

"Are you so blind that you don't see I grew to love you?" Persephone walked slowly toward him. "My love held me more than those six pomegranate seeds ever did. All I've ever wanted to hear was your voice calling me back because you loved me too."

He sighed and closed his eyes. "Come home, Persephone. I'm only a shade without you."

"Maybe there's a way that I can come home to you?"

His watery eyes snapped open. "Tell me! If there's something that'll keep you in my life, I'll gladly do it."

"Raise your castle," she replied. "Allow it to reside both in the underworld and in this world, so I can look on this place while nature slumbers. And sometimes – in spring or summer – walk with me in this world."

Hades thought for a moment, turning to stare at Elliott Bay. "What would Zeus say?"

"Does it matter?" Persephone asked. "You are lord of the underworld. What do *you* say?"

A faint smile lit his pale face for a moment. "I say that, without you, I'm dead inside."

At last he stepped toward her and took her in his arms. His kiss was long and deep, gentle as falling snow, but Persephone felt his passion, his urgency. She melted into his touch.

"With Poseidon's help," Hades whispered, "I'll raise my castle – if you'll stay with me."

She nodded and lifted her shirt, revealing the six pomegranate seeds tattooed across her stomach like little ruby teardrops. Finally they meant something permanent to her.

"The pomegranate seeds are forever," said Persephone, her coal black hair against her cheek.

Tenderly, he ran his fingers across the little teardrops. "Why, Persephone? The curse has been lifted."

"Because I love you."

Moved by the symbol, he could not speak for a moment, his eyes brimming with moisture.

After a long time, he took her hand in his. "In the spring, show me your world," he said in a soft voice. "But, please – come home now."

"Why?" Persephone asked.

"Because I love you," he said, a smile on his lips.

With his arms around her, Persephone led Hades toward the dock. They had a ferry to catch.

New Writings in the Fantastic
No Second Chance Paul L Bates

The most vivid part of the memory is how cool the barrel felt pressed against my temple. That and the hours I spent drilling and counterboring the soft lead tips, then filing those meticulous *X*s across the cone-shaped holes. The crazy part is that I actually prepped all six bullets when one was all I could possibly use. The strongest argument against the event ever really happening is obvious: had I pulled the trigger, my brain would have been splattered out the other side of my head. And it wasn't. That and the fact that I could never find the gun again.

I turn the key in the ignition. The car starts at once. I listen to the hum of the engine – not a ping, not a skip. Glancing at the clock I see it is 6:28. Shifting into reverse, I back out of the car port, turn, shift into drive, roll easily down the driveway, wait at the street, look for headlights washing pavement from either direction, take the hill at thirty-five. Deer and wild turkey cross the road at this hour – any faster and I might not stop in time.

I like the silence of the morning. It is the only time I can think. I let my thoughts arrive unbidden, do the analysis, find the conclusion, solve life's little problems on the way to work. This morning, it's Cathy. I know she's having an affair. I'm reasonably certain she's bedding Roger. When we're with him and Cynthia he's always avoiding me, or watching me from the corner of his eye. He's trying to figure out if I know – trying to figure out what I'll do.

At the intersection I wait. Two cars speed up in the slow lane, while a semi lumbers along in the passing lane. I hook a right behind them, give it a little more gas on the upgrade. The light at the top of the hill is still green. I've got it up to forty-five as I cross the intersection. A dozen sets of distant headlights make the rearview glitter. I let up on the gas as I crest the top. It's all downhill for the next half-mile or so.

I caught onto Cathy by accident. Figured it out on the morning commute. I'm not the jealous type, really. Not that this doesn't bother me, but I never minded her going out alone – never worried about her finding a lover. It was so good with us in the beginning. She'd do anything to satisfy me. I guess the fact that it didn't take all that much to gratify me got to her – that her best effort and her least were one to me became an insult to her. I just liked to touch her skin – feel her pressed against me. I liked to smell all her different smells, feel her hair, the sudden acceleration of her heartbeat, the gush of perspiration. How we got there was kind of like how I pick which road I take in the morning. Wherever the light is green, or the traffic is the lightest, that's the way I go.

I take my foot off the accelerator, turn onto the ramp, coast uphill, come to a stop at the crosswalk. This is a long light. At this hour, if no one's around, I usually run it after stopping. The visibility is good – I can see motorists and cops either way. This morning I have to wait for three cars turning left in front of me. Absently I look at the clock. It's 6:28. I decide not to run the light.

When it changes, I look again. It's still 6:28. I begin to calculate. At least thirty seconds to get out of the driveway. Half a mile down the hill at thirty-five – I've measured it – plus the wait at the bottom – that's another thirty seconds. It's three-quarters of a mile from the intersection to the top of the ramp. Even at an average speed of forty-five, that's another thirty seconds. And the light was red for at least a minute. I look at the clock again in time to see the number change. It's 6:29.

I just lived a two-and-a-half-minute minute. Every time something like this happens I feel the cool tip of the Colt Cobra pressed against my right temple. I try to remember the sound of the explosion, the smell of the gunpowder igniting, the sensation of my head dissolving. All I remember is the cool barrel, and the hours I spent, the night before, prepping the bullets. I waited a day, just in case I wanted to change my mind. No sense making a mistake.

I didn't change my mind.

So what happened? Why don't I remember?

I let it go. The answer will come to me eventually. It always does. Like Cathy's affair. I'm not given to anxiety attacks. But I began having them on Tuesday nights. About half an hour after Cathy left. I made the connection after the third one. I didn't say anything, but the following week took a good look at her when she came home complaining of a headache. She'd just had a shower. Her makeup was different. There was way too much perfume.

I noticed Roger watching me that weekend. For a laugh, I asked him to help me with a computer problem next Tuesday night. He dumped his coffee in his lap. After changing his trousers and exchanging a few hushed words with Cathy, he told me he was free on Wednesday. I told him I'd let him know.

I coast to a stop at the next intersection, turn right on the red light. There is no traffic on Evans Lane this morning. I see a skunk shambling across the road. The car reeks as I slow to let it cross. I roll down the window, feel the cool autumn air frolicking about the car, licking my skin, making off with the smell of the skunk as I speed up.

The day passes quickly. Cathy is home before me. She's already changed her clothes.

"Going somewhere?" I ask playfully.

"It's Tuesday night, remember?"

"So?"

"It's girls-night-out."

"Oh, yeah. When do I get to meet them?"

"If you behave, I might just invite them over some weekend. But I don't think you'd like them. Judy's fat, Ronnie smokes, and Sheila's the whining type."

I frown. Cathy smiles, blows me a kiss, slips out the door.

In the cellar I examine the little triangular file – one of the tools I inherited when my father died last year. I used it to make the *X*s in the bullets. I was what – eighteen? Funny how you can see your whole life unfolding before you as a young man. I just decided to pass on it. Not worth the effort – not worth the pain. I was right about everything – that much I remember. I run my finger over the crisscrossing, hoping to find some trace of the lead. There is nothing.

It starts. My hands feel like they're shaking. I hold them out. Not even a tremor. My mind begins to race. Nothing in particular. Just a jumble of nonsense that won't let up. My stomach knots, like it did when I was a kid about to get called out for something I'd done. Has it been half an hour? Anxiety on schedule.

I turn on the television. It's all so inconsequential, so trivial, so insulting that someone believes this fluff could be of interest to anyone else. Forty channels with nothing to watch. I go back downstairs – start rummaging through the boxes again. I can't remember if I ever sorted out all Dad's old stuff. There are a few cartons in back that look like they've never been opened. Yellowed nylon tape, half dissolved, wrapped about the pasteboard as if it would keep the past secret forever. I try to pull it apart, cut my forefinger near the nail. Sucking the blood, I find a Swiss Army knife. The little blade opens the first box. Faded books. From my grade school years. Leave it to Dad to hold on to junk like that.

I open the next box. His work clothes. They smell ancient. These two can go into the trash. A spasm in my midsection catches me unprepared. I drop the box. Pleated khaki pants and folded plaid shirts spill out. Something brown peeks out between them. My heart leaps. It's the pistol grip of the Cobra. I cannot breathe.

On my knees, I brush away the red plaid shirt, revealing gunmetal blue. Cool to the touch. I smell the barrel. It's been too long – all I smell is the clothes. Trembling, I open the cylinder. Six shells, one expended. My heart is pounding at my temples. Ejecting the bullets, I examine the tips. Counterbored and scored, just like I remember them. Reverently, I reload the gun, make sure the safety is on, slip it into my jacket pocket.

All I can remember about the drive out is the deer in the road. He froze midway across the street looking at me. I stopped the car about fifty feet away. Turned off the lights. Put them on again and he was gone. I don't recall how I knew where to drive, or how I got there. I must have remembered the name of the restaurant she gave me weeks ago. I saw Cathy's car in the lot by the restaurant, Roger's by the motel next door. I parked across the street, behind the dumpster, waiting. They came out together. It wasn't at all like I imagined it. They didn't kiss, hold hands, or even touch one another. As far as I could tell, they didn't even wish each other good night. It was kind of sad, actually.

Cathy heads west, Roger goes east, toward the parkway. I catch up to him at the next light, my passenger side by his driver's side, my window down. I lean over, waving. Roger looks startled, forces a smile. Lowers his window. He doesn't notice the little orange rubber plugs in my ears. I glance in the rearview. No headlamps there – none in front either. No one crossing the intersection. I flick off the safety, lift the Colt, aim between his eyes, fire. Even with the earplugs the sound is deafening. Roger's face still has that stupid guilty half-smile on it, but there is a neat red hole in his forehead, at the bridge of his nose. A dark trickle of blood on one cheek, and a lumpy dark smear all over the passenger side window. He slips out of view and his car rolls slowly forward.

The light turns green. I hang a left. Flick the safety back on. Leave the window open until the smoke and smell are gone. Accelerating, I finish the U-turn. I catch up with Cathy on the interstate. She doesn't drive this fast when I'm with her. The ringing in my ears hasn't subsided. Coming up close behind her, I go from parking-lights-only to brights, gunning my engine. She swerves right to avoid me. In the rearview I see her car going into a skid, riding up the low end of the guardrail, tumbling down the embankment. I slow down, heave a sigh, head for home. I'm the only one on the interstate.

It's been three days. Nothing in the paper about either one of them. No one calling for me to identify Cathy's body. I begin to think I should put in a missing person's report. Once again I have no idea where I left the Colt. I drove by Roger's place and saw Cynthia raking leaves. She waved and I waved back. Hardly the grieving widow.

I get rid of everything – all Dad's old stuff, all Cathy's. When I get back the phone is ringing. I stand still, in a cold sweat, just watching it. Finally I muster the courage to answer.

"Bob?"

"Yeah."

"It's Cynthia. Why didn't you stop this afternoon? I'm starting to feel unloved."

"How about I come over now?"

It's all getting fuzzy again. The only thing I'm sure of is Cynthia's voice.

"Only if you take me out someplace nice," she says.

"Of course. How about the Oasis?"
"Give me two hours to get ready."
"See you then."

I put down the receiver. I feel the cool tip of the gun barrel pressing into my right temple. I do my best to ignore it.

New Writings in the Fantastic
The Night Bride Stephen Kilpatrick

Anna pressed her face into the coarse fur of her love's goatskin and with closed eyes sucked in the tangy scent of man through the damp musk of his clothes. Her cheek itched where it touched the fleece, but she exhaled a long breath of contentment and tightened her arms about his belly. This was true love, and no amount of discomfort, not even the chafing of the horse's back against her thighs, would be sufficient to ruin her happiness.

She had never ridden bareback before, and had certainly never ridden with legs astride the mount like a man, skirts and petticoats hitched up to mid-thigh. She smiled to herself, thinking of how shocked her mother and brothers would be if they could see her now, and of how the women of her village had gasped in horror to see her ride away from her own wedding, abandoning her fiancé in front of the church.

"Where are you taking me, my love?"

The rider did not answer, but instead drove his spurs cruelly into the stallion's flank, urging it on to greater speed. Anna sighed in near rapture, and nuzzled her face deeper into the fleece of his jacket.

The increased pace of the horse caused Anna to bounce violently on its broad back and the rider's long saber to rattle by his side as the dark forest sped past them. She clung tighter still to her lover, relishing the sensation of her tender breasts crushed fiercely against the hard muscles of his back. The horse leapt a fallen tree, causing Ann's groin to collide hard with the saddle as it landed. There was a hot needle of pain from beneath her petticoats, followed by a sticky wetness on her inner thighs.

Blood, thought Anna. *Now I am no longer a maid, and there is no going back.*

The pain did not subside, but Anna did not cry. She felt elated. She was liberated. She had been prisoner to that thin membrane of flesh, but now she was free. Free to love. Free to be a woman. She released her grip on the rider for one moment and caressed the horse's sweating hide, making soothing sounds, as one might make to a resting lover. The smell of the beast's sweat stung her nostrils. An animal smell. More pungent, but not unlike that of the rider.

The rider violently dragged back on the reins, bringing the stallion rearing and whinnying to a halt. He slid silently from the beast's back, grabbed Anna roughly by the hips and swung her from the mount. As soon as her feet touched the ground, he pressed his body hard against hers. She could smell cooked meat on his breath and fancied she could see animal grease glinting off his thick, black moustache in the moonlight. Something hard and brutal pressed against her stomach, and she trembled with excitement.

She threw her head back in breathless anticipation, exposing her white throat to his hungry mouth. His lips came closer until Anna could feel his long whiskers brush her neck, then suddenly he drew back and grasped the bodice of her wedding dress in his fist, tearing furiously at the cloth. She felt him forcing her down onto the soft grass beneath an enormous oak tree.

Rough hands tugged at the laces and ribbons that, they and their kind, had bound her so tightly since childhood. There was no ceremony or ritual involved in this final step into maturity, only animal lust. Her most intimate places were touched without affection; she felt her soft body squeezed and rubbed almost raw. Anna cried out in pain as he moved inside her, despite the way having been prepared for him by the movement of his horse. This was not the act described by the old women of her village. This was no passive duty, but rather a bridge into a new life. A bridge that was burning as she left it in her wake.

Her lover tensed, then groaned and subsided, sinking onto her and crushing the air from her lungs. Anna lay there for a moment under his bruising weight, kissing his throat, tears of joy tracking across her cheeks, before the rider toppled from her with a groan.

"My love, my love," she whispered, "did I please you?"

There was no answer from him as he lay fading in the darkness.

"My love?"

The only response was his slowing breath.

How like a beast he is, thought Anna. *He is like the bear that takes what it wants and then sleeps until Spring.*

As her lover slept, Anna caressed his thick, black hair, losing her fingers in the midnight locks. His eyes were closed, but Anna remembered how they had burned like black fire when he had scooped her up from her wedding procession onto his horse. She had loved him from that moment. At first she had ridden slung across the horse on her belly, as if she had been no more than a saddlebag to him, but, as the distance between themselves and the village grew, he allowed her to ride behind him, like a man.

As they lay beneath the oak tree, Anna watched her lover in the moonlight, studying his features and burning the memory into her mind.

She opened her eyes. The branches of the tree, rustled in the whispering breeze. Something had awakened her. Sitting upright, she noticed something strange about the evening; no air played across her face, nor danced through her tousled hair.

She looked up into the bare branches of the oak tree. The tree resembled a cracked mirror, each twig and branch lined with silver moonlight. There was whispering in the higher branches, and twigs rustled as if jostled by the wind.

Anna silently rose to her feet and slipped into her knickers and boots. Without bothering to put on petticoats and skirt, she swung herself onto the horse's back and then, balancing herself with arms outstretched like a circus performer, stood upright. From here she could haul herself onto the lowest bough. Wet moss and lichen added new stains to her white linen.

Higher and higher into the tree she climbed. Moonlight threw every bough and branch into sharp contrast, each shape definable as only a nothingness edged with quicksilver.

She heard the creak of wood and hemp behind her and stopped silently, holding her breath, not wanting to turn.

"Hello, my pretty one."

The whisper slipped into her ear, as if rushing toward her from a great distance.

"A little early, aren't we?"

Anna did not turn, but instead screwed her eyes tight shut. The branch she perched on began to sway in time with the creaking behind her.

"No need to rush, deary," sighed a second voice. "You'll be joining us up here soon enough."

There were now three rhythmical creaking sounds behind her.

"You must be the bride of the night." This third voice sounded like breath squeezed between a strangler's fingers. "I was the first. I am Morning."

Anna gripped a branch tightly. She did not dare turn round.

"I am Evening, my pretty," hissed the first voice. "I preceded you."

"He named me Day," lamented the second voice. "But we will have time to get to know one another, deary."

"Go back down to him, Night, before he grows restless," all three voices intoned. "Go back down and accept his wedding band."

For a moment, Anna's curiosity overcame her fear and she turned quickly, almost losing her balance. Three moon-white young women faced her, each dressed in the finery of her wedding day, and each wedding dress bearing the rents of the rider's animal passion. Each held her head cocked at an impossible angle, and around each white throat wound a hempen cord, tied at the side in a hangman's knot. The women's eyes bulged and their tongues lolled, swollen like slugs.

Anna gasped, and in her fright lost her footing on the branch. She dropped through the boughs, trying to slow her descent by grabbing at splintering branches and twigs. Clawed limbs tore at her undergarments and scratched at her lily flesh as she passed until, finally, her hands found purchase on a strong branch. She hung there for a moment, breathing in great, sobbing gusts.

Below her, only a man's length from her feet, the rider lay naked, still sleeping. His broad chest rose and fell in a slow steady rhythm. Anna dropped from the tree and landed in the undergrowth with a dull thud. For a few moments she lay there, her ears sensitive to any signs of the rider waking. Once reassured the rider still slept, she began to creep toward him, a predatory feline stalking unwary prey.

Silently, on her hands and knees, she searched through their abandoned clothes, strewn around his sleeping body. Having located the rider's long, curved saber, she continued her advance upon him.

Once alongside, she held the covered blade across the bare throat of the slumbering man without touching the skin. Slowly and carefully, she began to draw the sword. The blade sang as it was gently unclothed. Reflected moonbeams illuminated the sleeper's face.

"You are Night, my love," whispered the man. "Now all is darkness."

Pinpricks of ice formed in Anna's veins as her gaze met the awakened eyes of the rider staring back at her.

A large cloud moved across the Moon, plunging the forest into blackness. Anna could no longer see the rider's face, but she could sense his presence. She was aware of his tanned neck trembling beneath the cold blade.

"Darkness."

She leaned onto the saber with all her weight, feeling his flesh give little resistance to the razor-sharp blade. Her hands grew slippery as they were washed in the warm liquid flowing from him.

Blood, she thought. *There is no turning back.*

Her dead lover's body finally buried, Anna swung herself onto the horse's back. The coarse fabric of his riding trousers irritated her raw thighs, but they were more practical than the skirts and petticoats she had arrived in. The goatskin waistcoat itched her neck, but its familiar smell had a calming effect on her spirit.

In the tree, she left one more adornment, a severed head, tied to one of the lower branches by a thick cord of shining, raven hair. Leaning from the horse's back, she placed a final kiss on the head's bloodless lips, its eyes rolled back in a mockery of ecstasy.

New Writings in the Fantastic
A Simple Gesture Stuart Jaffe

The bench sat deep in the park, cloistered by bushes and trees so that only those who had been around when the park first opened knew of its existence. Its sides created endless swirls of iron that transformed at the arms into lion-heads. Oak formed the seat and back; green paint dirtied to near-brown and worn down to the wood in some places.

The bench had been witness to entire generations. Babies were conceived upon it only then to play at its feet only then to grow into young children jumping from its seat. Soon those children were sitting with arms around each other, lips locked, as the sun descended with brilliant pinks and reds. Then the adults sat and watched their own children play only then to watch the years whittle by, leaving them still sitting on the bench – only nobody noticed.

That was Tim Ford.

So much of his life had been spent around this rusting bench that he considered it part of his family. It certainly knew his ass better than anyone else did. And, lately, it knew his slouch better, and his tired body sleeping away the daylight. He figured that one day, a day probably not too far from now, the damn' bench would know his dead body as well.

It'd know before anybody else. In fact, days might pass before another soul would notice, and those who did notice would not do much about it but wonder whatever happened to Old Tim. He guessed it would be the smell of his decaying corpse that would rouse some young couple on a love stroll through the park. They would poke through the bushes and discover an old bench and the wasting body that lay upon it.

No, that was wrong. Lately, he hardly saw people stroll in the park any more. People wouldn't be the ones to find him. Nowadays, it would be the C.

Their real name, as best as any human could figure it, was Cetamyzoprinetoahop – C for short. They were bulbous, goofy-looking aliens that waddled on wide-stretched legs, watched everything in all directions with eight well positioned eyes, and smelled worse than the subway during a heatwave. Not the invading hordes he had dreamt of battling as a child.

That would be his luck. A group of Cs would find his dead body and take it away to one of their orbiters. Probably wouldn't even report him. It could be years before anyone in his family knew he had died. Of course, the up-side would be that he'd finally get to experience spaceflight. If only he didn't have to be dead for it.

Tim chuckled and swigged a drink from his brown paper bag. At least that hadn't changed. The Wilkins Store still bagged his bottles.

He could have spent the rest of the day drinking and thinking and dreaming of old times. If he had better eyesight, he would have read a newspaper, but he managed to function in the world and that sufficed. The pleasant sun warmed him, and a gentle breeze rustled the bushes, disguising his few sounds from the even fewer ears around.

But, before he could get the slightest buzz going, a C stepped up unannounced and parked on the opposite side of his bench.

Tim pushed up his glasses, scowled at the intruder, and straightened on his side of the bench. He cleared his throat and gestured with his head that the thing should walk onward, but the C remained, its short legs swinging just above the ground. Tim drained a little more from his bottle, but the taste lacked much of the pleasure he sought. If he had been anyplace else he would have stormed off, huffing curses and vowing never to frequent that area again. But he wasn't just anyplace.

When the sun set that evening, the C stretched its thin arms, hopped off the bench, and sauntered away. Tim watched the display in disbelief. There was little to do, though – he had emptied his bottle. So he shook his head and left likewise, his jaw clenched.

The next afternoon the same happened. The C arrived, sat until sunset, and departed.

This would not do. Tim would never have let a punk kid do this, so he couldn't let a punk alien do it either. With a kid, he would cackle away like an old hag, knowing the teen wiseass would laugh at him but eventually be driven away by the nuisance. The tactic never failed.

The same wouldn't work here. Tim knew that from the start. The C would probably just mimic him, thinking the cackle to be a regional dialect or something. He had to come up with something more defined, something with rules the C would understand.

So, when he reached the bench the next day, he had a small box tucked under his arm. He stroked the lion-head armrest and sat down with a firm thump. Without waiting for the C, he opened the box, pulled out a chessboard, and set up the pieces.

The C turned up as usual. Tim did not look at it, choosing instead to concentrate on a beetle crawling nearby. He could hear the C studying the board, perhaps trying to figure out the game by communicating telepathically with its friends – he had heard they could do that. Of course, rumors had it the C could do just about anything, so Tim was willing to believe or disbelieve the telepathy thing, however it stood.

About an hour passed before he heard what he wanted – the soft but definite click of a pawn. For the first time since the C's arrival that day, Tim looked at the board. He moved his own pawn up to meet the C's, and turned away. The first several moves would be easy, he knew – he had spent enough time considering them. The game would become interesting later on, though, and he could be patient.

The C's moves came slow but they did come. With each little step, they pressured each other, maneuvered, feigned, trapped, and cut away the minutes of the day. When the sun had become no more than the barest arc at the horizon, the C stood, stared at the board one last time as if to memorize the pieces' positions, and waddled off. Tim had thought ahead – he pulled a small viewer from his pocket and imaged the board. Then he packed up.

The following day, Tim had just finished setting up when the C arrived. It was early. Tim let out a soft chuckle, placed the last piece where it had been at the end of yesterday, and waited for the C to move.

The game lasted more than a week. They set no time limit on each move, and often the C would require a few hours before settling on a course of action. On one day, they each moved just twice. Tim didn't mind, though. He had nowhere to be, and he figured he had to be lenient in this regard when considering that the C might still be learning as they played.

Where Tim planned no leniency, however, was with his victory. When he won, he would raise his right arm and point away from him and his bench. And that would be the end of this C bothering him.

As the week passed on and the game drew to a close, Tim found himself taking the majority of each day to make a move. Somehow, the little brat of a C had managed to get the upper hand. On the last day, Tim knew he could not win. The question no longer concerned winning or losing but rather how many moves it was going to take him to lose. He managed to find the best positions and forced the game on for three more hours.

And so the C stayed.

Tim sat on his side of the bench day after day, muttering sometimes when the C's odor got to be too strong. He could feel the C gazing at him on occasion – guessed the C wanted to play another game. However, the chessboard did not return, though the game always played in the back of his mind.

Other changes came along, too. Old Tim noticed them on his walks to and from the bench. The stores he had known throughout life melted away one by one, leaving behind empty fronts and ghostly memories. Most people were trying to move away, as if putting distance between themselves and all of the C could somehow protect them from change. The businesses just couldn't make money. Tim felt it the worst when the Wilkins Store closed.

Yet somehow the town pushed on, and a few more years passed. Then a new life grew. A few people came back, but mostly the town belonged to the many C that had moved in. The businesses sported strange signs in languages no human ever spoke. A mass of waddling creatures filled the streets, as if humans had never owned the town.

Tim shrugged it off. Every day he went to his bench, sat with a sigh and a soft stroke for the lion-head, and watched life roll. He tried to ignore his benchmate, taking great care never to look in its direction.

He probably would have let the world continue as such without a care for anything around, but he heard a bit of a rumor concerning these C and their strange abilities. Apparently, they were mighty good at fixing a human body, and Tim's eyesight was worsening with each day.

After a serious deliberation with himself, one day he offered the C that shared his bench a smile and set up the chessboard for the second time. Before he made his opening move, he pointed to his glasses and figured that would be enough. The bet was on. Then he grabbed his knight and moved it into the field.

The C spent the next hour staring at the board. Tim figured that, having played only one game in its life, the little guy didn't know what to do. It had to have expected him to put up a pawn in the standard opening gambit. But his eyesight depended on this game, he thought, and the C *had* played before. There was no point in going easy on it.

The first week went by rather quickly. The days were mild, for the most part, and only once did the players have to stop early because of a threatening storm. That day the rain came and went, and they both returned for the last hours of the evening. One move this day. Four on that. Another had a record eleven moves.

Tim could have played faster, but why? The C could not be hurried and, for Tim, the long periods between plays let him study the board so that he could research his next move overnight. No mercy this time. Without a win, he would be legally blind in a year. And, if he couldn't see... well, he just felt too old to start dealing with life as a blind person.

Despite all his patience, the game did pick up during the second week. He could taste the victory coming. He had already repelled two subtle attacks by the C, and each of these minor triumphs had left him in a stronger tactical position.

The closer he came to winning, the more impatient he grew. On one day, the C took five hours to make a move. There were only three safe possibilities; any other move would be either dangerous or pointless. Tim could not understand what was taking the alien so long. New eyes awaited him, and this C wanted to prolong the agony.

Against his better judgment, he decided to attempt a pressure tactic. Each time the C finally moved, Tim slammed his piece down within a second, forcing the C back into deep thought. He did not plan to afford the alien a moment's rest.

The problem, of course, was that Old Tim forgot himself at one crucial move, and to his surprise, after thrusting his rook across the board, the C did not delve into hours of thought but merely slid his bishop with great care until it captured Tim's queen.

Tim glared at the space now occupied by the C's bishop. He considered that this might be the last thing he'd remember seeing. He had lost, they both knew it, but that was one of the pains in chess – the game had to go on. Unless Tim wanted to surrender... but, for him, that was never a consideration.

The following day ended the game. The C did not pause much in its play – it had learned enough by now. It chipped away at Tim's final pieces and overwhelmed the king. Checkmate.

With a chuckle that bordered on a cry, Tim motioned to the board. Had the Wilkins Store still been around, he would have been able to raise a paper bag in toast to the victor. As it was, he offered a bitter smile.

The C watched him in a way he was not used to, and for a moment Tim grew angry, thinking the alien was rubbing in his defeat.

Then he chuckle-cried again, and it grew into a laugh. He had forgotten a key factor in the bet. He'd forgotten that now he owed the C something.

He raised his arms to show the emptiness of his hands, and shrugged. He had nothing to give.

Except that wasn't true. He had two things, still: the chessboard and the bench.

But he didn't want to give either of those away. The chessboard was not enough to match the fixing of his eyes. And the bench – that seemed like too much.

The good years had vanished, and the world no longer belonged to him and his kind. He had done his best, and it had served well for him for quite a time. He had always thought he would die on this bench, but that thought would now have to change. No matter what, he did not want this C thinking poorly of him... or of human beings in general.

He struggled to his feet, perhaps playing it up a bit, and took one last look at the bench – worn as ever. Rust spots invaded the lion-heads, and a crack in the wood threatened to splinter. Dirt covered the area beneath his side, and two grooves marked where his feet would kick and dig and, on occasion, swing.

He wanted to say something to the C, something about how the bench should be cared for, but, when he raised his eyes to the creature, the words stuck. He felt a stone in his chest and his lips quivered.

The C watched him with a concerned set of eyes and then, to Tim's surprise, it pointed toward the empty space on the bench.

Tim did not move. It was a nice gesture, a thoughtful one, perhaps the most thoughtful act he had ever witnessed, but he had to honor his bet. He turned to go, his feet dragging the moment out longer than his heart desired.

As he made the first full step, he heard the distinct clatter of the chessboard being set.

He glanced over his shoulder. With a smile he stepped back to the bench, wondering what the stakes would be this time – probably the chance to return to the bench. That made the most sense.

They began another game, yet, after several hours and a few moves, Tim frowned. He had been thinking little of the game and mostly of the C. It had won twice already, yet still it wanted him to play on. At least, that was the way it seemed.

A week later, he lost the game. And nothing happened. The C did not demand he leave the bench, and nor did it ask for some token payment. Nothing. It simply reset the board, switching black and white so Tim could play the first move this time, and concentrated on what was to come.

Years went by, and they played game after game. Tim won only once, and he suspected the C had a cold that week; its colour had faded, and its eyes were a puffy blue. Otherwise, the C always bested him. It never mattered, though. The playing of the game consumed them.

Some would think it a boring life or a wasted one. Some would see Old Tim as one who had given up on everything. To him, it was a new set of rules for living, and he guessed that was what it was for the C as well.

His eyesight lasted longer than he had expected, but eventually it did go. He found it difficult to admit, as if by doing so he was somehow letting his dying day come a little closer, but the C could tell by the way he played. It had to have figured it out somehow, and this was the explanation that made the most sense to him.

On that day, the C placed the chessboard on the ground and inched along the chipped wood seat. Tim could feel the body move closer. The classic fears rustled across his skin, but he did not squirm away. Even when he felt the C's spindly fingers on his face he did not move. The fingers seemed to grow, stretched up his cheeks like roots, or maybe snakes. Then the things slipped into his eyes, and he passed out.

Later, when he woke, his vision was perfect. It was that simple. The C sat on its side of the bench, and the chessboard lay between them.

Tears welled in these eyes that now could see. Tim's face contorted in a mixture of calm respect and a sob. The C just focused on the game.

The moment called for something more, though. The idea grew within him, surging upward through his chest. He had to do something. He had to do it right now. All the years they had spent together playing this game and all the years he now saw ahead of them had converged on this point. He could see that as well as he could see the chessboard and the bench and the C.

Only one thing came to mind. A simple gesture, true, but one that he hoped would convey all of his thoughts from all of this time, past and future.

Swallowing hard on a dry throat, he reached his hand halfway across the chessboard. The C stared for a moment, and then seemed to comprehend.

They shook hands.

New Writings in the Fantastic
Vice Cop Vincent L. Scarsella

My first day in vice, we raided an orgy house.
I barely had time to settle into my cubicle when one of my colleagues peeked around the divider and told me to get down to the conference room – "Pronto!" The Chief was just about to brief the entire squad.

My late arrival earned a scowl from the Chief. Hell of a first impression. He had already started and had to wait for me to squeeze into a seat at the back of the room.

"Nice of you to join us, Mr. Parsons," he said, and looked around the room packed with seasoned vice cops. I later learned that he called everyone Mister, even criminals, with his slight Irish brogue. "Mr. Parsons joins us from Narcotics. And, as we all know, those boys are always late."

There was a smattering of laughter.

"You're a lucky man, Mr. Parsons," he went on. "First day in the squad, you get some real excitement."

The Chief resumed the briefing. For weeks, they had been watching a house in a high-class subdivision, obviously an orgy house. The owners were hedons, hosting orgies sometimes two, three times a month.

"Like all hedons," said the Chief, "they got careless. Invited fuckers who couldn't keep a secret. We bitched a regular and she squealed. Became an insider. Told us the other day that another big orgy is being hosted there, and tonight's the night."

The entire squad of twenty or so vice cops had crammed into the small conference room, squeezing into desks appropriated from a local high school, knees scraping up against swinging desk tops. We worked out of the downtown headquarters of the county sheriff's department. The city cops had their own vice squads, of course, but they couldn't be trusted. Although the pure temptation of illicit sex sometimes soiled the reputation of even the county squad, there were just too many city vice cops either on the take or who had become hedons themselves. It was likely we'd pinch a couple during the raid tonight and have to let them go in the interest of inter-cop relations.

I guess county vice cops like us were just better motivated, run by guys like the Chief who still believed we were doing something vital for the protection of society. A former Marine, with a granite chin and steely gray eyes, he had blond hair cropped so short you could see his scalp shining in the bright light of the briefing room. Like all ex-Marines, he still believed in law and order, in this case the so-called "taboo" laws passed after the sex epidemics of the late 2020s, a hundred times worse than the AIDS epidemics of a generation before. They had almost wiped out the species.

The Chief got down to basics. Our intelligence suggested this was a nasty bunch of hedons, especially with one or two city vice cops included, and there would be resistance, even likely some violence. We were to show the usual restraint. But, if we had to kick them in the balls or snatch, we should do it. The key was to grab as many of the fuckers as we could and get the hell out. By the way, the Chief added, there might be some celebrities – a politician or two. They were to be sequestered with the city vice cops we nabbed. What was to become of them was for our superiors – and the District Attorney – to decide.

He wished us godspeed and dismissed us to our duty.

I followed the vice cops as they shuffled out of the briefing room and strolled to their lockers. It took me a minute to find one that wasn't occupied. Opening it, I saw a flak jacket, stun gun, billy club and handcuffs. Some of my new colleagues quickly got their gear, and by the time I was ready were already heading down a dark corridor to the garage to board three unmarked black vans that would transport us to the raid.

A gray-haired wizened old cop with the nametag *Petersen* sidled up to me as I slipped into my flak jacket and said: "Not to worry. Just follow me, kid. Your first day in vice is my last. Today you start, today I retire." He laughed, more to himself than anything. "And what a way to start, or go out for that matter. An orgy raid! Just hope I get some decent images of tits and ass to remember the place by." His flak jacket was worn and tattered and a cigarette dangled from the corner of his mouth. His teeth were grossly yellowed and his breath stank of old coffee. "Some decent pussy shots oozing with cream pies to help enliven my next hundred jack-off sessions."

I grimaced. Another cop grabbed my arm from behind and moved me away from Petersen.

"Don't listen to that old nut," he said. This one's tag said *Kyle*. He added: "The Chief asked me to look out for you."

I shrugged, offended that the Chief thought I needed looking out for. I had been one of the best cops in Narco, as evidenced by how many of my arrests had been successfully prosecuted.

"Just tag along with me tonight," Kyle said. "Raiding an orgy house ain't no drug bust."

I followed Kyle to the garage and stepped after him into the back of the same van. It was already crammed with disagreeable vice cops, all scowling except Petersen, who wore a wide, nonsensical grin. The others regarded me with a measure of distrust – I was the new guy in the squad, yet earn their respect. Well at least they wouldn't have to wait long to see how I reacted under pressure.

The drive was an uncomfortable, bumpy, blind fifteen minutes in the dank, stale-pissy and sweaty smell of the cramped rear of the van. Except for the lame comments that came out of Petersen's mouth, everyone else kept quiet, dwelling on the mission at hand.

The plan was, once we'd come to complete stop, to blitzkrieg. We'd jump out of the vans and go crashing into the orgy house, search warrant in tow, then tackle and immobilize as many fuckers as we could before the place cleared out. Our main advantage, of course, would be surprise, and the fact that our hosts and all their guests would be buck naked and likely interlocked in some or other deviant sex act.

"When we get there," Kyle told me on the way, "just follow me."

It went off as planned. The vans squealed to a stop a house down from the orgy house and we jumped out into the warm, humid night. I ran behind Kyle while Petersen broke protocol by letting out a battle cry as two vice cops rammed open the front door.

Before entering the house, I heard the shrieks of shocked fuckers and the scuttle and dash of escape.

The cops were yelling for fuckers to stay down or be stun-gunned; otherwise they just shouted curses. I followed Kyle – at first from a dark foyer into the living room until the lights were switched – into a mass, almost comical confusion of cops running about and tackling fuckers who, with tits and dicks flapping, were running every which way to escape from them – at least those who hadn't already been stunned and cuffed.

I spotted a blonde lady leap to her feet and make for the kitchen in the back of the house behind a couple other fuckers, probably hoping to sneak out a rear door. I broke off from Kyle and headed after her, anxious to chip in by making my first bust. It was hard not to keep my eyes off her ass as I quickly made up ground. Finally, I jumped and found my face right in it as I tackled her from behind. She screamed, and one of the fuckers ahead of her stopped and lowered a fist to the top of my head. I held tight and managed to cuff the lady around the ankles while the guy kept punching me. I pushed her off and saw her squirm helplessly, crying out indecipherable obscenities while I went after her accomplice with my stunner. I zapped the guy in his naked, hairy chest and he went limp. By that time Petersen was on the floor smothering the lady.

"She's down," I yelled at him. "Get the other one."

The third fucker was already at the back door and almost free and clear, but for some reason Petersen kept at the girl. I noticed his hand move down to her pubic area. He turned with a leering grin and said: "I need the smell for my dreams." He put his fingers to his nose and took a deep whiff. "Um! The smell of pussy cream."

The woman was screaming furiously. Petersen dry humped her for a time. I just sat there watching this, amazed, while the tumult continued around me. "You don't stop that right now, detective," I finally said, "I'll stun your ass."

Petersen continued humping a few moments longer before realizing he was gathering an audience, trying his luck. He rolled over onto his back, panting, and looked up at me with a sly, sick smile.

"Like I said," he said, "it's my last day and I need all the memories I can get."

Kyle peeked into the kitchen and shouted at us they needed help upstairs. The fuckers there were refusing to surrender.

I got to my feet and ran after him up a flight of stairs, ignoring the countless naked forms – skinny and fatassed men and women – writhing comically on the floor around me, cuffed from behind.

By the time I got upstairs, the mayhem was largely under control. There were a couple of naked hedons twisting arms in resistance, preventing themselves from being cuffed or stunned. But either Kyle or myself grabbed hold and helped the struggling vice cops gain control. It was all over in a couple minutes.

"Thanks" went all around, mixed in with the curses of arrested hedons, and I followed Kyle down a hallway to the stairs. On the way, I happened by an open door to a darkened room. Looking inside for a fraction of a second, I caught one of the vice cops leaning up against an immobilized naked blonde. His hand was down by her privates, stroking, and his mouth was up against her face. She seemed to be cooing.

"C'mon." Kyle grabbed at me. He gave the bedroom scene a look, scowled and pulled me away.

On our way downstairs he said, "That was Jed Carter, getting a thrill. He cuts it too close to the edge sometimes. But he's one damned good vice cop. Had the most arrests in the squad last year. So the Chief pretends what you just saw never happens. Looks the other way, as we all have learned to." We were in the living room by now. The mop-up cops charged with writing arrest sheets for the fuckers we had caught were already taking names and reading the suspects their rights.

As we stepped over a few bodies on our way out of the now former orgy house back to the vans, I turned and saw Carter and the blonde heading downstairs. I didn't think she was handcuffed any more.

The Chief briefed me personally in his office after we'd returned.

"Did you get hard?" he asked, scowling, dead serious. "Seeing that much tit and ass in the same damned place."

I swallowed. I had to admit that seeing, feeling and smelling snatch so close had slightly aroused me during the raid. I kept my eyes on the Chief and shrugged.

"Kinda, sir," I admitted with a shrug, guessing that was what he wanted to hear.

He nodded. "That's a healthy reaction. Beat off to it all you want at home, in private. That's your prerogative. As long as you can handle it – being exposed to it, the real thing, I mean." He sighed and his scowl narrowed. "Kyle said you did all right. Performed goddamn admirably. Better than that fuck Petersen. Glad to be rid of that nuisance."

I nodded, not sure if I'd been complimented or not. To be compared with Petersen, I felt, was kind of insulting.

"You on the list, Mr. Parsons?" he asked. For a moment, I didn't quite catch his meaning. "They lining up a mate for you?"

I shrugged. "Next year, I think," I said. "Nothing definite."

"Good," he said. "Once you get a bride, this'll be easier. At least you got a live body to relieve the aggravations of this job. Not that the temptation isn't still there." He sighed. "You understand, you'll be chasing men and women who have opted to violate the taboo laws. Scumbags who place themselves above the law – and who chose to risk all of mankind because they can't keep their dicks or pussies in their pants or skirts. The lowest, basest scum!"

He was getting into it now, like a reverend. Kyle had warned me on the way back from the orgy raid that the Chief would call me in almost immediately and give me the standard pep talk. He did that with all the new vice cops. It would make me one of them, a rite of passage.

"Just listen," Kyle had advised. "And smile."

"Believe me," the Chief went on, "I'd rather have a squad of married farmers or impotents. But the force ain't built like that, so we take what we can get. And you come highly recommended, mind you. Cream of the crop – to use a bad fucking pun. Anyway, I'm glad to have you. If you ever have a worry or a problem, you just bring it to me. And if I can't fix it I'll find somebody who goddamn will."

Just like that I was dismissed and let out into the world of the vice squad. I retired to my cubicle, prepared to be buried in a mound of paperwork, reports on the raid. And I was right.

My shift the next night, they sent me cruising with Carter as my partner. He worked cold and uncommunicative. There had been a report of some hanky-panky in a local coffee bar, heavy petting then parking lot blowjobs, that sort of stuff. A few months back, a couple had been arrested – teens mind you – going at it in the traditional sense in the back of his daddy's brand new hybrid Chevrolet.

Carter said nothing as we entered the bar, dressed the part, pretending to be on the prowl. We ordered some funky latte and occupied a table. Pretty soon, two lookers, one blonde, the other a ravenous brunette, asked if we'd like some company. I sensed Carter had had the go-around with these two before.

For a couple of minutes we made small talk. Carter seemed impressed how natural I was. For some reason, he must have thought I was uptight, perfectly straight. But I liked a pretty girl as much as the next guy, and thought I might have a good time jerking off to the brunette looker, who seemed to have taken a liking to me.

It didn't take long for Carter to invite them for a ride in our Caddy roadster, the newest hybrid widely advertised to possess some real kick – even for a mostly electric vehicle. The girls seemed excited about the prospect, and I thought to myself that Carter was good, real good. These two would be coming on to us, bare their chests and more even, and we'd make a couple arrests before the shift was a couple hours old.

But Carter had other ideas. Knowing exactly where he was going, he pulled into the girls' apartment complex, and we strolled in together. He even knew the alarm code. We went up three flights to their apartment, and he quickly led Carly – the blonde – to a back bedroom and left me alone with Hilde, the brunette.

"He's interrogating her," Hilde said flatly as she took my hand and led me to a couch in the middle of the wide, modern living room. She laughed seductively as we slumped close to each other, and my cock was rock hard. "She's been a bad girl."

"What about you?" I heard myself asking.

She smiled and pulled me close. I could smell a perfume like some kind of sweet powder. I started kissing her, wondering how many regulations had already been violated. She reached down to my crotch and started stroking. I let her do it for a time, then my thoughts drifted, for some reason, to the orgy raid. All those naked fuckers breaking the law, putting humanity at risk for a few moments' pleasure. Sex had almost exterminated mankind. Disease was inevitable unless procreation between men and women was strictly regulated. Not to mention the skewering of the gene pool which was the natural result of free sex.

I thought of what had been grilled into us in school – the evil and dirt that sex was.

A moment later, I found myself pushing Hilde away. She looked at me, horrified.

"You gonna arrest me?"

By then, Carter was out, with Carly in tow. "We got a problem here?" he asked, glaring.

Carly started giggling.

I got to my feet, and straightened my pants.

"No," I said. "No problem."

"Good," Carter said. "'Cause we're leaving." He let go of the blonde's hand. "There's nothing here. They're clean."

He said nothing to me on the way back from our patrol. It was as if nothing had happened. And what could I prove anyway. I had been the one with the obvious hard-on. He had been in the back bedroom "interrogating" the blonde.

Later that night he arrested a gray-haired, older broad who had slipped her hand down his pants in the back booth of the fifth or sixth coffee bar we had visited that patrol. His seventh arrest that month, not counting the raid on the orgy house. Another Carter record.

I got nothing that night.

The next day I sat in my cubicle wishing I was back in narcotics. There were occasional cheats there, too, scumbags like Carter, but it seemed easier, less consequential somehow, to play that game with drugs. Drugs ate away at the mind and soul of its abusers, for sure, but sex had killed, could kill, and would kill again. And this time it might kill everyone.

"You're looking glum." It was Kyle. He had peeked around the corner and seen me skulking. The Chief had likely asked him to take a look see how I was doing.

I shrugged. "No," I lied. "Just tired."

"Went out with Carter last night," he said, shaking his head. "I told the Chief that was a mistake."

I looked up at him, sick of his coddling.

"He made an arrest," I said. "And I didn't."

Kyle shrugged. "Heard you guys went up to Carly and Hilde's place," he said. "Carter's informants, so-called. Now that's a dangerous pair. Most of us think they're hedons, pure and simple."

I shrugged. "Maybe they are," I said. "And maybe they're not."

Kyle sat in the chair at the side of my desk, seeing he was getting nowhere. He knew Carter was too smart to reveal too much to a rookie.

After a moment, he nodded at my computer screen. "You got mail."

And so I did. I clicked on the e-mail icon and saw a long list.

"Most of it's bullshit," he said. "Personnel bulletins, procedure updates, unfunny jokes."

"I know," I said, and almost added: *I'm not a rookie, remember.* Instead, with a smirk, I added: "Been there, read that."

"So they fed you the same bullshit nonsense in narcotics?"

I nodded absently as I started clicking through about twenty messages.

"Ah!" Kyle said. "Slow down. One of them's orders."

Kyle was pointing to the e-mail I was just about to delete. Its subject line read: *Special Mission Directive.*

Now that was different. I never got a "directive" on my e-mail in narcotics.

I opened it and Kyle looked away. When I glanced at him, he said, "Usually, personal directives are secure: for your eyes only. The Chief should have told you that the other day."

I shrugged, irritated by such high-level nonsense.

"It's probably just a message putting you hot on a known hedon," he said. "A woman, I hope."

That was exactly it. Some informant had identified a lady exhibiting hedonistic tendencies. My mission was to find out if tendencies equated to reality and, if so, to make an arrest.

"That's it?" I said, looking back at Kyle with a laugh. "Top-secret spy shit for that. I have to find out if some lady likes to fuck?"

He shrugged. "That accusation in this day and age is worse than being tagged a drug lord, right?"

I had to admit that. Being a fucker and a drug dealer were two different things. While a drug lord might get a couple years in jail, the penalty for unregulated sex was at least exile, and possibly, death.

The suspect's name was Darlena Bolton. The lead page of the directive included her physical stats – height, weight, hair and eye colour, that sort of thing – and a photograph. She was a real looker. Hot. Blonde. Serious blue eyes, high cheekbones, nice slim hips sensually positioned. She was twenty-six years old, single, still on the list for a man, although she had passed on at least three Centrex selections and broken up with a fourth after only a couple months. Real picky, or maybe she simply enjoyed the single life. There was no law forcing marriage, only a strict rule against unregulated sex.

The snitch's information on page 2 was scant. She'd been arrested last week in a dance hall on the west side for performing mouth to pussy on some lady she'd just met. An undercover vice cop in the crowd had followed them into the bathroom and seen the whole sordid thing. In the snitch's subsequent haste for a favorable plea, she identified Darlena as someone who gave in to temptation on a regular basis – implying, I mused, that the snitch thought we all did it sometimes. Darlena was allegedly bi, although, to the snitch's chagrin, she liked men mostly. And that was it. Darlena had become a suspect on the strength of one desperate fucker's accusation.

Page 3 gave me Darlena's most frequent haunts, compiled after a couple days' surveillance. It was my task to flesh the list out (to use a bad pun) and get some hard evidence (to use another) that she engaged in illegal sex.

Kyle slapped me on the back.

"That's a hell of a lot better than my first job," he said. He went on to recount the story of that first job – an old lady, maybe seventy years old, who liked giving hand jobs to strangers on benches in public parks. "She stroked pretty good for an old hag," Kyle laughed, "but I had to end it before I let her finish. Took me three days of non-stop surveillance to finally weasel my way in for that hand-job. Wasn't even much of a motivation for late-night jerking off."

"What do I do with this one?" I asked Kyle. "Make the moves on her – see if she bites – to use a bad pun?"

He laughed. Bad puns were everywhere.

"Yep," he said. "Use your wiles. Sidle up to her wherever she hangs out and deploy your best pick-up lines. There's some real doozies in the procedure manual. Real laughers."

There was not much use for flirting these days, though people naturally did it sometimes, driven by subconscious instinct, forgetting that it was useful for nothing. Under the taboo laws, all sexual and romantic relationships had to be pre-arranged and monitored thereafter. Nothing was left to chance for fear of inevitable disease and genetic mischief.

Once I got away from Kyle, I checked out a car and drove to one of the target's regular haunts, a coffee bar in the West End named Pedigrees. She wasn't there. And neither was she at the next six or seven of the other common places – bookstores, a video malls, eateries – where she usually tramped. Must have stayed home tonight. After the sixth or seventh place, three hours after I had started the search, I shrugged and headed back with sore feet to headquarters and wrote a negative report.

At home that night, I couldn't help staring at Darlena's picture in the directive. She was a gorgeous and sexy blonde, every boy's jerk-off fantasy, and I had been given the job of identifying her as a fucker who deserved exile.

I couldn't help myself from thinking about her as a hedon slut and wondering what it would be like to pull a Carter and get her on the take for regular screw-jobs. Who would know? Carter got away with it. I pulled down Betty, my fuck doll, pulled her plug so that she inflated, and put a blonde wig on her. As she gave me a plastic blow job, I called out her name – "Darlena, oh, Darlena!" – as I came a load full.

The next night, a Friday, I hit pay dirt at the first coffee bar I stuck my head into – that place Pedigrees. Darlena occupied a small table in a back corner. She had her nose stuck in a book in front of her, some novel. A cup of exotic java cooled before her on the table.

I went to the bar and ordered myself a regular. As I stood at the counter after my order came, I couldn't remember a decent flirt line from the lame examples in the squad's procedure manual. After a couple sips of coffee, I decided to mosey over to Darlena's table and do or say whatever came to mind – trust my instincts. Standing there, paper coffee cup in hand, I stared down at her book for a time, craning my neck to take a better look. That got her attention.

"Can I help you?" she asked.

"That's, that's a great read," I said, although I still had no idea what the book was. She suddenly placed it flat on the table. I smirked, seeing that it was a romance novel.

"Oh, yeah," she said, smiling. "You read this?"

I shrugged, smiling sheepishly. "No," I said. "I don't think so, but it worked, didn't it? Got you to talk to me."

She smiled, and invited me to sit down.

"Never saw you here before," she said. "What brings you out?"

"I don't know," I told her, and took a sip of my coffee. Then, as if inspired, I looked up at her. "Maybe it was you."

That seemed to open up a wave of warmth in her. Her smile broadened, and I congratulated myself for such a good line. I seemed to be a natural at pick-up lines. Even Carter would have been proud of me.

It continued that way for a time, a real tit-for-tat exchange, nothing serious but still somewhat fun. I liked the girl, it was hard not to, with the way she looked and her silky voice. We got to talking about our jobs, and I lied that I was a spacecraft tech. She said she was a lawyer. I tipped my paper cup to her, impressed. She shrugged it off, and after one of those awkward pauses, the talk got deeper. She started to complain about how difficult life was under the taboo laws. Some government clerk deciding who and when and how you could "make love." Made the act disgusting, unnatural.

"Takes the romance out of it," I agreed.

She looked at me and nodded. "That's exactly it," she said. "There's no romance any more."

Ten minutes later, she had talked me into leaving Pedigrees.

"And go where?"

"My place?" she asked sheepishly.

I swallowed. That was one hell of a surprising proposition. Then I remembered I was a vice cop and what the mission was. So, after another swallow, I said, "Sure."

Her place was a small apartment in a singles' complex with security cams everywhere, ever watchful for the suspicious movement of bodies. In the parking lot of Pedigrees she'd told me how we could enter separately and avoid detection.

"We have to sneak," she said, leaning up against her car. "I'm not licensed for male guests."

"How?" I asked. "How do I get inside?"

She smiled. "I got a deal with the tenant downstairs," she said. "You go out a window of her place and climb up a special ladder into mine. There's a blind spot so the cams won't see you."

I nodded. It was probably the oldest trick in the book. Maybe the complex management looked the other way. I was getting giddy with the prospect of arresting not only this girl, but her girlfriend downstairs as an accomplice.

Then the suspect surprised me. She leaned forward and planted a kiss on my lips.

"You're cute," she said. Of course, I was – that's part of the reason I got picked for vice in the first place.

The kiss not only surprised me, it sent a rise you know where. I found myself leaning forward and returning it. This time our mouths opened and we just stood there for a time rolling and moving our tongues. The last girl I had kissed was a clean hooker at the sex clinic three months ago. Legal, regulated sex, under the taboo laws. But it was also damned expensive and you needed a doctor's prescription.

I backed up, thinking: *Wow!*

In her apartment, she latched onto my shoulders and pulled me onto the couch. We kissed a while until I was rock-hard. My thoughts turned to last night's fantasy with my plastic doll and I wondered if I should really breach duty and give in to her, pull a Carter. Once again I thought: *Who would know?*

Her left hand was suddenly down in my crotch, rubbing my already engorged member. Next thing I knew, she was unzipping my pants and her hand was reaching inside. Finally her fingers were on my erection, stroking me. Right now, I was still legitimate. I had to let her go on a little while before making an arrest. Unregulated physical intimacy was more than just a kiss, more than dry humping, more than stroking an erect penis inside denim jeans. But – as I had read in the procedure manual – an arrest could be made for something less than providing an orgasm.

So I let her stroke, giving me time to let my conscience wrestle with itself. Giving me time to taste her sweet, salty lips. The next move would be, of course, to pull her head down into my lap. If I did that, I'd be as far gone and crooked as Carter. And after less than a week in vice. At least Carter had been there two years.

"How's it feel, honey?" she said breathlessly. "I want to make you come."

That was all I needed. I threw caution to the wind and pulled her head down to my lap. She obeyed eagerly while I leaned back onto the armrest of the couch.

As she started trying to pulling down my pants one-handed, she said to me: "You know, I could bust you right now."

"What?" It came out something like a breathless whimper while I continued stroking her silky blonde hair on my lap. "What?"

"I'm a cop," she said. "A vice cop. From a city squad. Second Precinct."

That stopped me cold. My penis started to go limp.

"Don't worry," she said, still tugging at my pants. "I'm not gonna bust you. I decided I could use a decent fuck myself. And maybe we can become regulars."

I pushed her head away from my crotch and looked down at her with a bewildered grin.

"Sometimes they test new vice cops," she explained. "I guess, the other day, during some orgy raid, you exhibited some, well, tendencies that caused your superiors some concern. They pulled me from the city force to check you out. Give a full report." She laughed. "I guess I better not tell them what I found."

"You fucking hedon," I said. "You little bitch."

"Hey, man," she said, flashing her bright blue eyes at me. She reached over and stroked me once more, trying to get me hard again. "What's wrong?"

"I'm gonna bust *your* ass, bitch," I said. I grabbed her by her skinny shoulders and pushed her totally off me. Then I got to me feet, leaving her in a lump on the couch, frowning sorrowfully at me.

"What's the fucking *matter* with you?"

"I'm a vice cop, whore," I said. "Remember? And I'm gonna bust your ass for not busting mine."

She shook her head and laughed. "You got to be kidding me." She sat and straightened out her hair. "You have got to be fucking kidding me."

I didn't let her say another word. I did what we always did in narcotics to gain an immediate upper hand. I reached a fist back and thrust forward, slugging her fresh across her pretty nose, cracking it. As she tumbled, blood started streaming down from her face across the beige carpet of what was supposed to be her apartment.

The Chief was so proud of me you would have thought I'd nabbed a thousand freelance hookers. After the Internal Affairs nerds had heard my story and seemed to believe she was a rogue slut trying to blackmail me into illicit unregulated sex, they let me go and took her away on a stretcher for further interrogation.

"The power of sex," the Chief said. Veins throbbed along his thick forehead. "Now you see what it does to the best of them. I heard she had been Precinct Two's top vice cop."

"What'll happen to her?" I asked, feeling bad deep down that I'd had to save myself by fitting her up. But at least I hadn't sold my soul and become a hedon. In that moment, it was easy to convince myself she'd gotten exactly what she deserved. Still, I would forever wonder what would have become of us – would we have remained merely sex slaves to each other or would that have evolved into romance?

That, of course, I would never know.

"She'll be kicked out of vice." he laughed. "Of that I can assure you."
I laughed too – gently, though.
"Can I go, Chief? I'm bushed."
The Chief got up and came around his desk to my chair.
"Sure, you can go," he said, sitting on the armrest. "But not before I give you your penance."
"Penance?"
He smirked. "I know you were about ready to fuck that girl until she slipped up and told you she was a vice cop," he said, and I didn't move a muscle in protest. "That's her story, anyway. And it fits, somehow. But what's done is done and we got no proof either way. So here's what I want you to do."
"What's that?"
"Know Carter?"
"Detective Carter?"
"Yes. I want you to finally bust that scumbag's ass." He smiled. "And guess who's gonna help you?"
I smiled. The beauty in the Chief's plan was priceless.
"At least when the swelling in her nose goes down," he said.
"Can't wait," I said.
The Chief gestured for me to stand, and shook my hand as I did so.
"Welcome to Vice," he said.
And, this time, I knew he meant it.

New Writings in the Fantastic
The Clouds Roll By-hi Greg Beatty

After a quarter of an hour, Dr. Evans said, "So, if I may sum up, you're here because you're having trouble sleeping due to a crushing sense of responsibility."

"I would not call it 'crushing'... Actually, yes, I suppose I would. Yes, that summation is essentially correct."

"And, again to review, you're single and haven't suffered any recent personal tragedies. Nor is your work, as a grammarian, particularly stressful."

Henry smiled at his therapist. "Well put, but when you say it that way the situation sounds ridiculous. Irrational, even. Which is why I sought clinical help."

Dr. Evans smiled gently back. "And we're going to see that you get all the help you need. I'd like to start by making an observation, and filling in a few areas of your history that aren't quite clear to me yet."

"By all means," Henry said. "I salute your desire for a systematic approach."

"Well, since you mentioned salutes, do you see your gestures as having any particular connection to your insomnia and lack of ease?"

"Pardon me?"

"Your gestures." Dr. Evans made a rolling motion with one hand and presented the palm of another, as if shoving a car.

"Excuse me?"

Had Evans been a cat, his tail might have twitched. As it was, he limited himself to saying, "Henry, would you look down for me?"

Henry did. "Well I, I would say 'I never,' but clearly I do. Would it surprise you to learn that I'd never noticed these motions?" Henry did a few self-tests. When he picked up a pen in his right hand to occupy it, his left alternated between the shoving and the twirling motions. When he put the pen down, the left returned to shoving while the right twirled smoothly. "How. Curious."

"It's clear that you experience your surprise as genuine."

"Again, sir, may I say that I appreciate your precision? My, this certainly explains some of the heretofore cryptic asides my students have been making. How distracting. How pointless. And I seem unable to stop. Strange. Dr. Evans, would you say there's something that could be done? May we move this to the top of the list of priorities?"

Evans was about to suggest his new client allow himself to speak in a more natural fashion, but stopped. Did Henry *have* one such? All Evans said out loud was, "Well, if it hasn't bothered you yet, I wouldn't be concerned. But it does draw the attention. There are things we could try."

"Let us attempt them, then."

Most of the rest of the session was spent ruling things out. There were no toxins in Henry's work environment, as might produce involuntary physical spasms or repetitive motions. There was no dulling of memory of the sort that might accompany neurological disorders, though Evans made a note to order tests to be sure. There were no traumatic incidents that might have established movement patterns below the level of consciousness, and Henry remained calm and rational, even hyper-rational, when discussing them. In short, Evans saw little reason for Henry's rolling and shoving motions. On the plus side, he saw no reason not to try to stop them.

"We're almost out of time, Henry. We may have to take this up next time. Before you go, however, would you be willing to give hypnosis a try?"

"By all means," Henry said.

Dr. Evans closed the drapes to reduce distractions, and began the process. To his surprise, despite Henry's habitual rationality, he was a perfect subject, entering a deep trance with ease. Henry was no more able to explain the gestures while hypnotized than he had been in normal consciousness, but Dr. Evans was quite satisfied at his readiness to accept suggestion, and even more satisfied to see Henry's hands settled relaxedly in his lap.

"And when I count down to one you'll return to normal consciousness. Three, two one," Evans said.

Henry opened his eyes, glanced at his hands, and smiled broadly. "How wonderful! And though I had thought the matters unrelated, that feeling of – forgive the cliché – the whole world resting on my shoulders is gone!"

Dr. Evans smiled as he walked over to open the curtains, almost grinning at the unexpected sound of Henry humming. "Well, I'd like to address the matter in one of our following sessions, to make sure that everything... that's peculiar."

"What is it?" Henry asked.

"It almost looks like—" Evans stopped speaking, unable to tear his eyes from the sky, but unwilling to name what he seemed to be seeing. "Henry, we're out of time, so I understand if you need to go, but would you do me a favor and tell me what you see?"

Obligingly, Henry hummed his way over to the window. "I see a golden day – thank you, doctor. Blue skies, yes. I see how wonderful the world is, and a host of graceful, fluffy clouds... that aren't moving at all. Heavens, they're just hanging there."

Despite his real and very evident consternation, Henry did not lose his formality, or, curiously, his tune.

As the two men stood staring at clouds that did not move in a sky that was completely still, Dr. Evans slowly asked, "What's that you're humming, Henry?"

"Oh, my. Was I humming? Is that rude? Is it another symptom?"

"What's the song?"

"It escapes me. Something from *My Fair Lady*, I believe. I have always been fond of musicals. Such an ordered world."

With a sense of foreboding, Dr. Evans said, "Would you do me the favor of singing the lines for me?"

"As good as I feel, I would gladly *dance* for you, doctor." In a light tenor, Henry sang, "'I shall not feel alone without you. I can stand on my own without you.' I see what you mean," he continued, letting the song lapse. "The words are a perfect paradigm for the therapeutic relationship."

"No! I mean, would you sing the lines before those?"

"Certainly. 'Without your twirling it, the earth can spin. Without your pushing them, the clouds roll by-hi." Henry stopped with a cough. "Oh, my."

"'Oh, my.' indeed," Dr. Evans said as the clouds continued to not roll by and, by implication, the earth to not spin. He yanked on the cord, pulling the drapes sharply shut.

There was a knock on the door. "In session!" Evans yelled. "Henry, sit down! We've got to get you back to spinning and pushing – and fast!"

"But, Dr. Evans, I feel so much better, and this urge feels precisely like the sort of pressure that has been troubling me. I am simply not comfortable with it."

Beyond the room's drawn curtain, things began to heat up, from the sun not shifting. The world began to grumble and shake as the moon kept moving but the earth stood still. Evans thought of his son, on a surfing trip to San Diego, and of what was likely to be happening to the tides there.

Most days, what happened in therapy was interesting only to those involved. Today, the fate of the world depended on how fast Dr. Evans could hypnotize a recalcitrant grammarian.

"Okay, I want you to try to relax," he said, speaking louder to be heard over the growing roar of the earth's displeasure.

New Writings in the Fantastic
Employment Gremlins Holden Herbert

Ryan's confidence was at its peak. He had been speaking with the hiring manager for an hour, and nailing every question. All the interviewing practice he had done with the employment agency, though terribly expensive, was paying off. This was the third and final interview, covering more than a month of letters, telephone calls and internet research. Just a few more minutes and the job would be in the bag.

He scratched his thigh, imagining a pocket full of money. He was on a roll. Bring it on.

"This is an example of a problem that's happened in the past, and I'm curious how you would handle it," said the hiring manager. "Suppose you had a worker reporting to you who was having discipline problems. The person is integral to the project but isn't coming through with quality work. How would you handle the situation?"

"I would string the faggot up by the balls and skullfuck him," Ryan said.

"Excuse me?"

"Yes, I had a similar problem at my previous job. I found that dealing with the problem early and staying open to communication brought the worker in line quickly."

"No, what was it you said before?" The hiring manager set his pen on the table and clasped his hands in front of him.

"I'd commented about how open communication and dealing with problems early prevented problems from getting out of hand."

"Before that. You said something about faggots."

"'Faggots'?" Ryan's shoulders slumped forward.

"I'm assuming you knew I was gay." The hiring manager took a cellphone from his coat pocket and punched in a number.

"Yes, but it doesn't matter to me," said Ryan. "You can slip your skinny dick into any shit-filled asshole you want." He tilted his head to the side and smiled. "I've worked with gay men before and it's never been a problem."

"Get security up here right away. Fourth floor. Conference room D," said the hiring manager into the cellphone. Then, to Ryan, "This interview's over. Security will escort you out of the building."

The man stood, walked to the door, opened it and started to leave, shaking his head.

"Wait! I don't understand." Ryan heard laughter. He turned to see its source, but there was nothing except a white board and two chairs.

"You're kidding me," said the hiring manager. "Is this some kind of joke?"

The security guard held the door open for Ryan to leave the building. He walked several rows into the parking lot before it dawned on him that he was looking for his car. Where had he parked?

He wandered for a half-hour, walking past his Toyota Tercel three times before he stopped and took out his keys. He looked at his reflection in the driver-side window. The new suit Cheryl had bought him for this interview looked perfect. He'd knotted the tie just right. His shirt was crisp. He got his hair cut yesterday, shaved this morning.

What the hell had happened in there?

He opened the door and paused. What was he going to tell Cheryl? All he'd talked about for the last month was this job. He was a perfect fit – slightly overqualified, enthusiastic. He'd done his homework. Damn. His wife was going to leave him. She'd tolerated his joblessness for a year, but everyone had their limits.

While he stood holding the car door, two beings, a foot and a half tall, circled around him and jumped up to the front seat. They pushed each other's shoulders. The smaller one pinched the other's nose, then hopped over the headrest to the back seat. She laughed, bobbing her head and showing sharp brown teeth. Spittle dripped from her mouth and landed on the scales of her green skin. She motioned to her mate to join her, winking her bulging yellow cat eyes.

"Hurry up before he sits on you," said Striptease. She slid next to the back window, patting the seat with her bone-thin hand and its black nails. "If we dally, he'll be able to see us. C'mon."

Shitforbrains leaped over to the back seat. He punched Striptease on the shoulder, and she pulled his hefty, pointed ears. They put their hands over their round stomachs and cackled.

"You're a genius," said Striptease. "I had no idea he was gay. That 'skullfuck' thing, where'd you hear that?"

"A drill sergeant who was trying to get promoted during the Vietnam War used to say it all the time."

"I get to use it next," she said.

"This guy's smart," said Shitforbrains. "He's catching on. We need to look for another host."

Striptease closed her eyes, bowed her head and turned away. "But I like him. Let's ride this pony into Chapter Eleven."

Ryan drove home from the job interview doing forty miles an hour in the freeway's fast lane. Cars honked as they sped past, the drivers giving him the finger. Occasionally he looked over at them, and saw that everyone had the hiring manager's face. The voices in his head distracted him every day. Some days they showed no mercy, chattering from morning until night.

"Look, idiot, see that deranged woman in the lane next to you," said Shitforbrains. "She's pissed at you 'cause you're driving like a ninety-year-old woman. Don't just sit there; ram her with your car. Flip her the bird, wimp. She's better than you. She's got a job." He sat on the headrest, leaning against the driver-side window. "Loser, look down the road. Everyone has a job but you."

Striptease sat on the headrest opposite Shitforbrains. She whispered in Ryan's ear, "If it wasn't for the money you get from your wife, you wouldn't be able to feed yourself. Loser. Penniless loser. No one's going to hire you."

Beads of sweat rolled down Ryan's cheeks. *My God, I'm going crazy. I can't go crazy now. I haven't got any health insurance. I can't tell Cheryl I'm hearing voices. She'd be out the door before I finished telling her.* He looked to the side and saw he was passing his exit.

"Get a grip on yourself. You've got to tell Cheryl you blew the interview. Tell her first thing she walks through the door," said Striptease. "Blame it on the faggot hiring manager. Lie to her. She isn't going to believe you, anyway."

In Seattle, during the month of January, it's cold and black outside by five o'clock in the evening. Ryan sat on the couch with his feet up on the coffee table, still wearing his navy blue suit. His shirt was untucked and his tie hung lose. He held his fifth beer on his knee. He should get up and turn on the heat, flip a couple of light switches, make the place warm and comfortable before Cheryl came home. Every time he blinked his eyes, he imagined the hiring manager's shocked expression.

Cheryl gasped when she came in the house and flipped on the lights. "My God, I didn't think you were here. Why are you sitting in the dark? It's freezing in here." She turned on the furnace.

"I didn't get the job."

"Oh, baby, what happened? This morning you thought it was a sure thing."

Ryan related the story as best he could remember.

"You must've said something to make him angry," she said.

"I don't know. I don't get it."

"I was hoping we could rob our piggy bank and go out and celebrate tonight." She set a couple of magazines and several envelopes on the coffee table, tearing one open. "Shit, another fifteen-day notice from Puget Power. Damn, Ryan, we're behind $365. I'm tired of this. It's the same thing every month from the power company and the telephone. You've got to get a job, that's all there is to it."

"That was the best shot I've had in months. Now I'm back to square one."

"Jenny from the gaming company called me today. I asked her about the jobs there you applied for. You're perfect for their company. I'd been surprised no one had called you. She said she wanted to show me something, and faxed me a copy of the resume you sent her." She held out the paper, but he didn't glance at it. "Look at this, dammit. I need you to explain what's going on."

He took and read it. At the bottom of the first page was

I am a member of the White Aryans for Freedom, and we are less than a month away from an assassination attempt on the President.

At the bottom of the last page was:

My wife and I are having serious financial problems. Either of us will do you for the night for $75.

"I don't understand, Ryan. Why would you put something like that on your resume?"

"I... I... I didn't do that." He could hear the laughter again to either side, but when he looked he saw nothing.

"Jenny isn't lying. This is what you sent her. That's why you never heard from them. She couldn't forward this. With all the problems she's been having with her boss, she's afraid to bring you in. She thinks you'll screw up and get her in trouble. She's not willing to take the risk." Cheryl held her hands out to her side and shook her head. "I'm beginning to wonder if you *want* to get a job. You say you're sending out resumes and making calls. Then the interview today. You said something, must have." She sat beside him. "Since your unemployment ran out, we've fallen behind on everything. I'm totally stressed out. I don't care what you do, but you've *got* to get a job. Any job."

Ryan felt a tingling in his ear and he scratched it.

A voice said, "Tell her to fuck off. Go get another beer. See if you can get her to borrow money from her brother. He's a real-estate broker. He can afford to give you five hundred bucks. Tell him you've got a hot tip. Show some balls here, Dude."

Ryan covered his ears. Damn those voices.

"I've thought about this a lot, Ryan," Cheryl said. "I'm sorry, but I have to say it. Either you have a job in thirty days or I'm moving out. I love you, I truly do. But this is making me crazy."

Ryan had seen the Help Wanted sign in the pet store window for a couple of weeks. Hell, what could it pay? Not much more than minimum wage, but it didn't matter. Any job was better than losing his wife, and that would be only the start of the things that would disappear from his life if he didn't find work soon. It would be fun to work with animals, and he could lift a fifty-pound bag of grain as well as anybody. Besides, the pet store was close enough to his house that he could ride his bicycle there each day. Brainless as the job might be, it would be a relief to get up in the morning and have a place to go, to have people depending on him.

He didn't want to overdo it. He wore his blue slacks and gray shirt, and decided against a tie. He saw himself reflected in the store window. *Hey, what a stud.* If they needed somebody, he was the man. Who could resist a college-educated man with an impressive work history? He walked up to the counter.

"I'm interested in the job you have advertised in the window. Could I speak to the manager?" he said, straightening his back and squaring his shoulders.

The clerk was a pimply-faced boy in his late teens. He looked Ryan up and down, shaking his head. "You're kidding?"

"No, I'm dead serious. Can I speak to the manager?"

The clerk went into a back room and came out accompanied by a tall woman in her mid-twenties. She wore a black T-shirt and studded jeans with ripped knees. She had made her face pale with white makeup and eyes her dark red with eye shadow. Her hair was dyed black and shaved three inches above her ears. She looked Ryan over and stepped back.

"You sure you're interested in this job? It don't pay much."

"I can assure you I am," said Ryan.

"Okay, fill out this application. Got a pen?"

Ryan nodded.

"You can sit at my desk. I was eating lunch, but I'll clear you a spot." She led him into a dark room at the back of the store. She pushed aside Burger King bags, plastic packets of catsup and paper cups containing brown water.

Ryan sat at a metal desk with a Formica top and rusted sides and filled out the application. What the hell could he put for education? Surely not a PhD and an MBA? That would impress a software-development company, but was definite overkill for a pet store. Employment history? It wouldn't improve his chances to say he'd worked as a Project Manager for software companies. It wasn't likely he'd need his C++ and JAVA skills at the pet store. He stared at the application form, tapped his pen on the desk, and ran through a hundred lies. What could he say that would be believable?

He decided to use four jobs he'd had while he was an undergraduate over fifteen years ago. He wrote down his retail experience at the Gap clothing store. It was true he had worked there, but he stretched out the time from six months to six years. The previous job was at Tower Records. Would they check to see if he'd really worked there for five years? He had worked at Kinkead Industries his freshman year, and, most likely, this manager had no idea what a sink frame was. He wasn't sure what Mustang Ridge Ranch was, but he had a strong impulse to put it down. He'd worked there for four years, or so he said. What was the difference between the voices in his head and his intuition?

He handed the application to the manager and stood by while she read it, shifting his weight from one foot to the other. Looking around the store, he took mental notes of the clientele. He ran his hand through a bin filled with green pellet rabbit food.

"What? You got to pee or something?" said the manager. "What's a Rectal Rolly Polly anyway?"

"Huh?" Ryan looked past the manager's shoulder. There was a creature he had never seen before, not even on PBS, opening the birdcage doors. A red parrot jumped from its cage and took flight. "What's that thing?" he said pointing to the creature. Several parakeets flew out of their cages and circled overhead.

"Oh, shit. If you can catch those birds, the job's yours."

Ryan looked down and saw another of the creatures push over the bin of rabbit food. The green pellets spilled over his shoes.

The manager stopped running after the birds and turned to Ryan. "Shit, first you let my birds out and now you dump the rabbit food. You're a real pain in the ass. Get out of here."

"But I didn't do anything." Ryan saw the creature run past him and open the front door. It motioned for him to come. He shook his head but moved in the creature's direction. Just as he got to the door, the red parrot flew past him. The store manager pushed by, knocking him to the floor.

"Goddamn you, you're going to have to pay for that bird," she yelled as she ran down the sidewalk. "I'm going to call the cops."

Ryan was online looking at his profile on Monster, the granddaddy of the job search sites. Everything seemed in order. He had a couple different resumes online suitable for several types of jobs. After the mess at the pet store yesterday, he was not interested in cold calls for jobs. He clicked on his search agent and brought up five jobs that matched his criteria. That was the most he had seen in a couple of weeks. He clicked on the first job and read the description. Excellent, a good match to his skills. There was a link to send an e-mail, and he clicked on it. When the e-mail form came up, he looked at the address – employment@limbo.com. Ryan laughed at that one. It would be terrific to work for a firm that had a sense of humor, sorely lacking at most software companies. He copied and pasted his resume, then sent it off.

The next job on his list was for a software trainer. It was a bit of a stretch, but he had great computer skills and had been a teaching assistant at UC Berkeley while working on his PhD. They might be interested. He made some changes to his resume and wrote a new cover letter. When he clicked on the link to bring up an e-mail, the address was hr@limbo.com.

That's funny. Same organization? He read the listing and found that, no, it was a different company. What the hell, maybe Monster made a mistake. Perhaps a recruiting firm had posted the jobs.

All five of the positions on offer had an @limbo.com address. *Must* be an agency. He customized the cover letters and resumes and sent them off.

He opened his bookmarks and clicked on FlipDog.com, and then ran a search, coming up with two more jobs that were a decent match. He clicked on the e-mail link and brought up one.

jokesonyou@limbo.com?

No way. Someone had been screwing with his computer. Cheryl?

He closed the browser and disconnected. At the lower left corner of his screen he saw an animated version of the creature at the pet store. It was chewing on the shortcut to Photoshop, which was soon devoured.

Holy shit, a virus. Ryan had never heard of a virus like this. He clicked on the gremlin. It turned to face him and stuck out its tongue. He did a right click and the creature turned and bent over. A fart sound came from his speakers.

"Don't you wish it was that easy?" he heard from behind him. When Ryan turned, there was no one there.

Someone must have sent him an e-mail with a virus attached. He couldn't remember downloading anything from the internet recently. Perhaps Cheryl had done something to his computer without telling him. It wasn't her style, but...

He opened Explore and looked in his Windows directory. That little shit was somewhere among the thousands of files. Chances were he wouldn't recognize the file if it was right in his face.

Striptease jumped on his shoulder and whispered in his ear, "Life's like that sometimes – in your case, *all* the time."

I've got to get some health insurance. I need to see a doctor before I totally lose my mind. Maybe I'm already too late...

Ryan brushed his shoulder with the back of his hand, felt a chill of rough scales, and saw a ghost image of Striptease as she jumped to the floor.

"Hey, asshole, leave her alone," blared from his computer speakers.

Ryan turned and saw the gremlin icon grow until its head filled the screen. It twisted, and a foot, a leg, then the whole figure of Shitforbrains popped out from the monitor.

Shitforbrains scratched his chin and said, "Tell me your greatest weakness, and what you do to overcome it."

Ryan pushed his chair back and wiped spittle off his face with his shirtsleeve. "Who're you? What're you? What do you want?"

"I'm the thumbtack in your chair, the sugar in your gas tank, the aphids on your fuchsias, the voice mail of your job leads. I'm what you feel climbing up your butt during job interviews. Don't you worry, Bud, I'm your guardian angel," said Shitforbrains.

He jumped off the desk to stand next to Striptease. They giggled, then disappeared.

That night, while he and Cheryl were in bed, Ryan said, "I need you to do me a favor. I know you won't understand, but you've got to trust me. Don't ask questions, just do it. Please."

"So what is it?"

"I can't tell you now. Walls have ears."

"You're too weird, Ryan."

"Trust me." He put his arms around her and held her tight. She twirled his chest hairs between two fingers. "I love you," he said. "I wish you were someone else, a redhead with a small ass instead of a big one like yours."

"You asshole," she said, sliding as far away as she could and still be on the bed.

"What?"

"Screw you."

"Honey, please. Forget about everything. Trust me. Just for a couple more days."

He was dressed to kill in his new blue suit. When he walked into Jenny's office, he held the door open for a few extra seconds. "I appreciate your seeing me on such short notice," he said. "Cheryl had many good things to say about you. I hope we're on the same page."

"Yes, she showed me a copy of your resume, and, from what I know of you, I understood what she meant. So, tell me a little about yourself. Why would you like to work here? Where do you think you'll be in five years?"

"Well..."

Ryan gave his two-minute pitch without a hitch. He ended strong, but his eyes showed he had an unasked question.

He and Jenny went back and forth with the interview for several minutes. Ryan's answers were sharp and to the point.

"Could you give me an instance where you had a plan that would increase productivity in the software development cycle? And tell me how you implemented it?"

Ryan felt a tingling sensation at his ear. He tugged at his earlobe, brushing against Shitforbrains's rough skin. Ryan nodded and smiled.

Jenny lifted her hands from the desk, turned them palms-up, and shrugged.

"I'd like to pull your dress up past your thighs and do it to you right here on your desk. You'd certainly see my productivity rise," said Ryan, a big smile on his face.

"Ah, well, ah." Jenny reached into her desk drawer and took out a burlap bag. "Cheryl said you would need this."

"Yes, thank you."

But, instead of reaching for the bag, Ryan grabbed Shitforbrains. He couldn't see the gremlin, but could feel him struggle to get away.

Ryan jumped up, twisting from side to side, throwing his arms in one direction then the other. To Jenny it looked as if he were in a death brawl with the wind, except there was no wind.

Jenny stood motionless until blood began streaming from Ryan's hand. "Goddammit," he shouted. "Get that bag open. Hurry."

She opened the bag and held it toward him.

He stuffed his hands inside, then jerked them out, closed the bag, and tied it with a piece of twine.

When he held it up, the bag twitched and joggled.

"Show yourself," said Ryan to the empty air. "Show yourself or I'll smash this little bugger against the wall."

Ryan and Jenny watched as Striptease materialized. She looked back and forth between them, took backward steps, bit her knuckles. "Please, please don't hurt him. He's a genius, really."

Jenny called to the lobby and told Cheryl to come up to her office.

When Ryan's wife came through the door she gasped and staggered.

"My God, they're real! I thought you'd gone way over the deep end, but..."

"We don't mean you any harm," said Striptease. "A little mischief maybe. Please let him go."

"You're ruining my life. You've got to leave me alone or I'm going to throw you in the Puget Sound," Ryan said.

"We can't leave you alone. We need you. If we don't have you, we don't have anything. No reason to exist, sorta speak."

"Then it's the Puget Sound." Ryan reached for Striptease. She moved back against the wall, her arms above her head.

"Wait," said Jenny. "I've got an idea. What would happen if you had someone else to torment?"

Striptease looked at Ryan, eyes widening with a sudden hope. "I'd miss you, though. I really like you."

"I've got just the thing," said Jenny. Then, to Striptease, "You've got to get in the bag."

Jenny knocked on the door of Mike Tierny's office and opened it before he had a chance to answer. "Hello, Mike. This is Ryan Hopkins. He's interviewing for the Project Manager position. If you have a few minutes, would you talk to him?"

Ryan set the bag next to a chair, shook hands with Jenny's supervisor, and sat down.

Mike Tierny leaned back in his seat. "So, tell me a little bit about yourself."

Ryan reached down, untied the bag, and spread it open.

New Writings in the Fantastic
The Wishbone Harry R. Campion

"Trina!" Her mother's voice floated in from the back yard. "Have you finished the carrots?"

Trina ignored her, staring instead at the wishbone. It hung on its nail above the doorway, a simple arc of bone, waiting for the turn of the time. The carrots lay unpeeled before her on the cutting board.

Patience, she heard her Gram say. *You needed Patience as a first name, 'stead of a middle.* Gram, who had always been the one to calm her, to listen to her, was gone three... no, almost four years. There had been more sadness than heat in these words when her grandmother said them, so Katrina Patience Bellise had cultivated patience and waiting at an age when most children were still concerned with not falling over at every step.

The wanting – that was how Trina thought of her desire – remained a dull ache within her, but it was tolerable.

The screen door to the sideyard opened hesitantly and Stephen poked his head in.

"They around?"

"They're out back with the Weasel," she said.

He slipped up and twined his arm through and around hers so that his hand ended up resting just beneath the swell of her breast. She took a deep breath and felt his fingertips brush her nipple.

Tremulous butterflies sank through her stomach to melt in her loins, and she raised her hips to press against him.

"You sure they know I'm going to be here?"

He was still scared. He'd been scared to ask her out, almost too scared to kiss her on the first date. A month later at the drive-in, his hands had shaken so badly he'd been unable to unhook her bra. Their first sex, despite its brevity, had been a terrifying experience for him. He was afraid of her Dad and even more afraid of her Mom.

He knew where to touch her; he'd learned.

But he was weak.

"They said it was fine," she told him. His face was still a shadow beneath his blond hair. "They said they wanted you to come."

He relaxed.

Through the open window floated the laugh of the Weasel. Stephen dropped his arm away hastily and slouched over against the wall to stare up at the wishbone hanging over the kitchen doorway.

"So," he said at last, "whatcha going to wish for?"

"You know I can't tell you," she replied quickly.

He studied her face as if he were trying to resolve an optical illusion.

"Like I said," she went on more softly, "it won't work if I tell."

"Not even me?"

He didn't believe. Sarcasm hung from the words at all the wrong angles. He would hurt her with his disbelief if she let him. He thought it was nothing more than a silly old grandmother-tale. *Keep your heart, your thoughts and especially your darn mouth quiet, Trinie,* she heard Gram saying. Four years dead and the words still floated in the air from a rocking chair in another house, in another city. *Heart, thoughts and darn mouth,* Trina thought, *shut the hell up. If he even guesses...*

The door banged open and the Weasel bounded in, huge, torn sneakers clapping the linoleum. Stephen straightened himself with the air of a wealthy man whose car gives out in the bad part of town.

"Roller skates!" the Weasel yelled in Trina's face.

"Jesus," she said, pulling a face. "Isn't it about the time of year you brush your teeth?"

"Ha! I knew it!" he yelled. "I got your wish, got your wish! You want rollerblades!"

She smiled sweetly and held up three fingers for him. "Pick your favorite, Weasel-boy. Wrong again."

The Weasel scowled and noticed Stephen. "What's *he* doin' here?"

"Mom and Dad invited him," Trina answered. "He's a guest." She emphasized the last word just enough to remind your average brain-dead eleven-year-old of the rules and consequences associated with terrorizing guests. "So I guess you're going away crying." She cocked her head. "Mom wants you."

"Edwin!" called their mother from the yard. "Bring the juice from the fridge."

His scowl deepened into a gargoylean mask. "I'm still gonna guess it and spoil you," he promised. "Then *you'll* be the one going away crying!"

"You have five minutes," she said airily. "At the rate you think, maybe you can get out another thought and a half if you hold your breath."

With another glare at Stephen, who seemed less impervious to them, the Weasel departed the field.

Blessed silence descended on the kitchen. Trina scraped at the carrots, waiting to see if Stephen would offer to help her.

"Why does he want to guess your wish?" he asked instead. "He's trying to wreck it even if you win."

"Of course," she said. "It'd be the highlight of his miserable existence." *But he doesn't stand a chance.*

"Why did you want me to come?" Stephen said. "I thought this was a family thing."

In more ways than you know, Stevie. She swallowed and took in his expression with her peripheral vision. There was something watchful in him, something that didn't seem to trust her any more.

"Can you tell me your wish afterwards?"

She didn't trust herself to answer or even look at him, so she peeled carrots briskly and shook her head.

"Then why?"

She swung on him, a part of her viciously glad to see him shy back as if she were going to emasculate him with the peeler. In the next moment she was filled with a sorrow so deep it threatened to drown her in despair. She wanted to shout, *I invited you out of courtesy! I invited you because you're weak and I want you, but I never want to see you and the back seat of your car again! I invited you because I don't commit murder every day...*

Keep quiet your mind, hissed grammy. *Close down your face.*

Trina schooled her expression and forced her heartbeat to slow. *Patience,* she told herself. *Your name is Patience.*

I'm scared.

That does no good, she reproved. *None at all.*

Her eyes strayed up to the wishbone hanging from the nail over the doorway.

It was only a few months old, but like all dried bone it had acquired the dry, timeless look of something belonging in a temple.

She grew calm again.

"I wish I could tell you," she lied, reaching down to touch him lightly, then squeezing. "I know it's just silly superstition," she lied again, leaning forward to lick at his ear. The back-seat monster to which she had just been wishing a speedy farewell grew hard beneath his jeans zipper. His mouth hung open in sudden ecstasy, probably forgetting that he'd even asked a question. "I just don't want this to... come between us," she lied a last time, feeling a healthy traitorous warmth between her own legs as she pressed herself to him.

"It won't," he gasped, his hands moving down...

"Trina!" her mother called from the yard. Stephen jumped away from her as if stung, panting heavily. "The sun's setting. Bring the wishbone."

She turned from him, raised herself on tiptoe and brought down the tiny gray arch that had been the very personal property of a tender young chicken. She held it for him to see. Stephen shrugged and she smiled.

Her family waited on the patio.

"Concert tickets for the Barenaked Ladies!" the Weasel said in his "gotcha!" voice.

"Oh, hush, Edwin," said Mom. "Trina isn't trying to spoil *your* fun, is she?"

"She does that just by living," the Weasel muttered.

"You okay, honey?" Her dad, wearing his grease-splotched Kiss-the-Cook apron, was watching her intently. Ever since she'd begun dating Stephen, Dad's face had held that look. Her father was a devotee of Sir Arthur Conan Doyle and prided himself on his ability to guess at people's motivations from tiny behavioral clues. He was looking curiously at her hands, and Trina realized with alarm that they were knotted fiercely in front of her stomach. She forced her fingers out of their secret handshake and deepened her breathing. She could do nothing about the pallor of her face, but she could crack a smile.

"Sure, Dad. You doing the honors?"

He appraised her for a moment, and she could see the gears meshing behind his eyes. He lifted one eyebrow as if daring her to maintain her composure. She took the dare and returned the quizzical look with such aptness that he laughed, and the suspicious look drained away.

"Mom's turn," he said, and turned his attention back to the grill.

Trina nodded and presented the wishbone gravely to her mother. Sylvia Bellise took the wishbone by the top and held it between her two children, turning it slowly back and forth.

"Five," Trina blurted.

"Not fair!" cried the Weasel. "She always picks in the middle and I get stuck!"

"If I have to spend one more second feeling like I'm refereeing a prize fight in Vegas," Mom said ruefully, "I'm tossing this thing in the trash."

"Six," spat the Weasel.

"The lucky number is seven," said Dad.

"Ha!" The Weasel stuck out his large and offensive tongue. "You goin' down, sucka!"

"Edwin!"

"Just pick a clavicle," Dad said. "Save the trash talk for the post-game show."

The Weasel made a grand show of reaching and pulling back before he finally picked the end closer to Trina. Mom rotated the wishbone so that the other faced her.

"By the power vested in me by the state of Michigan, I now pronounce you man and wife, you may kiss the chicken."

"*Mo–om!*" both her children chorused.

"Say it right," Trina asked. "Please?"

Trina could feel her father focus in on her again, but she kept her own focus on the bone.

Mom rolled her eyes at the solemnity of teenage wishes and intoned, "Do you, Edwin Clinton Bellise, have a wish?"

"I sure do," said the Weasel, bouncing up and down on his toes, careful not to move his hand at all.

"Do you, Katrina Patience Bellise, have a wish?"

"Yes," whispered Trina.

"Then may it come true for one," said Mom, and released the top of the wishbone.

For a second, Trina was afraid she would not have the strength to pull – the Weasel would just yank it out of her grasp and they'd have to start all over. Then she heard the crack begin and gave a tiny convulsive pull.

There was a dull snap.

"Aw, *man*...!"

She was holding her side of the arch, and atop it was the prize middle.

"This *sucks*!" complained the Weasel. He threw down his end and started to stomp away. Mom snagged him by the ear.

"In the trash, please."

"Burgers are on," Dad announced, still watching his daughter carefully. "Congratulations, T."

"Thanks, Daddy." She felt slightly lightheaded and tried to take a deep breath without trembling. If she fainted now, all sorts of things might go wrong.

"How do you like your burger, Steve?" Apparently her father had misread her tension and was working to alleviate it.

"Medium, sir." Stephen was looking at Trina. She in turn had eyes only for the wish in her hand. "You okay?"

She looked at him with eyes that felt like cold pools. "Yeah." She closed the broken bone in her palm, feeling the sharp, jagged end with her fingertips. "Excuse me." She turned toward the house.

Stephen's furtive hand on her arm stopped her. "Would it wreck the wish," he whispered, "to ask now if you were wishing for us to get married someday?"

So that's what he's been afraid of. "It would," she said, and raised herself to look directly at him. "If that had been the wish."

She pulled free.

"Hey, the burgers are hot now," Dad called in protest.

She didn't look back. "I'll just be a minute."

In the bathroom upstairs, Trina stood leaning against the vanity, looking in the mirror and clutching the winning wishbone. She unsnapped her shorts and pulled them down. Her panties were the silky blue ones she'd never let her mother find in the wash. Wishbone still in hand, she slid them down and sat on the toilet in one motion.

The pad was there. She'd put it on this morning in a paroxysm of optimism. After all, five weeks late was five weeks late, was the rest of your life...

There was a bright spot of crimson on the absorbent fibers of the pad.

Relief blew through her in a nauseating flood, and she doubled over to keep from falling off the seat. She felt the nasty cramp of what Mom had introduced at the age of thirteen as "the monthlies." Now, four years later, Trina had never been so happy to be in pain. She was unaware that she whispered, "Thank you, Grammy."

Trina spared a last glance at the wishbone in her hand and dropped it into the waste can.

New Writings in the Fantastic
When... Paul Finch

"So which is the bigger sin, father?" the boy asked. "The fact that I wank, or the fact that I wank over my victims?"

The plain-clothes priest's cheeks paled a little. His warm smile faltered. He cleared his throat.

It was a spacious, well appointed office: wide, airy, looking out over the lush school grounds on two different sides. The deputy head clearly believed in gentle contemplation. Light streamed in, the positive energy flowed – hence the well ordered nature of his books and files, the neatly stacked shelves, the cleared desk-top, the nodding plants on the windowsills.

The boy was seated on a chair in the middle, but he didn't look marooned; more enthroned. His arms were folded – idly, as if boredom was sneaking up. Not that he seemed bored with the interview thus far. Black hair flopped to his brows, but he wore a handsome smile, and his green eyes shone. "That doesn't surprise you, does it?" he asked. "I mean, one thing leads to another."

Again the priest cleared his throat. "If you're trying to shock me, Matthew, I advise you, I've heard it all before."

The boy began to fiddle with his fingernails. They were dirty and chewed, and didn't sit well with his otherwise immaculate appearance. He wore the navy-blue blazer well. Even the top button of his shirt was fastened, the school-tie knotted smartly. "You've been all over the country, haven't you?" he asked.

The priest nodded, warming up his smile again, which wasn't hard – young people needed guidance, not punishment, no matter how disturbed their behavior.

"Spoken to all sorts of people," the boy added. "Every crummy bastard there is." He gave a rasping chuckle. "As far as you know."

"I don't claim to know everything, Matthew."

"You've met the cheats?"

"Of course."

"The bullies?"

Now the priest laughed.

The boy sat back, jammed his hands in his pockets. "The crackheads? The drunks? The habitual thieves? The pyromaniacs? The knifers?"

The priest's smiled faded again.

"The fourteen-year-old slappers who'll let you have a feel of anything you like for a drag on your cig? All the usual rabble who make school life such a misery these days?"

"I've met them all, I assure you."

The boy's eyes gleamed. "But you haven't met anyone like me."

The priest sighed in a sorry-to-disappoint-you sort of way. "Matthew... masturbation in the school library is not the most serious thing I've ever come across."

The boy clucked irritably. "You're not listening to me, are you?"

"I don't think *you're* listening to *me*, Matthew. I've already told you, I'm not here to reprimand you, to warn you, to fight you. I represent The Inner Flame. Our mission is to keep the Christian message alive in modern schools."

The boy began to slouch. He stretched his legs out and sniffed. "Difficult job, I suppose."

He sounded vaguely genuine about that, and the priest wondered if at last he were getting through to the youngster. From what he'd seen on the disciplinary report, this lad Compeyson was regarded as having an above-average intellect, even by grammar school standards. The deputy head had felt that reasoned argument might make an impression.

"Mind if I smoke?" the boy asked.

"Er..." The priest was uncertain. It was forbidden on school premises, of course. Still... this was long after hours, and who else would know? If it helped settle the atmosphere – bad pun. "Not at all."

The boy sniggered. "In that case I won't bother."

The priest licked his fingers and flattened his thinning hair. He was only in his early forties, but like so many in his profession was ageing prematurely. His sidelocks were gray, his pate already balding. He was determined to maintain his composure. It wasn't so hard; he'd dealt with much tougher cases than this.

"We tour the nation's schools," he said, strolling around the office, "addressing assemblies, giving sermons to classes, having private one-to-ones with troubled individuals like yourself."

"'Troubled'? What's 'troubled' about spanking the monkey? It's fun. Don't tell me you don't do it."

The priest shrugged. "My habits aren't the issue here."

"No. Mine are." The boy sat forward. "Yet I dropped a rather large hint a couple of minutes ago that I might've done something a bit more serious."

The priest refused to meet the youth's disconcerting gaze. He didn't want to lecture too much – that wasn't suitable for occasions like this – but he had to overcome this deliberate subversion of the interview. "On the whole, Matthew, your disciplinary record is good. You've been occasionally disruptive, but this incident is by far the..."

"Yeah, I know what the paperwork says. I'm talking about real life, though. Which is something the modern Church seems happy to ignore."

"I don't know what you mean."

The boy smiled. "You're not remotely concerned about my victims. You're more interested in my dirty habits."

The priest began to walk again. "Dirty habits can be very destructive."

"So can murder."

"Your body is the Lord's Temple. Self-abuse is profaning that Temple. It causes deep spiritual harm."

"And murder doesn't?"

The priest sat down behind the desk. He gazed at its polished surface for a moment. He didn't want to play this childish game, but perhaps there might be no option. He glanced up. "You expect me to believe you've killed someone?"

The boy dug a fleck of snot from his nose and flicked it. "Why is it that every priest I've ever met is more ready to condemn the dirty-book reader than the robber or the murderer?"

The priest steepled his fingers. "Matthew, The Inner Flame is just trying to meet young people on their own level. Trying to show them there's more to life than this secular hedonism the western world is currently besotted with."

The boy leaned back. "I'm a great reader of the religious press, father. Would you believe that?"

The priest couldn't answer. Ordinarily, no, he wouldn't, but now... who knew?

The boy continued. "And it never ceases to amaze me how ready the modern Church is to blame the most innocent members of society. Do you know what I mean? The ordinary people going about their lives. It seems these people are responsible for the druggie wrecks we see on the street corners, rather than the dealers and gangsters who've put them there. The common man's also responsible for Third World debt because he happened to have been born in Britain or America and buys training shoes made in some crappy Brazilian glue-factory which he doesn't even know about. It's all his fault, not the fault of the evil dictators who built the factories."

"Matthew," said the priest quietly, "are you seriously telling me you have committed murder?"

"You still don't believe me. Why's that? Because I'm a good Catholic boy." The boy's lip curled scornfully. "Check that report again, father. Why do you think I was wanking in the school library rather than in the shithouse with all the rest of them?"

"Why don't you tell me?" said the priest.

The boy leaned forward confidentially. "I was wanking over a history book, father. Over a photograph, in fact. Want to know which one?"

The priest didn't, but the boy told him anyway, hoarsely, wet-lipped, with great glee and relish: "Death-camp victims. A great heap of them. Naked, emaciated, lying in a jumble of arms and legs on a cart."

For a moment, the priest wasn't quite sure what to say. He didn't have the report forms in front of him at the moment, but he would certainly look at them again. Death-camp victims... *dear God!*

"*Now* tell me you're here to guide and not punish," the boy said.

The priest stared him squarely in the face. "So you've murdered?"

The boy sucked air in between clenched teeth, as if wondering whether it was worth it or not, spilling the beans. He scratched his head, then stood up. "Suppose it depends on what you mean by 'murder.'"

"We both know the meaning of the word 'murder,' Matthew, but I have to warn you I won't be drawn along this route indefinitely. I'll ask you one more time. Have you actually killed someone?"

The boy made no reply, wandering across to the antique fireplace. which was filled with sports shields and silver-framed photo-prints – all sepia-toned, of course – displaying glories past. In the center, in a position of utmost honor, stood an old cricket bat.

"Now this I like," said the boy, crouching down.

The bat was an original, from that legendary Test match of September 1880. Each member of the victorious England team had signed it, including the skipper Lord Harris and his Gloucester County star Doctor Grace, who'd flattened Australia almost single-handed with a knock of one-five-two.

The boy knew it was the deputy-head's pride and joy. He picked it up and placed himself at an imaginary crease, leaning forward to attack the Aussie pacemen.

"Matthew," said the priest. "I'll ask you one more time..."

"No," said the boy, looking up, though now his eyes had clouded and there was a stern look on his face, which no longer seemed so young. He hefted the bat to his shoulder. "At least... not yet."

The interview terminated fifteen minutes later. Before leaving, the boy put his blazer back on and straightened his tie. He glanced at the priest, who was lying over the deputy-head's desk, very limp but moving slightly. *That* at least was something, the boy thought. He was damned if he was granting the old bastard a martyrdom.

Outside the office, in the long-drawn shadows of evening, a nervous-looking thin-faced youth, also in school uniform, was waiting on a bench.

"You Compeyson?" the boy asked him, as he closed the door behind him. "The one they caught tossing off in the library?"

The nervous youth flushed pink and nodded.

"You're a bit late," said the boy.

"Cross-country training," was the lame excuse.

The boy nodded, then thumbed the quiet office behind him. "Well, he's in there, waiting for you." Then inspiration struck. "Bit dodgy, though."

"Why?" asked Compeyson.

The boy gave him a sly look. "Wanted me to suck his cock. Asked if he could fuck me in the arse as well. Wasn't even going to wear a condom. Fucking wufter."

Compeyson swallowed and glanced at the door. The boy knew what was going through the pupil's mind: Why had he been asked to meet this bloke, who wasn't even on the school staff, so late on in the evening, after everyone else had gone home? And what about him being a priest? These days, whenever you looked in the paper, one of that lot was at it. And wasn't he supposed to be a trendy priest as well? Sort of social-worker type, who wanted to talk to young people about their problems, sexual ones top of the list?

Compeyson decided that discretion was the better part of valor. He began to retreat along the corridor. "You haven't seen me, all right?" he said.

The boy nodded, silently, impressed that such a little white lie had achieved so much so quickly when such a vast outpouring of brute force had totally failed.

Once he was alone, he glanced back at the office; there was a faint shuffling from within, as of someone crawling across the carpet.

Maybe there was something in this "small sins first" lark after all, he thought. He'd have to give it a bit more consideration.

A few minutes later, he'd left the premises. The tie and blazer he dumped in a skip at the end of the road. It didn't really matter. He didn't go to that school.

He didn't go to any.

New Writings in the Fantastic
Borderline Charm Paul Pinn

So there I am in a ramshackle joint somewhere on the borderline 'tween Texas and Louisiana, sitting at a bar that looks like it's been made from bayou driftwood by drunk rednecks. When the bartender asks me what I want, it's like being addressed by an alligator. He delivers my beer with the same panache.

Everything in the place creaks and smells of bourbon, beer, skin-dust and musk – and that includes my four fellow drinkers, a motley lot suggestive of what might be expected from a womb polluted with oil and seeped in stagnant water infiltrated by tree roots: grimy, wizened, and looking like the spawn of wayward family behaviour.

The guy nearest me asks where I'm from.

"England," I reply. "London."

He nods, says, "Jus what I'm looking for."

"Why's that?" I enquire, disguising my apprehension with a soft neutral tone.

"My sister needs to get out. You marry her an she'd be English."

"Oh."

"She's eighteen. You can marry her here. Say you been courting her."

"I've only been in America nine days."

"Been here before?"

"Twelve years ago."

"She would have been six then. You can show love letters as proof."

"She could write letters at six years old?"

"I dunno but she's a bright gal. She could do them now and backdate them."

"But six? C'mon, I was twenty back then. The authorities would think I was a pedophile."

"Some marriages are planned long in advance."

"Usually between the same sort of people."

"How so?"

"Same religion or culture. Like Hindus."

"Like what?"

"Hindus."

"What're they?"

"Indians."

"Ain't never heard of em."

"They come from India, in Asia."

"Well, that might be so, but her name's Prissy an she lives on the banks of the Mississippi."

"On the Mississippi or Louisiana side?"

"Depends what side of the river she's on. She's a ferry hand for fisher folk."

"So she can stay on either side depending on which side she finishes that day?"

"You're smart. She'll like that."

"Does she stay with family?"

"Yeah. We got places on both banks."

I thought he was playing out some lengthy joke, but it dawns on me now that he's serious. I wait a few seconds before announcing I'm married.

"So what? I ain't asking you to live with her once you get to England. She'll make her own way in life."

"Yeah, right." I take a much-needed slug of beer. "So why is she so eager to get away?"

"She ain't. I am. I want her away from here."

"Why?"

"There are some things in life best not known about."

I glance at the others in the place. All are acting stone deaf and staring at a fixed point a few feet in front of their noses. It's still-life multiplied, like staring at an old sepia photograph from the inside.

"What do you mean?" I finally ask.

"Too much information can cramp a man's style."

He calls the bartender over, gets us a refill. I glance again at the other drinkers, knowing they've heard everything. They remain as motionless as tree trunks, but their eyes are now fixed on their beers. The bartender is briskly efficient. I wonder what the marriage broker's last comment means. Is it my style or his he's concerned about?

Before I can ask him, he asks me something.

"You wanna know what she's like?"

"Yes."

"She got all her bits."

"That's good."

He glances malevolently at me.

"For getting on in life," I explain. "It helps."

"Yeah?"

"So I've been led to believe."

He nods, slugs back his beer. I slug back mine.

"She's got hair like a water rat."

My slug turns to a choking gulp. I manage, "Like a what?"

"A water rat."

I feel like laughing. "What hair's that like?"

"Thick brown hair. Short."

"How short."

"Shoulder-length."

"What's the rest of her like – I mean, is she tall? Short? Pretty? You know?"

"I'm her brother, ain't I?"

"Yes. I'm just trying to picture her." I imagine a ratlike fat girl with eyes gazing in opposite directions and hair on her upper lip.

Big brother wipes the image away. "Why bother picturing her? You gonna meet her soon enough. You can see for yerself."

"I'd like to know a little more before I meet her."

"Curious, eh?"

I shrug. "Guess so."

He turns to face me for the first time. He's a bit ratlike himself, but with a bit of gator chucked in for good measure.

"She's a crippled dwarf. You gotta problem with that?"

"No, I don't have a problem with that." *Not much.*

We finish our beers in silence. He orders two more. I want to decline, get out of the place, but all eyes are on me. I can sense them.

"Has she got a nice personality?" I venture.

"No. She's a goddamn little witch."

"Really?"

"Yeah."

I choose my next question none-too-carefully. "So why should I marry her?"

"You're English, ain'tcha?"

"Yes. So?"

"So it's a better life, even if my ancestors did kick yer butts outta state."

"What makes you think it's a better life?"

"You got a queen an welfare an cops without guns... What else you wanna hear?"

"British immigration control might not let her in," I counter with suppressed enthusiasm. "Or your immigration people might not let her out."

"She'll be married with a passport and documents, so what's the problem?"

This guy was so definite I was beginning to doubt my own future.

"What's in it for me?" I say.

"How should I know? I ain't you and you ain't married her yet."

"But why should I accept your offer?"

"It ain't no offer. It's a foregone conclusion."

"How so?"

"That's the way we are out here."

"And if I refuse?"

"You won't."

"You seem very sure about that."

"She's a witch. It's already done. I'm goin' to the john. You make sure I got a beer waiting for me when I git back and we'll talk some more."

He slides off his stool like an alligator slips off the bank, and heads to the john. I quickly finish my beer, order another.

"You mean two?" says the bartender.

"No, I mean one. For him."

I jerk my head toward the john, flick a note on the bar, and get the hell out of there.

I hit the road and rise to fifty in quick time, cruise from there until about twenty miles into Texas. As I approach a derelict gas station a teenage girl appears from behind the pumps, stands by the roadside and waves at me to stop. I check her over as I slow. She's short, about five-four, with shoulder-length brown hair. She doesn't look too bad in the face or figure, so I pull over, lower the window. She sticks her face in: green eyes, nose pointed, chin and cheekbones well defined. Plain but interesting. Her voice has a southern drawl.

"Heading for Mississippi," she says. "You coming? Texas got a storm brewing. It'll be hitting in a lit' while. Could be a twister or two."

"You're on the wrong side of the road."

"I don't think so. You may be heading this way but you really mean to be going the other."

"How do you work that out?"

"Logarithms," and her smile is undeniably saucy.

"Wish I could help you. How come you're out here anyway? You walk from somewhere, or get dropped off?"

"I just slipped through the veils, like so."

"Really?" Then I realize she's sitting next to me. "*Wha*...? How did you get *there*?" I push back against my door. "What are you? Get the hell out my car."

"Quit crying and turn the car round. We don't get going that storm'll be on top of us no time. Come on! We got things to be doing."

"Like what?"

She sighs, smiles, raises an eyebrow. Her eyes sparkle like a pair of highly polished emeralds. Her lips look kissable. Her pert breasts look lonely. Her jeans are dusty and I feel like ripping them off.

"Plenty of time for that later. Come on, let's get going."

I turn the car round without giving it a moment's thought, accelerate up to forty. "What are you – really?" A rush of images crowd my brain.

"Well I ain't no alien or man-killing witch or voodoo trucker trash as you got pictured."

She reading my mind? I shoot her a side glance.

The girl chuckles. "Ain't nothing to read in that movie head of yours."

Tires screech as I stop the car so sharply she nearly hits the windscreen. The guy in the bar said his sister was a witch with thick brown shoulder-length hair *just like hers*.

"Are you related to the man I was having a beer with a while ago?"

"You know, you're lucky there weren't nothing behind us. You didn't even check your mirror when you braked. You really gotta be more careful."

"And you should wear your seat belt. Now, tell me, are you related to that guy in the bar or what?"

She laughs lightly. "How the hell should I know? I wasn't there."

"Logarithms?"

Her laughter peaks then drops. "Some things ain't responsive to logarithms. You gotta use other means."

"Like what?"

"Mississippi magic."

"What's that?"

"River tunes. Catfish runes. Whispering of the wind. You ever swam with a gator?"

"Can't say I have."

"Gator's got mean eyes if you don't know what you're looking for. Like some men."

"Fascinating. So where are we heading with all this nonsense?"

"That bar where you left a drink for ma brother Johnny."

"I'm not going there. I had enough of that place and his crazy talk."

"Here, pull over. We're there."

And she's right. Yet it's impossible. We haven't covered the miles or the time. "How've we got here so quickly?" I demand loudly, freaked out by the whole thing.

"Slipped through the veils. Like so."

"Knew you wouldn't be too long," says Johnny as I look around the bar, the stool under my ass, my head in never-never land. "Hey, my crippled dwarf, come to your big brother."

"You call me that agin I'm gonna feed your balls to Uncle Mervin's pitbull. Now buy me a beer, you stinking mud flapper, 'fore I do something truly regrettable."

Johnny slaps me on the back. "Ain't she got some spice in her veins? Ain't she?"

"Why do you call her a crippled dwarf?" And to her: "What's your real name, anyway?"

Johnny answers first. "I call her that cause on the day ma found her she was cripple-legged an so small we thought she'd been dumped by some freak show carnies who didn't have the nerve to finish her off. We took her in an she blossomed, an made us blossom too, didn't yer? Soon came obvious she had magic in her soul. Soon the whole family doing well an she had the best legs this side o' Mississippi an any other damned place. That right, sis?"

"Sure, Johnny. An I got the best figure, too. Name's Prissy-Ellen."

"Mine is Jonathan. I'm thirty-two. Are you really eighteen?"

Prissy laughs and gives her brother a playful slap on the arm. "You don't wanna take any notice of him. His words are the size of the catfish and crays he never catches. I'm twenty-two. Hey, Frankie, " she calls to a fellow at the other end of the bar, "stick a dime in the juke. I wanna dance with my new man here."

Frankie does as he's told. Prissy takes my arm and pulls me off the stool. Clasps her hands behind my neck. Makes me dance slow and close to some finger-pickin' cajun blues. Her breath travels in waves across the side of my neck; it smells of sweet pickles. Her breasts press against the base of my ribcage. Her hands slide down my spine and hook into the back of my jeans. It all feels very comfortable, lazy, timeless. When I eventually open my eyes and look over her shoulder, night paints the windows and the bar is empty. Even the bartender has vanished.

"What time is it? Where's everyone gone?"

"It doesn't matter what time it is, or where everyone's gone." She moves back to the bar. A couple of kids, a boy and girl, look over the top. "Give ma and pa one small beer each. Ellen-May, you pour mine. John Richard, you do your pa's."

I walk behind the bar, lift the boy and sit him on the top. "Skip the beer. I've had enough." I survey the room, taking in the tables and chairs, the wall hangings and pictures, the CD juke. The bar is small and cozy. Homely.

"Time for bed," I announce.

Prissy finishes her beer. "No sooner said than done."

I look at her lying next to me. The kids are in their adjacent bedroom. She is beautiful. I am lucky. Our kids are great. Our friends a pleasure to be with. Our customers an interesting and respectful crowd. We have a lot of fun. Even Prissy's family are a good bunch to know, and Johnny and I often laugh over the first day we met, and how strange life is, Prissy buying that same bar and me never going home – not that I could, even if I wanted to, because being a drifter I don't know where or what home is, although Johnny don't know this any more than I know his private business. Prissy might, what with her abilities and all, but I guess, truth be told, everything is just so damned comfortable no one wants to change it.

We fall asleep, and as usual I dream of Prissy and the kids and me having a picnic on the other side of the state, by the wide old Mississippi River. The dream unfolds as it always does:

The weather is bright and dry, the food good, the river calm, and we all laugh a lot. Until, that is, a small crowd gathers on the opposite bank and calls my name to join them. They are the family and friends I was supposed to have left behind in England, people I didn't contact because I didn't know who the hell they were.

Usually, in the dream, their presence makes me tense and Prissy has to whisper calming words to help me relax until the crowd disperses and we can no longer see or hear them, which due to the width of the river should have been the case anyway.

This night, though, something different slips into the dream. As I stare at the crowd across the river, something pricks the back of my neck. It doesn't feel like an insect – rather, the tip of a knife. I turn quickly, and for a fraction of a second I think I see a naked Prissy embracing her brother Johnny, the children naked too, sitting astride an alligator. I turn back to the crowd, then look behind me again, not so quick this time, and see nothing unusual. Prissy asks if I'm okay. The children argue by the water's edge as they fish with cane rods. I touch the back of my neck, feel something, look at blood on my finger.

"Probably a mud fly," says Prissy. She looks at the sky. "Turning moody. Better be movin' on."

"We haven't been here that long."

"Most the day is long enough." She kisses my cheek. "You been mesmerized by them England folk. C'mon, help me pack."

Johnny appears from between some bushes. "Thought I'd catch you here."

"Must be important if it's got you off yer ass," says Prissy.

"You got cops at the bar asking questions about some private investigator from England found chewed up in these parts a while back. They reckon he was looking for an Englishman who disappeared on holiday out here. Name of Jonathan something." He smiles, shows long stained teeth. "That sure as hell gave the regulars a good belly laugh."

"Yeah, I'm sure," Prissy replies without amusement. "Guess we better git back an' sort this nonsense out." She looks straight at me. "You homesick?"

I shake my head.

"Then it seems your people over in England got bigger feelings for you than you thought. Maybe it's 'bout time you wrote to 'em and told 'em you're okay and not to bother you agin."

I nod, kind of caught out by her tone of voice. She sounds like an actress running through her lines, maybe for Johnny's benefit rather than mine. Then something not wholly relevant strikes me out of the blue and tumbles out my mouth. "You know, Johnny originally wanted me to take you to England to live – didn't you, Johnny?"

"Yeah, that's right. Thought you'd be happier over there."

Prissy looks sharply at him. "You mean 'safer,' Johnny, cause I know that sometimes you don't portray reality as the rest of us experience it."

"I don't know about that, little sister," Johnny replies with a flush. "I just stepped out to let you know what's happening."

"Sure you did, Johnny." Suddenly she's looking real deep into *my* eyes. She whispers, "And I know *your* reality ain't the same as the one you think I believe. Now I guess we'd better slip back in and see what needs repairing."

And everything is normal as she wakes me in the morning and the kids jump on the bed and we all have breakfast together. Strange how certain things in my life seem to disappear from my thoughts, like bad memories buried so deep I'm no longer aware of them. My childhood, for example, that was bad and I know it was bad and I used to get flashbacks, but now it's all blank spots where I can't remember the details or even recall an image, and for that I'm grateful, but it still leaves me feeling weird on occasions, like I'm not fully myself.

I guess Prissy knew from the first day we met that the closest I ever came to being an Englishman was impersonating one on that very same day. Wouldn't have taken much to work out the rest, at least for the likes of her. I even had the guy's passport for a while but the picture didn't look like me so I got rid of it, like I'd got rid of him. It wasn't no bother to me.

He was a thieving opportunity and I took it, but he had to play hero and make things difficult so he stayed in the bayou. He had a hire car so I drove it around for as long as the agreement lasted, then dumped it. This much I know, but I don't know the precise details, and can't recall the images to go with them, but it doesn't matter. And it doesn't matter why Prissy chose me, a regular-looking guy who was never much good at anything other than getting away with things. And I've never asked her cause I figure most things in life, especially round these parts, are best left alone.

Now I'm a reformed man with a business to run, a wife to love, and two beautiful kids to keep an eye on. Better keep an eye on Johnny, too. He's beginning to make me feel a bit uneasy. Something about the way he looks at Prissy and me, like he's hungry for something we got. Maybe it's envy. Maybe he fancies her; after all, they ain't blood kin. I reckon he should marry one of them girls he goes with, but they never last long. Out-of-town types mostly, passing through for a while. They come, they go, and Johnny just hangs out for more. Guess that's his magic. Apart from the time they found one of them half-eaten up by the river. Alligator for sure, but Johnny was pretty tetchy for a while. Guess he missed the girl, kept thinking of what happened to her, especially as he was the one volunteered to identify the body.

Oddly enough, a week later he was rushed into hospital with abdominal pains. X-rays showed something lodged in his intestine, where it meets the stomach. Had to have an operation to remove it. Turned out to be a girl's ankle chain. That gave everyone a good laugh, and pushed Johnny well up the Wild Romeo league. Ended up being exaggerated with people saying Johnny gave girls such a good time he even ate their clothes. Only Johnny didn't find it that pleasing. Guess he missed that girl.

Well, that's the life in these parts, and you'll soon get used to it. Beats a life of drifting and bad living, an I talk from experience, that's why I know your kind and can tell the mistakes you've made. Like those small bloodstains on your left sleeve, the dollars too crisp and clean to be yours, and the look in your eyes. Yeah, almost like a mirror image. Where'd you say you're from? *And I'll have the truth this time.* That's good. Good strong stock from there. Here, have another beer. The ladies'll be here soon. You do like ladies, I take it? We got some real nice ones drinking here at nights. Man ain't complete without one. It's like losing what magic there is in life. And I got a feeling the magic's about to come back for you, mister.

"Hi, Johnny. You're early tonight. Usual?"

"Yeah, and one for Alice. She's talkin' outside. And one for the stranger here – yeah, we're known for our hospitality in this bar, mister – bit like my cousin Alice. You'll like her. Real nice girl. Kinda bewitching, ain't she, Jonathan?"

"Sure is, Johnny. And stranger, when you meet her you ain't ever again gonna think my storytelling's false...

"That's right, you jus relax and have a real nice night now."

New Writings in the Fantastic
The Letter Editor Kim Sheard

It began as just another news item about just another weirdo. Dr. Carl Torbin rushed into his hacienda with the March wind at his back and flattened what was left of his dark hair back down to his head before flipping on the television and sinking gratefully into his black leather recliner. He vowed once again to lose the twenty extra pounds that made him so happy to put his feet up. When the story came on the local news, he was sorting through the mail, barely paying attention to the newscaster. (Later, though, he was surprised at how much he had heard and retained.) A forty-year-old Las Vegas native, Davis Feebs, had accosted visitors to Caesar's Palace earlier in the day. Police found him standing on a fountain wall preaching that the time had come for all residents of Earth to join together and take their rightful place in the Galaxy. He had been arrested for disturbing the peace, but was released only a few hours later.

After hearing the story, Carl simply chuckled, shook his head, and returned to his bills.

By the first of May, Davis Feebs had made the national news. Carl, again in his recliner, caught the name at the end of the evening broadcast as a note of interest just before the closing credits.

"Are there aliens among us?" the anchor asked. "According to Davis Feebs, there are, and he is one of them. Always considered a native of Las Vegas, Feebs now claims to actually hail from another planet and that he was sent to Earth to aid in our entry into the space age. Feebs had this to say when last seen outside the Capitol Building in Washington."

A lanky blond man was shown speaking passionately to a small group outside the white domed building.

"Humankind has reached a crossroads," he said. "Earth will survive or fall based on the decisions you make in the next several years. I can guide you if you will let me speak."

The anchorman turned to his pretty young colleague with an amused expression. "So, E.T. is back, and this time he's not trying to get home, he's going to save Earth."

"It looks that way, John," she replied, equally amused. To the camera she said, "That's the news for tonight. Thank you for joining us."

"Sounds like a classic case of paranoid schizophrenia," Carl mumbled, focusing on his newspaper.

By Labor Day, Feebs had moved on to UN Headquarters in New York. Carl discovered later that the police sent him back to Vegas under the condition he seek psychiatric help. The local government was forced to take custody and to oversee his treatment.

Feebs, allowed to choose his own doctor, picked Carl out of the phone book.

"That's the last time I get one of those bold-faced entries in the Yellow Pages," Carl groused to himself.

This was how Carl became directly involved with the weirdo named Davis Feebs.

After finishing some notes from a session with a sixteen-year-old girl who was fighting her parents, Carl glanced at the pile of other files from today that still needed to be updated, including one belonging to a mildly depressive housewife who was improving with a course of serotonin reuptake inhibitors and an elderly gentleman who still considered himself scarred by emotional abuse as a small child.

Carl frowned. His practice was comfortable. He made a respectable living and had an ordered career. Taking on Davis Feebs as a patient was bound to change that.

The man was delusional, for crying out loud! Not that Carl didn't have the background to deal with delusional patients. Early in his career he had worked with psychotic and dangerous patients at the public hospital. But that had been a long time ago, when he had still thought he could change the world and make every patient well. Carl no longer believed in "causes." Before he was out of his thirties, he had accepted the fact that some patients could never be helped, regardless what treatments were tried. By his forty-first birthday, he had established his current practice which, ten years later, still served some of the same patients. Why had he ever agreed to take Davis Feebs's case?

Before Carl could answer his own question, Davis and his police escort arrived. The officer sat down uneasily in the waiting room.

Carl forced a smile as he greeted his new patient.

"Hello, Davis. I'm Doctor Torbin, but you can call me Carl. Come on in and make yourself comfortable."

He studied the younger man. Feebs certainly didn't look forty. His fair skin was wrinkle-free and his dirty-blond hair was thick and free of any gray. He was lean and fit, and moved to the overstuffed sofa with grace. He settled into the sofa cushions and waited patiently for his doctor to take the lead.

After leaning back into his easy chair, Carl did so.

"Do you understand that anything you say to me will be kept confidential, Davis?"

Feebs nodded and smiled. His teeth were white and perfectly straight.

"I'll probably be asking you many questions while you're here," Carl went on, "but don't feel you can't bring up other subjects or ask your own questions. We're here to explore your thoughts and feelings, so don't let me lead the conversation too much. On the other hand, therapy often gets into areas of discussion that are not easily dealt with, and we won't always be able to shy away from such things. Do you understand?"

"Yes, sir," Feebs said.

"I have to admit that your case is a little different than most I handle." Carl took a deep breath. "I understand the law requires that you come to me. Suppose you tell me about that."

"Certainly." Feebs straightened as much as the sofa would allow and folded his hands in his lap. "I went to the UN building to talk with some of the delegates, and the police saw fit to arrest me. They decided I could avoid going to jail if I'd speak with a psychiatrist."

"What did you want to discuss with the UN representatives?"

Feebs raised his right hand toward the ceiling. "I wanted to talk to them about Earth taking its rightful place in a Galaxy full of occupied planets. About Earth surviving or falling based on the decisions humans make in the next few years."

Carl tried to look understanding. "Does this have anything to do with the new millennium? I thought we were over all that stuff."

Feebs shook his head. "No. The label of the new millennium, the year 2000 or 2001, your choice, is an arbitrary one assigned by Western humans. It means nothing, particularly to off-worlders." He chuckled. "Although it is an interesting coincidence that you stand at such an important crossroads just now."

He already knew what Feebs's answer would be, but still Carl asked, "What do you know about other occupied planets? What about 'off-worlders'?"

Feebs looked him straight in the eye. "I am from one of those other planets, Carl. I know more about the Galaxy than anyone else on Earth."

He truly believes that, Carl thought, trying to keep the doubt off his face. Aloud, he said, "Please tell me about your home planet."

"I'm not allowed to tell you much," the patient replied. "It would give Earth an unfair advantage over other developing planets. But I can tell you that there are many planets like yours out there with beings that are like humans in many ways. They may not look like you or talk like you, but they do think much like you and have lives similar to yours. Soon you will want to join them and gather them to you as parts of your lives."

"Why just now?"

"Human civilization is changing extremely quickly, more quickly than it ever has before. What's amazing is how easily humans themselves have adapted. This tells us that you now have the capability to explore space and other worlds and to understand them. At the same time, you can enjoy the full potential of your home planet."

Carl cocked his head. "Are you talking about technology?"

Excited, Feebs moved forward until he sat on the very edge of the couch. His hands gestured wildly. "That's part of it, yes. Computers and technology are expanding and growing at an astonishing rate. In fact, that technology is growing at a much faster pace than your current economy allows it to spread. You are making large strides in medicine and are building rudimentary space stations and sending spacecraft out of your solar system. You've figured out how you're abusing your planet and are coming up with ways to fix it. But it's more than that. The human *mind* is growing. Now, societies are changing every decade, every year, rather than requiring centuries for significant change." Breathlessly, he added, "There's not much more growing your race can do while locked on this planet."

"Well, world peace might be a nice aspiration," Carl suggested, trying not to sound flippant.

"Of course. I'm not saying that humanity is perfect or that you have everything figured out." Feebs paused thoughtfully. "Don't you think knowledge of everything else out there would be the perfect impetus for world peace? Most other planets haven't unified either until faced with the same situation Earth is in today."

"And what, exactly, *is* that situation?"

"Others are coming. Ones who are not as friendly as me. If they think you are tough enough and brave enough and can add something positive to the Galaxy, they will welcome you as brothers. On the other hand, if they find you weak and stupid they will take your planet and use humans as slave labor for their own purposes."

"Changing the subject a bit, if I may?"

"Feel free, Doctor."

"Are you aware that these claims you are making lead many people to believe you are... well, there's no delicate way to put this... insane?"

"A typical reaction. It doesn't disturb me at all," Feebs answered.

"Do you know of any way we could prove your assertion that you're from another planet? You look human. You speak like an American and, aside from your claims, act like one. Is there anything tangible that sets you apart?"

"Only my knowledge, and that's not very tangible, is it?"

Carl weighed his words carefully. Sometimes delusional patients could become dangerous if their stories were challenged. "The police are requiring a report on you, including the results of a physical examination and some tests. These are completely standard for new psychiatric patients, so don't be upset by them. You'll need to sign a release so I can share the results of the tests with the authorities. That in no way compromises the confidentiality of our talks; it just allows me to compile those specific results into a report that will be provided in layman's terms to the police. Is that all right?"

"Perfectly, Doctor. I understand completely."

After their session, Carl began Davis Feebs's file with:

> Patient is obviously delusional, but a more specific diagnosis cannot be made at this time. He is surprisingly intelligent, articulate, polite, and well groomed. I do not believe he is lying when he says he is from another planet. He is confident that what he is saying is the truth. Prescribe complete physical and neurological workup and DSM-IV testing prior to diagnosis.

Over the next several weeks, Carl and Feebs continued sessions together as the results of the latter's tests were compiled. Unfortunately, the report that Carl provided to the authorities was still inconclusive.

> According to his medical examinations, Mr. Feebs is in excellent physical and neurological condition. His CT scan, blood tests, and urinalysis were normal; no thyroid, adrenal, or liver problems were detected, and all tests for drugs and alcohol were negative. While Mr. Feebs displays one symptom of paranoid schizophrenia (delusions), I don't endorse that as a final diagnosis. His DSM-IV psychological profile simply doesn't show any schizophrenic tendencies. His intellectual capacity is not diminished in any way, and he suffers no apparent emotional difficulties or confusion. Aside from his statement that he is from another planet, his behavior is completely normal. It is my belief that Mr. Feebs poses no danger to himself or others. He should be allowed to continue with his normal activities, while continuing therapy at least once a week.

As a footnote, Carl added that, since Feebs had not actually been diagnosed with any physical or psychiatric disorders, it was his opinion that medication was not necessary or advisable. The drugs currently in use for schizophrenia and related problems had negative side-effects that would definitely outweigh any slight chance of benefit.

Carl read the finished report to Feebs at one of their sessions.

"Thank you, Doctor," Feebs said. "I feel like you defended me."

Carl watched his patient carefully. He still hesitated to attack the man's claims, but Feebs remained calm after the report. It was the first time Carl had actually used the word "delusions" in the patient's presence. He decided to try challenging him even further.

"Davis, if you are from another planet, how is it that none of our medical tests showed you as anything but human, and a perfectly normal one at that?"

"Because I've taken human form for this mission."

"How?"

"I can't tell you that."

"Is it a body-snatching kind of thing?"

Feebs smiled. "No, nothing like that."

"What do you really look like, then?"

Feebs lowered his eyes. "I'm sorry, I can't tell you." Then he studied Carl's face. "Do you believe me?"

Carl rose from his chair and wandered over to his mahogany desk. He had known this question would arise sooner or later, but was still unsure how to answer. "I know you believe what you're saying, and I can find absolutely no reason why you would lie about your claims."

"But you don't believe me."

Carl sighed. "When I was a teenager, I read every science-fiction story I could find. I especially loved the ones where the unsuspecting Earthling met an alien visitor for the first time. At that point in my life, I truly believed such a thing could happen. Even when I wasn't reading those stories, I would think about the possibility of aliens coming to Earth and wonder how it would happen. I never doubted that someday it would." Carl realized he was pacing, and stopped suddenly in the middle of the oriental rug. "As an adult, though, I have a really difficult time believing that Earth's first alien visitor would appear, looking and acting like any other human being, and would end up in my office for therapy." He finally returned to his chair, perching on the arm. "I'm sorry. It seems just a bit too far-fetched. I'm just not important enough."

Feebs leaned forward on the couch and looked kindly into Carl's face. "Who *is* important enough, then, Carl? Aren't all you humans created equal? Can't one person who believes prompt change?"

Carl had the eerie sensation that their counselor/patient roles had been reversed. Before he could ponder that too closely, Feebs continued.

"So, Doctor, even if I accept the fact that no one will believe my heritage, there must be some way I can get my points across. Any ideas?"

Carl cleared his throat and sat back, trying to regain his mental balance. "Well, obviously your physical presence near our world leaders gets you only negative attention. But perhaps you could write them letters."

Davis grinned, suddenly stimulated. "This time I'll leave out the part about being from outer space," he said.

Within a week Feebs had drafted a letter and compiled a mailing list of governmental representatives around the world. The letter was ignored by those officials, of course – it was only one of many they received every day – but the act of composing it seemed to inspire him. He immediately began looking for other ways to get his points across and other people to reach. He had tried the world's leaders but, as he reminded Carl, everyone is equal and anyone can exact change, so he searched for ways to reach the common people. He enthusiastically wrote letters to the editors of major newspapers.

To Carl's surprise, they were well received. Quite a few were published.

After only a few months, Feebs was offered his own syndicated newspaper column, which was titled "The Letter Editor" in honor of his beginning. Carl encouraged his patient's pursuits, feeling that any positive outlet for his energies was beneficial, but privately he considered Feebs's writings flowery and overly sentimental. Still, he carefully cut each one out of the newspaper and added it to his patient file already thick with clippings like:

The Letter Editor: Development
By Davis Feebs

One would assume that humanity has developed much like a redwood tree, reaching slowly but steadily for the stars at a rate of only an inch or two a year. In reality, though, humans are more like a tiger lily grown from seed. It takes several slow months before it even sprouts, and even longer for the bulb to form. Then the bulb goes dormant through the winter. Finally, with a little warmth and care, tender growth emerges slowly in the spring. As the air grows warmer, the stem grows more and more quickly until it is strong and tall. Then, suddenly, the bud bursts into bloom. The lily's progress was slow – it even stopped along the way – but eventually it grew rapidly until the flower, its ultimate beauty, appeared.

It took thousands and millions of years for humans to evolve from apes. Then, over the ages, humans slowly learned to use bone and stone tools, to smelt metal, and to write. Progress was extremely slow. Eventually humans spread across the globe, and then they learned faster ways to get back to each other. Mankind is still developing and still learning, and at an exponential rate. Humans are about to burst into bloom.

Consider the progress of the last century alone.

In science, humans discovered and developed quantum theory, the theory of Relativity, atomic theory, nuclear fission, and DNA. They learned volumes about the natural laws of the Universe.

In medicine, humans created the electrocardiograph, Freudian psychology, antibiotics, the polio vaccine, the pacemaker, birth control, and infertility treatments. They learned how to take care of themselves.

In technology, humans invented air conditioning, talking motion pictures, nylon, insecticides, holography, transistors, lasers, space shuttles, personal computers, nuclear power, and compact disks. They learned how to improve their lives.

But, perhaps most importantly, humans are learning unity. By introducing the airplane, the automobile, the Nobel prizes, radio, radar, television, the World Bank, the United Nations, artificial satellites, environmental awareness, space stations, and the internet, humans have shrunk the globe and allowed peoples of all nations to begin to know and understand each other.

Congratulations, and keep up the good work!

Feebs was becoming successful, but he continued his weekly therapy sessions. He regaled Carl with his plans for new columns and for the speeches he was beginning to present at university graduations and Daughters of the American Revolution meetings. He spoke and wrote in favor of environmental awareness, cooperation in scientific research, and population control, and was a strong supporter of the space programs. People were really listening to him, and were beginning to speak out themselves by writing to their leaders and quoting his ideas. Feebs was always cheerful and hopeful, and he thrived on having his opinions heard. He no longer seemed like a patient to Carl. The man's enthusiasm always lifted Carl's spirits on rough days. Their relationship became more that of mentor-to-student or friend-to-friend than doctor-to-patient.

But, to Carl's surprise, Feebs never dropped his story about being an alien. He never mentioned it to anyone but Carl any more, but he never abandoned the delusion. *He should have given up on that by now*, Carl often thought. *He doesn't need that fantasy any more*. Still, Feebs persisted.

"So, Carl, do you believe me yet?" Feebs asked for the hundredth time one day in May.

Carl gave his usual response. "Believe what, Davis?"

Rolling his eyes and grinning, Feebs said, "That I'm from another planet and I'm here to help you humans."

"Yeah, sure, Davis, I believe you," Carl said, but it was clear to both of them that he did not.

"Just make sure you catch my column this Sunday, Carl, okay?"

"I always catch your column, Davis."

"Good," he said on his way out the door. "Goodbye, Carl."

On Sunday morning, Carl climbed into his recliner with his paper. He usually read the weekend news in bed, but both he and the paper were too damp from a spring rain for that. As soon as he opened to the front page of the Opinion section, he understood Feebs's insistence. The column was about... Carl.

The Letter Editor: Carl
By Davis Feebs

Today I want to tell you about a man named Carl. Carl and I didn't start out as friends. In fact, Carl was forced to meet and talk with me, even though he didn't trust me. But Carl didn't trust me because he didn't know me. All he knew of me was what he had been told by others, who also didn't know me. He was biased coming into our relationship.

But the special thing about Carl is that he gave me a chance. He didn't rely on what others told him about me. He talked to me. He got to know me. He asked me questions and listened to the answers. He even wrote some of them down. He got to know me, and then formed his own opinions about me.

Now, I believe, Carl trusts me. He may even like me – I'm not sure. Either way, it doesn't really matter to me, because Carl has formed his convictions on his own, by knowing me, rather than through prejudice, gossip, or fear. That's all we can ask of each other as individuals.

I'm sure you can guess where I'm going with this. Carl and I could easily be two different races, two different nations, or even two different planets. Unless we truly know each other, we have no basis for judgment, fear, or hate.

Carl helps me to remember that all humans are on the same team.

Thank you, Carl.

Carl's mouth was agape when he finished reading the column. Feebs was a very smart man. Certainly he realized that Carl listened to his stories and "got to know him" simply to earn a paycheck. Surely he knew it had taken months for Carl to trust him. And Feebs was *thanking* him! Carl didn't even believe the man's stories. He thought Feebs was delusional.

Or did he?

In all those months, with all their talking and all his tests, Carl had never found a single reason for Feebs to hide behind delusions. Carl had to admit that some small part of him wanted to believe his patient was what he said he was. The little bit of dreamy teenager that was left in Carl kept Feebs out of police custody or a mental institution. He certainly would not have treated in the same way a patient who claimed he was the Tooth Fairy or Adolf Hitler. He didn't think so, anyway.

Ugh, he shook his head. *I'm getting all sappy.* Feebs was insane, he reminded himself. He was smart and a nice guy, and he was definitely not dangerous, but he *was* insane. There was no other explanation for his behavior.

Glancing down at the column again, Carl smiled. On the other hand, it didn't really matter. Feebs was inspiring people, helping them to work together, to explore their beliefs. That was a good thing. And maybe, in some small way, Carl had helped.

Yes, I think I like that, he mused, leaning contentedly back with his hands behind his head. *I could get used to helping inspire people. I can inspire the inspirer.* He chuckled, nodding his head decisively. *We can make the world a better place.*

Unfortunately, he never saw Davis Feebs again. Television and newspaper stories reported the disappearance. The tabloid headlines claimed "The Letter Editor Vanishes Off the Face of the Planet!"

If they only knew, Carl thought as he sat down to his typewriter to compose a letter to his congressman.

New Writings in the Fantastic
The Jesus Autopsy
M.F. Korn *and* Hertzan Chimera RIP

Todd had just spent his entire allowance on comic books, but that is what he did every time. *Wolverine, Incredible Hulk, X-Men, Silver Surfer*. The comics were devoured reading that sublime afternoon, after riding his bike home from the drugstore with the precious items. His mom still continued to threaten to throw his comics out: "At least keep them in order, Todd! Not thrown all over the room!" Todd had just finished reading *Weird War Stories* and was stuffed with anticipation of reading through twenty of the newest DCs and Marvels.

Right before he threw the *Silver Surfer* comic on the floor, before turning the last page, he saw the usual adverts:

"X-Ray Specs!"
"Sea Monkeys! Watch Them Play!"
"Hot Pepper Bubble Gum! Black Soap! Trick Your Friends!"
"100 Military Army Men Set!"
"Throw Your Voice! Be a Ventriloquist!"

But at the bottom left corner was this:

Jesus Autopsy Videos for Sale!
$19.99 plus $5.99 shipping and handling!
Not a fake! • Show your friends!
Diamond Video Services, Ft. Lauderdale, Florida.

Todd blinked.
What? He *had* to get that! Was it true? His mom and dad made him go to church, but...
He fell asleep on the green plaid bedspread, surrounded by spent comic books.

They came for him as he slept, the Autopsiers. Those faceless beasts who take characters from their restful slumber and subject them to paralysed but conscious autopsies. A blast of lurid light and he was there on the cold slab. All round him the accoutrements of surgery and anatomical investigation. Long chrome arms tipped with powerdrills and bone saws and syringes loomed over him, right near his open yet totally paralysed eyes. The Autopsiers shuffled about behind the light. You could smell thoughts – hideous visions of burning chrome terror subjecting flesh to in-depth investigation. They spoke in abstract whispers. They left en masse with a loud crackle of feet on packaging, but he knew they would be back.

As much as Todd tried, he couldn't move. He would surely be Autopsied Alive. They might even film him like they did the Blessed Christ off the Cross, his left side still dripping vinegar and sorrow.

Just then he caught something shimmer in the corner of his peripheral vision, like a scared cat balancing on a treacherous log in a raging Spring mountain thaw. He heard those kitten cries but wasn't convinced, something had gotten muddled up. Reality was infected.

"Little child," croaked a man's terrorized voice. It sounded like the man had been screaming for millennia, so rough was his throat, tearing the soft coating off each of the two words "little" and "child." A torture of endless retribution.

Todd looked to his right, where he saw a blurred vision, still crowned in thorns. It was like the guy had a blood-encrusted halo. The face of the man looked vaguely Iranian or Egyptian. Definitely not Roman in origin. Nor American. He was in some sort of cloth nappy. There was blood dripping down off the many wounds of the man's body. You could hear them still dripping onto the chrome slab he lay on. On his face was a look of utter terror.

"Little child." He spoke again, weaker still. "Are you The Lord my Father come to visit me in this place of rest as a mirror of my boyself on Earth?"

"My name is Todd," said Todd, the words seemed manufactured – they felt like they were from a bad script.

"Todd! Supper!"

"Huh?" Todd mumbled.

"Who said you could use my Visa card, huh, Todd?"

"I didn't, I swear, Mama!"

"Come to the supper table now!"

"I already ate!"

The doorbell rang.

"It's your little friend Peter!" his mom yelled up the stairs. "Go on up, Peter."

Todd's door peeked open. Todd heard a "Dude! Look what I got in the mail!"

Peter showed the tape to Todd:

JESUS AUTOPSY!
SCIENTISTS CUT OPEN JESUS'S BODY!
SCANDALOUS! BANNED IN 100 COUNTRIES!

"I was dreaming about that. I just ordered my copy. My mom's mad at me for using her Visa card," Todd said.

"Mine too! I ordered this thing a week ago. I haven't seen it yet. I was too scared to watch it by myself. So I waited until I could come over. All that blood and guts!"

They popped it in the VCR.

The opening graphics were very tacky – looked like they had been done on an amateur deck in the '80s. The filmers were even using wipeovers and twisting plane transforms. The colours were hacked from a battered palette of inadequacy, and the overall feel of the production was not good.

Repeating the familiar blasting rhetoric –

JESUS AUTOPSY!
SCIENTISTS CUT OPEN JESUS'S BODY!
SCANDALOUS! BANNED IN 100 COUNTRIES!

– the VHS cranked into action.

+++++Once the ludicrous titles had been dispensed with, the two young lads sat on the edges of their seats, biting their nails. A soft excited whine rose from them as the cameraman bustled through an operating theater door. Todd grabbed his friend's arm. He really thought he was gonna see an autopsy performed on Jesus Christ himself. The video shown a pearly incandescent white light of beatific origin.

There were two boys on an autopsy table: Todd and Peter.

Todd saw it was the same set of doctors as in his dream.

The screen fell into a coma of static.

"No!" the lads screamed in unison.

They thought about complaining to Peter's mother, but that would have done no good – *Jesus Autopsy* was exactly the sort of heinous thing impressionable young boys get into real trouble for having in their possession. Basically, they had gotten ripped off (hadn't we all?) and had not one leg to stand on.

But what of Todd and Peter? The boys on the autopsy slab?

That *was* Todd and Peter, right?

The boys *had* seen themselves in the video – of that you can be sure.

That night Jesus came to visit Todd. Not in his dreams this time but at his bedside, in his bedroom, in his house, breaching the walls of the castle. The bed Todd lay on felt disturbingly hard and cold to the touch. He looked up at the blood soaked Messiah looming over him and couldn't move. A dot of blood spilled off his visitor's skull-piercing crown of thorns. An angry smile grew on Jesus's face.

"Peter!" Todd shouted for his friend to come and help him, but the words never escaped his mouth. Everything had been planned with perfect precision. This was to be *Jesus's* autopsy, and no one could stop the Good Lord from having his fun.

Jesus took out a scalpel and held it close to Todd's eye. A puddle of urine grew on the cold hard bed.

The first incision went straight across Todd's left eye. The super-sharp edge of the blade tore across his vision making the room go all blurry. The tip of the scalpel dented the cornea until it popped.

"Breakfast, Todd! And come dump the garbage and kitty litter too, young man!"

Todd breathed gobs of air, shivering. Where was he? He looked down on the bed and saw the Shroud of Turin draping his body.

He studied the cheap video container that held the ratty cheap autopsy tape. He tore it into pieces.

"What are you doing up there, son?" his mother yelled.

Todd stood and looked into the mirror. Jesus put his arm around Todd.

"Are you real?" Todd asked him.

Jesus disappeared – he didn't even cross himself as he faded away into the Mickey Mouse wallpaper.

Todd's mother was coming up the stairs.

"Todd, time to nail you to the cross!"

"Coming, mom!" and he dove back into his comic books as the glass of water on his nightstand turned into red wine.

His mother opened the door, banging the cross against the wall as she squeezed through, three nails in her mouth and a hammer in her free hand, smiling and grinning a grin of evil.

New Writings in the Fantastic

An Incomplete Palindrome Alphabet for Dyslexic Deliverymen Derek J. Goodman

P is for Pizza. Thirty minutes or less or else it's free. Of course, pizza places don't do that any more. Too many accidents. The drivers, in their rush to get the pie to its destination on time, had a tendency to hit pedestrians or other cars. The thirty-minute guarantee has now gone the way of the Sega Dreamcast. Drivers don't get hurt, people on the street don't get hurt, and everybody waits an hour and a half for a pizza that has already grown cold. Everybody's happy.

H is for Honda. Brand new, or at least new to its current owner. A steal at twenty-five hundred, only one hundred and twenty thousand miles on it. Its owner is still making payments. There's a small dent in the side, but otherwise there's absolutely nothing wrong with it. Unless you count the muffler, the windshield wipers, the rear window defogger, the tires, the transmission, the etc. etc. etc.

J is for Job. Part-time only, evenings and weekends, occasional overtime if you can swing it. You have your own car, right? Apply in person at our nearest store. Perfect for making a little cash on the side if you need money for something.

W is for Wallet. Real imitation leather, because the person who bought it as a gift is a fucking cheapskate. Inside are a library card and discount cards for two different grocery stores. The fold-out plastic flaps for pictures contain only a single snapshot. The girl in the picture is pretty, trendy hairstyle, perfect white teeth. She's giving the camera something of a come-hither look, like she can see right out through the picture at the wallet's owner. The edges of the picture are frayed from persistent handling.

Hidden behind the library card is a lonely quarter. Other than that, there is no money in the wallet, and on the few occasions where small amounts of cash come to rest there, it rarely stays for long.

M is for Map, the sort you can download from those destination-finding places online. The printer at the pizza place is running out of ink, so all the map's colours are washed out. It's still mostly legible, with a red line connecting the pizza place to the deliveryman's destination, although the ink was still wet when the paper came out of the printer and the address got smeared. That's fine, since the address is also printed onto a label on the pizza box, but that's not very clear either. Whatever. It's not like it's a hard address to remember.

D is for Doorbell on a house that looks like it's seen better days. The grass on the lawn is shabby and an ancient swing set is rusting in the backyard. The gray siding may have been white once and darkened with dust, or it may have been black and faded in the sun. If someone were walking down the street and glanced at it casually, he or she would think the house abandoned, but it isn't. *Someone* has to have ordered the pizza.

C is for the Cracked Mirror in the house's front hall. A mirror simply reflects the image of whatever is in front of it, but what if it could record the gaze of all who looked upon it? Could it tell us the last person to come through the front door? Could it tell us *who* opened the front door? Could it tell us *what* opened the front door?

A is for Ammonia, pungent, rancid, like the smell of week-old cat urine. The stench infects the outer hallway, impregnating the walls with an odor that will never wash away. It's strongest at the floor, however, where a thick, viscous, clear fluid makes a trail from the front door, through the hall, across the mildewed kitchen floor to an open basement door. Look very closely at that trail. Do you see it? Here and there, at what looks like random intervals, there are places where the trail is interrupted, brushed aside like something has been slipping around in it. Look even closer at where the trail first hits the kitchen and an imprint in the liquid is easily visible. It appears to be a tread, roughly foot-shaped. Smack in the middle of the tread is a Swoosh. The imprint's not there for long, though. The gelatinous substance fills it in like the incoming tide washing away a sand castle, eventually leaving no trace it was ever even there.

C is for the Cracked Mirror. There is no one around to bother asking how it was cracked. Some folks believe that some images are so disgusting, so horrid that a mirror will crack rather than reflect them. That's bullshit. Nothing is that bad.

D is for the Doorbell of the house next door that was never rung. It's a whole heck of a lot later than thirty minutes, honey. I'm telling you, the professionalism of these places has really gone to hell ever since they got rid of that guarantee. It's not just the pizza place, either. This whole town is just going to hell. I really think we should move sometime soon. If not out of the town then at least somewhere away from that abandoned place next door. I really don't like raising the kids next door to a rot trap like that. Do you realize I caught them over there not even fifteen minutes ago? They said they heard something from inside. Yes, yes, I *know* they have active imaginations, but still... You mean to tell me you've never heard anything from... Are you okay? You're going pale...

I'll call the real estate agent first thing tomorrow.

M is for Map. Look at one. In fact, look at every map of the entire town. If you can find the gray house on one, I'll give you a cookie. It's not there. Look in the records at City Hall. You won't find any mention of it even being built, and yet there it is. It's kind of quaint, now that I think of it. What exactly would you call that architectural style? Yeah, I'm not sure either.

W is for Wallet, the first thing anyone finds. A twelve-year-old down by the river accidentally hooks it on his line. Something sharp and ragged has punched through it, snapping the library card into little plastic pieces like broken tile. Everything in the wallet is stained maroon. Covered in dark stains, the picture of the girl no longer looks so sexy. She looks horrified, like she has seen something to permanently damage her sense of reality. The lucky quarter is nowhere to be found.

J is for Job. Yes, we do have a position open. Part-time only, evenings and weekends, occasional overtime if you can swing it. Huh? The last guy? There's, uh, nothing to say. One day out of the blue he just quit. No, the rumors are not true. You really should be more careful about where you get your information. The internet is notorious for those sorts of half-truths. I assure you the whole thing's just an urban legend that has popped up. So, when can you start?

H is for Honda. It wasn't like it was hard to find. The people next door saw the Honda sitting there abandoned, recognized the description from the news, and called the police. The faded and smudged map was still on the passenger seat. The keys were still in the ignition and the car was out of gas. The owner had left it running. He hadn't expected to be away from it more than a minute.

P is for Pizza, the only thing the cops found. The entire house was empty, completely devoid of furniture or decoration. A trail from the front door to the basement was eaten away like someone had spread acid along it. The pizza lay forgotten next to the door, the box slightly open and flies buzzing lazily around it. A few maggots crawled about their maggoty little business over its putrefying surface. A bite had been taken from a single slice, but otherwise it was completely untouched.

New Writings in the Fantastic
Way of Life Craig Sernotti

I couldn't help but stare at the underarm hair of the recent cluster of guilties. Bloated maggots dangled and dropped from dirty strands, landing in the banana split sundaes of several young and bemused onlookers.

One guilty cried hysterically, "Save the three-toed sloth before it's too late!" Another said that war was "never" the answer. A third insisted we "eat a queer fetus for Jesus!"

"Enough with the speeches!" said a man to my right, his one hand moving questionably in his pants. "Die already!"

"Jesus? Wow. That name takes me back," said a female to my left, her index finger two knuckles deep in the ear sprouting from her forehead.

"Are people supposed to bend that way, Mommy?" queried the quadriplegic child in front of me, nodding his pinhead toward a nearby guilty.

"Yes, sweetie," his mother responded. "This is what happens when people are bad. He's like this because" – she read the guilty's crime, the text carved into his chest – "he's a... a libertarian."

For those scarce incognizant citizens of our world, crucifixion was, being archaic and far too humane a method of punishment, replaced centuries ago by the Ouroboros Method. Idolaters and enemies of the state were bent backwards until their toes and mouths connected. Through a special and top-secret scientific process, recipients of said method remained alive. Following the treatment, the guilties were suspended naked from trees outside the court building and left to die, which, on average, took three weeks to a month. Once the last of the top-secret chemicals were excreted/micturated, death came in a sudden explosion of splintered bone, black blood, and shredded organs.

Transparent umbrellas were available on site for the minuscule monetary payment of $1,444.99.

I listened further to what people had to say as I strolled casually among the trees, noticing words, not the people who spoke them.

"Where do you think a guilty goes when he dies?"

"I like the naked lady guilties. Even though they're evil, and despicable, and impious, some of them sure are pretty."

"I hope one pops soon. My lunch break is over in fifteen minutes."

"Did you hear the one about the two guilties and the bucket of water?" (I had not.)

One man stood below a bulbous, tomentose guilty. He shook his fist, yelling, "How do you like it, you bastard! You took Mr. Sniffles from me! You killed my warthog! How do you feel now, huh? How do you feel, you bastard?"

I stopped in front of the fourth tree. (The trees continued for miles and miles.) A guilty, male, thin, covered in acne and lashing scars, was shaking violently. His eyes were open and bulging from their sockets. One popped out as I watched, a red-veined orb dangling from multicoloured nervestrings. Guttural, wet sounds dribbled from him.

A small crowd formed around me. Someone said, "Hey everyone! This one's about to burst!"

Several umbrellas opened. People stared expectantly at his expanding body.

An animalistic shriek, a stentorian tearing sound, and...

Cheers as bone, blood, feces, and guts splattered the lot of us. I heard hands slap in approval, prayers, and jovial banter.

Behind me, among the noise, I heard two men talking:

"How great was that?"

"Fine. But..."

"But what?"

"I don't know. All this seems... excessive."

"What?"

"I mean, they deserve what they get, don't get me wrong. But isn't there a... less exploitative way than this?"

"Are you questioning the way things are? That sounds like near-blasphemy to me, man. You better be careful with talk like that. You never know who's listening."

At which point I turned and faced them. The men, among several others, gasped, realizing who I was.

"H–h–hello, sir! So happy to see you today!"

"W–what a fine day to w–watch the guilties, is it not?"

"Hello," I said. "Indeed, it is a fine day," I said.

I stared down at both men. Their eyes – seven between the two of them – went elsewhere; to their feet, to the trees. I paused for a moment, then moved past them.

"Can't wait for your next column, sir!" cried one of the men. "What edition will it be appearing in again?"

"The Thursday evening edition," I said, not bothering to turn round.

"God bless our way of life!" It was the man who had questioned the guilty's demise.

I stopped, glanced over my shoulder. He was visibly shaking. Children hid behind their parents. A woman bit her bottom lip. Eyes went from him to me, me to him.

I smiled. "God bless our way of life," I said.

New Writings in the Fantastic
Martin's Walk Mark Justice

The walks had been Emma's idea.

They bought the sixty acres nearly twenty years ago. She was still teaching then, third grade at Harmony Elementary. Being around all those kids every day gave Emma a great deal of gratification and, Martin guessed, satisfied whatever it was in a woman that drew fulfillment from raising children. So the idea of having children of their own was never a pressing matter. Indeed, when Emma was 37, her doctor recommended she opt for surgery that made having their own kids impossible. Martin had given his support and blessing to her, though he secretly grieved for the son or daughter he would never know. Still, they had each other and their dogs and their many interests. And, when the farm had come up for sale, they dipped into their savings, put down twenty percent, and sold their little house downtown on Riverfront Drive. They left behind the sounds of close neighbors. They craved a little solitude.

The property was really a farm in name only. It was mostly rolling tree-covered hills. The two-story house, with its wide porch, sat on the only flat piece of land on their property.

So they owned a farm (in partnership with Harmony County Savings and Trust) but they weren't farmers. Martin was a civil engineer in Ashland. He could design things, though he wasn't that competent when the tools were actually in his hands. Emma grew tomatoes and peppers in a little garden behind their house. Neither had the desire to plow or harvest. They treasured the time they had together, when Emma had finished her day of teaching and Martin had left behind the bitter office politics and a supervisor who wouldn't be out of place running a Nazi concentration camp. They talked and read and watched movies.

And they walked. Emma suggested it after seeing how stressed Martin was becoming. He had always been an even-tempered man, slow to anger. But his new boss had begun to leach the kindness out of him. One summer evening, after they had finished dinner, Emma took him by the hand before he could settle into his recliner with a scotch and the newspaper, and she led him out into the back yard and up the hill behind their house. They walked with their two dogs along the elevated land, then down into the dip between the hills, passing by the farm's pond – which Martin had stocked with bass and blue gill – and into the woods, where Martin swore he could smell the approach of Autumn. They held hands, tightly, and Martin found himself opening up again, growing aware of the things that made his life good. The problems at work dimmed to insignificance. Martin felt lighter, happier.

So the tradition of the nightly walk was born. The walk became a way for them to deal with the pressures they both encountered during the day.

It also gave them a means of working out problems between them. Emma had made him promise they would walk every evening, even if they were mad at each other. And, almost always, whatever grievance had briefly divided them was forgotten at their journey's end. The walks made them closer.

They had grown closer still when Emma retired after thirty years in the classroom. Martin's job had grown even more unbearable, until she convinced him to take an early retirement. The money wasn't a full pension, but between them they had enough to live on.

Freedom from work meant they were able to do the things they had promised each other they would, like traveling (as much as they could on their limited budget) and taking pottery classes at the community college. Martin felt like the two of them were finally living life the way they were always meant to. He looked forward to many years of exploration, of trying new things and sharing them with the person he was meant to be with.

Later, he would blame himself.

He was too happy – was too cocky, perhaps, about the future. That's when the powers-that-be smack you in the head, as his father used to say. Martin wasn't exactly religious or spiritual. He only went to church when Emma dragged him. She herself certainly wasn't sanctimonious: she could cuss like a sailor when she wanted to and – to the chagrin of the women at Harmony Methodist Church – liked to wear an Egyptian ankh on a silver chain around her neck. At least she believed in something.

Still, one shouldn't tempt fate. *That* philosophy came from Martin's mother.

But he had tempted the fates or the gods or the great karmic wheel. He had tempted *something*. And whatever it was he'd tempted chose to swat him down *hard*.

Emma had gone to the doctor on a cold Tuesday in February. Martin was certain it was just for a checkup. If there had been a problem, she would have told him. So he sat in his favorite chair in their den and read a Dick Francis book while his wife found out she was dying.

"It's ovarian cancer," she told him later that day. She fixed tea and made him sit at the kitchen table, next to the window with its view of the first hill, the starting point of all their walks. She held his hand, which was a good thing. Otherwise, he would have just spun away from the earth. It felt like gravity had taken a day off.

"Wh–What—?" He stopped to suck in more air, but it was so hard to breathe. "What can they do?"

Emma sighed. The ghost of a smile touched her mouth. "Nothing. It's too far along."

She pulled him forward into an awkward embrace. "I'm so sorry."

Always the caregiver, she was still trying to bring him comfort, even now.

It didn't take long.

Her strength went first. She tired so easily. The evening walks became first a challenge, then a memory. She grew thin, and her skin seemed transparent. Martin imagined he could sometimes see the skull beneath the face he loved.

Later, near the end, they brought Hospice in, at her request.

"You can't do it all on your own," she said in a whisper, the strongest voice she could offer. He argued, of course. He needed to care for her. It was the last thing he could do for her. In the end, though, she was right, as always. The extra help was a relief. He could get a bit more rest, and he actually thought he was handling things pretty well.

And then, one evening toward the end of March, she passed. It wasn't dramatic movie-of-the-week stuff. It was long and painful. The cancer and the drugs had taken her away days before her body finally surrendered. She gave one last rattle of breath. And Martin was alone. Even with the two Hospice nurses swirling around, disconnecting tubes and offering a brief condolence, he was alone.

At the funeral home he had a moment to himself with her before anyone else arrived. His wife looked like a wax doll. He kissed her cold forehead and touched her cold hand. He arranged the ankh around her neck. And he knew it was such a joke. Emma wasn't here. She wasn't anywhere. Anything else was just a desperate wish, a need to be assured that he would be with her again someday.

Martin felt as empty as the corpse before him in the mahogany box.

Over the next few days, as family and friends called at their home, Martin was stoic, contained. He accepted the proffered comfort as intended, provided a quiet word of thanks to every mourner. But it was as if his heart had gone into the earth with Emma.

After the funeral, after the neighbors had delivered the last cake and plate of fried chicken, and after the last out-of-town relative had given him an awkward hug and gone, Martin locked the front door, fixed himself a scotch, and sat in his favorite chair and cried. Bawled like a child, in fact, great gasping, unmanly sobs which shook his whole body and doubled him over like he had the dry heaves. He wailed until his voice was only a rasp and his eyes were swollen. He wept for the loss of his best friend, and for the pain she'd endured. And he knew that, most of all, he selfishly cried for himself. For his loneliness. For all the empty days to come.

For several weeks, Martin seldom left the house. When he did, it was just to the end of the driveway to fetch the mail – whenever Bill Lambert decided to deliver it – or a brief trip to the bank or the grocery store or the liquor store. At home, he mostly sat in the recliner, watching TV and drinking until he passed out. He woke up each morning disgusted with himself, and anxious to fill the emptiness inside of him.

Sometimes he wondered how long he had left to live, to endure this awful existence.

Sometimes he even thought about ending it now. On his own schedule.

But he always sobered up.

Emma wouldn't want you to be like this, he thought. But Emma wasn't here. She wasn't anywhere.

Still, as time passed, something changed. His grief lightened a little. Or perhaps he had adjusted to its weight. He woke up one morning and found that the touches of Emma about the house – from the pictures, the flowers, even their one surviving Golden Lab – didn't hurt as much as they had the day before. In fact, he found a very small bit of comfort in them. That comfort grew more each day, until Martin realized he had achieved a precarious balance between pain and love.

At the end of the summer, Martin was ready to go for a walk again.

He had cooked a couple of pork chops for dinner, splitting one with Matilda, the Lab.

After he cleaned up the mess, he put on his Bassmaster ball cap and Nikes and let Matilda lead the way up the hill.

His first sight of his property as seen from the rise behind the house was both exhilarating and frightening. His heart beat so fast that for a moment – a long, frightening moment – he thought he was having a "cardiac incident." As he rubbed his chest and felt sweat forming on his forehead, Martin couldn't help but smile. To spend days thinking about suicide only to be felled by a heart attack on his first journey out of the house had to qualify for the irony hall of fame.

Finally, his heart rate slowed.

What did you expect? You spent nearly four months lying drunk in the house.

The sweat was pouring freely down his face. He wiped it away. Matilda had stopped about fifty yards ahead of him, looking back, her tail sweeping slowly back and forth.

"Just a minute, girl," he said, winded. He straightened up and nearly gasped again when he saw the vista before him, the acres of trees and valleys that Emma had loved so much.

He thought for a moment that he might cry, but the feeling passed. He wiped the sweat from his face again.

"Come on, Matilda." He started back down to the house. "That's enough for one day."

He walked the next day, and the one after that, a little farther each day, loyal Matilda bravely leading the way. On the morning of the fourth day, Martin saw that rain had fallen before sunup. It was close enough to autumn that the light drizzle had cooled the air, so Martin put on the windbreaker Emma had given him for his birthday nearly twenty years ago. It was white, with the logo of the Cincinnati Reds prominently displayed on the back and above his heart. While he zipped it up, Matilda was dancing from foot to foot in front of him, her nails tip-tapping on the wooden floor, her wagging tail nearly a blur.

"All right, all right. Don't rush me." He reached for the door, causing Matilda to lift her front half off the floor and emit a warbling whimper. She burst out of the house the instant he opened the door and was racing up the hill before Martin had cleared the threshold. She stopped – as usual – halfway up the hill. "I know," he said. "I'm old and slow. You don't have to rub it in."

Martin found the going to be slippery. It must have rained more than he had realized. At one point his left foot slid on a muddy patch and he fell to one knee.

I'm getting too old for this shit.

Farther up the hill, Matilda made a whining sound.

"Okay, I hear you."

Martin pushed himself up and resumed his climb. He reached the top of the rise and greeted his dog, who came back to run circles around him. They continued on, trekking up and down the hills on Martin's property, finally reaching the Water Tower Hill. That's what Emma had dubbed it, the first time they had climbed up it, one late October. With most of the leaves gone from the trees, you could see the town's water tower, a pale green monstrosity with HARMONY, KENTUCKY painted on it in red. Today the tower was still hidden.

"Be a good six, eight weeks before I can see it, girl," Martin said to Matilda, who sprawled on the grass beside him, licking a forepaw. He shivered, imagining the late autumn wind on this hill. Emma would have loved it.

For Emma, he tried to find a slightly better vantage point. He moved forward a few steps, then raised up on his toes.

By God, there it was. He could make out the very top of the tower.

"I see it, Emma," he whispered.

He tried to lift himself higher. The toe of one of his sneakers slipped on the damp grass. His right leg shot out in front of him. As he tried to regain his balance, his back foot also slipped, and Martin tumbled down the hill. He grasped at the hillside, tearing out clumps of mud and vegetation, the wet soil offering no support, nothing he could use to slow himself. It was like the water slide he had ridden years ago when Emma's sister invited them down to Florida to see the kids. He was speeding up, his entire world a jumble of green, bumping against him, prodding him downward.

What's down there?

He tried frantically to remember the terrain, but he was too panicked to focus. He had slid maybe seventy yards when he struck something. He heard a sickening crunch. The pain didn't come until a second later and, when it did, it was thunderous, an agony that traveled from his leg to his eyes in an instant, turning the world yellow. Then black.

Martin knew he wasn't out long. The light hadn't changed. The pain in his leg was still there, too, and it was Biblical.

He was on his stomach, his face turned sideways in the grass and mud. He had no idea how badly he was damaged. As much as the idea scared him, he had to find out.

He bit his lip, got both hands under him and pushed up.

Martin screamed.

The world swam before his eyes. He fought to stay conscious. He turned his torso as far as possible, each movement bringing from him whimpering sounds, noises he would otherwise be ashamed of. Finally he was able to see his right leg. From the hip down it looked okay. But at the knee it twisted sideways away from his body at almost a ninety-degree angle.

"Okay, that's no good," he said. His voice sounded funny, thin and quivery.

He sucked in a breath and turned his upper body until he could look up the hill.

Matilda stood atop the rise, her tail hanging down, her Lab face a knot of concern.

"'S okay, girl. Everything's fine." It was the same thing he had said to her when she was a pup, afraid of thunderstorms. Emma would hold little Matilda in her lap and Martin would stroke the shaking animal until she calmed down.

Martin turned as far as he could to survey where he had landed. He was in a gully, like the bottom of a bowl, with the hill in front of him and a rising slope of wooded land behind him. The ground beneath him was very damp, and the wetness was beginning to spread a chill through his body.

The dog started carefully down the hill. Martin braced his hands against the wet ground and tried to pull himself forward. He was screaming before he even realized it. It was the worst pain he had ever experienced.

Thankfully, he didn't feel it for long.

He passed out again.

When he awoke again, it was late afternoon, judging by the sun. It was cloudier, too, and he smelled rain in the air.

Matilda was curled up next to him, pressing against his side. He could feel her warmth through his jacket. The pain in his leg was a low throbbing. Martin was quite happy to leave it that way for a while. His right pants leg was tight at the knee, and he felt feverish. His throat was raw. He slowly moved his left arm until it was wrapped around the dog. He got a tail-thump in response. "Good girl," he whispered. He stayed in that position for a half hour or so, he judged, until he felt it was time to make another attempt.

Removing his arm from around Matilda, he braced his hands against the ground again, this time trying to place more of his weight on the left side of his body. He pulled himself an inch or two toward the hill.

"*Oh, Jesus!*"

Everything – the ground, Matilda, his damp clothes – was blasted away by the jolt of agony from his broken leg. Fire raced along his nerve endings, sending fish-hooks of torment into his brain. The pain was all-consuming. For what seemed like an eternity, it was his entire world.

The worst part of it was that this time he remained conscious. His vision swam, turning yellow, then red. Finally, he was able to see and hear and think again. And what he thought was: *I'm going to die here.*

There was no way to make it up the hill. He didn't expect anyone to come looking for him since he had pushed away family and friends after the funeral. And, while Matilda was a good dog – a *great* dog – she wasn't going to go fetch Fire and Rescue.

"Go tell 'em Timmy's in the well again."

Martin laughed at his own joke until the laughter turned into a cough. Matilda cocked her lovely head to the side and watched him.

"Go on home, girl," he said, shoving at her, surprised by his lack of strength.

She stepped away from him, her brow furrowed again in concern as she tried to figure out what kind of game this was.

Martin feebly shoved at her once more. He was afraid she would stick with him, and he knew he wasn't going home.

Matilda chuffed, then circled three times and curled up next to him.

Martin waited for panic to set in, for fear to twist his guts into bowel-loosening knots of desperation.

It didn't happen.

He hurt. He wanted some Tylenol. And maybe a glass of Dewar's.

Mostly, he wanted to sleep. He put his head down on his arm and closed his eyes. "Let's take a little nap, old girl." Next to him, Matilda whined softly

The rain woke him up. It was soft and carried with it the sweetness of summer nights from his boyhood. He let himself enjoy its fragrance before he opened his eyes. Then he made the mistake of trying to turn over.

He was instantly awake – and painfully aware – of his situation. While the pain wasn't as sharp as before, it seemed to be spreading through his entire leg and into his hip. His right leg was swollen and heavy, like part of a statue, connected to him only through his discomfort.

He was light-headed. His fever had risen.

The sun was almost gone and his wet clothes – further soaked by the light rain – were making him shiver.

Despite all of that, he was hungry. He caught the scent of something sharp and metallic. His neck seemed to creak as he turned to the right. Matilda was lying a few feet away. She was eating something.

Martin could see blood and strips of meat and a gray leg. He guessed she'd caught a squirrel. Matilda's muzzle was now red.

"What do you have, girlie?" He could barely speak above a whisper. His voice sounded like a gangster in a B movie. Matilda didn't even look up from her supper.

Martin had never been a hunter – though he did enjoy fishing, mostly for the quiet – and he'd never eaten raw game. But he had left the house after only a cup of coffee, and last night's dinner had been a long time ago.

He reached toward the dog with his right arm, extending it as far as he could. "Let me have some, Matilda. 'M hungry." At the mention of her name, the Lab twitched her ears. Otherwise, she ignored him.

Martin hesitated for only a moment before twisting his body toward the dog. He tried to support his weight on his arms, but he was too weak. Instead, he used his good leg and his arms to pull himself along the soaked ground. He was surprised to find that his broken leg was growing numb. At least he could move it without passing out. He dragged the bad leg behind him until he reached Matilda.

The Lab stopped eating to watch his progress. Her coat was drenched. She smelled like wet dog and blood. Martin could now see that her meal had indeed once been a squirrel. Its bushy tail was the only part of the animal that hadn't been mangled.

When he was within a foot of her, Martin extended his hand. "Can I have a bite?"

Matilda bared her fangs and growled at him. He could see thin strings of meat hanging from her teeth.

"Matilda," he said as firmly as he could muster. She dropped her eyes and backed away, whining as she went.

He pulled himself forward and looked at the meal she had left him. In addition to the tail, part of the head remained attached to the squirrel's body, canted at an unnatural angle, the eyes two small black BBs. The belly had been torn open. The front legs were gone. Ordinarily, the sight of the mangled animal would have sickened Martin. Now he raised it to his mouth and tore into it, tearing off a hunk of what might have been intestine, chewing only once or twice before swallowing a hunk of meat and organ.

The food seemed to hang in his throat for a second before his stomach protested and he vomited it all up on the ground.

Okay, he thought, *maybe food isn't such a priority.*

He propped himself up on one arm and wiped his mouth with the back of the other hand. The rain was coming harder, and Martin's chills now alternated with moments of feverish sweats.

He had to find shelter.

Over the next hour, he pulled himself across the thirty or so yards to the incline that led to the woods. Matilda had stayed behind at first, eating more of the squirrel. Then she followed Martin, always a few feet behind him, as though ashamed of her earlier behavior.

The rain had increased in intensity. He could hear thunder in the distance and knew Matilda would soon flee. He would be alone.

At the base of the hill, Martin saw several large tree limbs that must have fallen during an earlier storm. He crawled toward them, a wild notion forming.

He reached them quickly, his excitement adding strength to his effort. There were five or six branches strewn across a ten-foot area at the base of the hill. Most were too thin or too short. One was much too large. One, however, was about four feet long and as big around as his wrist.

He took hold of it. It was solid. No cracks or breaks.

This might work.

If he could use the limb as a crutch, he could stand and maybe – a *big* maybe – make it into the shelter of the trees and wait out the storm, then circle around the gully and head back to the house.

He knew it would be a long journey with his broken leg and his fever. And he knew he might not make it. But he was driven to try. Martin was astounded by his desire to survive, to have another day to draw breath.

Thunder boomed above him like a shotgun fired by God. He turned and saw the rear end of Matilda as she raced up the slippery hill on the other side of the gully.

Good luck, girl.

His first two attempts to stand were abysmal failures. He was right-handed and, apparently, right-footed, as well. He couldn't wrap his feverish brain around the idea of starting off with his left foot. Twice he slid back down to what was quickly becoming a swamp. On the third try he concentrated on using his left leg for support and holding his right leg slightly off the ground, keeping all weight off it. With both hands on his makeshift crutch, he finally stood, every muscle on fire and trembling.

He didn't move at first, afraid to upset this balance he had achieved. Martin sucked in a deep breath. His skin seemed to be dancing on his bones, and the edge of his vision was marked by trails of red and yellow, as if shooting stars were bombarding the gully in which he finally stood.

He leaned on the branch and stepped forward with his left foot. His right foot touched the ground, forcing a whimper from him. He caught his balance, then tried again. Two good steps.

I can do this.

But not very fast. He took his time, setting up each step like the engineer he had been, moving his broken right leg with extreme care. Within five or six minutes, he had reached the base of the hill. Thrilled with his accomplishment, and utterly fatigued, he turned and slid into a sitting position, his back against the slope of the hill, letting the rain wash over him. The thunder had grown distant, though the rain had not slackened. Maybe he wouldn't be struck by lightning when he reached the woods.

I'm doing this, Emma. I think I can make it.

He looked across the bowl-shaped gully and saw Matilda's paw prints on the hill. He missed the dog terribly, and was determined to see her again.

He struggled once more to a standing position. He hopped round on his good leg until he was facing the hill. It was growing darker, and he wanted to be at the top of the hill while he could still see the way home.

His plan was to plant the tip of his crutch in the ground and pull himself up like a mountain climber. Once he'd secured his position, he would plant the crutch a few feet ahead and repeat the process. That was the theory, at least.

Martin's first step up the hill worked out pretty well, though he fell to his good knee when he pulled himself forward. He managed to keep his bad leg from striking the ground, so it wasn't a total disaster. He gained his footing again, and pulled the crutch out of the mud. He planted it three feet in front of him, where it sank in a good six inches. He dragged himself to the new position without slipping.

Great. Now just do that a hundred and fifty more times and you're home free.

He chuckled. His throat felt like he had swallowed barbed wire and his head pounded from the fever and the exertion. He planted his crutch ahead of him, and pulled himself after it.

His progress was slow, but successful. He had scaled approximately one-third of the hillside when the rain – which had been steady throughout his climb – turned into a deluge. He was in the middle of planting his crutch for the next step when the piece of wood slid along the ground instead of sinking into it. Martin leaned forward, attempting to force it into the soil, and lost his balance. The makeshift crutch flew from his hand and for one second he stood on the muddy slope, arms extended like a high-wire acrobat, standing on one foot, teetering for balance.

Then he fell.

He slid down the hill on his back, his bad leg banging again and again against the ground. Near the bottom he tried to slow himself with his hands, wrenching his right arm nearly out of its socket. He came to rest at the bottom on his back, his hips and legs elevated on the hill. The rain poured into his eyes and his open mouth. He wondered if he could drown that way, and again felt laughter bubbling up from his chest, laughter that he couldn't stop. His cackling sounded mad to his ears. He continued to laugh until tears poured from his eyes and became indistinguishable from the rain on his face.

Martin didn't have he strength to stand again. His left leg was aching.

He didn't have a stick to use for support.

His chest ached when he drew a breath, and he could feel a gurgling in his lungs.

I don't want to die, he thought. But it seemed he no longer had a choice.

He thought sleep was a very good idea. So he closed his eyes. He hated to give up. He hated not being the kind of man Emma had believed him to be.

Now he just hoped the end came soon.

The rain had stopped and the sky had cleared. He could see stars above him.

Martin heard a rustling somewhere nearby. He lifted his neck so he could look up the hill. In the shadows of the trees, four robed figures were looking back at him. Though their faces were hidden in the shadow of their hoods, Martin could feel their heavy gaze on him. They were impossibly tall, bigger even than basketball players. And, while he knew they were a hallucination, they seemed so real. They seemed purposeful.

Judging me.

"Tell—" he began. His voice was barely a soft croak. It didn't matter. They weren't actually there, yet he had to say it anyway. "Tell Emma I thought about her every minute of every day."

There. He'd gotten it out. He smiled and let sleep claim him again.

I'm not dead yet.

Either that or he was dead and in Hell.

He opened his eyes and instantly closed them again. The sun was directly overhead. While the previous day had been mild for late summer, this day was right in character.

Martin had never been as thirsty as he was now. Each swallow burned like napalm in his throat, the passage so swollen he was surprised he could even breathe.

Okay. So the end was going to be slow in coming.

He looked up at the wooded hill, remembering the robed figures from his dream. He briefly wondered if there would be someone to welcome him after he passed. He decided it wasn't very likely.

He tried to move his right leg, but he couldn't even feel it. He could feel his right arm, though. If he hadn't broken it, he had certainly torn ligaments.

He laid his head back on the now-dry ground. He wished he had some sunscreen.

He wished he had never started the walk.

Someone was wiping a warm, wet cloth across his face.

Emma?

He opened his eyes and Matilda licked him again.

He tried to smile. His lips cracked, but he barely registered the pain. Matilda continued to lick his face.

"You're my good girl," he said in a voice so soft he doubted the dog could hear it.

The sun was nearly down again, and he wondered why he was still alive, how long this was going to take.

Matilda curled up next to him once more, pressing against his side. He wanted to tell her goodbye but his voice had finally failed him.

He drifted in and out of consciousness over the next few hours. When he was lucid he felt comforted by the presence of his dog.

At least be alone when I go. He hoped someone would take Matilda in and give her a good home.

"Martin?"

He almost smiled. He must be close to the end now. He could hear Emma's voice.

"Honey?"

Emma.

"Open your eyes, baby."

I don't have the strength.

"You do now."

Martin opened his eyes.

On the stump of a chestnut tree – a stump he had never noticed until this moment – sat his beautiful, deceased wife.

Emma was wearing faded jeans and a flannel work shirt she had taken from his closet years ago. It was far too big for her, and she wore it open with a white T-shirt underneath and the sleeves rolled up. Her hands were on her knees. She was smiling at him.

She was beautiful. She glowed.

Martin swallowed. He coughed once, then tried to speak. To his amazement, he still had a voice, albeit a raspy one. "Missed you... so much."

"Poor baby. I'm so sorry I had to leave you." Her smile had softened. She seemed to be radiating love. It was a palpable force that caressed his skin and drove the pain away.

"Soon. Be with you soon."

Emma was kneeling next to him. He hadn't seen her move. She gently caressed his face, the same touch that he had awakened to on many mornings.

"Not yet, Martin. It's not your time."

"Please." He felt tears well up in his eyes, moisture he didn't know he had. "Emma, please."

She took one of his hands in hers and clasped it tightly. It felt like he was grabbing an electric fence. "You have another twenty or so years, honey, if you'll take them." She squeezed his hand. "Please tell me you'll take them."

"Why?"

"Because life is a gift."

"Not... not any more."

"Especially now. You have lives yet to touch, Martin. And you have those who depend on you." Emma turned to Matilda and smiled. The Lab thumped her tail against the ground. "Please live, Martin."

"Never... never could refuse you."

"You never could," she agreed. She kissed him on his dry, cracked lips. Like a soothing balm, the kiss softened his skin, and more of his pain faded.

"Nice dream," he said.

"Yes," Emma said, "it is."

She stood up, and for the first time Martin noticed a silhouette behind her, and another one behind the first, and still more stretching up to the sky. Golden shapes, arrayed to the heavens.

"Who...?"

"It's *everyone*," Emma said. "Everyone who knew you, who loved you, who came before."

"Oh, my."

"I know it's a lot to take in, baby, so just close your eyes. It won't be long now."

He couldn't keep his eyes open, despite his best effort. As he blinked and grew sleepy, the dream that was Emma seemed to break apart into a million blazing fireflies.

"Remember I love you, Martin."

He couldn't fight it; his eyes closed.

I love you, Martin.

He knew it was a dream. Still, it was good to hear Emma's voice again.

Love you, Martin.

He settled back against the ground, knowing his final moments were here.

Martin.

Odd, how her voice had changed. Deeper now.

"Martin?"

Deeper. And frightened

"Martin? Can you hear me? Oh, Jesus! I found him! Over here!"

Martin managed to open his eyes enough to see the ridiculous spectacle of Bill Lambert, nearly unrecognizable out of his Postal Service uniform, sliding down the muddy hill on his ass. Others were standing at the top of the hill. He made out two men in deputy sheriff uniforms.

Then Bill was next to him.

"Martin? Oh, lord." Bill was out of breath. He also sounded like he might cry. "Are you with me, Martin? Oh, geez, please don't be dead."

"Give me... another ten minutes. See... what I can do."

Bill's eyes widened so much he looked like a cartoon character. "You're alive! Sweet Jesus!" He turned to the deputies who were carefully making their way down the hill. "He's alive!"

Bill put both of his hands around Martin's clenched fist – the one that, in his dream, Emma had been holding.

"Hang on, buddy. We're getting you some help."

"Okay," Martin said, and then realized he'd only thought he'd said it. In the distance he heard sirens.

A horn bleated twice from the driveway.

"Okay, okay. Give me a second." Martin rose from the chair and stepped carefully over Matilda. She raised a doggie eyebrow and gave him the look that said *I know you're going out.*

He steadied himself with the cane – he was still getting used to the walking cast – and made his way to the window, where he pulled aside the curtain and held up one finger. From the warmth of the pickup, Bill Lambert waved back.

Martin turned and took a moment, experiencing the same conflicting emotions he felt every time he looked at the Christmas decorations. Emma's niece Marcy and her two girls had shown up on Thanksgiving Day with a bushel of food and a couple of boxes of decorations. Despite his objections, the three of them had brought the artificial tree up from the basement, assembled it, and decorated it. They'd added a few lights around the windows, a wreath on the door and, atop the fireplace mantel, a bunch of figurines of Santa and his reindeer. Then Marcy had warmed up the food and made him eat while the girls laughed as they fed turkey to Matilda.

Now, when he saw the tree, he missed Emma all over again.

But, strangely, he also felt hopeful.

Marcy and her kids had been back several times. And Martin had welcomed the friends and other extended family members who had visited him after the accident.

He thought he might be piecing a life together. Bit by tiny bit. Every handshake, every hug, every call was another brick in the foundation.

One ornament on the tree caught his attention. It was the first one Emma's niece had picked out on Thanksgiving evening.

It was a small heart-shaped picture frame, its red and green border faded from the years.

The bottom of the frame bore – in candy-striped letters – the inscription "OUR FIRST CHRISTMAS." It held a photograph of an impossibly young Martin and his beautiful wife. Martin wore a Santa Claus hat titled rakishly to the side. They held up champagne glasses full of eggnog.

Martin touched the frame, and he remembered.

He remembered the hospital room, a fuzzy white place made indistinct by the painkillers. His right leg was immobilized and full of metal. Needles in both arms fed God-knew-what into his veins.

"Hiya, Martin."

Martin blinked and managed to turn his head to his visitor. Bill Lambert stood there in his Postal Service uniform, holding several magazines, including *Sports Illustrated* and *Entertainment Weekly*. Martin thought he saw mailing labels on the magazines and wondered if Bill's mailbag was a bit lighter than it should be.

"Didn't need to spend money on me, Bill."

"Don't worry. I didn't," Bill said with a sly smile. The tips of his very large ears turned red.

Martin searched with his finger until he found the button that would raise the bed.

In a moment, his head was level with Bill's.

"Thank you, Bill. I would have died out there."

Bill's ears grew redder and he looked away. "Aw, come on. I just saw a couple of days' worth of mail and you hadn't said you were going anywhere. So I looked through the garage window and saw the car. That's when I called the sheriff. I just wish we'd found you sooner. Man, you were talking out of your head."

"I was?" Martin said, remembering the dream of Emma and the golden shapes that floated behind her.

"Where'd they put it?"

"What?"

"That thing, you know. The *thing*." Bill made a motion with his fingers that was apparently supposed to clear up everything. Bill sorted through the hospital items on the nightstand next to the bed. "Aw hell!"

"What are you talking about?"

"It was in your hand," Bill said. He opened the top drawer in the nightstand "It fell out when the fire department was carrying you up the hill. I gave it to one of the nurses. She said they'd get it to you. I knew I should've held on to it."

"Bill, I have no idea—"

"Ah–ha!" Bill removed his hand from the drawer and, a triumphant smile lighting up his face, held up the object of his search.

Martin touched the photo ornament once more, then he hobbled to the hall and opened a drawer on the old roll-top desk. He pulled out the thin gold chain and carried it back to the Christmas tree.

A hallucination, brought on by pain and dehydration. He knew that's what the dream had been. As much as he wanted to see Emma again, he knew it could never be.

Until the hospital room.

Until Bill had held up the object that had been clenched in Martin's fist when his rescuers had discovered him.

A simple gold chain with a small Egyptian ankh. The very one that he had placed in his wife's casket at the funeral home.

The same one he now hung from the tree.

"Merry Christmas, baby."

Bill tooted his horn again.

Christ, Martin thought. *I can't believe I'm doing this.*

He made his way back to the hall and retrieved his coat from the wall peg. He was still surprised he'd let Bill talk him into going to the party. Especially since he knew Jennifer Dowdy would be there. The recently widowed, very attractive Jennifer Dowdy.

"I hope she likes gimps," Martin said aloud. From her perch in front of his chair, Matilda raised her head and gave him a quizzical look.

"I'll be home later, girl," he told her. Then added, "Don't wait up."

Martin walked out into the winter night and began the rest of his life.

New Writings in the Fantastic
The Catherine Wheel Geoffrey Maloney

In a darkened room not yet touched by the weak light of morning, a young man turned in his sleep. In his mind it was the end of the year, his final exams were approaching, but he had forgotten he was studying for a degree, forgotten his exams were due, and knew there was no way he would be ever able to pass. In the distance he heard a woman singing a plaintive, lilting song, barely audible and melancholic; a song he had never heard before. His ears strained to hear it.

He woke to a banging on his door and a feeling of failure in his heart as the last notes of the song died away to be replaced by a woman's harsh voice calling his name. As he rolled out of bed his eyes fell upon a desk littered with textbooks, papers and a computer that was very nearly an antique. The sight of his desk dismayed him. A groan escaped his lips. It was true. He was at university and there was a good chance he would fail his exams. He had hoped for a moment he would wake up in his own bed back in Wagga, in his parents' home, and had never won the scholarship to study medicine in Sydney.

The banging on his door sounded again, demanding his sleepy attention, forcing him to open it. Sylvia, his landlady, stood there, wearing a pink chenille dressing gown, her hair uncombed, proclaiming she too had been woken abruptly from her sleep.

"Jesus, you took your time, Jamie," she said. "Frank Whylie down the hall's in pretty bad shape. I want you to take a look at him."

Frank Whylie, in his late sixties or early seventies, thin and clean shaven, with short crewcut hair that had never thinned, lay on his bed. He wore a grubby cotton singlet and his mouth hung open. His lips had begun to blue.

Jamie felt for a pulse. It was faint. He put an ear to the man's mouth. No breath. The landlady stood at the door, watching anxiously, not keen on the prospect of having dead people in her boarding house. Too many questions to answer, too many papers to fill out. She watched with a mixture of fascination and revulsion as Jamie's lips met those of the old man in an attempt to revive him.

Jamie breathed hard, counted slowly, looked at the old guy's chest, searching for any movement that would indicate the natural rhythm of his lungs was working again.

As Frank's lungs began to rise and fall of their own volition, Jamie moved away, to the end of the bed, feeling slightly dizzy and breathing deeply to restore oxygen to his own lungs. It was then that he saw her, at the edge of the room, tucked away in the corner, up against the old wooden wardrobe: a thin woman, almost childlike, with long dark hair, big round eyes and a short sharp little nose. A young girl, he thought at first, but then decided not; her breasts were too round and too full beneath the dirty cotton T-shirt she wore.

Jamie stood at the banister railing outside the room, breathing more steadily now. The old guy could have died, he knew that. Sleep apnea. It could happen to anyone. Sometimes, especially during sleep, the body could forget to breathe, as if it had lost its instinctive memory, misplaced its natural rhythm. Mostly it remembered again, before any damage was done, and the sleeper slept on, oblivious to the crisis they had passed through.

Behind him, he heard Sylvia close the door to Frank's room. "He's breathing fine now," she said. "He'll be OK."

"He could have died," Jamie said. "I think he should go to the hospital, see a real doctor."

"No," Sylvia said. "That wouldn't do him any good. Francis is an illegal immigrant. He's a Yank who jumped ship. He's got no Medicare card. He'd just run the chance of being arrested and deported."

Jamie nodded his head. He understood. There were always problems with illegal immigrants.

"I bet you're wondering how I knew something was up?" Sylvia asked. But he hadn't been wondering about that at all. He'd thought the girl, the woman he had seen hiding next to the wardrobe, had called her.

"I had this dream," Sylvia said. "I was at the opera. There was a woman singing a lovely, sad, sweet song, but it was in a language I couldn't understand. There was man sitting next to me. He said, 'I'll translate for you.' Then he said, 'Francis Whylie in Number 10 is dying. Call the doctor!' And I was out of bed and up the stairs like a shot. Used the spare key to open Frank's room and there he was, lying on the bed, turning blue. I trust things like that, trust my dreams, have real faith in them. They've never let me down yet."

"I thought it was his girlfriend," Jamie said, feeling better now, feeling glad he'd been able to help, even if it was only his high-school first aid he'd remember and not something they'd taught him at medical school. "Thought she must have called you for help."

"Girlfriend?" Sylvia said, and shook her head. "Frank's been here for two years now and he's never had no woman friends in his room. I don't allow it. Besides Frank's an old man, no ways a woman'd look twice at an old codger like that."

He wanted to tell her he had definitely seen a woman in Frank's room, but thought better of it. Maybe Sylvia already knew, maybe she was just trying to cover up for Frank, and didn't want it known she was willing to let some of her guests and not others break the house rules. Still, he had to admire her. The story about the dream was creative if nothing else.

Sylvia patted him on the shoulder. "Sleep, my young doctor," she said. "You have more than earned your rest on this earth for one night and I, for one, am grateful. I don't like my boys snuffing it on the premises, no matter how old they might be."

And he did try to sleep in the gray griminess of his bedsitter, but his desk continued to bother him. With its open books, full of the knowledge he had to transfer to his mind, it loomed large and dominating in the small room, a heavy burden he felt unable to lift. Too much work and only four weeks left before the finals. It was almost too late. He felt he should have been studying twenty-four hours a day, seven days a week, popping caffeine pills like peppermints, and keeping his eyelids peeled open with sticky tape.

Before dawn, falling through a light doze, the dream came to him again. It was the morning of the finals, and he had done nothing, no study, no preparation. Failure loomed large. How had he done this to himself, how had he gotten into such a mess? Then he was at the examination desk, his pen in his hand, the question paper before him and his mind one long dark blank. Anxiety twisted a savage knot in his stomach. He closed his eyes, trying to conjure up the words that had floated across the lecture theater, the words that had leapt up from the white paper of his textbooks and out of the computer screen, hoping to remember them as sounds, as images, to capture them and give them meaning, but the impressions they had left were faint, like lemon-juice ink on blotting paper, and no candle flame, no match light, could be found to illuminate them. It was then he heard the singing again, sad and melancholic, a famous aria from a tragic opera, perhaps, and his hand began to write of its own volition, writing the words to the answers, answers so detailed and so complex he barely understood them as his eyes watched the pen dance across the page.

Six hours' study the next day after waking late, and he felt exhausted. It was first-year revision: The function and structure of the cranial nerves. It should have been easy; there weren't that many of them. He knew the mnemonic, had known it for years: "On Old Olympus Towering Top A Fin And German Viewed A Hop." Olfactory, optic, oculomotor, trochlear... and that was it. His memory failed him, becoming lost in a jumble of words.

When the knock came on the door, he felt a sense of relief at the interruption. Anything that would get him away from his books was welcome.

"You the doctor?" Frank Whylie said when Jamie opened the door.

The man spoke with an American accent, but one that sounded as if it had been softened by many years spent outside the States.

"Hope to be," Jamie said.

"I've got a bottle of whiskey in my room," Frank said. "I want you to come and have a drink. Sylvia told me what happened last night."

Jamie rubbed his hand across his face, dug his fingers into his eyes. "I've got to get through these books," he said, looking back at his desk.

"One drink," Frank said, grabbing him by the arm. "My way of saying thanks. I don't have much else."

Frank's room was similar to Jamie's own: a bedsitter, with just enough room for a bed, a table and couple of chairs, and an old wardrobe. There was a separate bathroom and a kitchen alcove with a single gas jet and a small hot-water heater over the sink, but the room smelt musty, damp, the smell of an old person who didn't like to wash too often. On the table were two glasses and a bottle of whiskey already opened. One of the glasses had been used, for a couple of drinks at least, judging by what was left in the bottle.

"That's Grant, pure malt," Frank said. "The last of a case given to me by an admirer many years ago. I've been saving it for a special occasion, and my last-minute resurrection is about as special as things get these days."

He had meant it as a joke, but Jamie detected something tragic in the old man's voice. As he sat down, his eyes flickered round the room, looking for the young woman he had seen the previous night, but she wasn't there and anyway he knew it wasn't his business who Frank had in his room.

"You find me in straightened circumstances," Frank said as he sloshed some whiskey into the glasses. "No money, no family, no country. But it wasn't always like this. I used to be an astronaut. I once walked on Mars."

Jamie kept a poker face, but smiled to himself as he took a sip of his whiskey. "That must have been interesting," he said, trying to be polite, but already wanting to leave. He could see what was coming. Frank would keep him here all night, if he let him, spinning out some fantastic yarn.

"Interesting?" Frank said and drained his glass. "Yeah, it *was* fucking interesting. But if you believed me, if you really believed me, you wouldn't have said 'That must have been interesting.' You would have said, 'God, that's fucking amazing.' Or you could have been honest, you could have said you didn't believe me. I can take that. It's what everybody else says, when I tell them."

Jamie looked at his glass. He wanted to get away, be back in his own room or out in the street, anywhere but where he was.

"I'm sorry," he said.

"No use being sorry around me, doctor," Frank said, standing up and pushing his chair back. "Sorry's one word I've never had time for."

Frank walked across the room to his wardrobe in a exaggerated steady fashion, trying to act like the three glasses of whiskey he'd drunk hadn't affected him at all. Jamie thought he should make a dash for the door, leave while Frank's attention was occupied. He made to rise from his chair, but then he saw her, sitting on the bed, the same young woman from the night before. She was staring straight back at him. He noticed her eyes were dark, almost black, that her hair – the deepest blackest brown – trailed about her, falling to her waist. The thin cotton T-shirt she wore was wrapped tightly around her knees. The skin of her face, arms and legs was so white, so translucent, it seemed to contain its own light, as though shining softly with a pale phosphorescence. He hadn't heard the door open. Had she been there all the time, hidden away among the shadows beside the wardrobe?

Frank slammed a thick photo album down on the table, causing the whiskey bottle and the glasses to shake.

"Don't you look at her," he said, his voice loud, shouting. "Don't you dare look at her! Go on, get out!"

Jamie stood up, backed away from the table, looked across to the bed, saw the woman, a flash of white, her dark hair flying, rolling away and off the bed, moving until she had melted into the shadow between the wardrobe and the wall, until she had almost disappeared. He looked back at Frank.

The man's face was red, blotched with anger. He held his arms stiffly at the side of his body with hard clenched fists.

Jamie moved to the door slowly and let himself out into the quiet of the hallway.

More troubled sleep, more dreams of exams and studies neglected. These night terrors and anxieties would give him no peace. And so too Frank, Frank in many disguises, appearing throughout the dreams: The lecturer, the examiner, the superintendent at the hospital, threatening him, cursing him, with many voices raised in anger, his life under constant threat. Then at four o'clock in the morning the real chaos started. He heard a woman moaning, a low guttural sound like a wild animal's night cry and, beneath this, the crooning tones of an old man's voice, pleading and imploring.

Still feeling captured by his dreams, Jamie climbed from his bed, crept to the door, opened it just a little. Frank's girlfriend stood in the hallway with her back to him. Her hair rose above her head, defying gravity, swirling and twisting and snaking into the air. Frank stood in the doorway of his room, one hand stretched before him, frozen in midair. His lips moved rapidly, spluttering forth words in a mad rush, encouraging, cajoling, pleading with the woman to return to the room. Then she turned, swiveling at the ankles, until she stared straight at Jamie. His eyes met hers and his mind was touched by a brilliant yellow glow. Like a giant sunflower blooming and spreading its petals, the light unfolded into every corner of his consciousness. He staggered backward, away from the door, and fell into the gray dawn of the early morning.

When Jamie came to, Frank was sitting on the floor beside his bed, another whiskey bottle in his hand.

"And so I became the 97th person to set foot on Mars," Frank said as though he'd been talking to Jamie for hours. "I thought it was a big deal, but it was nothing. We covered the same ground that had already been covered many times. We discovered nothing new, we didn't achieve anything. And soon all the others were dead. Oxygen deprivation. They died on re-entry. Me the only one to survive – because of her. She just turned up, maybe she'd been there all along, maybe we brought her back from Mars. I don't know. But she got me through re-entry, and I was Francis-Whylie-the-sole-survivor-of-the-16th-mission-to-Mars. Famous for a while, but then the war came and she wanted me to stay and go into politics. With her behind me, I could have done anything. But I've got no stomach for politics. I wanted out, and I got out. Came here and did nothing. Done nothing for twenty years now."

Jamie rolled over in bed and looked at Frank. "Who is she?"

Frank took a swig from the whiskey bottle and chuckled quietly. "Who is she? What is she? I gave up asking those questions a long time ago. Martian, angel, devil, muse, spirit, fairy? I've been through them all. None of them seems to fit. For a long time I thought I'd made her up, something my brain dreamed up when it was deprived of oxygen, something I had created to help me survive. At first I thought that explained why I was the only one who could see her. But I was wrong. Other people can see her, if she wants them to."

The yellow light had faded, the sunflower was gone, leaving Jamie's head throbbing gently between the eyes. The doctor in him clicked in, searching for an explanation. He felt as if he were still trapped in a dream, a crazy dream of Frank's making.

"I call her Tess," Frank said, "for no other reason than that I like the name and she has to have a name. I said she could visit you. Had to agree to that to stop the argument, to calm her down. She gets so angry when she doesn't get her own way. You must promise me you won't take her away. You saved my life, doctor, just like she did once, and you can't take her away from me. I found her and she's all I've got left."

"It's a dream, Frank," Jamie said. "It's all just a dream. Go back to bed. Sleep it off. You won't remember any of this when you wake up."

"She doesn't like to be touched," Frank said. "She's a half-wild creature sometimes, hasn't learnt the ways of our world yet. I've tried, but it just doesn't work. She can hardly speak, but she sings beautifully in her own language."

"Stop it!"

"She likes to play games. She's very good at them, chess especially."

"I don't believe this," Jamie said. "I don't believe any of it."

Frank heaved himself to his feet, staggered back from the bed. "You'll believe, young doctor. Oh yes, you're going to believe it. Because she told me last night she won't have it any other way and I'm an old man; I don't have the power or energy to defy her."

Jamie slept peacefully after Frank left, late into the morning, finally waking towards midday with the remnants of the night's events sticking in his mind like pieces of a tattered collage. Most of it had been a dream, of that he was sure, but Frank had certainly been in his room. He could still smell the stench of the old man's alcoholic breath in the stuffy air. And the woman was real enough, he decided – he had seen her twice now. Some poor waif Frank had captured off the street and woven into his web of fantasy. It was debatable whether Frank was an ex-Martian astronaut, Jamie decided, but he was most certainly crazy. Rational thought was a cure for all evils, he told himself, as he made a cup of coffee and attacked the books on his desk.

After three hours of study that took him through to the afternoon, he felt he was getting somewhere, felt the words he read were no longer as meaningless as they had been the day before. The bits and pieces of his studies were beginning to come together, no longer just isolated facts floating in the space of his mind; now connections came into being, patterns formed, taking on the shadowy shape of a sphere. But he knew the surface of that sphere had to be coloured in, etched over, and then the sphere filled down to its core, so it became a hard solid ball of knowledge that could be unwound and its facts regurgitated, bit by bit, onto something as mundane and lifeless as an examination paper.

It was while he was thinking this that he heard his door open. He turned quickly, swiveling in his chair, to see the woman, Tess, standing there. She wore the same thin cotton T-shirt he had seen her in before. Her hair fell past her shoulders in a thick mass that looked as if she never brushed it. In her hands she held a chessboard, and a wooden box he guessed contained the playing pieces. She stared straight at him, her eyes unblinking, her face pensive, a little frightened. She made a gesture with the board and the wooden box, an invitation to play.

"No," Jamie said politely, indicating his books. "I have to study. You shouldn't be here. Frank will get angry."

She did not speak, but slowly bent her knees and placed the chessboard and the box beside the door. Leaning against the doorway, she looked at the chessboard once more, then back at Jamie.

He shook his head. He found her actions strange, almost childlike, nothing like those of the creature he had seen in his dreams. The thought struck him that perhaps she suffered from some form of intellectual disability. This would explain her relationship with Frank.

She pointed to the chessboard, more insistent now.

"No," Jamie said. "You should go."

But she took no notice of his words. Her hand grasped the hem of her T-shirt and her face broke into a soft smile as she dragged it upwards. She wore no underwear beneath. Her belly was white and smooth, falling into a soft gentle V between her legs that was only sparsely covered in dark curly hair.

Jamie felt a sudden urge to touch her, to feel if her skin was as smooth as it looked, and he imagined for a moment it would feel like silk, that if he only touched her he would have everything he had ever wanted, be completely satisfied with that one, almost innocent act. But he had no wish to be dragged into such games, no wish to become part of the world that Tess and Frank lived in, no wish to take advantage of a poor creature who seemed incapable of understanding the meaning of her own actions, nor anything of what she was signifying.

"You shouldn't do that," he said. "It's wrong. I think you'd better leave."

"Now!" he said, more sternly, when she made no move to go, but she reacted to the harshness in his voice. She let her T-shirt fall to cover her again, looked sad for a moment, then stepped through the open door and closed it softly behind her.

Jamie tried to return to his books, but his concentration was fragmented. Images of Tess and her nakedness kept flitting through his mind. He was right not to touch her, he knew that, but somewhere the temptation remained, a bittersweet taste that clung to the back of his tongue. In the end he had to get out. He grabbed his coat and left the boarding house.

The Vishnu Fish Café bustled that evening with a crowd seeking strong coffee and cheap food in their refuge from a sudden thunderstorm. It was a short distance from Jamie's lodgings. Just a stroll from Sydney University, the café was a casual place frequented by money-conscious students and junior lecturers, a place where Jamie, always on the brink of poverty, didn't feel out of place.

After a light meal and two cups of black coffee, he felt refueled and ready to hit the books again, but not quite ready to face the gloom and madness of the boarding house. He dawdled at the table for a little longer, wishing he had been able to afford more expensive accommodation, like he wished for many things, but he was in the big city, studying at medical school by the good graces of a government scholarship. You couldn't afford to dream or wish for too much when the taxpayers were supporting you.

He was about to leave and head back to his room when a glass of wine appeared before him. He looked up to see Helen, a fellow student, take the chair opposite him.

"You look so gloomy," she said, "sitting here all by yourself. I thought I'd come and cheer you up."

"Not so gloomy," he said. "Just thinking about the books waiting for me."

Helen brushed blonde hair out of her eyes, took a sip from her glass of wine. "Looks like you've been studying too much. The dark rings under the eyes are a dead giveaway. You shouldn't force it."

"It's not the study," he said. "Too many late nights. There's a strange couple in the room next to mine. A half-crazy old guy and a young woman who's missing something upstairs. They seem to have taken an interest in me, can't leave me alone."

"Maybe they like you," she said. "Maybe they find your gloominess and your intensity attractive, think you've got something they want. Perhaps lots of people take an interest in you for the same reason."

"Like who?" Jamie said, giving in to temptation and taking a sip from the glass before him.

"Like me, for instance."

"I'm flattered," he said, and meant it. He liked Helen, felt she was one of the few other students he could deal with. She didn't drive an expensive car and she didn't always talk about how much money she was going to make from being a doctor. She was the sort of person who wanted to be a doctor because that was all she had ever wanted to be. He admired her for that, wished he had the same dedication for himself.

"Hey, don't get carried away," she said. "It's not like I'm going to sleep with you or anything."

"I didn't ask," he said, chasing one throwaway line with another.

"No," she said, "you wouldn't, would you? You wouldn't want to give me the pleasure of saying no."

She was right. He would never have asked her because he would never wish to hear her say no, never want that rejection. You didn't ask things of people, you didn't want things from them, and you didn't get rejected. It was a simple formula he believed in, something almost innate in him. He could approach life no other way. Was that the gloominess she had mentioned, the intensity others found attractive? He didn't know. He was incapable of standing outside himself and seeing the world as others did. But... he could call her bluff. He could give her the pleasure of saying "no" and be satisfied in that, because it had been his idea she would say "no," and so that wouldn't be a rejection but a reaction in the soft-shoed game they were playing, a game he was beginning to enjoy because it had nothing to do with the boarding house and nothing to do with his studies. It gave him, for the moment, a delightful sense of freedom.

He toyed with his glass as he asked, watching the moon-coloured wine swimming in the glass's rounded bottom, "Would you like to sleep with me?"

He thought Helen wouldn't answer straight away, that she would study her own drink, toy with it as he did, play the game, string it out, and relish the "no" she had planned for her lips.

But Helen did not hesitate at all. She placed her hand beneath his chin and lifted it until his eyes were forced to look at hers.

"Yes," she said.

Moonlight guided them through the streets of the city, night vision past the landlady's downstairs apartment and up the stairs, past Frank's door and into Jamie's room. They made love in the darkness, their bodies slipping into each other, fitting together in a grateful, peaceful harmony.

Later, after the quietness set in, Jamie rose to make some coffee. While he busied himself with the coffee pot, he heard Helen stir behind him. There was a soft click as the desk lamp flashed on, bathing the room in light and shadows.

"Too much study, eh?" she said in a friendly tone. "I didn't know you played chess."

He moved from the kitchen into the main room, past the bed, until he was standing behind Helen, looking where she looked. His computer had been pushed up into one corner. His books were piled in neat little stacks against the wall. The desk was clean, tidy, not like he had left it, and in the middle sat a chess board, the pieces on it positioned halfway through a game.

"The white queen is in a vulnerable position," Helen said. "Threatened by the black knight and the bishop, with a rook in support."

He moved up close to her, touching her naked body with his, seeking her reassuring warmth. "It's Frank," he said. "The old guy who lives next door. He plays chess with his girlfriend. They must have been here while I was out. They've left it here."

"Strange. But we could finish the game. I'll be white. It's a challenge. The queen's position can be salvaged."

"No," he said. "I don't play chess. Come and have some coffee, come back to bed."

And he knew she was eager to please him, that she liked him, that she had wanted him. She turned out the desk lamp, drank the coffee he had made and lay back on the bed in the moonlight, seeming happy and pleased with herself. "We must do this more often," she whispered in his ear as they both fell asleep.

As the night turned in on itself and began its descent into morning, Jamie woke abruptly to find himself in bed alone. The door of his room was open, revealing a crack of blazing yellow light. He rose from the bed, approached the doorway, wanting to believe it was all a dream and wishing, as his hand reached for the door, he could wake and find himself in bed, beside Helen.

Tess was there again, staring at him, as he opened the door. Her hair scattered above her head in a swirling mass as though caught in the winds of a hurricane. Her eyes burned with green fire, red fire, orange fire, throwing out the images of a kaleidoscope, twirling and spinning and sparking like twin catherine wheels.

Half-collapsed down the staircase was a giant sunflower, its center burning like the sun, its green stem broken, its richly coloured petals drooping and torn. *This is a dream,* he told himself. *My dream. I am in control.* Beyond the sunflower, further up the hall, Helen leant against the wall. Her eyes were closed, her body was naked, her breasts glistened with a thin film of sweat. Her hair hung lankly across her shoulders, damp where it touched her skin, but her face pointed upward as though feeling for the sun, and her lips were curved into a sweet, blissful smile. In her hand she clasped a golden petal from the sunflower.

Jamie eased himself past Tess and slowly walked the hallway toward Helen. Behind him Tess began to sing, the same melancholic song he had heard before in his dreams. When he picked Helen up in his arms – her body was limp and light, like a marionette with broken strings – the singing stopped and he turned to find the hallway empty.

In his room Jamie placed Helen on the bed. She remained unconscious, but her breathing was steady and the smile still shone upon her face. When his eyes fell upon the sunflower petal in her hand, he tore it away and cast it out the door.

Jamie watched Helen during what was left of the night, watched her for any signs of distress, and wondered when he would be released from the dream. But she showed no distress and the dream refused to release him. When the morning sun climbed through the window, he cleaned the coffee pot, refilled it and placed it on the stove.

As Helen woke he handed her a cup of coffee. She squeezed the sleep from her eyes and looked up at him, saw the rings under his eyes darker than the night before.

"You haven't slept," she said. "All night I could feel your eyes upon my body."

He wanted to say something, wanted to tell her they hadn't woken from the dream, Frank's dream, that strange creature's dream. *It's their dreams we're dreaming,* he thought, but she stopped him before he spoke, held her fingers up to his mouth.

"Don't speak," she said. "Don't break the spell. I liked it, you watching me while I slept, your eyes searching over me and liking what they saw. It was all part of the dream I had. I dreamt I woke and you were still asleep. The door was open, there was a yellow glow. I slipped out of bed and into the hallway and there was a giant sunflower, raised on a green stalk, its leaves alive and green, its flower glowing like the sun. I reached up and grasped a petal, pulled on the petal until it tore free. I was so excited, I was so happy. It was like that petal, that single golden petal, was everything I had ever wanted – and I held it in my hand. I had attained it. It was mine."

Jamie kissed her on the forehead, stroked her hair down the curve of her back. "A wonderful dream. You slept with a such a sweet smile on your face," he said. "I'll make some more coffee."

Helen slipped away during the silent morning, returning to her own studies. Jamie remained on the bed, not wanting to deal with what lay on his desk, the unfinished chess game, begging for players. Now he believed, or thought he believed, it was no longer a dream. He had woken once, not a second time. Reality had arrived in the shape of the morning, stretching a continuous unbroken line from the night's events to his present point in time.

When the door opened and Tess eased herself into his room, he was not surprised. She glanced at him, then moved to the chessboard. Her hand took hold of the black bishop and pressed the attack against the white queen. Jamie sighed and wondered what he was doing as he climbed out of bed, took a kitchen chair and moved it across to his desk.

Helen had been right, the white queen was in danger, but the game could be salvaged. As the day stole on and he became lost in the game, Jamie staved off the attack of the black knight and its bishop, defended with his pawns and counterattacked with a rook. Not once did he speak, not once did he dare to look at his opponent, for fear her eyes would start spinning again and the reality he had carefully reconstructed with the playing of the game would vanish with a single stolen glance.

The game turned. The black knight was vanquished and the threatening bishop disposed of. The king was vulnerable. The black queen could be captured. Tess moved, exposing her queen to further danger, but it was a silly move and for the first time since they had begun playing Jamie looked up at her. There were no spinning catherine wheels. Her eyes were dark and sad. Her hand moved up and touched his face. She drew near to him and kissed him softly on the lips. He remained passive, willing himself not to respond. If he kissed her, he felt he would be lost, damned and lost. She kissed him again, stronger now, then pulled back a little, but still held him with her eyes. The image of a sunflower suddenly appeared in his mind, and he felt that if he returned her kiss he could have anything he wanted, that, even if damned, he would never be lost again. The temptation which had lingered at the back of his tongue burst forth into his mouth, carrying with it a sweet illicit taste he had never known before.

He kissed her and his hands began pulling at her clothing. She raised her arms, allowing the T-shirt to slide free from her body. Then he was touching her, feeling the softness of her skin, smoother and more intoxicating than the silk he had imagined, and she responded to his touch. Her nipples hardened beneath his fingertips. He moved his hand lower and felt the wetness between her legs.

Now he had gone too far. He could not draw back and he knew she did not want him to. He carried her to the bed and entered her in a crazy rush of madness and abandonment. Sunflowers burst into bloom in his mind. If he was damned and lost then he welcomed it with open arms. Tess heaved against him, drawing him into her, grasping him so tightly he felt he would never be released. When he came it shattered him, sending his head spinning like the catherine wheels he had seen in her eyes.

When had he lost consciousness? This was the first thought that came to him when he opened his eyes, expecting to find Tess beside him. But the bed was empty, its sheets cool to his touch. He peered at the clock on the fridge. It was evening, barely seven o'clock. He rose from the bed and went to Frank's room in search of Tess.

Frank already had more than a few drinks under his belt when he opened the door. Jamie pushed past him into the room. Tess sat on the bed. Her eyes downcast, she refused to look at him.

"Come with me," he said. "I'll look after you."

"Heh, heh, heh," Frank said behind him. "The young doctor comes to claim his prize. What happened, did she let you fuck her?"

Jamie turned to face him, his eyes angry, his jaw quivering, unable to get the words out. Frank laughed again.

"You were wrong," Jamie said. "She likes to be touched. She wanted to be touched by me."

"You think you're the first one?" Frank said. "You think this hasn't happened before? That it won't happen again? You're a fool, young doctor, an absolute fool. I told you she didn't like to be touched because I wanted to save you from yourself."

Jamie stretched his arm towards the bed. "Tess," he said, "come with me. I promise I'll look after you."

"She won't go," Frank said. "She can't. You don't understand, man. You just don't understand. I made her. I created her. During re-entry, I was near death. I conjured her up from the air and the wind, brought her into being out of my imagination. I created her to help me survive. Death has that power. Without me she's nothing. She's *my* image of what she should be, not yours. You can't take her away. You can't. So you'd better leave and forget about us, forget you ever saw her."

But Jamie believed none of it. He wanted Tess, more than he had ever wanted anything, and he believed she wanted him. She was a street child Frank had made his captive, but he would release her, give her what she wanted, what she needed, as long as she stayed with him. And he was confident in this, confident she would come with him.

"All right," he said. "I'll leave. Tess will choose what she wants to do. But if you try to stop her from making that choice I'll come and wring your bloody neck."

"Fine words for a doctor," Frank said as Jamie left. "Fine fucking words for a young would-be-if-he-could-be bloody doctor."

As the evening stretched into night, Jamie lay on his bed, waiting for Tess to arrive as he was sure she would. But, when the knock sounded on his door and he opened it, he was disappointed to find Helen standing there, beaming a smile and cradling a bottle of wine in one arm.

"I know," she said, "you've got study to do, but after last night, Jamie, I just had to come and see you. That sunflower. I haven't been able to get it out of my mind all day."

And he could not refuse her entry, although there was nothing but Tess on his mind. Helen went straight to the kitchen, where she rummaged through the drawers until she found a corkscrew.

Jamie sat at the kitchen table, drinking the wine, as Helen wandered around his bedsitter.

"You played the game through," she said when her eyes spied the chessboard. "You reversed the position. The white queen is protected and the black queen is vulnerable. It must have been interesting, changing things that way, turning defeat into near-victory. Did you play with Frank?"

Jamie said nothing. He felt if he spoke he would reveal all, but he knew Helen would not understand, that he could not expect her to understand. He thought nobody would be capable of understanding the tumult of emotions he felt, as if he alone, of all the living and all the dead, was the first, the only one to feel the way he did. As if he had found something nobody else was looking for and, in that finding, had discovered a rare but unrecognizable jewel. He poured himself some more wine, did not offer to fill Helen's glass. She walked across to the table and filled it herself.

"You're very pensive," she said, "much more than your usual self. I get the impression I'm not wanted."

"No," he said, thinking, *Not unwanted, just not wanted.* There was a difference, a distinct difference. Of that he was sure. "No, it's not you. I'm just worried, worried about a lot of things."

"Like what? Tell me," Helen said, but as she did so the door opened and Tess entered.

Quiet as a cat, Tess wandered over to the bed and curled herself upon it. Her eyes, from the moment she walked in the door, were on Helen.

"You shouldn't be here," Jamie said. "I have to ask you to leave."

Helen followed Jamie's eyes across the room to where his gaze fell upon the empty bed.

"Look at me," she said. He looked up at her briefly, then down again, unable to face the questions in her eyes. He could feel his life changing, shifting away from him, as he moved from the past to the future, through a present that was intangible and confusing. To make that transition he would have to release everything. *Damned and lost.* Again those words came to him, but they were the words of pessimist, one who found fault with everything and danger in every shadow because they would not try to understand, would not dare to understand those things they had never known before. But the pessimist had not seen the sunflower, nor made love to Tess. Such joys were beyond them.

Helen placed her hand beneath his chin and forced his eyes to look into her own. She saw yellow sunflowers burning in the depths of his pupils, as brilliant as the sunflower that had come to her in her dreams. And that was enough for her. Something had happened. Everything had changed, and she knew she shouldn't have come. She kissed him gently on the forehead and left. He thought he would never see her again.

Jamie reconstructed Tess. He started by buying her clothes: jeans and shirts, nice underwear and new shoes, a jacket and a belt – all expenses paid on credit. He even coaxed her out of the boarding house, forced her to reveal herself, so she could have her hair cut and trimmed. And in return Tess opened his mind, or perhaps Jamie imagined she did, and revealed to him all the knowledge he already knew, so that the words of his lecturers and textbooks came alive. He did no further study, yet in his exams he wrote complex answers to complex questions, remembering everything he had ever learnt.

With his first appointment as a doctor, they moved from the boarding house across to the other side of the city, where Frank became a distant memory to them. In the months that followed, Jamie taught Tess to speak, and success followed success. He became a good doctor and began studying to become a specialist, something he had never dreamt of when he had started at medical school.

What Tess was and where she had come from were unknowns that rarely troubled Jamie. Her origins remained a question mark. For Tess herself they seemed to hold little interest. Before her life with Jamie, there had been Frank. This she admitted grudgingly at times, usually late at night when they lay in bed, but before Frank she seemed to have no memory, no knowledge of who she was or where she had been. At other times she would even try to deny the existence of Frank, as though that part of her life meant nothing to her, as though Frank had never existed and she had always been with Jamie and that would be the way it would forever remain. For his part, Jamie accepted Tess on her own terms and never once regretted the day he had become lost to her. If he had been forced to reveal his inner thoughts, he would have admitted his fantasies first, would have said Tess had come from Mars, as Frank had once said, because he enjoyed the exotic nature of the story. To some extent, it answered the question of the powers he believed she had, her ability to affect other people, to force strange dreams upon them, to open up their minds and release the knowledge that was held within. But in his heart of hearts he suspected the reality was more mundane. Tess *was* a street child with a damaged mind who had begun to rejuvenate under Frank's care, as limited as that was, and had blossomed and healed after Jamie had come into her life.

The years passed with hardly a wrinkle. Jamie's reputation grew as a doctor of skill and intelligence, as a man with a beautiful if somewhat eccentric wife who was impossible to beat at chess. Life with Tess was perfect, and Jamie enjoyed it as it came, never having any fears for the future and never once thinking of Frank who had brought Tess into his life.

Then one night Tess rose from the bed and said, "I must go now."

He believed it was a whim of hers, like the night he had driven her to the beach when he learned she had never seen the sea, or the day he had taken her to the mountains, in the dead of winter, so she could touch snow, a thing as mysterious to her as sand and ocean waves. Tonight she made him drive her across the city until they reached the place where they had first met.

The boarding house had changed little in the intervening years. It was a little more rundown than before and in need of a coat of paint, but stepping inside it was like stepping back in time. The same staircase was there, the same upstairs hallway, and the same stealth was needed to creep past Sylvia's downstairs apartment.

Tess led him up the stairs and opened the door into the room where he had first seen her. Here nothing had changed. Time had moved on yet everything had remained the same. Frank lay on the bed, the same man he had known before; a little thinner, a little weaker and more sickly-looking, but it was still the same Frank with his gray stubble crewcut and his dirty cotton singlets. The old man's eyes stared straight up at the ceiling. Déjà vu, Jamie felt, as if by crossing the city he was experiencing part of his life all over again.

Tess went to Frank's side, touched his forehead, then eased herself onto the bed, lay next to him and cradled his head.

"Tess," Frank said. "I knew you'd come back. I knew you wouldn't stay in his room for too long. I knew you'd couldn't leave me."

"It's been years, Frank," Jamie said. Tess flashed him a look that held the spark of old catherine wheels.

"Do something," she said. "He's dying. You're a doctor."

"What? You're talking now?" Frank said and almost managed a laugh. "He taught you that? What a clever man!"

Tess looked up at Jamie, eyes imploring. He moved across the room, took Frank's arm, felt the faint pulse at his wrist.

Frank blinked up at him. "The young doctor," he said.

"We need to get you to a hospital," Jamie said.

"No point," Frank said. "No point at all. I'd be dead before they got a chance to ship me back to the States. Cancer, it's too far gone. They wouldn't be able to do a thing."

"No," Tess said, "no, you can't die. You can't do this to me, not now..."

"Not now," Frank said, "not now when you've found happiness. That's how it goes, isn't it, Tess? Not now, when you left me, when you went away with him. We kept each other alive, girl. You knew that, you must have known, but still you left me, thinking you could survive on your own. Without me you're nothing. Without me, you *will be* nothing."

Tess stood up, moved away from the bed. Her head went back, pulling her neck taut. As her hair began to rise up from her shoulders, her eyes glazed over, revealing yellow sunflowers in their pupils. When she spoke her voice sounded as a far-off echo.

"He can't die, Jamie," she said. "You can't let him die. You mustn't."

Frank rolled his head on the pillow to look at her. "It's too late, Tess. You can't pretend any longer. You're not real. You never were. You're a link on a chain, a chain that's wrapped around someone's mind. It's my mind. It's my chain. Not his, not yours. You don't exist. You never did."

"No," Tess said. "It's not true."

"Stop it," Jamie said. "Please, Frank."

Frank looked up at Jamie. "But I *am* stopping it," he said. "I'm stopping it because I can't go on any longer. I'm dying, young doctor, and I know there's nothing you or anybody else can do about it. I've sat in this room for years, thinking about her, thinking about you, keeping her alive with my thoughts. It hasn't been you! No, not you! You don't have that power in your mind, that imagination, that creativity. You're too gloomy, too intense. You've never walked on Mars, never seen the things I've seen. You can't keep her alive without me. She's like a paper doll, something created out of next to nothing. During re-entry, I took a piece of paper, a pair of scissors, and I cut and fashioned her from my mind, then I breathed breath into her and the paper became flesh."

Tess moved to his side, her hair streaming wildly about her. "You can't die," she said. "I won't let you. Hear me! I won't let you!"

Frank shook his head slowly and closed his eyes.

"No!" Tess screamed.

Jamie took her arm. "Come away," he said. "There's nothing you can do."

She spun around. "Look at me," she said. "You want me, think of me the way you want me. Hold that image in your mind. See the sunflowers, like the sun, from it we draw our essence. Draw on that power, think of me, create me, believe in me."

"Tess," he said. "Stop this."

She backed away from him. Her hair collapsed, falling limp about her shoulders. She shook her head sadly from side to side.

"Frank was right," she said. "It is too late."

He reached out to grab her, to draw her near, to console her, but found his hands grasping at the air, until they clutched upon something soft and moist, the wilted petal of a sunflower. He looked down at Frank, like he had that first night, when he had breathed life back into the old man's lungs. Now Frank was dead.

Jamie's eyes fell off the edge of the bed, searching the space between the wardrobe and the wall, but there was nothing there, perhaps there never had been.

"Tess," he whispered into the empty room.

"Jamie." He heard his name spoken behind him, turned to see Sylvia standing in the doorway, still wearing the same old pink dressing-gown. Life switched and changed, realities cascaded and collapsed. In the corner of his mind a catherine wheel spun, sparked, then burnt out.

Jamie drove home, across the bridge, to the other side of the city, feeling like he was returning from a night call to one of his patients. In bed, he snuggled up close to his wife, seeking her warmth and pressing a gift into her hands.

"I took this from you years ago," he said.

Helen murmured sleepily and rolled away, clasping a sunflower petal to her breast.

New Writings in the Fantastic
Eclipsing Edd Vick

When she rapped at the door, the detective looked up from his battered paperback copy of *The Big Sleep* and growled, "It's open!"

She turned the knob and used the tiniest jot of her power to open the door. Wrenched off its hinges, the door sailed through his window and down to the street. "You're the investigator?" Her voice held a suggestion of twilight, filling his room with the rosy warmth of neon.

"You got it" – he consulted the book – "sister!"

She floated across the floor and hovered above his best chair. "Then you must help me."

"Yeah. Sure." He offered her a cigarette. She stared at it, then took it and began picking at it. "So, sweetheart, what can I do you for?" He frowned and moved the bartending guide further away on his desk.

"It's my husband." Beneath her misty veil, the moon stared at him in placid fury. Her eyes were seas, her mouth a pale crescent.

"Hmm," he hummed.

"I never see him any more."

"Some skirt gettin' plowed in your field, eh?" He pocketed the book. "I get a *per diem*."

"Will this be enough?"

"Sister, that'll keep me on your payroll a century or so. Let's go." When he got to the door, he found the moon rising through his shattered window. Cursing, he took a step, then another, and jumped to ride her into the sky. Flexing his fingers into claws, he thought he could stand to do just this forever.

"First, I investigate," he growled.

"And how do you do that?"

"Give me a list of the places your husband frequents."

"Why? What would you do with it?"

"And a list of the dames he knows."

"Just look in the phone book. He sees everyone, every day."

"Then I shadow him, and catch him in the act."

"Will he stop? If you do catch him?"

"Sure, baby. Sure."

The detective took himself away with his camera and his notebook and his gun. He followed the curvature of the earth until he found the sun. Hiding behind a satellite, he brought out his camera and snapped a quick shot. He suspected he should have brought faster film. Sunglasses, too.

All that day he shadowed his client's husband. The sun plodded his stately course from horizon to horizon, favoring no one. He shone on the just and the unjust, it seemed to the detective.

Then night fell, but the detective was not there to see it, so intent was he on following the sun and snapping more shots. Forty days and forty more days he followed, until finally he stopped to let the moon catch up.

She was dark. She said she always felt dark, eclipsed, without the sun's gaze. The detective pitied the emptiness of her... and used the darkness to develop his photos. When they showed nothing, the moon wept bitter rocks.

"Listen, sister. The guy's clean. He never even looked sideways at another woman. I dunno why he's giving you the cold shoulder, but it's not because he's got a frail on the side."

"It's me, I know it is."

"OK, doll. OK. Dry up the rockworks. Let's go back to my office. I got a copy of *Consolation for Dummies* there."

"What seems to be the problem?"

"I told you, my husband avoids me."

"How does this make you feel?"

"Dark, sad, empty. Like I'm nothing, a mere reflection of him."

"And how does that make you feel?"

"Like his negation. As if were we to meet we would cancel each other out. Maybe he knows that."

"OK, how does that make—?"

"Is that all you do? Ask the same question over and over again?"

"Sorry." The detective turned a page. "Trial separation? No. Couples therapy? Mmm, no." He let the pages flip past his thumb, then set the book on its spine atop his desk. When he let go, it fell open. He spoke again after reading. "Listen. I think it's time for you to move on. You were attracted to him once, sure, but it's over. Done with. Kaput." He spread his hands out, palms down. "Leave him."

"I did not hire you to advise me. You were to help me." She reached into her purse, put her hand on something inside.

The detective felt the attraction, the tidal force pulling him into her orbit. Hair sprouted. Fangs grew. "You *will* help me," she said.

He felt his heart heaving at the inside of his chest.

"All right," he snarled. "Back off, sister. I'll take another run at it."

A sliver, a fingernail of light, glinted at him from her face. "Thank you," she said. When she pulled her hand out, it was holding a slim volume. She placed it carefully on a shelf far from his desk, but not so far he couldn't read the word "garou" on its spine.

"No way," he said. "That's what I should have said," he said. "Take your money back. Leave me alone. Stop stealing my heart and turning me into a wolf.

"That's what I should have said," he said.

The detective slouched over the horizon into darkness. Not as surprised as he expected to be, he hurried forward to find the great dead orb. Chalk marks already in place, and the coroner scraping bits of this and that from walls and roofs and Mercury and Venus.

"It was murder," he heard, and "Solly never saw it coming."

"I doubt that," said the detective to himself. "She's either one thing or the other: either victim or victor."

He felt tired.

She was dark, invisible, when he returned to her. He knew where she would be: a hundred and eighty degrees removed from the scene. Eclipsed.

Weak. Needing his strength.

He caught her up in his arms and carried her into his office. Put her on the couch.

"He's dead," she said, and it was not a question.

The detective nodded. "He was keeping you at a distance. He knew he was going down. He didn't want you involved."

"You did it for me."

"I–? Did what?"

"You never remember what you do," she said, "at night."

He snapped on his desk lamp. Its sterile cone of light lit no more than a parabola of desk.

She struggled up. Her hand fell on one of his books, and she pushed it into the light. "*Cosmos*," she read. "Why not *The Sun Also Rises*?"

"You're mistaking the title for the territory," he replied. "Pamplona's not hot enough for me."

"Curious, that I'd find the one item I most needed. You think big, too."

"Bigger than the both of us." The detective felt a glow eat his heart, a warmth a heat a burning that intensified until he was the source. His heart was no longer alone in its pull toward hers. He could feel his mass pulling at her, could see her expression melting from bleak comprehension to sour acceptance.

"Not so curious," he said. "Call it inevitable."

He spared not a look for the tools of his trade. The camera. The notebook.

The gun.

As the building around them melted away he rose and she with him. Together they rode into the sky, no longer separated by the planet between them.

New Writings in the Fantastic
The Career of Edward Northam Naomi Alderman

In the early years of the 1890s, as is well known, a young artist named Edward Northam came to prominence. His road to success had been a peculiarly rocky one. A younger son of an ancient English family, he attended a minor public school and an obscure Oxford college before vanishing from the London scene almost entirely. Northam was determined to become an artist and had the independent income, if not the talent, to pursue his dream. He drifted across Europe, in search of inspiration for what he called his artistic muse but his friends and family called an insufferable waste of time. Northam spent ten years on this pursuit, producing hundreds of canvases, but found no market for his work. He became increasingly depressed, although a certain stubbornness of temperament kept him at the work for which he was so unsuited.

Then, in an instant, he was discovered. A small gallery owner on the Rive Gauche took him up, and his work began to sell with remarkable swiftness. The galleries of London, Paris and Berlin vied to host his exhibitions. Within a year, the world of art seemed to have no words on its lips but "Edward Northam." Publications that had previously taken little interest in fine art began to devote articles to his works. It is said that Mrs. Langtry performed a song about his paintings at several private parties. This much is well known and can be reviewed in several excellent biographies.

My story is a little more obscure, however. It was during this period of what has been called Northam-fever that I first encountered the artist's work. I do not hesitate to confess that I had never taken notice of art. I have an interest in a small but highly regarded private bank in the City, and it is there I spend most of my days. I rarely read any paper but *The Times*, and I had not paid one jot of attention to the murmurings about this great new artist. However, a business acquaintance, a writer on art for a weekly paper, insisted that I see his latest exhibition, "so daring, so brilliant." Thus it was that, around two years after Edward Northam first came to the attention of the public, I finally saw some of the hallowed works of the great genius. I hated them, instantly.

All Northam's paintings seemed to me a debasement of the very word "art." Certainly, I am a mere man of business, but even to my untrained eye it was clear these were just daubings. To the amazement of my friend, I became eloquent, even heated, on the subject. I have never experienced such an outpouring of criticism as I did (and do) when viewing the artistic works of Edward Northam.

Such was my fervor that my journalist acquaintance instantly asked me to write a review of the show to accompany his own piece. It was impossible, he said, to find anyone who had anything but praise for

Northam's work – my opinions (though, as he thought, clearly misguided) would add colour to the paper. I wrote on Northam, and only on Northam, from that day on. I have never been remotely interested in other art; but his paintings excited in me such a violent distaste that it could not but be expressed. My reviews became rather popular, in a queer sort of way, and, since no one else showed any sign of sharing my opinion, I did not feel that I was doing Northam any harm.

It was thus that matters stood until a certain day in August, 1896. I can recall the evening quite clearly. I had dined at my club, and at 10pm was sitting in my study, reading the paper and thinking of bed, when my man informed me that Edward Northam was calling to see me. I confess I was a little nervous. The lateness of the hour did not suggest a pleasant social call, and I had given his latest exhibition – some childlike studies of feet and hands – a scathing review in that week's *Conversationalist*. However, if the man wished to protest, he would have to be faced eventually. I asked Jamieson to show him in.

The man who entered my study did not seem aggressive. He walked in, hands in his pockets, looking about him a little nervously. I put out my hand and he shook it. We both declared how delighted we were finally to meet the other. I was surprised at his youth – he could not have been more than forty; I had somehow been expecting an older man. He did appear a little strained, though: his skin was pale, his dark hair unruly, and there was a certain redness to his eyes. I invited him to sit and he did so, still looking around him. He remarked suddenly:

"Rather dull place you have here, Masterson – no paintings."

I did not know what reply to make to this. To state honestly that I had no particular love of painting would be to invite an argument about my fitness to be a critic. Instead, I offered him a sherry and took one myself. He refused and looked about him once more. I made some remark about the fineness of the weather. Northam sat silently. After a long moment, he turned to face me, jerking his whole body round in a twitching motion.

"You don't like my work, do you?"

I was taken off my guard.

"No," I replied. "It is not to my taste."

"It is not to your taste," he repeated, seeming to savor the words. "It is not to your taste. Do you trust your taste, Masterson?"

I did not know where this conversation was leading, but I tried to be placatory. "Every man trusts his taste, I think. But it is only taste – each of us enjoys something different, do we not? Your work has many admirers."

He seemed to consider that for a moment before responding.

"Yes, my work is admired. But somehow I cannot seem to care for anyone's opinion but yours. What do you say to that?"

What I wished to say was that the hour was late, that my opinions of his art were of no import, that I had not asked for this meeting. I replied:

"It is natural that you should become interested in the opinions of your critic, especially when praise for your work is otherwise so uniform, but the truth is that I stand against the multitude, Northam." I smiled. "I have made a pleasant little secondary career of being clearly wrong in my assessment of you and your painting."

At that, Northam rose violently from his chair, almost knocking it to the ground, and began to pace the room. I must confess that I was concerned some unpleasantness might ensue. He rounded on me and declared:

"Do you wish to know the truth, Masterson? The truth is that you are the only man alive who can see my work for what it is. You see clearly; the others see only illusion. You, when you say my work is trash, that I no more deserve my place in the Royal Academy than a menagerie-monkey, you speak the truth."

I believe at this point I may have protested, not wishing to take back my words but, rather, pained to hear a man stoop to such abasement. He made an impatient gesture.

"No, no. You are the only one who can see the truth; I shall not allow you to lie. My work is trash, and all the world judges it wrongly. Shall I tell you how it happened? You can't imagine how I have longed to tell someone, but I have always been afraid to do so. Afraid they would not believe me. Afraid they would. Sometimes I think I am going mad, you know."

At this, he gave me such a ghastly grin that I shudder now, in the quiet peace of my study, to think of it.

"She was not at all as you read of them in books, you know, not at all. You hear of them being beautiful, you see, clever, malign and beautiful. She was rather plain, and I knew from the moment I saw her that she was stupid. She had the vapid look of a cow, but also that rather cunning air which stupid people sometimes have."

He broke off, suddenly, and gave a hideous cackle.

"Not as stupid as I was, though, eh!"

I managed to get out a few quick words, trying to be calming, for it was clear the man was in a state of nerves which would soon make him physically unwell:

"Now, now old man. Try to calm yourself. We've all had our troubles with women. Lord knows I've had a few, but the thing is not to pay them too much mind. Now, what's the difficulty? Is she married? You would not be the first."

I put a friendly hand on his shoulder, but he pushed me away. He gave a brief derisive laugh, then seemed to collect himself for a moment. He breathed deeply and turned a face to me which was more calm than I had hoped.

"Masterson," he said, "I wish to explain myself to you." He drummed his fingers nervously on the tabletop. "I must explain the thing to you, and once I have done so, you will understand why it must be you and no other." He took a long breath. "Five years ago, I encountered a genie."

He must have seen me start in my chair, and indeed I feared the fellow might be nearing some sort of mental crisis. But he began to speak so calmly that he was almost unrecognizable as the near-deranged individual who had entered my house a short while before.

"No, no, Masterson, I must tell my story and you must listen. For what I have given you, you owe me that at least. Five years ago, I encountered a genie. This is a rather astonishing thing, especially for men of science such as we."

"Did she...? Did she live in a lamp?" I managed to stutter out, half-hoping to laugh the fellow out of his delusion. Northam looked at me almost gratefully.

"No, she did not. She lived in a small enamel box. You may recall that I spent much of the winter of 18– in various opium dens, hoping to capture the life I found there. The Wyckham Gallery recently exhibited some of the paintings I made during that time. Universally acclaimed as shockingly honest, though you, I believe, called the works 'execrable daubings.'"

Northam gave a sudden sharp laugh and I looked down, not knowing what answer to make to this.

"You were correct, of course, Masterson, but no matter, no matter. Let me see... in the course of that winter, I met several interesting and unusual characters, including Lord Q___ " – he named a scion of a Tory family of some renown. "He had traveled widely in the East and had picked up the love of the pipe and hookah there. He was wild-eyed and, though only in his forties, could have been taken for seventy. He had allowed his beard to grow long, in the Oriental fashion, and his nails were yellowed and curled. He was full of ravings and fantastic tales of strange monsters and mythical journeys. You may understand, therefore, that I paid little heed to his claim to have a woman in a box, although he made it often.

"I came to know the fellow tolerably well. I made some studies of him, and in return gave him a few shillings. As it happened, I arrived at his usual spot one day, and found him at a low ebb. He owed a great deal of money, and was unable even to pay the interest the rogues claimed was due. They threatened to cast him onto the streets, and he feared he would be left utterly destitute. He begged me for money, clinging to my clothes in the most pitiful manner. I would gladly have given the fellow a few guineas, simply to stop his pleading, but he was struck with a sudden fancy, as opium-smokers often are, that I must have something for my money – it must be some kind of bargain. From inside his robe, he drew a slim, black enamel box, decorated with golden flowers, and tied round about with several firmly knotted ribbons.

"'This,' he declared, 'is the finest jewel of the East. It is without price. It is without equal. The secrets to your heart's desire lie within this box.'

"I examined it without much enthusiasm. Frankly, I had no interest in this bauble, which I could not conceive had any value. Although the workmanship was fine, it was clearly old and had been damaged by the passing years. The enamel was chipped in several places, and the wood had warped. But he was in need. I gave him twenty pounds for it, and felt I had performed an act of charity. I tried to untie the ribbons there and then, but Lord Q___ prevented me, wrapping his gnarled hands around mine and entreating me to open it only in private. The man pleaded so pathetically that I promised to open the box only when I had reached my own chambers. As it was, I spent several hours on business in town before I returned home. The box entirely slipped my mind until the evening, when I was relaxing with my pipe. Immediately, I retrieved it from the pocket of my greatcoat and, taking up a letter-opener from my desk, cut through the ribbons and opened the box.

"My suspicions of Lord Q___'s mental state were confirmed when I found that the box was but an empty compartment lined with pink and cream satin. But, at once, I caught the trace of an aroma which I later came to associate with *her* appearance – a smell at once acrid and spicy, as though of some exotic dish – burned. I looked at the box in bewilderment. Then, a slight noise in the room made me look up. She was standing there, a woman. A rather stupid, cruel-looking woman, dressed in a sort of pajama-like satin affair. A genie.

"You will believe me when I tell you, Masterson, that, in the five years since that moment, I have made genies an object of special study. I believe that very few enslaved genies still exist. It is possible that mine is the last remaining. Certainly, the secret of how to snare these creatures died a long time ago, and it may be that all the others have been freed by grateful masters. According to the legends, of course, that is the only wish which the genies will grant without in some way perverting its aim. I believe, too, that it is a by-product of whatever esoteric arts were used to capture them in the first place that each 'master' receives but three wishes. As far as I can ascertain, there is no theoretical limit to these creatures' power; perhaps the ancient magicians of old decided in their wisdom to limit each man's access to it, or perhaps they were able to bind the genies only thus and no further. In any case, that is what I received: three wishes."

"Just a moment, Northam," I interjected. "Are you really to have me believe that you found a genie in a box and received three wishes? Why, the notion is too fantastic to be countenanced!"

Northam sighed. Whatever nervous energy had inspired and enabled him to make his way to my door seemed to be ebbing. Yet, the man had an air of sincerity to him that could not be denied.

"Yes, Masterson. That is exactly what I would have you believe, for it is the truth. Five years ago, or thereabouts, I found a genie in a box and received three wishes. Could you but meet her, you would have no further doubts." He chuckled a little. "I have half a mind to engineer such a meeting, in fact. You would doubtless find each other excellent company; you are both so literal-minded. In any case, to return to the matter in hand: The genie herself is of little interest. Her face is cruel, her manner throughout our acquaintance has been insolent in the extreme and her conversation perfunctory. She has always given the impression that she despises me, and, although I have made many attempts, has never engaged in any discussion regarding her origins or powers. On that first day, she offered me three wishes rather as a shop-girl might offer one a soiled pair of gloves. But, like any man, I did not refuse."

He sighed again, a deep, long breath, almost a moan.

"To understand what I did, you must attempt to enter into my state of mind at that moment. As you know, I had spent ten years in the corners and byways of Europe, painting, always painting. I was – ha! at that time! – fairly well convinced of my own talent, but I had received such constant rejection that my spirit was almost crushed. Every gallery turned me away, every critic whom my position could influence to view my work considered it to be without merit. I had become a monomaniac, Masterson. All that I wished, all that I desired, was that a single work of mine should be shown in a gallery of good reputation, or purchased by an influential patron, or praised in a widely read journal. Just one such success, I felt, would buoy me up for another ten years of work.

"I did not act hastily, however. I spent two days in contemplating other wishes I might make. I could wish for money – but what would that do for me? I already had all the money I needed – more would not make me any more content. Power? I could become Prime Minister, or King! More than that – I could become ruler of the world. But all these prospects, while interesting, held little thrill for me. I could imagine that I would quickly tire of ruling the world, and that I would not do so especially well. Fantastic powers, then? I could wish to be able to fly, to move items with the power of my mind, as music-hall entertainers claim to do. But what would I be but a music-hall entertainer? I would become a freak. No, there was but one wish to interest me.

"After two days of thought, I opened the box once more. The genie stood before me, and I made my wish: that my paintings, both past and future, should be held in the highest esteem by all who saw them, that anyone who saw one of my works should see in them all the qualities they would wish to see in the finest masterpiece.

"The genie, as I recall, curled her mouth into a half smile. I thought she was recognizing that I had defeated her; that she would not be able to turn this wish against me. She looked at me for a moment, then asked:

"'You are sure this is what you wish?'

"She was trying to trick me, I was convinced. 'I am certain.'

"'You wish for all others to adore your paintings?'

"'In essence.'

"'Very well, then, it is so.'

"She had not made any motion, or cast any spell – I must confess that I was a little unconvinced. My face must have shown this, for she looked at me sullenly:

"'Do you wish to test me? Take one of your paintings, then. Thrust it in the face of any passer-by in the street, and you will see that I speak the truth.'

"She stepped again toward her box and was gone.

"Thus began probably the most wonderful period of my life. Acting on the genie's words, I took three or four of my canvases to a small but exclusive gallery. The owner adored them. The public adored them. They were all bought within a day of being put on display, and there were orders for another thirty. Within a month I had sold a large proportion of the canvases I had produced over the previous ten years, even those I considered myself to be failures. I kept back only the very cream, in anticipation of a show. As you will know, the show was an enormous success. The press had nothing but praise for me; I was invited to lecture at the Slade, St. Martin's, the Royal Academy. There was talk of a knighthood..."

Northam's voice slowly faded away, as though the act of describing these triumphs was sapping him of vital energy. He stared down at his hands. I felt that perhaps he was deriving some benefit from telling the story of his instant success. It was only natural that he might find his rapid rise rather difficult to accept, that he might need to go over the events again and again. Perhaps I could help – for I knew the story from this point:

"Yes, it was then that I first saw one of your shows," I began, tentatively.

He looked up and gave a short barking laugh. I stopped, uncertain of the best course of action.

"Go on," he urged. "I've often wondered how you came to see my works first. Had you seen them before, and loved them, or were you the only person in the world who had never seen 'a Northam'?"

I recounted, briefly, the tale of how blind luck had brought me into contact with his work for the first time at the very moment that I was also in a position to share my opinions with the world. Northam listened intently, and when I had finished threw back his head in the first healthy laughter I had seen him give.

"So, you were never a critic!" he exclaimed. "For some reason I had presumed you would be." He sighed. "You are a banker, are you?"

I confessed that I was.

"With no knowledge of art, no expertise at all?"

"None."

He barked out another laugh.

"And had you ever had the urge to analyze a piece of art, to criticize it, to write about it, before?"

"Never."

"Then, my friend" – and with this he leaned towards me conspiratorially – "I have given you a greater gift than I thought. You and I will always be bound together by this."

I hesitated to ask him what he meant, for fear of sending him back to melancholy, but he saw that I did not understand his words.

"I will continue with my story and all will become clear, my friend. All will become clear..." And, chuckling to himself, he continued:

"I had reached a peak of fame. Only a banker, it seems, concerned purely with the flow of Her Majesty's coin, could fail to know of my work. I was, in general, full of delight to hear the praise I had hardly dared to imagine heaped upon me. I had, in some moments, almost convinced myself that the genie had done nothing – that I had simply been lucky to find a gallery owner who recognized my skill and that all which had happened since then had been natural.

"But there were times when I was troubled. The adulation I received began to seem harsh, hysterical. Every time I unveiled a new painting there was *no criticism* – can you understand that? Not one word. I will tell you honestly, Masterson, it came to gnaw at me. I remember a show I had in Brussels – Sir ___ " – he named an elderly artist of great standing – "overflowed with simpering praise for my work. I wanted to shake him, or knock him to the ground.

"I began to become obsessed with the idea of finding an unbiased observer, who could give me his opinion of my work, so that I would know, for certain, which of the praise was genuine and which derived from my wish, where my weaknesses lay, how I could become a better artist. Once this notion had taken possession of me it would not let me rest. And so I summoned the genie to make my wish. She appeared amused when I told her what I wanted.

"'You wish for the truth? You have wished for the entire world to be deceived, but now you wish for the truth? Why, Northam, do you think there is truth to be had? This person's opinion, that one's, perhaps this is all an artist's reputation consists in. Why do you not wish that you yourself would be convinced, and then you would not need any truth?'

"But I was adamant. I wanted to know – I, of all people, should be able to know. Thinking now about her words, I wonder if she was not right. Perhaps I should have wished to be taken in by the deception myself – to be dull and lifeless and lacking in curiosity. To believe my own lie. But I did not. I wished that one man in all the world should be able to see the truth of my work, and that I should know this man's opinion.

"Again, it did not seem to me that the genie had done anything to grant my wish, but two or three days later, walking past a news vendor, I had the sudden whim to buy a copy of a certain paper. And when I found your piece on my exhibition, I knew that you were the one, that you spoke the truth. I remember what you wrote in that first piece: 'Art is a combination of technique and emotion. If Northam's emotions were sincerely felt, his technique could be forgiven; if his technique were strong, he could succeed without passion. As it is, his work has nothing to recommend it other than the strength of his name.' It was all I had feared and more. My despair, since reading that first article, has grown day by day."

Northam began to speak more slowly now. The energy seemed utterly gone from him, and I feared he might topple from his chair at any moment. He looked up at me, blankly.

"Well, Masterson, you have the truth of it now. My wishing has not done me as much good as I hoped, although it seems to have opened your eyes to the world of art, at least. I came here tonight to lay my final hope to rest. I have read your pieces, all of them, in great detail. You pour nothing but scorn and contempt upon all my artistic endeavors. You find no redeeming features in my work. You appear to feel that I should never have been allowed to put brush to canvas. But, as I sank into despair, it came to me to wonder – you are a journalist, writing for a magazine. Have you exaggerated your opinions in any way? Have you, perhaps, concealed a grain of praise that your writing might be more forceful, more appealing? Is there anything you can tell me?"

I swear now, by all that is good and holy, that I wanted to praise him. This poor, broken man needed comfort now that only I could give. I wished, with all my heart, to praise one painting, one angle, one brushstroke even. I opened my mouth aiming to speak some kind of platitude, using only my banker's knowledge of art, but what I said, in a level tone, was:

"Northam, you are no artist. Your pictures have no merit. You could work for a thousand years and still you would lack that which you need – were it not for your wish, your art would never have succeeded, no matter the fashion, no matter the viewers."

Northam buried his head in his hands at my words, and let out one or two low sobs. He looked up at me, and said, in a voice which was almost a whisper:

"Then it is ended. I needed nothing more than this. Thank you, Masterson, for your honesty, and for listening to my tale."

He stood up, making to leave the room, but I had regained control of my own voice by this point, and said:

"But, where do you intend to go? What will you do? Will you reverse the wish?"

His eyes were infinitely sad.

"That is how these tales are supposed to end, is it not? Remember the tale of the poor woodcutter, who was granted three wishes? He wished for a sausage. His wife was angry with him and, in a rage, he wished the sausage onto his wife's nose, and was then forced to use the last wish to rid her of the sausage, and so had nothing. I believe the genies wish us to have nothing. But they shall not have me so easily. My fame may be based on a lie, but that fame will endure. No, I shall find another wish. I shall find a wish more to my taste. I shall search myself and I shall search the world until I find that which will truly please me, and I shall then wish for it. I have been given a great gift, Masterson, a great gift. I shall not let it slip from me."

"But, Northam," I protested, "have you not done with wishing now? It has not brought you happiness. It has brought you close to madness. Why not let it be over?"

In answer he simply smiled and, before I could stop him, marched to the door, opened it, and raced out into the dark.

I passed a restless night, thinking over the fantastic story Northam had told me. My mind came back again and again to the convictions I held about his art. It was unthinkable to me that I should hold any other opinions. The very sight of his artworks repelled me. But whence did these impressions emerge? I tried, again and again, to follow my own mind, from the consideration of one of his artworks, to the formation of opinions. It seemed very like they were coming from myself alone – I felt under no one's control. I examined a daguerreotype of one of his most obnoxious efforts – a still life of a bowl of peaches. The fruits were nothing more than two swirls of orange paint – there was no texture to them. The light seemed to be coming from at least a dozen angles; the table on which the bowl rested would hardly have been able to stand upright had it really existed, so skewed was the perspective of the piece. These thoughts arose in me quite naturally as I looked at the painting; they followed one after another as thoughts of my work in the bank would have done.

I then took down a book sent to me by my artistic friend; prints of the works of Van Gogh. I opened it at a random page – a picture of a pair of boots. I gazed at the picture for five minutes or so, and all I could think was that they looked like they needed a jolly good clean, or possibly to be thrown out. Nothing more. I thought for a long while about that, as the endless night wore on. I slept a little, sitting in my chair, and jerked awake, suddenly. I jotted a few notes, which have become the basis of this account. Finally, though it seemed a lifetime in coming, the sun rose, pale and watery, casting a thin light over the city.

At 7am – which, though not a cordial hour was at least a decent one – I took a carriage over to Northam's lavish townhouse on the other side of St. James's. The maidservant, a little overwhelmed by receiving visitors so early, informed me that her master was "not at 'ome." I called again at midday and again at 4pm. The answer remained the same, although the anxiety with which it was delivered increased on each occasion.

For most people in England, I dare say, the circumstances of the disappearance of Edward Northam will remain vivid in the memory. The servants, questioned by the police, said that their master had left the house in some agitation at around 9pm, had returned at around midnight, entered his private study, and left ten minutes later. They had not seen him again. The house was searched, and it was found that he had taken no clothing nor a traveling bag. The safe in his study, however, was found to be empty, though his servants could not say what it had contained.

As the last man to see him alive, I was questioned myself. Although all suspicion of my own involvement was cleared early on, I remained interested in the case, and Northam's family were, I think, glad of my support. For their sakes, I chose not to divulge to the police the substance of my conversation with Northam that night. I simply said that he wished to discuss my opinion of his work, that we talked, rather than argued, and that there was no anger between us when we parted.

Around a year later, I was privileged to be allowed to peruse the police reports of the investigation. As is the method of modern policing, every item in Northam's house was documented and recorded, but no black lacquer box was ever found. I noted with interest that the study was found to be perfumed with a lingering acrid scent, perhaps of burned spices, which did not dissipate for several days.

Ten years have passed since then, and there has been no sign of the

Honourable Edward Northam. Although the case is still officially open, I believe that the police rather tend to the conviction that Northam chose to end his own life, suffering from some form of artistic self-doubt for which I certainly cannot be held responsible.

Some, I hear, believe that he "faked" his own disappearance, in order to increase the value of his works. Whatever the truth, it is clear that his continued absence has had this effect. The fame of Edward Northam continues to increase. That painting of a bowl of peaches recently sold at Sotheby's for close to one thousand pounds, and there seems to be no ceiling to the estimates of the future value of even the smallest of his paintings. His art decorates the finest drawing-rooms in Europe; the Louvre, the National Gallery, the Uffizi and the Metropolitan all own examples. He is studied by young painters, by art historians. Several books have already been written; more will surely follow.

There is less demand for my thoughts on Edward Northam now, although certain broadsheets will call on me for "one of my humorous pieces" when Northam retrospectives are organized by major galleries. If Edward Northam, as seems certain, becomes known as the finest artist of his century, I may find a footnote in history as the misguided critic who detested his work. For it becomes increasingly clear to me that, although Northam is gone, the effects of his final wish live on as potently as ever. His work is trash. I know it plainly. But, loudly as I may speak this truth, it seems that not one person will ever agree with me.

New Writings in the Fantastic
11:11 Jamie Shanks

There was almost a physical tug as Zoe was yanked, roughly, back to reality. Reality was a thin sheaf of faxed news releases being placed on her desk by one of the clerical staff. The clerics, Zoe liked to call them.

"For you," the cleric said politely, and then disappeared around the filing cabinet, her stout legs whisking furiously back and forth beneath her. Zoe peeled the tips of her fingers from the phone where they had been lightly resting, leaving behind a series of fading oval prints from the warmth of her skin.

She blinked as she fine-tuned her reception. What had she been doing? As always, there was the automatic rewinding of her memory, like a tape, as she carefully traced her mental steps backward.

She had been wondering what her super-power was.

It was ten minutes ago. "Were you aware," Newman had asked her, "that I have a super-power?"

"No, I was not," Zoe replied in a deliberately false tone of lavish interest.

"Oh, yes," he said. He was leaning back in his chair, legs crossed, an agricultural feature article half-written on his computer. He wasn't even trying to look busy. He was a good enough reporter that he could afford not to bother with pretenses, but he also seemed surrounded by an almost palpable forcefield that deflected criticism of any sort originating from positions of authority. He was slightly younger than Zoe and still warm from the college oven that emitted racks of fresh journalism students into the real world. He would probably do another year or two out here in the sticks, perhaps less, and then jump straight to one of the big dailies. She found him quite annoying. At the same time, she was faintly glad he was around.

She gazed at him expectantly.

"Everybody has one," he said after a theatrical pause he deemed suitable. "I'm serious. I don't mean flying or X-ray vision or whatever, obviously. It could be something like never being late for anything, ever. Or having perfect hair no matter what. Or always having the perfect comeback exactly when you need a witty retort."

"Or getting sucked into idiotic conversations."

He snapped his fingers. "Witty retort, see? Perfect timing. Do you always do that?"

"No."

"Then that's not your super-power. It'll be something else. Everybody's got one, even if they don't know it."

"Hey, I've got one," blurted Chase, a husky young man sitting at an adjoining desk which faced them both. It was a huge mahogany creation of monstrous dimensions that was probably older than the three reporters combined. "Yeah," he added as though reassuring them, talking around the phone receiver jammed between his cheek and shoulder as he put a few hundred more ticks on his life's clock of total time spent in the abyss of being on hold. "Cigarette smoke. If someone lights up a butt in a room, it doesn't matter where I'm sitting. The smoke goes straight into my eyes." With a pen he traced a line in the air from the tip of an imaginary cigarette. "Not just, you know, around or in clouds or whatever. Straight into my eyes. Never fails."

For a brief instant Zoe sensed that Newman was unsure if Chase was cramping his style deliberately, unknowingly, or was actually contributing in a useful way.

"See, there you go," Newman said, apparently deciding on the latter option, turning back to Zoe. "I had a friend in college who was a persuader. He could convince anyone of just about anything. He was just irresistible."

"That's charisma," Zoe said, checking through her day planner. She had to leave soon to do an interview.

"That was his super-power," Newman corrected her.

"All right, then. What's yours?"

"Well," he said slowly, "something strange always happens at 11:11."

She stared at him. "At 11:11? You mean, at eleven minutes after eleven o'clock?"

"Yeah."

"Something strange happens, like, to you?"

"Yeah. I'll have a strange experience," he said, waving his hands slowly in the air and wiggling his fingers to illustrate general mysteriousness.

"Uh huh. Which one, morning or night?"

"Doesn't matter," Newman said thoughtfully. "If I happen to note the time at exactly 11:11, something happens. If I miss it, nothing. It took me a long time to pin it down."

Zoe laced her fingers together on her desk and leaned closer. She glanced up at the fluorescent lights embedded in the ceiling tiles and then back at him. "That's the dumbest super-power I ever heard of," she said, letting a laugh escape from her throat. "I mean, no offense, but it's kind of useless. Aren't you disappointed?"

Newman smiled and shrugged. "Could be worse."

And then she had grudgingly taken the bait and asked what sort of strange and mysterious things transpired at 11:11 – or, more accurately, at 11:11 when he happened to know it was 11:11. And he had described some examples, and then asked her what, or what she thought, her own super-power was...

Zoe woke up to her surroundings once more, catching up to the present again like a trundling wave overtaking a surfer.

She was in her car driving to the interview, which was with a self-described "fulfillment counsellor" who was in town to conduct a day-long series of seminars on reaching one's full potential, realizing one's goals, making dreams reality and blah blah blah. Zoe had imagined there would be a modest turnout of locals seeking enlightenment and self-empowerment by way of spending forty dollars, and she was not wrong. She slipped into the rented hotel banquet room and quietly worked her way around the periphery, snapping a few unobtrusive photos for the story.

As the opening session was wrapping up Zoe took a few moments to jot down some questions, trying to anticipate possible gaps of useful information in the story she would write later. She was asking them a few moments later.

"It's about potential," the man was explaining emphatically, trying to make every second count in what was essentially a plug. He had taken out a sizeable ad in the paper, and in return was getting a bit of gratuitous coverage. It rankled with Zoe, since she felt she had at least an idea of what journalistic integrity should be. But at the end of the day it was the nature of things in a small pond, and she accepted it with a degree of stoicism that had seen her through much of her life.

"For some people," he was saying – as her pen whispered on the paper a detached part of Zoe thought he really should have said "many people" from a marketing perspective, but it didn't matter – "it's more comfortable, or more satisfying, to maintain a potential rather than living up to it or fulfilling it. Because a potential is always there, and it's like a drug. Right? Someone can always imagine what it could be, and it can be different each time depending on what their needs are at a given moment, and it can be whatever you want. You can live off it. It's comforting. But when you actually make the choice, when you take action, and you reach that potential" (here he actually clawed a handful of air for emphasis; later, as she got behind the wheel of her car, Zoe would realize despairingly that his recent audience had probably eaten this stuff up and come back for seconds) "it's gone and you don't have that security blanket any more. Those possibilities that were so easy and fun to imagine are now gone, and they might not have turned out exactly, precisely the way you envisioned they would have, or could have. And..."

Blah, blah, blah. It's the way it is in the pond, she kept telling herself. It was like a martial art, or a religious philosophy. The Way of The Pond. Om.

She was already writing the lede in her head and was thinking about Newman. It was clear he wanted to sleep with her. How tacky. She thought about the incident in the darkroom some weeks ago, where they had been choosing prints together for a sports-section photo essay, alone, and for a second he had seemed about to try something. She had prepared herself to crack him a good one. But nothing had happened, and the moment had passed and vanished. It was probably all in her head. He had made a comment about the light, and she'd said something about being able to see well enough, and there was the sudden sensation of expectancy like a static charge about to go off with a pop in one's innards, and then nothing. In a way it was too bad – she had kind of wanted to hit him. She visualized doing it and smiled. Perhaps if she had used a different inflection in what she'd said about being able to see in the dim red light, he would have seen an opening. What exactly had she said?

Zoe caught herself repeating the words out loud with different variants of emphasis, analyzing them like an actor rehearsing for a bit part. She realized she was easing her car into the parking lot beside the long, flat gray newspaper building. She felt a flash of embarrassment until she confirmed that no one had been standing around close enough to see or hear her.

She checked the clock as she walked to her desk and sat down, pleased. Not quite eleven. Newman was in the darkroom and would be out momentarily.

She wanted to see this. What would happen, she wondered? Something mundane? Like the power outage at the drive-in he had described? He had looked at his car's LED clock, seen the time, and bang, the screen and sound had winked out. Or another instance in his car, more ominous if you wanted it to be: heading home one day after picking up a bargain-bin volume of Poe and hitting a raven that spread its wings across his windshield and affixed him with one black beady eye that seemed to say "Nevermore!" Or watching television in a seedy apartment he used to rent and having his door knocked down by a man who tore straight through the room without a word, flung himself out through the open window, rattled and crashed his way down the fire escape and disappeared into the night.

Or maybe nothing would happen since it was all a crock.

Newman appeared from the hallway with some fresh photographs and placed them carefully on a layout table before sitting down at his desk.

"How'd it go?" he asked.

"Fine. Marginally interesting," Zoe said. "You'll note the time."

"What time is it?" he asked innocently.

"It's 11:08."

"Oh, I see. I go by my watch." He looked at it. "It's 11:09."

"Good," Zoe said. She settled back in her chair. "Let's see what happens."

He returned her gaze and leaned back. "Yes," he said pleasantly, and smiled. "Let's."

They waited.

A Close Personal Relationship Thomas Marcinko

Five years into Junior's Surprise Visit, Ted got a call at the office from Clare of Assisi, patron saint of television since her appointment to that post by Pope Pius XII in 1958.

Ted recognized Clare's picturephone image immediately, but who wouldn't? Her late-night talk show had been a hit on all 1,057 v-channels since Junior's return to earth. Ted felt his teeth grind, but he turned it into a smile. He couldn't stand her show, but of course he had to watch it. He had no choice.

Clare beamed him a beatific smile. "Ted Stevski?"

"Yes?" Ted's mouth dried up.

"Your Interview is this afternoon."

Something inside Ted turned instantly to ice. His tongue suddenly felt like a dirty gym sock. It stuck to the roof of his mouth.

"Three o'clock," continued Clare. "Your place." She leaned closer to the screen. "This is your lucky afternoon."

I'm dead, he thought. It's all over for me.

"Why – why thanks!" he said.

"Think nothing of it," Clare replied. "Good luck." She logged off.

Ted's heart triphammered as he called up his appointment calendar and canceled everything. Next he called up the message system to let his boss, Kevin, know he was leaving the office early.

He saw a prompt:

Call me. K.

Dammit, Ted thought. *Damn* it. Bad enough that he had to sign a loyalty oath, and take back everything he'd ever said or written or thought, and go to work for the Bureau of Values. Now he had to pretend to *like* it.

He rang up Kevin, whose bright-eyed, smiling face sported a new beard in imitation of Junior. Kevin had had his Interview last month; since then, he'd talked of little else.

"Looks like it's time to talk to the Big Man," Kevin said. "Congratulations."

"Thanks." It didn't surprise Ted that Kevin knew. All the post-Interviewees seemed to be of one mind.

"Nervous?" Kevin asked. "Hey, I can understand that. But you've got nothing to worry about. My Interview went great. I came out of it a new man."

"I'm glad." It seemed to Ted that Kevin hadn't changed much. But then Kevin had always believed. He'd joined the Bureau in the beginning, ten years ago, back before Junior's return. It seemed like a long time ago.

"Relax," Kevin said, "You've been a model employee."

Yes, thought Ted. *Model employee. Great.*

His oilburner was parked at the far end of the Bureau's lot. He covered his mouth with his breathing mask and began the long walk. No point in environmental regulations these days; after years of being gnawed away, they'd all been scrapped since He showed up. Junior had actually ordered the laws repealed; He considered them a Personal affront to His dictum about using up the world.

Ted still remembered the broadcast. *My Father gave you this planet to use up; you're saving it as if there actually were a tomorrow. Your lack of faith wounds Me. See?* And He'd held up his bleeding stigmata for a global v-audience of billions.

You couldn't help but believe.

Everybody believes but me, Ted thought. And cringed.

He'd be found out. Everybody was, sooner or later. Kevin had been a believer from day one. But Tyrone in Accounting was a rabid atheist, Tina in Word Processing thought Junior was a space alien in disguise. After their Interviews, they'd come out perfect believers.

Ted didn't want that to happen to him. Just why, he could not say. Surely it would be a more comfortable world if he fit in a little better?

I must not think bad thoughts. I must not think bad thoughts.

As he revved up his federally mandated 32-cylinder engine, the radio automatically exploded to life with a Bureau-sponsored broadcast. You could turn it down but not off. He punched in his destination and, as the car roared onto the freeway, one of the Bureau Spokesmen – Pat or Jerry or Oral; they all sounded alike to Ted – lectured the audience on the folly of pre-Junior societal behavior. As if anybody alive still favored gun control, or birth control, or equal rights for homosexuals, or teaching evolution.

Ted turned the volume down as far as it would go. The scent of incense, always present in the interior of the car, increased to choking point. That, too, you could turn down but not off. Ted dialed the knob down as far as it would go.

He took a Halcion Lite from the glove compartment, choked it down without water, leaned back in the driver's seat, and closed his eyes. Nothing to worry about. Sure. Oh, Kevin had done fine with his Interview, and Charlie and Tyrone in Accounting, and Tina in Word Processing.

Sooner or later everybody had an Interview with Junior. Everybody.

But Kevin believed. Ted did not. Surely He would see it. If He didn't know already.

This wasn't the Second Coming Ted had expected. If Second Coming it truly was.

Junior wasn't saying.

New Writings in the Fantastic
* * *

As a child Ted had tried hard to be devout. He'd loved Junior with all his heart, and considered Him a close personal friend. He would pray to Him whenever he was in trouble, when his mother lay dying, when his father kept hitting the bottle. Ted didn't always get what he asked for, but he'd always figured there must be a reason.

He knew exactly when his faith had begun to desert him. Ted remembered the day, twenty years before Junior's Surprise Visit, when the people in black came to take away his copy of *The World We Live In*, by the Editors of *Life* Magazine.

He'd been in fifth grade, devouring the book before classes began, lingering over a panoramic fold-out page showing the Age of Dinosaurs. Men and women in black casually strolled into the room and had a brief whispered discussion with the teacher. Ted didn't notice till the whispering grew loud. The people in black showed papers and badges. Miss Clement bit her lip and nodded grimly. Ted froze as her footsteps clacked towards him in a classroom that was now otherwise silent.

"Ted," she said, leaning over him, speaking quietly but urgently, "that book is overdue from the library."

"But I just checked it out yesterday," Ted said.

She leaned closer. "Ted, I'm going to have to take the book now. You can check it out again later."

Ted looked up at the men and women in black. They nodded and smiled at him. Their smiles were way too sweet.

Later he tried to find the book again, but it was gone from the school library. In its place were books about Noah's Ark, and Jonah and the Whale, and the Tower of Babel. The illustrations in them were nice, too. But they weren't the same.

Fortunately the public libraries were still open. And there were always bookstores, too. He collected books on dinosaurs, books on astronomy, books on evolution. Sometimes he hid them under the bed, and he read them with a flashlight, the covers pulled over his head.

He didn't understand. There were a billion copies of the Bible in print, and very few copies left of *The World We Live In*. Where was the threat?

He read the underground copies of forbidden texts. Science and philosophy, mostly. Blurry photocopies and crumbling volumes helped him piece together what had happened to the world when the Pats and Jerries and Orals took over.

Ted came to the conclusion that, if Junior ever came back, He would have nothing to do with the people who claimed His support.

All right, Ted thought. *So I was wrong.*

Ted prepared to meet his Maker. Or his Maker's Son. One and the same, according to some. Junior was vague on that point. Ted didn't think it mattered just now. He wondered if there were any nice people in Hell. The dashboard clock read 2:54 when Ted's '00 Chief Seattle sixdoor pulled into his driveway.

Junior wore an expensive three-piece blue pinstripe suit. His ash-blond hair was combed back and parted; it was a little long in the back, but the beard was neatly trimmed. He had put on a few pounds since his return to earth. He wore several rings on each hand, including a pinkie ring on his right.

Junior sat in Ted's favorite chair, idly leafing through the Bureau's weekly newsletter. Ted had been editing the newsletter since he'd joined the Bureau five years ago, when all jobs in the communications field had become the property of Church and State overnight. At the time Ted had hoped the Visit would be a short one. Either Junior would go away, or it really would be the end of the world, and it would all be over mercifully quick.

No such luck.

Stop thinking like that, Ted ordered himself. *I must not think bad thoughts. I must not think bad thoughts.*

He wondered how Junior had gotten past the house's security system.

"A miracle," Junior replied to Ted's unvoiced thought. Junior shrugged and looked at His fingernails. "What else?"

"Of course," Ted said. "Sorry."

"Sit down."

Ted sat. Now that they were face-to-face, he felt strangely at ease. He knew the punishment was close at hand, but there was no point in squirming now. He'd spent the last five years hiding what he really thought. He'd recanted his earlier beliefs and writings, and mentally crossed his fingers. It moves, anyway.

But Junior could see through all that. You couldn't avoid Him. That's what everybody said.

"Which of course is true," Junior said. "But it's not what you think it is. I'm not here to punish you."

"I sure don't expect You to give me a reward," Ted said. He was getting tired of hiding his thoughts. What difference did it make now?

Junior leaned forward. His ice-blue eyes burned like distant stars.

"You don't much like Me, Ted. Do you?"

Ted reached for his collar and loosened the tie. This was not what he'd expected.

"I'm not sure I know what You mean," Ted replied.

Junior sighed and got up. He put his hands in his back pockets and began to pace the room.

"I mean, it's not a question of belief," He said. "I've brought peace and prosperity to the world. This is an age of miracles. You can't help but believe I exist. That choice I've taken away from you. But *you* don't believe in me. Do you?"

He stopped and looked Ted straight in the eye.

Ted said: "I don't suppose it would do any good to say—"

Junior whirled around. "—that you've 'been good'? Yes, you've kept all the outward signs of belief. But the time has come for you to give Us more than just your obedience."

Ted swallowed. "Isn't obedience what You want?"

Junior smiled, stuck His hands in His back pockets, looked at the ceiling, and rocked on His heels. "Well, outward signs of obedience are just fine, Ted. Especially for Catholics. But we're not Catholics, are we? I'm certainly not."

Ted wiped his palms on the upholstery. "Then what is it You want?"

"Oh, I dunno, Ted. You tell Me. Like, oh, take a look at this!"

Junior pointed to a picture hanging on the wall. Ted had burned it for his own protection, five years ago, but now it was back, something he'd kept above his desk when he'd been teaching Creation Science 101, and slipped kids blurrily photocopied books on Darwin without written permission slips from their parents.

It was a print of the famous 16th-century woodcut showing a scholarly type poking his head through the dome of the heavens, staring in wonder at the gears and wheels of the greater cosmos beyond.

"This," Junior said, "fucking offends Me, if you want the truth."

"Well, I don't see why; it's only a picture..."

"'It moves, anyway,' eh, Ted?"

"What do You mean?"

"That Catholic thing again. The Church pardoned Galileo. Does that mean I have to? That guy, he fucking offended Me, too."

What did He want? And where had that print come from?

"I told you, a miracle. Get used to them. Now, the point is – well, let Me put it this way. I expect certain things to be taken on faith. Out of sheer adoration of Me. If I say 'believe' I mean *believe*. If I say two and two are five, believe that. You got it?"

Ted felt his jaw and mouth tighten. *I must not think bad thoughts.*

"Certainly," he said.

Junior twisted His face and mouth into a mincing expression.

"'Certainly,'" he said in a mocking falsetto. He gave an elaborate shrug. "And what is that supposed to mean?"

He pointed to a poster on the wall. It was another item Ted had lost a long time ago. It showed the evolution of life, from a single cell, to simple organisms, through dinosaurs, smaller mammals, through the apes and hominids and finally to modern man.

"You loved the dinosaurs more than Me," He said. "You always did."

Yes, Ted thought. *But I needed to, don't you see?*

If Junior heard that thought, He did not acknowledge it. Instead, He reached into his pocket, removed something small, and tossed it.

Ted caught a small toy model of a triceratops. He turned it over and over in his fingers. It was made of blue plastic. The horns bent when he fingered them.

"This really bothers You?" Ted asked, looking up.

"Not the thing itself," said Junior. "What it stands for."

"What's that?"

Junior sighed. He flopped onto the couch, stretched out, and let his foot dangle over the back. "Let Me tell you a little story. Once upon a time there was a Son, and He had a very demanding Father. His Father asked Him to do a certain Thing, and the Son did so, even though He didn't particularly want to; even though, to tell the truth, the Son found this Task quite painful. But the Son was under the impression that, after He did this Deed, people would straighten up and fly right."

Junior made a spitting noise. "Talk about your original dysfunctional family... Yeah, after the Big Sleep I sat at the right hand of My Father. Not a word from Him about all I did for Him; not so much as a fucking Thanks, Son, well done. I sat there at His right hand and sort of basked in His radiance. Which is a little like watching paint dry, if you ask Me. I mean, that's all it is with Him: Me, Me, Me. The Great I Am... Not that I really got along any better with my Mother. I always talked back. I couldn't help it. Everything she said seemed so inane. I think I was angry at her for being such a doormat.

"So next time, I thought... next time... I decided I'm going to do it differently. I came back once before, in the 15th century. You thought that was fiction, something that crazy Russian novelist dreamed up? It's a true story.

"Yeah, I came back for a little visit. I was doing a few miracles. Raised a girl from the dead. The Grand Inquisitor – old cardinal, ninety years at least – told the crowd to grab Me. They were so used to following his orders that they locked Me up! And he told Me I had no right to add anything to what I'd already said!

"So then I thought... one more time. I wasn't going to go through any of that again. No more run-ins with the law. No more conflict with the established order.

"Playing along is the one thing I've never done. 'Render unto Caesar.' To hell with that. Render unto Me for once in My lives; how's that sound?"

Junior gave Ted a meaningful glance. "I made compromises," He said.

Ted blinked. "Compromises?"

Junior nodded. "With Pat, and Jerry, and Oral. With the Bureau. They'd been doing pretty well for years. Congress, the Supreme Court, the White House, the media – I watched their influence grow and I said to myself, 'Why not?' My coming back just helped to give them momentum. Compromise. No reason I shouldn't play along.

"At first I didn't feel quite right about it. I was still following those old codependent patterns. I felt guilty. I felt I should be giving, giving, giving.

"But I got used to it. It turned out to be easy. It turned out to be fun. When I think of all that sacrifice, all that blood... Well, this time, we're going to do it My way. I've bled. Now it's your turn."

Ted, confused, gestured helplessly with the triceratops.

"Get that thing out of My sight!" Junior said.

Ted put it in his pocket.

Junior shook his head. "Not good enough. Look."

Ted found himself in his bedroom in the house he grew up in. Laid out before him was all the paraphernalia of his childhood, before the people in black came after it. Models of dinosaurs, and books about them too. A map of the solar system and the evolution of the galaxies. A three-inch reflecting telescope, a toy gyroscope, and the Visible Man, all courtesy of the Edmund Scientific Company.

"Miracle," Junior said as Ted adjusted to the change.

Ted's heart filled with awe. Never mind Junior's attitude. By bringing him here, He was showing Ted how much He understood him. Why, He must know everything there was to know about him.

Junior looked at it all and frowned, and shook His head, and gave the thumbs-down.

"It's got to go."

How? Ted thought, and knew the answer at once. *Miracles.*

"Damn' straight," Junior said.

Ted picked up an Estes model of the Saturn V rocket. "Why? All this threatens You somehow?" He waved the rocket.

Junior shook His head. "It doesn't threaten me. It *offends* Me. It's a threat to you, though."

How so? Ted wondered.

"I should think it would be obvious," replied Junior. "Everything in this room is a sign of a dismaying lack of faith. Some people can take or leave a universe that's billions of years old, but you... Well, during this Visit I'm demanding a sacrifice from everybody. Some people are giving up sex; some people are giving up money; some people are giving up power. Kevin and Tyrone and Tina in Word Processing all gave up something. And I'm Interviewing hundreds of other people right now, simultaneously. They're all making the sacrifice, because, you see, Ted, thou shalt have no other gods before me.

"And *some* people, Ted – *some* people are giving up a worldview. And whatever sense of wonder goes with it."

Next stop – miracle – was the late Cretaceous era.

A dragonfly the size of a housecat buzzed by Ted's ear. Lizards glided through the air on leather wings. A tyrannosaurus feasted on raw pink meat. A brontosaurus bounced lazily through a lake, wading to the far side, where tastier fronds grew.

The scene wasn't even accurate, Ted realized. It was the prehistoric bestiary of his childhood, long ago supplanted by theories of quick-moving, warm-blooded lizards. But it was enough to make him stare in wonder.

Ted was getting used to sudden shifts in the scenery. But he felt his face split into a grin, now that he was in a place he'd always wanted to be. But his grin was tinged with sadness.

He had spent hours contemplating the dinosaurs: reading about them, drawing them, imagining them mindlessly whiling away their hundred-million-year afternoon. It was where Ted went, in his mind, when Dad stumbled home and passed out on the couch, when the news about Mom got worse and worse.

Here everything seemed friendly and clear, and when the nuns and priests tried to talk him out of this world of wonders, and replace it with Eden, Ted always wanted to say, "Don't you get it?" This was a world without sin and evil. This *was* Eden, or something better than Eden.

He loosened his tie completely, letting it hang around his neck, down the front of his shirt. He was already half-soaked with sweat. His feet sank inches into the fetid swamp, his shoes filling with water.

Junior, of course, looked air-conditioned cool. And He knew how to deal with a body of water. He stood right on top of it. He tapped one foot impatiently.

Ted glanced worriedly at the ancient world around him. *No,* he thought. *I don't want to let it go.*

Junior was right. Ted loved the dinosaurs more than he loved Junior. Far more.

Junior clapped him on the back. "Well, Ted, you got it. Kiss it all goodbye."

White flecks filled the sky and fell slowly toward the ground. At first Ted thought they were snow. But, as he held out his hand to catch a flake, he felt an ectoplasmic nothingness fall onto his outstretched palm.

He looked closer. It was a kind of snow, but more like video snow. It was blankness, negation.

The flakes were getting bigger. The world-tapestry before him was filling full of holes.

"You're going to destroy it?" Ted's gesture took in the entire modern universe. "All of it?"

"No," He said. "You are."

The hell I will, Ted thought. *You sleazy, pompous, infantile excuse for a god...*

"Now, is that any way to talk to Me, Ted? Me? Isn't it about time you accepted Me as your Personal Savior, that we had a Close Personal Relationship?"

"You do this with everybody?" Ted asked. "Everybody with a mind of their own?"

"Pretty much," Junior admitted. "Watch."

Ted looked closer. Junior was forming something in His hand. It was a round, white object. He leaned back for a long throw and lobbed it hard, straight at the brontosaurus. It splattered and exploded against the creature's head. It covered up the head like invisible paint; the white nothingness dripped down and covered the great gray bulk. Soon the creature was gone.

Junior made an even bigger snowball of the stuff. He shoved it into Ted's hands. "Toss."

"No."

"I said 'toss.' I can make you do it. Look."

And, without his will, Ted lobbed the white ball at a docile stegosaurus absently munching a clump of fronds. The creature was covered with the white stuff; it vanished.

Ted didn't care until it was over. Then he was sorry he'd done it, but even sorrier that he hadn't cared. He felt like he'd killed a favorite pet – not one that needed to be mercy-killed, but one that was perfectly healthy.

"Want to do it that way?" Junior asked. "We could do it that way, if that's what you want."

More of the white stuff appeared in Ted's hands. It had the consistency of slush rather than snow, but it was only slightly cool to the touch.

"What is this stuff?" Ted asked.

"Holiness," said Junior. "Blind faith."

Ted frowned. "It looks like this?" Warm snow, as far as he could tell.

Junior shook His head impatiently. "It doesn't matter what it is. It's the mechanism I've chosen. I could bring on an ice age; I could bring down the head of a comet and cover this stinking little globe with a nice cool dust. But you'd like that, wouldn't you? It would fit your precious theories. Instead, let's try something else. Let's say your theories never existed.

"It's up to you to make the toss," Junior continued. "I can make you do it. Or you can do it as yourself. Your choice."

"Will I remember what I know, after I'm done?" Ted asked. "Will all this still exist?"

Junior nodded. "In your mind, yes. Who knows? I might bring it back sometime. Or let you visit."

"Really?"

Junior shrugged. "Take your chances. If you want, I can remove completely your memory of this time and place."

"Why are You giving me a choice?" Ted asked. "Why not just make me do Your will and be done with it?"

Junior leaned forward. "Because I care, Ted. I care deeply. I want you to love Me of your own free will. Like Father, like Son. It's the way We've always run our business. So, choose."

Yes, Ted thought. *Better to do it myself. Better to do the deed to a loved one than to have somebody else do it for you.*

At least he would remember.

Ted lobbed one at a triceratops. And another at a tyrannosaur. He caught a pterodactyl in mid-flight. He pummeled an ankylosaur. He kept throwing.

By the end of the day his arm was sore from throwing snowballs of the stuff. Ted was surprised at how far he could throw it, how much it could cover. Exhaustion muffled his grief.

The universe he'd lived in and loved as a child was gone. In its place was a thing without form, and void. Nothing.

Ted remembered how things used to be.

But he couldn't have proved it to save his life.

Junior took him back to his apartment. He put his arm around Ted's shoulder, and regaled him with anecdotes about how He used to drive Joseph crazy every time He reminded him that he wasn't His real father. "His face would get all red, especially around the ears," said Junior. "That's what I remember. The ears got red as a beet, red as blood."

Ted smiled. "That's a great story, Junior."

"Oh, I've got plenty more." He slapped Ted on the back. "We're going to be great friends, I can tell."

"I'm sure too, Junior," Ted said through a tight, bright smile. "I don't know what took me so long."

"It doesn't matter, Ted. What matters is that we now have a Close Personal Relationship. Oh, look who's here," He said as he escorted Ted into the kitchen. "All your friends."

Kevin was there, and Charlie from Accounting, and Tina from Word Processing. "Surprise!" They'd draped a banner across his living room: "Congratulations On Your Interview." Junior popped open a bottle of fizzy water and took a swig.

"Water!" He cried in mock surprise. "Well, I'll fix that!"

Laughter all around.

Ted just smiled.

Junior caught Ted's eye. "Not so glum, kid," He said, throwing his arm around Ted again. "Everything's going to be great from now on. I'll never leave you now. We'll talk later."

"I'd like that," said Ted. "I'd like that very much."

By the time the party had broken up, Ted had found another framed print on his wall. He hadn't noticed it before. It was done in a 16th-century style and showed the dome of heaven. A man sat beneath it and contemplated the splendor of the skies beneath the dome, beyond which was blank nothingness. The man seemed happy in his little universe.

Ted began to wonder if he shouldn't try to follow this example.

He never managed to do it. Junior never took him back to the prehistoric garden, either.

And, like everybody else, Ted lived forever.

New Writings in the Fantastic
Stray Barbara Nickless

Shortly before 10pm on a Friday night, Detective Natasha Valerya entered the Halt 'n' Salt Café armed with only a toggle gun and her anger, which she figured was at least as important as the gun for dealing with the cannibals. The thing about cannibals, Detective Valerya knew, was that they could get under your skin in more ways than one. They were designed for it. It was part of what made them so lethal.

The anger, her partner Mike would have told her, was dangerous. Better to keep cool, he'd always said. But he was dead, so his cool hadn't gotten him anywhere. Valerya had tried on her anger that night in front of her mirror, held it up for size as if it were a new uniform, watching the way it flattened her lips into a line and crushed the image-ruining compassion right out of her eyes. She'd nodded. It was better than the suffocating depression that had enfolded her ever since she'd sat in the chair next to her supervisor's desk and listened to him explain what had happened to Mike while she stared at the forensic shots before throwing up in the supervisor's trashcan. It was better than that long, shaky moment two nights ago when – convinced she'd let Mike down and that she had nothing left to live for – she'd laid out a gleaming line of razor blades, marching them up to a full glass of scotch like little flags of death. She'd ended the evening by sweeping the blades onto the floor, downing the scotch and stumbling off to bed, unwilling to die, unable to live.

She paused inside the glass door. The diner, like all the others in the cannibal chain, hummed with activity, gleamed with neon sparkle-lights, and reeked of roasting human flesh. Valerya felt her gorge rise as she took a seat at the end of the counter. A week after Mike had vanished while searching for the leader of the cannibals, Valerya still found it hard to believe this was where he had met his end. He would have said he'd died serving the public.

Mike was always one with the lame jokes.

She discretely flipped her badge open for the tall, pale waiter and held it in the shadow of her jacket. "Keep mum about it or your hunting days are over," she murmured.

His sharp teeth flashed as he grinned. "More's the challenge," he said. "I won't tell tales about you." He peered closer at her name on the badge. "New Russia, eh? You sure you don't want to cross? Some of your countrymen –"

She tucked the badge away. "Bring some coffee and leave the pot here," she said. "Act like I'm a regular customer. When you get a chance, come back. I need to ask you some questions."

He licked his lips. "Mmm, a forceful Slavic policewoman." He bounded away before she could threaten him with anything else.

Valerya watched his energy with envy. She, like every other honest citizen, was perpetually malnourished, forever fatigued. Sometimes it was almost too much effort to blame the cannibals for the choice they had made. It was only survival.

Saturday night, and the diner was filled with cannibals. Feral and sleek-skinned, charged with the kind of vitality only a high-protein diet could supply. They were dressed in flash clothes, and many were surgically altered to sport night-seeing eyes and elongated canines. Most of them, Valerya knew, were perfectly legit. Staying within their quota, hunting only their own kind. But a renegade gang had spread like gangrene on the open wound of Denver, consuming the innocent, the uninitiated, the desperately poor who couldn't afford to go off-world. They'd snatched Mike last week while Valerya was laid up in bed, and now Valerya had a real beef with them. So to speak.

The waiter brought a pot of coffee and a mug, smiled wolfishly at her, and went to wait on other customers. She forced herself to sip her coffee even as her stomach heaved. If she vomited, one of two things would happen. Either the other diners would assume she was new and share a laugh with her, or they would realize she wasn't one of them at all. In that case, only her gun stood between her and becoming the Blue Plate Special.

Valerya watched the customers in the mirror behind the bar. She had a blurry photograph of the leader of the gang that had killed Mike, snapped by a security camera at an apartment building where the gang had made a hit. Ben Lopez, the leader, was a youthful-looking man with black hair and a thick mustache that drooped over thin lips. She knew from computer records that he was thirty-two, and had been born off-world before being brought to earth at the tender age of six. His parents had died a year later, killed in a demonstration protesting beef exports. Ben had disappeared until he was sixteen, when his name had shown up on the weekly roster of legitimate cannibals. In the photograph, he stared directly at the camera with an expression of sorrow. There was nothing in his eyes of the rapaciousness she had expected to see. The picture infuriated her. Mike had been a good man, fighting off a cancer that had finally gone into remission, managing, despite his illness, to keep his wife and kid off-world. Then Lopez's group had brought him down.

The images of both men haunted her dreams.

"More coffee?" asked the waiter, pouring.

"I'm looking for Ben Lopez," said Valerya, pushing her cup closer to the waiter.

His hand faltered, and most of the coffee spilled on the counter. He set the pot down. "Let me clean that up."

Her hand shot out and she grabbed his wrist. "Lopez," she mouthed.

"Haven't seen him."

"I can close this place so fast you'll feel like your ass has grown eyeballs so that it can see the door slam behind you on your way out. And I'll be sure to tell the owner it was your fault. You'll lose your allegiances. I'm sure I don't need to explain how bad *that* would be, a cannibal without a gang."

He laughed nervously. A lock of his thick, brown hair fell over one eye. "You don't understand. I haven't seen him. Lopez used to be in every night around midnight. But he hasn't been by in nearly a week."

Not since killing Mike. She released the bartender's wrist and glanced at her watch. Midnight was more than two hours away. "What's the word?"

"Word is, something happened to him." He winked at her and suddenly ran his fingers along her throat, the meaty tip of his middle finger lingering near her jugular.

Valerya held still. "Clean up the mess."

"Of course."

She dumped sugar into her cup and poured more coffee. What if Lopez had skipped town, gone to another city-state where she had no jurisdiction? How would she go forward without even revenge to give her strength?

The door opened and a woman entered, pausing on the threshold. Her expression was uncertain, her hands clutching at the hem of her flash jacket. She stepped to the phone and stared at the Out of Order sign hung across it. *Another lost soul,* thought Valerya. *New cannibal? Or simply someone with an unfortunate choice in eating establishments?* It happened occasionally, despite the graphic names of the diners. The courts were still deciding whether this turned the ignorant intruders into legitimate prey.

The woman glanced around the diner with wide eyes that practically screamed *victim*. A male cannibal leaned over her, baring teeth in a false smile, laying his large hands on her shoulders. The woman gave a little shriek followed by a sickly smile that must have been meant to radiate confidence. Two other men sidled over, their shoulders hunched, muscles rippling beneath their flash shirts.

Valerya slid from her seat, feeling the toggle gun in her jacket. *Always a sucker for a victim.* That's what Mike had said, laughing gently when she'd cried at the news that he was ill and probably dying.

She walked over to the woman and grabbed her hand.

"Glad you made it," she said loudly. "I was beginning to wonder."

The woman blinked at her and then smiled again. The cannibals raised their hands as if to show they meant no harm, laughing as they backed off.

Valerya dropped the woman's hand. The stranger followed her back to the counter.

Nodding at the seat next to her, Valerya hunched over her coffee. *I am tired, so very tired of all of this,* she thought. *The good guys, the bad guys. The pain and the deaths. Maybe, in some stupid way, Mike was the lucky one. Maybe I'll get lucky tonight, too. But not before Lopez has his own little fortuitous moment.*

The stool next to hers creaked as the woman sat down. The waiter, slowly swirling a rag through the coffee on the countertop, lifted his eyebrows at Valerya.

"Friend of yours?"

"Yes," said the woman.

"Never seen her before," said Valerya, not wanting the waiter to link the woman with the police.

The waiter chuckled. "Curiouser and curiouser," he said as he moved off to mop other parts of the counter.

Valerya turned a cold eye on the new arrival. "I don't want to know you. You don't want to know me. I've saved your ass for now, but you'd better figure a way to get out of here on your own."

The woman couldn't be more than twenty-five. She shivered and crossed her arms over her small breasts. "I – I need help. I'm not supposed to be here. You look –"

"Careful," said Valerya, "who you confide in."

The woman frowned. She had bleached blonde hair which she wore in a frizzy halo about her face. She'd sprayed a black, raccoon-like mask over her eyes. Beneath the flash jacket, she wore a black dress and fishnet stockings. Valerya felt her resolve soften even as a tongue of fear licked down her spine. She'd always had a weakness for strays. Mike had once asked her why she didn't marry and become a mommy instead of looking for poor creatures about to become road-kill. He'd grossly overestimated her ability to commit.

"What are you doing here?" she asked the girl.

"I was supposed to meet my boyfriend. He said it was time I – time to – oh, God, I don't think I can do it."

"Do what?"

"Become... you know." She gave a little jerk with her head. "One of them."

"Your boyfriend didn't show?"

The woman sniffed. Faint tear tracks marred the black mask. "No."

"Did you sign an agreement? To become prey?"

"The law says you have to sign to show intention."

"And did you?"

Her voice was almost inaudible. "Yes."

Shit, thought Valerya. Another innocent suckered into the perfect setup. Without a benefactor, and by wider implication a gang, to protect her, this woman had just given permission for every cannibal on the planet to hunt her down in the vehicle of their choice, and either kill her immediately or string her up and hack off choice parts, keeping the meat fresh for days until she finally died from shock and loss of blood. She remained a potential victim even of her benefactor's gang until she made a witnessed kill of her own.

The woman sobbed into her sleeve, her back turned to the hunters in the diner. "I know how stupid I was. But I love Ben."

Valerya stared in surprise. "Ben Lopez?"

Her face invisible, the woman's hazy blonde hair floated about as she nodded.

"You were supposed to meet Ben Lopez tonight?"

The woman lifted her head. The raccoon mask was smeared, and her nose was reddened, but she was still beautiful. Valerya looked back down at her coffee. Mike had been the truly compassionate one. The strays she cared for until they could care for themselves were merely her way of getting around her inability to become seriously involved with anyone. Mike had been the only one she'd loved since the two of them had been childhood friends. He and his wife had been her family. Until Elisabeth went off-world and Mike was killed.

"Ben said to meet him at Sixteenth and Dakota," the woman said. "I waited for him for half an hour, but I got scared. There were cannibals going by. This was the first place I found that was open. I thought I'd use the phone. You could kill me, I know, but you saved me just now."

"Do I have sucker stamped all over me?"

"You have a kind face."

Valerya rubbed her temples. "Look," she began, then interrupted herself. "What's your name?"

"Beatrice."

"Look, Beatrice, I might be able to help you. But, in return, you've got to help me. Tell me about Lopez. When was the last time you saw him?"

"Three days ago. At Memorial Park, near the capitol. Why? You looking to jump gangs? He won't take just anyone." She sniffed, pulled a napkin from the dispenser, and blew her nose. "Not even me, apparently."

"Maybe you were set up, Beatrice."

"Ben wouldn't do that. He –"

"Has killed scores of innocent people."

"No, it's not like that. He told me. They only pick those who want to be... who are –"

"Who are what? Harboring a secret desire to be eaten by their own kind? Don't be stupid."

The girl flinched. "No. Those who are already dying."

"What? How would he know something like that?"

She shrugged. "He says it's inbred. He's a gencan, you know."

Valerya felt her heart surge like an engine on overdrive. A gencan. A bred cannibal rather than a superficial, surgically altered one. Ben Lopez had been raised on Cannan II. Born in 2156. It made sense. His parents could have had him genetically altered in the womb to restore long-lost predator traits. With earth now a world of hunger and desperate poverty, it was becoming a matter of survival.

"Like a wolf," the girl was saying, "hunting caribou. They kill the sick and the old, those that slow the herd."

"It doesn't matter whether the victims are dying or not," said Valerya, thinking of her partner and his cancer. "They're humans with free will. Lopez has no right to prey on them. And sometimes he screws up." Mike's cancer had been in remission.

Even as it angered her, Valerya felt a profound satisfaction at this news. Lopez's genetics, plus his murder of a cop, meant an automatic death sentence if she could bring him in.

"The wolf–caribou logic doesn't apply to humans," she said.

"We're hardly human, any more," murmured Beatrice.

Valerya knew this girl might be of use to her in the future, but for now the two of them were attracting way too much attention. "Come on," she said, tossing some money down for the coffee. "I need information from you. In return, I'll get you out of here, find a place for you to stay. I know where the safe places are."

"So does Ben," said the girl, standing. "It won't help."

"He doesn't know them all," Valerya answered, thinking of the hidden places she'd discovered over the years. Places where one could be self-sufficient for years. Places she'd preserved in her mind like gold coins, hoarding them until the time to spend.

"I gotta pee."

"Can't you wait?"

The girl shook her head.

Drugs. All the cannibals took them. "Be quick."

She turned her back as Beatrice made her way down the narrow aisle between the counters and the bar. The reflective glass allowed her to watch the girl unobtrusively. For the most part, the cannibals moved out of the girl's way. At the doors to the bathrooms, Beatrice reached toward the women's door, then suddenly darted left, into the men's.

Valerya realized she had been duped, just as Mike must have been. The girl's boyfriend was probably waiting in there. She hadn't intended to corner Lopez here, among his allies. She'd meant to follow him, arrest him where there were fewer witnesses. She felt a moment of panic and considered making a dash for the door. But an unusual congregation of cannibals was now standing between her and flight. Coincidence, or something else? It didn't matter. She'd come to avenge her partner's death. She had to follow through. Beatrice was the key, as either bait or guide.

Furtively, Valerya slipped her hand into her jacket and toggled the switch on the police special, changing it from a tool designed to slow an enemy into a weapon guaranteed to stop even the most determined cannibal.

When Beatrice emerged from the bathroom, she came alone. Valerya still calmly sipped her coffee. She smiled and stood when the girl approached. "Let's go," she said, softly. Beatrice shivered and nodded. What an actress the girl was, Valerya thought. Did she and Lopez intend the cop to be the girl's first kill?

Beatrice led the way out the door. The male cannibals moved aside, leering and whistling at both of them. Valerya felt her gun riding snugly beneath her arm. Her unmarked car was parked directly in front on the one-way street.

"Get in," she said, unlocking the driver's door, her hand on her gun.

The girl glanced up and down the street, then slid into the car and across to the passenger side. Valerya spared a glance back at the diner before following Beatrice inside. The cannibals were watching through the window. None of the faces looked like Lopez's.

She started the car and swung out into the nearly empty street. Cars were a rarity these days, owned by the elite who had chosen to stay on earth, by the occasional criminal, and by the cops. Valerya had taken a risk in bringing the car to the diner, but she'd wanted a fast escape. She'd expected Beatrice, or whatever her name was, to refuse to get in, or to at least express surprise. But the girl was silent. Valerya drove with one hand on the wheel and kept the other on the gun in her jacket. Her pulse thrummed loudly in her throat and she felt a cold trickle of sweat at her hairline.

"OK, the game is up. Where do you really want to go?" she asked, watching the girl out of the corner of her eye while she steered around boulder-sized debris in the street.

"I want you to turn me in," the girl said in a calm, male voice.

As Valerya watched, Beatrice removed her wig and slipped plastic breasts from beneath her dress. She/he used the sleeve of her/his jacket to wipe the makeup away.

"Holy shit," said Valerya, stopping the car in the middle of the street. "Ben Lopez."

Lopez stared at her with sorrowful eyes in which a predator still lurked. "Pleased to meet you, Natasha Valerya."

Valerya felt the bead of sweat run down along her ear and under her collar. She pulled her gun and aimed it at him. "First my partner and now me. Why?"

"I am sorry about your partner. But he was dying anyway."

"You had no right."

"Perhaps. But he asked for my help."

"*What?*"

"His widow is now set for life. Her husband is a hero, killed in the line of duty. If he'd died in a hospital somewhere, she would have gotten nothing. Why not be a bit pragmatic? It was what he wanted. It was what he asked for."

Valerya saw that her hands were shaking. "His cancer was in remission."

"If that's what he told you, he was lying."

She clenched the gun, thinking: Was it true? Had Mike asked this man to kill him, knowing that Elisabeth and their daughter would then never have another cause for worry? Payoff to the relatives of killed cops was immense. It was one of the biggest recruiting factors in a world of violence and short lifespans.

"You still had no right." She was surprised at the sob that scorched her throat. She had thought the tears had burned themselves out.

"I'm sorry," said Lopez. "But I won't hurt you, if I can help it. I need you to turn me in."

"Why?"

"Because I'm just like you. I want to die."

She wiped her nose with the back of her hand. She thought of the razor blades. Of her decision not to ask for backup. Just like Mike. *Just like Mike*. He hadn't asked for backup. "What do you know about me?"

His face was feral. "I can smell your death-desire. You smell like the grave. You're half there already."

She recalled her anger, drew it onto her like a suit of armor. "Your sense of smell is off. Why don't you just shoot yourself? You can use my gun. Save me the trouble."

"I can't."

Realization dawned. "The survival instinct. As a gencan, you can't kill yourself." Kind of like a cop. If Mike had committed suicide, Elisabeth would have collected nothing. So Mike had sought out this man with the sorrowful eyes to do it for him. *Oh, Mike, Mike, what the hell must you have been thinking the night you died?*

"Your partner gave me an opportunity I could never have given myself. His death will mean my own. They will execute me." Lopez's eyes flashed and he clenched his teeth. "But you need to hurry," he muttered through his teeth.

"Why?"

"I still have a survival instinct," he said, looking as if it was all he could do not to leap at her.

"That's good," she said, finger on the trigger. "So do I."

She released the brake and began driving again, half-watching the road, half-watching Lopez, thinking furiously. The gencan stared out the window at the passing lights. She flipped the gun back to a mode designed merely to incapacitate, and settled it in her lap.

It would be a fairly simple matter to keep the two of them alive in the hour it would take to reach the nearest police station, where she could lock him up. But then what? Ben Lopez would be tried, found guilty and put to death. And what would that make him?

A martyr. Every cause needs a martyr.

If Lopez died, it would draw more to his cause. More dead cops. More dead innocents. Already earth hung in the balance between those who maintained order and those who sought a new order. His could be the single death that started a war.

And what if he talked about Mike before he died? The serums they had these days could make a vegetable talk.

"I can't let you be a martyr. Or betray Mike."

He looked away from the window. "No," he said, "it won't be like that. I'll serve as an example. The others will back off, leave the police alone."

"You know that isn't true, Lopez. Think. Your people don't want an example, they want a cause. If you die, you'll give them that."

He stared at her. The predator came and went in his eyes, replaced by a darkness that rattled her. It was the agonizing pain of a man bound by something too large for him to encompass. He threw back his head and howled. His voice ripped his throat. "I don't want to live any more!"

She lifted the gun at the same moment he lunged across the length of the seat. The pellet caught him high, through the meaty flesh of his upper arm. Blood sprayed the window and door and rushed over her hands, causing a flame to ignite in his eyes. For a few seconds, as his hands scrabbled for her throat, she thought the pellet wasn't going to be enough. For an even worse second, she wondered if it mattered.

But then the light in his eyes dimmed, turned to ash, and his lids sank even as his body did. Valerya pulled over and wept to find herself still alive.

She glanced at him from time to time as she drove.

Turn him into the police, he would rat on Mike, robbing Elisabeth and their daughter of a future. He would then be made a martyr and all hell would break loose.

Her foot pushed down on the accelerator as they neared and then passed the exit bearing the sign Northeastern Police Station, Urban Areas.

Kill him herself, bury his body, no one would be the wiser. Lopez would be an unmarked casualty, and life would grind on.

She slowed, watching him. He slept on in his drug-induced stupor. The blood had dried on his shirt. His breathing was deep and even. She looked away, staring out at the darkness where her headlights cut a thin path.

She'd heard of nanosurgery that could change a person's genetic programming even in adulthood. The project had reached its heyday in the 2020s, before anyone went off-world, when there had been a concerted effort to eliminate congenital diseases.

It should work for Ben. She knew someone who would do it. Another friend could spread tales that Ben had gone off-world. She would take him to one of her safe places and he could have something like a normal life.

She could retire. Maybe have something like a normal life herself.

She retoggled the gun to termination. When he awoke, she would give him a choice, and his choice would be hers.

Life or death.

It was time to make a commitment.

New Writings in the Fantastic
The Colonoscopy of My Beloved
Ian Watson & Roberto Quaglia

My beloved Katrina is a multi-orgasmic woman, which is one reason why she's so beloved to me (as well as her mind – never forget the mind, which plays a huge role in excitement). Even quite gentle caresses provoke fireworks, which is great for a man's self-esteem, because he feels very competent. Sometimes, indeed, Katrina and I used to joke that her whole body seemed to behave like a clitoris.

Little did we realize!

One morning, when Katrina did a crap, a lot of blood came out of her bottom too, a truly disconcerting amount, bright red. The water in the toilet bowl looked like wine.

We both feared she had a tumor up in her entrails.

Katrina's doctor tried to calm her fears – "It might be nothing much, just a polyp which has burst" – but he immediately arranged for an inspection of her bowels by a specialist at the city hospital.

The specialist's name was Dr. Schmidt. Schmidt explained to us both about polyps, which grow naturally in the intestines and resemble closed-up sea anemones in a rock pool.

"Trauma is another possible cause," he went on. "Do you bugger much?"

Well, most people know that there are clitoral orgasms and vaginal orgasms and anal orgasms also.

"And there's diverticular disease, where the inside wall of the bowel splits because of hard constipatory turds, not enough fiber in the diet. The inside wall can look like a colonnade in a painting by Chirico." (This is when I decided that Katrina was in excellent, appreciative hands.) "A tumor rarely produces as much blood as you describe, although it can on occasion."

Katrina's interior could be investigated either by means of a sigmoidoscopy or a colonoscopy. Because of Sigmoid Freud's theories about constipatory anal retention I surmised that the former procedure might be named in honor of him. As for the latter, I thought of Christopher Colon crossing the Atlantic to spy out a new world, and about the Panama Canal. Both procedures employed instruments resembling long flexible silvery snakes the thickness of an average thumb tipped with a fiber-optic light for illumination, a mini-camera which would display the view from within on a colour TV monitor, and a small hoop of sharp wire which could be tightened to take a biopsy sample or to decapitate a polyp which might be growing too much and might cease to be benign.

The sigmoidoscope could be pushed partway up the intestines; the colonoscope could be pushed up all the way. Just to be on the safe side, Schmidt favored a colonoscopy.

"Anyway," he told Katrina, "a sigmoidoscopy can be a bit uncomfortable, whereas we need you completely relaxed for a colonoscopy, so you'll receive a strong sedative as well as muscle relaxants. Probably you'll sleep through the whole thing."

Katrina needed to starve for a couple of days and to take powders to empty herself completely, but three days later we returned to the city hospital.

Schmidt introduced us to Dr. Mohammad Hassan, who was on a fellowship from Morocco to perfect his skills, and who would observe and assist. Then I was left in the waiting room. Once the relaxants and sedatives had done their work the investigation should take no more than twenty minutes. Katrina would be separated from me for only about an hour in all.

Imagine my alarm when quite soon a nurse came from the examination room and requested my presence. Immediately I thought that they had found a tumor inside my Beloved.

Katrina lay on her side, knees drawn up, the silvery snake inserted up her anus. She was giggling.

Dr. Schmidt looked distracted.

"This is very rare," he said. "The sedative is acting as a euphoric, and I need to concentrate."

"Ah, so you want me to hold her hand?"

"No." He gestured at the TV monitor where in glorious colour I saw for the first time the truly intimate private inside of my beloved, seen by no one else before this day – a pink tunnel, upon the wall of which...

"That is no polyp," declared Schmidt. "That is a *clitoris*. A clitoris in the big bowel!"

My Beloved had always seemed to revel in the aftermath of a meal, several hours later.

"Does she have a clitoris in the normal place?" he demanded of me. I suppose he could easily have discovered this for himself, but he wasn't a gynae specialist, and besides there are protocols of behavior.

"Of course she does," I replied.

"Then this is a secondary clitoris."

"Supernumerary," said Dr. Hassan. "I know how to perform a clitoridectomy. That is quite customary in parts of Morocco."

Schmidt turned upon him in a momentary fury.

"Clitoridectomy is an obscenity."

Hassan showed his teeth. "Is it not obscenity when the clitoris is inside the shit of a bowel?"

Schmidt controlled himself. "Besides, it isn't the clitoris that bled. Even you can see it's a perfectly normal healthy clitoris."

Perhaps to prevent Hassan from seizing the initiative and decapitating the clitoris, Schmidt hastily pushed more of the colonoscope up my Beloved's anus. Maybe because of the sudden rubbing of the instrument across her internal clitoris, Katrina squirmed pleasurably.

"Madam, try to lie still!"

This was only the *first* additional clitoris that Schmidt's voyage of internal exploration discovered. In fact we witnessed several clitorises, at intervals.

Schmidt paused and lectured Hassan. "It's a good thing men do not have additional *penises* in their intestines. No matter how small those penises might normally be, if erect they could block the passage. Wonderful pieces of food, or more exactly wonderful turds, might excite them. They might think, *Ah, we're going to be caressed!* Awful constipation would occur."

"Surely the penises would soon ejaculate," said Hassan, "and the semen from them would lubricate the bowel?"

"Perhaps they can't produce semen. Dry ejaculations won't help with constipation."

The two doctors fell silent, for the colonoscope had arrived at the site of damage, from which some blood still oozed.

"My God," exclaimed Schmidt, "her *appendix* – look, the appendix was covered by a hymen. A particularly hard turd must have broken the hymen. Imagine continuing to be a virgin deep within your body, no matter how much intercourse has taken place! You could honestly swear to a prospective husband that you're still *intacta*."

To my eye, that little tube of the appendix looked a bit like a tiny additional womb.

"I wonder," said Schmidt, "if she will have periods of the bowels, now that the hymen is gone – instead of the bloodshed being resorbed, which it must have been previously. I think that the appendix–hymen was a total seal, not merely partial. Well, we've solved the mystery of the patient's sudden hemorrhage. She really is a remarkable patient. Supplementary sexual organs." (My Beloved giggled again.) "I wonder whether the body-scanner room is free..."

A body-scan cannot distinguish perfectly between similar tissue, and the technician seemed astonished by Schmidt's interpretation, but the good doctor declared that he could perceive yet other clitorises within my Beloved – a small one in a little finger, for example, and another in the back of her neck – and that her nervous system was additionally a clitoral system. Knowing my multi-orgasmic Beloved as I did, I didn't doubt him.

I don't know why I thought that oral sex would help soothe my Beloved's entrails. Oh yes I do: it's because semen is white – symbolically this would counteract bleeding. Anyway, once we were home that night, we did as we had done on other special occasions, and I came fulsomely in her mouth, all of which she swallowed.

Schmidt telephoned a week later. Prior to her colonoscopy Katrina had signed a medical consent form, but Schmidt now wished to discuss a different kind of consent. He wanted to purchase some expensive new equipment from Japan. Also, he hoped to make patients more sanguine about sigmoidoscopies and colonoscopies in general – by sanguine I mean cheerful, not bloody – and he had realized that, because of her clitorises, the videotape of my beloved's internal examination was in fact the world's first colonoscopy porn movie. Consequently he wished to enter it for the Erotic Festival held in Barcelona, Spain, each October. With Katrina's consent. True, her participation in the porn movie would be incognito, since no friends nor family nor neighbors would easily recognize Katrina from her intestines, but Schmidt was a man of probity and integrity. (And I'd already recognized his artistic penchant when he alluded to the paintings of Chirico.)

Katrina was delighted.

"You're a woman in a million," Schmidt said gratefully. "You're a star."

"Hmm," said my Beloved. "I always wanted to star in a movie. You know, I think I would rather appreciate screen credit – my name on the silver screen for a couple of seconds. You can simply call me Katrina in the credits. I'm thinking about a title for the film." My Beloved can get very excited about ideas. "We've had *Deep Throat*. How about *Deep Bowel*? Does the festival give out prizes?"

"It wouldn't be a festival without prizes," Schmidt assured her. "Erotic journalists often call its Grand Prix for films *The Grand Prick*. The runner-up gets a consolation prize called *El Consolador*."

"What do the prizes look like?"

"Rather long dildos. Actually, they're telescopic. Specially made."

"You can *see* through them, like you see through a telescope?"

"No, but they're adjustable. They extend."

"Far enough to reach that first clitoris inside of me?"

Maybe Katrina could retain custody of the prize for a while, although Schmidt craved such a trophy for his own office, where it might encourage male homosexuals to look forward to sigmoidoscopies and colonoscopies.

When my Beloved began to experience morning sickness several weeks later we suspected what had happened. She must have swallowed so much semen sticking together protectively that some survived the digestive juices in the stomach and the juices of the small intestine. She must be pregnant in that additional womb which was her appendix, opened for fertilization now that the hymen had been torn away by a hard turd.

"My love, that means you must have an extra ovary at the back of the appendix!"

"Unless," she said inspiredly, "there's such a thing as... Well now, the word for a virgin pregnancy is parthenogenesis. So what's the male counterpart? What's the name for a self-fertilizing *sperm* pregnancy. It's a possibility."

Parthenos is Greek for maiden, and *pais* is Greek for boy, as in pedophile and pedophilia. Maybe the correct term might be *pedogenesis*. A pedogenetic pregnancy.

"That sounds a bit like a buggered boy becoming pregnant," said Katrina. "I once read a horror novel about that theme. It was called *The Worm* or something."

"Well, whatever." The name didn't matter. The *term* that did matter was the likely length and outcome of her pregnancy, which we now took to be an indisputable fact.

I hesitated. "Ectopic pregnancies are ones which take place outside the womb. They can be dangerous. You might need an abortion."

"An appendix abortion? Shall I eat a masochistically hot curry? Or take part in a Mexican chili-eating contest? Beloved," for Katrina also calls me thus, "this pregnancy *isn't* happening outside of a womb – merely in a *different* womb, an auxiliary womb."

"Hmm, that's true." Between two such kindred spirits as my Beloved and myself, talking often makes unusual things seem very true, truer than ordinary banal things.

To avoid any risk of an officious impulsive ectopic appendectomy occurring if the gynecological equivalent of Dr. Hassan were involved, my Beloved did not consult her doctor at all about our intuitions. During the further subsequent weeks I inspected Katrina's belly by hand pressure periodically – and we also noted the absence of any menstruation from her anus, which might have been expected normally subsequent to the loss of her seal-tight hymen.

"Any tenderness?" I would enquire.

"Only tenderness for you, my Beloved," she would reply, and she might experience a minor orgasm.

"Will our baby look like you, or like me?" she mused. "Even if this pregnancy arises principally from your sperm which I swallowed, every cell in me still contains my own DNA. Osmosis of genetic material seems quite possible."

"Maybe it'll be like both of us, then!"

In all, three months had passed since Katrina's colonoscopy, and soon it would be October, the time of the Barcelona Erotic Festival. For weeks now, whenever my Beloved went to the toilet to crap, she'd been holding a sieve, since it would be terrible if our baby drowned. And then, one wonderful morning...

Well, this is the true story of the birth of Tom Thumb, known as Pulgarcito in Spain and by other names in other lands – which proves that the same kind of birth must have happened previously elsewhere; otherwise the tale would not exist, let alone be widespread. The development of flush toilets may have prevented more recent reports.

During her pregnancy Katrina had eaten as richly as she could so that good semi-digested nourishment would reach the foetus, but our son had gestated in my Beloved's appendix which, unlike the primary womb, could not swell otherwise it would burst. Thus he was only the size of a thumb, and he may never grow much larger.

Don't get the idea, though, that our diminutive son is of deficient intellect! He's very bright and communicative. He brings joy to the lives of me and Latrina, I mean Katrina, damn this keyboard.

In addition to combating contraception and abortion, maybe the Pope ought to start a campaign for *coproconsciousness* – in other words, shit-inspection by all women. He might use as the motto for this campaign that famous remark by Saint Augustine, *Inter faeces et urinam nascimur* – "we are born between [or, in this case, among] shit and piss." Even so, the birth of a miniature person, a bonsai baby, must be a rare occurrence.

If Dr. Schmidt's film wins a prize in Barcelona, Katrina talks of a career in intestinal porn to build a sizable nest-egg for our son, who mightn't be able to earn a normal living. If enough people become imprinted upon bowel-porn – the clitoris in the colon – they'll need more than merely one video to watch.

Hector Meets the King
E Sedia

"I never was good at saying goodbye, and you were never good at letting go. So it starts, between me and you, and so it will end. I and you, inhale and exhale, a sigh and a kiss into a flat, adenoid face of the world.

"I know, I do not look much like a hero nowadays – gravity, the eternal bitch, has me in its hold, my fingertips are stained with ink, and my shoulders wrap around my chest as a pair of wide, anemic wings. But, believe me, I am a hero.

"There are ties in the world, son. Nothing binds more securely than another's pain. I watch your mother sleeping, her translucent skin flushed with dreams, her stately knees drawn at the pit of her stomach. I would have loved her even if she were short of leg and black of tooth; even then, hurting her would not be a possibility. Mediocrity is the only painless state in the world, or so I thought.

"There is a finite, immutable amount of pain in the world, and what you spare others you must swallow yourself. I swallowed my pride and my honor. I did not walk through the gates that day unable to hurt her. I would rather be a coward than a torturer. The legends lie – they tell the story as it should have been, they tell of Hector felled in the spray of warm sticky blood and splintered bone, they tell of his body dragged behind a chariot, of his orphaned son. The truth is sadder. Hector lived to see his son grow up. He watched him through the shroud of swallowed shame, and his eyes teared, as if from acrid smoke of burning Troy. And so it ends."

I sing of what has not been sung before. I sing of Hector and his sacrifice, I sing his unlamented mediocrity. I sing his cowering, and I sing his end.

I sing the dry wooden rain of arrows that drummed on the roofs of the palace and the hovels, monotonous, growing too familiar to be noticed. I sing the braying of donkeys in their stables, the crowing of roosters at dawn, and the lowing of oxen. Smells of manure and hay. Incessant gnawing of saws and hacking of axes outside the city walls. The siege. I sing guilt like manacles.

Hector took off his helm with horsehair crest that had scared the infant. With this gesture he dispensed with the heroism forever. He took his son into the crook of his arm, and his wife by her hand. He was familiar with the labyrinth of narrow streets, and with vast open space by the city walls.

As Cassandra's mad cries hung over the city like a cloud, he led them to the well hidden entrance into an underground tunnel that took them outside, into the thicket of scrub and hazelnuts. Swift, straight branches – future arrows – lashed their faces as they walked away from the doomed city.

I sing Hector, as he cranes his neck surveying a tall, gleaming building, and I sing his new job, I sing eight hours at the office, every day, excepting the holidays and two-week vacation. I sing the plastic smile of the receptionist that greets him every morning, as the elevator spews him forth, in the crowd of other overheated bodies. I sing Hector's sacrifice.

I put on my helm, the horsehair crest of it moth-eaten and ready to fall apart into dust. I fold the note addressed to my son and leave it on the kitchen table. I do not dare to kiss Andromache, for fear of waking her and letting the yoke of her white arms hold me back again.

I find my spear in the back of a coat closet, and my arthritic fingers close over its smooth, cool shaft. I do not even attempt to put on my old armor – my girth is too great now, and my back is too bent and weakened by years at the desk to bear its terrible weight. But I brush my fingertips against the polished bronze of the breastplate. I pick up my shield and strap on my sword.

I pause in the driveway, thinking whether I should take my car. I decide against it – it seems undignified somehow. I let my feet carry me past and out of the sleeping development.

I pass green lawns and neatly trimmed hedges; somebody's dog follows me, its docked tail wagging in tentative friendship. I do not know where I am going, but I am certain that I will find it, and all mistakes of the past will be rectified. I think of what will become of Andromache, of her delayed widowhood. I find comfort in thoughts about pension, Social Security, life insurance. With all that, she won't have to do any more telemarketing, and she will drop her pretense of happiness. As I think this, I do not notice as I arrive here, at the miniature golf course.

Hector stopped, the trimmed grass soft and submissive under the soles of his scuffed brown shoes. He surveyed the battlefield from under drawn, graying eyebrows. His eyes squinted against the lashings of the wind and hardened to narrow slits.

A windmill chopped the air into thick, humid slices, and the wind whistled between its four wings. A giant ape, its low forehead wrinkled with malice, grinned with bright wooden teeth and shuffled its massive foot back and forth, exposing and covering a narrow pipe, just wide enough for a golf ball. A dinosaur reared up as its mouth opened in and closed in silent screams of presumed pain.

These were the only worthy adversaries, and Hector hefted his spear, choosing his target. The ape seemed the most malignant of all, and he shouted his challenge to it. The ape grinned and shuffled in one place, too dumb or too conceited to take cover.

Hector's arm felt weak as he raised his spear and hurled it toward the ape. The spear hit its shoulder and sank into the wooden flesh, trembling from impact. The shaft swayed, and the spear fell to the ground.

The ape roared and cowered for a moment, and then stood to its full height, its fists the size of millstones pounding on its chest. It swung at Hector, but he ducked the blow. The giant fist passed inches over his head, and his gray hair ruffled in the wind.

Hector ripped his sword from the sheath, and lunged for the ape's unprotected side. The gash his blade left dripped with ichor the colour of papier-mâché, and the ape howled in pain.

Hector retreated, waiting for his chance to strike, as the enraged ape chased after him, its cries piercing like Andromache's tears. Hector was running out of breath, weighed as he was by age and manacles of guilt. He remembered the ape's name: King Kong. It was too young and too strong for him, and he retreated until the back wall of the windmill blocked his passage – he could feel it with his shoulder blades. The ape's fists swung in an easy rhythm: king–kong, sigh–kill, maim–kiss.

Hector's sword slashed across the ape's knuckles, making it cry out again, but inflicted as little damage as a toothpick. He still waved his weapon about as the ape picked him into one of its fists, as his ribs cracked, as his world narrowed to a swirling, rolling singularity of darkness.

In his last moments his thoughts sped up so that his short time of lingering lucidity between blindness and death stretched forever. Hector dreamed of Achilles, guilt and ape, of the forces that grinded him into a bloodied, limp husk, of the destiny of loss and defeat. He dreamed of Andromache's peppy voice traveling over the telephone wires: "Have you considered switching your long-distance provider?" He had spared her degradation in the Grecian hands, he had saved her from a lifetime of slavery. She would be grateful.

And he thought of his son, of his legacy, of a sigh and a kiss. He would graduate from college and enter a law school, and become a king – like King Menelaus, King Priam, the King o' Cats, King Kong. And Hector smiled.

New Writings in the Fantastic
May Day, May Day
Liza Granville

She hadn't wanted to come. When it came to anything natural, she never did.

"Someone has to go," Nigel said. "Her father's an important client."

Because she was ambitious, Jane agreed, even though it meant leaving at dawn. After all, it was only a wedding. And May the first was a Saturday.

The church was ancient, only halfheartedly Christian. Its carved doorway writhed with serpents devouring each other's tails. Shela-na-gig, the Celtic fertility goddess, crouched over the entrance exposing herself. The nave was massed with flowers flaunting their reproductive organs. Jane averted her eyes. Disgusting, all of it.

She sat at the back, on the end of a pew. Smoothing down her chic suit, she forced a tight smile for the old man on her left. He mumbled something to her chest. Jane yawned. Her eyes drifted upwards to focus on the roof bosses.

Nature again. Each was carved to represent foliage. Then she saw the face, half-hidden, leering. It was the Green Man, master of May Day ceremonies. Fertility ceremonies, she recalled, shuddering. Unbridled goings-on in the greenwood.

A couple of hairpins sprang from the sleek chignon. A few wisps of hair escaped.

The congregation stirred. Heads turned. The organ choked on Mendelssohn as the bride sailed past.

A dark figure hesitated by Jane's pew. Her eyes flicked sideways and a quiver ran up her spine. He was huge. A beast in an expensive suit, with a tight, icy white rosebud in his buttonhole. She frowned. Surely he didn't think he could sit here. There was no room...

But already he was moving in on her, pushing his body into that tiny space, forcing her to slide further along, pressing her up against the old man's spindly frame. Jane squeezed her thighs together, to avoid touching him. Her arms crossed over her chest to escape the pressure of his shoulder. When they stood, his big hands rested on the pew in front. Thick hair erupted from his sleeves, lay like a pelt on his hands, coiled across his finger joints. Slowly but surely the flower fragrance was overlaid by a dense musky smell.

More pins erupted. She could feel the chignon slowly unwinding, lying heavy on her nape.

She began to sweat. Jane *never* sweated.

They sat down. Suddenly he was there again, jammed tight against her. She noticed the rosebud had changed colour. Its petals were flushed a delicate pink. And they were opening.

"Do you...?"

He caught her looking. His eyes held hers. They were dark brown. Passionate. Full of secrets. His mouth was full too. The sensuous lips, curved in a smile, suggested he knew more than she wanted him to. Her own lips parted. Her breaths became quick and shallow. Her skin tingled.

"Take this woman..."

Furious, she tore her eyes away. This time, when they knelt, she prayed.

Impossible not to sneak another look at the rose. The pink had deepened. A space opened in its heart. Bud had become chalice.

"And do you...."

Against her will, her body began responding to his male energy. An electrical charge passed between them. A wordless conversation. Her mind was invaded by fleeting images that were nothing and everything to do with the ceremony. The remaining pins slid to the floor. Her hair cascaded round her shoulders. Her nipples erected. An ache began deep in the pit of her stomach: an old memory, reawakened, brought fierce waves of desire.

"Take this man..."

She pulled herself together. Ignore these feelings and they went away. Concentrate on thinking about something loathsome: bluebottles on liver; dog turd on shoes; extra pounds on the hips. It always worked.

It didn't.

The rose blushed deep red. A flower in full bloom, the moist petals turned back. Open. Waiting.

His hand brushed hers. Jane's body swayed toward him. But he'd only reached into his pocket. The panpipes lay on his palm like a silver toy. He left as silently as he'd come. From beyond the door, sweet notes soared above the death-march groan of the hymn. They beckoned. She resisted.

But the sound was irresistible: a Pied Piper's tune, it drew her on, across meadows, into the roaring boiling green of the woods. The trees shivered with anticipation. Twigs tugged at her jacket. Ivy uncurled to finger her buttons. Ferns unzipped her skirt with tiny green teeth. Moss tugged at her shoes. Brambles shredded her tights. When he stopped, she sank down, catching her breath; music curled round her, dark as enchanter's nightshade.

She didn't pull away when his lips touched her cheek, her neck, her shoulders, soft as butterfly wings. Nor when his tongue probed with the insistence of a hummingbird reaching deep between the petals for nectar. His big hands moved over her body, rough and gentle as a cat's tongue, playing her as expertly as he played the pipes.

She was lost in another place. The only way out was to go further in. A swarm of bees erupted from her navel. Rain forests tingled symphonies on her thighs. A rainbow arched her back. Flowers blossomed from her perineum. The trees absorbed her primeval wail. Nothing mattered.

An explosion of triumph from the church organ announced that the deed was done. The knot was tied. Jane sat up damp and disorientated. The old man snored. On her right was an empty space. She hugged herself, hoping nobody had noticed.

It was a dream. Just a bizarre dream. Of course it was.

Even so, something had happened. In those brief minutes of... sleep... a shell had been cracked, an iceberg melted, a door opened. The tune lingered. She'd go back to her old life, but nothing would ever be the same again.

Above her head the Green Man grinned. Jane hadn't noticed her ruined tights. Nor the fern fronds in her shoes. Not even the may blossom in her hair.

But when she opened her clenched fist her hand was full of red rose petals.

New Writings in the Fantastic
Killing Mr. Softly
Scott Emerson Bull

Mr. Softly had to die.

There were just no two ways about it. I'd reached the end of my rope. Mr. Softly had to die and he had to die soon.

Margaret would not agree – not that I ever considered discussing the idea with her. Poor, sweet, Margaret. She would just shake her gray, curly-haired head and say, "Killing is wrong, Max. It's just wrong. I swear, that temper of yours..." But sometimes it's necessary to kill. We can try to hide those murderous feelings in the dark corners of our hearts, but sometimes we have to let them out. Sometimes we have no choice.

Mr. Softly knew that. He knew where the dark thoughts hid and he knew how to coax them out. It was all part of the game. Tit for tat, as he would say. But then he would say this, wouldn't he? He was winning.

We'd see about that.

I found Mr. Softly, as I always did, watching the morning shuffleboard game.

"Morning, Max."

"Softly," I said, tipping my hat. He was dressed, as always, in an outrageous red jogging suit and virginal white high-top sneakers. I doubt he had ever jogged in his life, but sweatsuits seemed to have become the uniform of choice for most of the active elderly in the community. A style that seemed utterly pathetic to me.

"Nice day," he said, looking up at the gray sky.

"What's nice about it?"

He pushed a wisp of gray hair back from his forehead and pulled the road map of wrinkles on his face into a puckering smirk. It took every bit of will power I had not to bust it down his throat. I could hear Margaret warning "Temper, temper" *in absentia*.

"Care to finish our game?" he asked.

"Not interested."

"Come on, Max. I'll make it interesting. Besides, I believe you owe me."

I let out a sigh of exasperation and watched the action on the shuffleboard court. Miss Ransom had just knocked one of her own disks out of the scoring triangle and was cursing a blue streak.

"I'm tired of our game, Softly."

The creature in red bent closer towards me. Hot breath burned my cheek as he squeezed my arm.

"Which is exactly why we have to make it more interesting," he said. "Raise the stakes a bit."

"The stakes are already too high," I said, pulling my arm free.

We stood silently for a moment, listening to the scrape of shuffleboard disks on concrete. My heart beat a tick faster.

"Be a shame if Margaret found out," Softly said finally.

My hands squeezed into fists. Softly saw the anger in my face.

"Now, now," he said. "That hot streak of yours will be your undoing one day."

"And you'd know all about that, wouldn't you?"

Mr. Softly cleared his throat and spat on the grass. "You disappoint me, Max. Just because I get, shall we say, persnickety from time to time..."

"'Persnickety,'" I scoffed. "You're a goddam lunatic."

Mr. Softly smiled. "Yes," he said. "I suppose I am. But that doesn't change the fact that you owe me, and the game's not over until that debt is settled." He slipped his clawlike hand around my arm again. "So, what do you say?"

There was a sharp cry of victory from the shuffleboard court as Miss Ransom defeated her opponent.

"All right," I said. "What do you want?"

It was Winky who raised the stakes of our game, though she would have had no way of knowing.

I suppose I should explain a little about our game. It was Softly's idea of course. It started on a drunken evening late last spring. I had liked Softly then. He was a loner and about the only other senior male in the retirement community with a lick of sense about him. He had a taste for good whiskey and so did I, and, as is often the case between men our age, that was enough for us to form a bond. We were sitting on the porch of his house – Softly had one of the few detached homes in the community – whining about the boredom of advancing age when the conversation turned to the shapely nurse who had just been hired to tend to the bedridden in the permanent care center. Playing the dirty old man, I wondered out loud how she might look without that starched white uniform. Mr. Softly said he'd be happy to find out for me, but for a price.

"What price?" I asked.

Softly leaned forward on his chair. I'll never forget the look on his face. Like a spider sizing up an entangled fly.

"Drusilla Hawkins," he said.

"Old 'Squinty' Hawkins?"

"Yes. I provide you with pictures of the lusty young nurse and you get me Drusilla Hawkins."

I eyed Softy suspiciously. I should have known something was up by the quickness of his answer, as if he had planned this moment all along, which I am sure now that he had. But I was an old fool.

"What do you want with her?"

"My reasons are of no importance," Softly said, grinning smugly. "Have we got a deal?"

"Seeing as how there's no way you're gonna catch Nurse Lusty in the buff, sure, why not?"

So I shook hands with the old devil.

When I ran into Softly the next day, he was holding an unlabeled videotape in his hand.

"Nurse Lusty, as requested." He smiled, handing it to me.

I stared blankly at the tape. "But how did you...?"

"Trade secret," he grinned. "Suffice it to say you owe me one Miss Drusilla Hawkins."

I felt lightheaded. "I'll have to see the video first," I stammered.

"By all means. Then arrange for Drusilla to be at my house by six for dinner. Tell her any lie you have to. I'll take care of the rest." And with a squeak of his tennis-shoe heels, Softly turned and disappeared into the community clubhouse.

The video was grainy and poorly focused, but there was no doubting it was Nurse Lusty. I hid the tape with the other things I had decided Margaret didn't need to know about and went to find Drusilla Hawkins. I felt like I'd been used, but figured what the hell, so the old man wanted a little romance in his life, though I had to admit that Squinty was an odd choice. She was one of the older residents of the home and known for being outlandishly frugal. She earned her nickname from the way she screwed up her eyes to look through spectacles several prescriptions out of date because she was too cheap to buy herself new ones. She had lost her husband last year, and I was afraid she might be tentative in accepting a strange man's invitation to dinner. But, like many of the single residents here, she was lonely, and convincing her to visit Softly was the work of only a few minutes. I must say I actually felt kind of good about fixing them up.

But the next day...

"How was your date?" I asked Drusilla. We had run into each other in the laundry room.

She looked at me, confused. "Date?"

"With Mr. Softly," I said. "Last night."

"I don't know what you mean."

I shrugged my shoulders and threw some towels into the dryer. I was in the process of writing off Squinty as just another flaky old broad when I noticed something was different about her. Then it hit me.

"New glasses?" I asked.

"Why, yes! Got them this morning at the mall. Only took an hour. Aren't they nice?"

Actually they weren't nice. They were big and thick and gaudy, with sides that twisted like a child's drinking straw. "They look expensive," I said.

"My goodness, were they ever! Nearly three hundred dollars. Designer frames, you know."

"Really." Again I shrugged my shoulders. It seemed odd to hear Squinty bragging about spending money as opposed to squeezing each nickel dry, but I figured, So what? So the old broad finally splurged on something.

But then things got really weird. As I reached to deposit my quarters into the dryer's coin slot, Mrs. Hawkins frantically pushed my hand away and deposited four quarters of her own.

"There you go," she said, smiling. "Today it's on me. In fact, today they're *all* on me!"

Slack-jawed, I watched as Mrs. Hawkins proceeded to fill the coin slot of every washer and dryer in the laundry room with quarters out of a worn change purse, the kind that used to produce only stray flies when Jack Benny opened them. Having used up her quarters, she gave me a half-cocked moonbeam smile and exited the laundry room in a flourish.

Something was wrong. Immediately, I went looking for Softly. I found him sipping lemonade by the shuffleboard courts.

"How was your date?" I asked.

"Splendid," he replied.

"Seems Mrs. Hawkins has no remembrance of it."

Mr. Softly raised a crooked finger to his lips. "Swore her to secrecy. Don't want people talking."

I sat down in the lawn chair next to him. "There's something wrong with her," I said.

"Nonsense."

"I mean it, Softly. Suddenly the woman's a spendthrift. You know she bought a pair of three-hundred-dollar glasses today?"

"Of course," he said. "I helped her pick them out myself."

"But she *never* spends money. She's the tightest woman I've ever met. She calculates her share of the tip to the penny when we go out to eat. I swear, something is wrong."

"Pisshaw," Softly said, with a twinkle in his eye. "Woman's just in love."

But, if Mrs. Hawkins was suddenly in love, it was with spending money. Within a week she had bought a new Cadillac, a new set of teeth, and a diamond tennis bracelet so laden with carats she could hardly lift her arm. Feeling guilty, I spent most of this time going about my own business, trying to avoid both Mrs. Hawkins and Mr. Softly. I enjoyed a brief respite in early summer when Margaret and I spent two months with her son in Delaware, but when we got back the whole community was abuzz about Mrs. Hawkins having to move out.

"She's gone?" Margaret asked Clara Meddleton over tea and cookies in our dining-room.

"Well, oh my, yes," Clara said. Clara was a busybody and someone I made a habit of ignoring, but this time I tuned her in, listening as I pretended to read the newspaper.

"According to Gina Munshaur, one of the secretaries said that Mrs. Hawkins was dead broke. Couldn't pay her rent any more. They claimed she went through two hundred thousand dollars of her dead husband's money in less than a month."

"But what about all those nice things she bought? That new Cadillac?"

"All gone. She had to sell them to pay off debts. Apparently, after she'd spent all her husband's money, she began spending money she didn't have..."

"Well, where did she go?"

"Nobody knows. She didn't have any family left. Tom Parker swears he saw her downtown carrying a suitcase and a trash bag filled with clothes, but you know what a storyteller he is."

"Oh dear Lord! I hope she's not living on the streets."

I'd heard enough. I bid Margaret and Clara goodbye and went out to look for Mr. Softly. Something was wrong, though I had no idea what. I knew only that Softly was somehow at the bottom of it. With each step, I felt my temper flare, and visions of doing bodily harm to Mr. Softly clouded my mind. I wanted to twist the little bastard's neck in my hands. I stalked down the sidewalk, determined more than ever to find him.

Which was when I ran into the aforementioned Winky.

Winky was Mrs. Atkinson's dog. I don't know much about breeds, but let's just say that Winky was one of those nasty, yappy little mutts. A hairball that would have been better left uncoughed-up. I was passing Mrs. Atkinson's apartment building, daydreaming about doing Mr. Softly bodily harm, when Winky charged out from behind the azaleas, barking her fool head off. The rotten little bitch nearly gave me a heart attack. I must have leapt a foot off the ground, no mean feat for someone my age.

"Winky," Mrs. Atkinson cried from the screen door of her apartment. "Don't bark at Mr. Max."

Hearing her owner's voice, Winky scampered back to the apartment building, stopping once to give me a quick look, no doubt wanting to satisfy herself that she had indeed removed another year from what little time I had left on earth.

"Goddamn little monster," I muttered. "I wish someone should shut that creature up permanently."

Behind me I heard footsteps. It was Mr. Softly.

"Consider it done," he said, with a neighborly pat on my shoulder. "Consider it done."

They buried Winky two weeks later. The vet said he had never seen anything like it. Winky had simply stopped barking. He couldn't find any medical reason for it, nor could he find any marks on the dog. It was as if divine providence, or providence of some other kind, had relieved the dog of its ability to speak, which was bad since Winky was the type of dog that lived to bark and did so at absolutely everything that moved within a whisker of her path. Once her reason to live had gone, she took to sulking about in hiding places. Unfortunately, one of these hiding places was a dryer in the laundry room. Perhaps if she'd still had her bark she could have saved herself, but as it was she stayed in for the full forty-five-minute cycle. She came out nice and fluffy, but quite dead.

Mrs. Atkinson was beside herself, ranting and raving about the weird cults and religious organizations she believed had put a spell on her dear departed dog.

But I knew who the culprit was, and soon it would be his turn to die.

I chewed my dinner slowly. Margaret was normally a wonderful cook, but tonight she had burned the pork chops out of all recognition. Even the fat, which is, after all, the best part, was completely inedible. She probably assumed that her culinary *faux pas* was the reason for my black mood, but nothing could have been further from the truth. I was still replaying the conversation I'd had with Softly today in my head. I was watching his chicken-thin lips move as he told me what, or rather who, he wanted me to provide to even the game.

"Max?" Margaret said.

"What?"

"I don't like it when you get like this. I told you I was sorry about dinner."

"Forget it. A simple mistake. We'll buy you a new kitchen timer tomorrow." Tomorrow, I thought. How strange to think about tomorrow. There might not even be a tomorrow.

Margaret absently pushed her peas around her plate with her fork. She looked at me, saw the anger in my eyes, and got up suddenly from the table. She threw some dirty pots and pans into the sink, then whirled around on me. "Then what's eating you?" she asked.

"Nothing," I said quietly.

"Come on, Max. You know I hate it when you get these moods. I swear your temper's getting worse than your father's."

I looked at Margaret and took a deep breath. Her soft brow was creased with concern and her flowered apron was twisted in her hands. I tried to smile, but no smile was getting past the scowl on my face. I thought I saw the beginnings of a tear in one of her brown eyes, and realized how desperately I still loved her after all these years.

"Can we just drop this, please?" I said. "I'm entitled to a bad mood now and again, aren't I?"

She smoothed her apron against her thighs and let her gaze drop to the floor. "I'm going to Clara's for a while tonight," she said. "If that's OK with you?"

I took another deep breath. "No."

Margaret glared at me.

"Who died and left *you* in charge?"

"I don't want you going out tonight," I said.

She turned the hot water on full blast, drowning the dirty dishes. "I'll go out if I damn' well please," she said. Margaret was mad now. She hardly ever cursed.

"No," I said again. I stood abruptly, scraping the floor with the steel legs of the dinette chair. "Now, you listen to me, Margaret. I want you to stay home. Under no circumstances are you to leave this house." I grabbed my hat and made for the door.

"And just where are you going?" Margaret said.

"Out."

She said something else, but the door slammed, cutting off her words. Already I was on the sidewalk moving fast, and with each step my anger rose. My father's temper, the temper I had inherited, was well on the boil. The time had come to settle things.

I took a shortcut past the permanent care center. In the parking lot I saw Nurse Lusty getting out of her car. It was the first time I had seen her since Softly had given me the videotape, and I must say I hardly recognized her. She seemed plain to me now; her eyes sullen, her hair hanging in greasy strands, her figure bloated by a few too many extra pounds. All of her sexiness was gone, as if the videotape had stolen it from her. Was Softly responsible for this as well?

I entered the retirement community's one street of detached bungalows. The door to Softly's house was ajar. He was waiting for me.

"Come in," he said.

He was sitting at his dining-room table. The same one at which we had played many a drunken round of gin rummy. A pistol was lying on the table. The hand grip was facing me. The barrel was pointed at Softly.

"What the hell's that?" I asked.

"It's why you came here, isn't?" Mr. Softly smiled. "You did come here to kill me, didn't you?"

I looked down at the gun. I felt ashamed, but my temper pushed aside any thoughts of backing down.

"You deserve to die," I said.

"Perhaps." Softly twisted the cap off a bottle of whiskey and poured some into an empty tumbler. "Please," he said, shoving the glass toward me, "sit down."

I took a seat in the chair across from him. The whiskey tasted hot in my mouth. I locked my eyes onto his. The gun hovered just below my peripheral vision.

"I must say I am disappointed, Max," Softly said, pouring himself some whiskey. "I always thought you an honorable man. Thought you would uphold your end of the bargain no matter what the consequences."

"What bargain? You tricked me."

"Nevertheless, there's only one way out."

"You're not getting her," I said.

Softly smiled. "We'll see about that. More whiskey?"

I covered the top of my glass with my hand. "What are you?" I asked. "I mean what do you...?"

Softly raised his hand as if to say he knew what I was trying to ask. He swirled the whiskey in his glass, then drank it down in one swallow. "How do I explain this?" he said. "I guess you could call me a thief."

"A thief?"

"Yes. A thief. A common criminal. You wouldn't put someone to death for stealing, would you?"

"That depends," I said, glancing down at the gun. It appeared to be closer than before. "What is it that you steal?"

Softly leaned forward on the table with his elbows. "The essence of people," he said. "I take that one quality which determines a person's individuality."

"Like Mrs. Hawkins's cheapness?" I asked.

"Exactly."

"But why?"

Softly poured himself another whiskey. "To be honest, I really don't know any more. It's become a sort of obsession, I suppose. The odd thing is, I really don't get much pleasure from it any longer. It's sort of like sex as you get older: it doesn't feel as good, but you still do it because you remember how good it used to feel."

My hand crept closer to the gun. "You're sick," I said. "You ruined Mrs. Hawkins. They say she's living on the streets."

"Oh, nonsense. She spent maybe one night on the streets. Two, tops. A church took her in. She'll be fine."

Hatred gripped my soul. "Bastard. Don't you have a heart under that stupid sweatsuit?"

Softly smiled. "Why don't you shoot me and find out?"

I ground my teeth together and looked down at the shiny black metal of the gun. "Maybe I will."

The old man chuckled. "You're quite famous for your temper, aren't you, Max? You know that's the most difficult quality for me to steal from someone. Very unpredictable, but oh so satisfying once it's been taken."

I looked down again. The gun was in my hand. I wasn't even aware I had picked it up. "What the hell are you? Some sort of demon?"

Softly drank another glass of whiskey. If he was worried about my holding the gun, he was doing a good job of not showing it. "I really don't know," he said. "I've just always been this way, long as I can remember. I suppose my parents could have told me, but then they both died when I was very young. Drove their car off a cliff. I've always wondered if I had anything to do with their sudden perishing."

The gun felt heavy in my hand. My thumb found the safety and released it.

"So why me?" I asked. "Why involve me in this stupid game?"

"It's a funny thing," he said. "It's easier for me to steal a person's essence if they come to me of their own free will. Take Mrs. Hawkins, for example. If I had approached her on my own, her defenses would have been up. It's the natural distrust people have for other people. You know, that 'Now, what does he want from *me*?' attitude. But, when it's them who approach me, their defenses are down." Softly's smile broadened. "As yours are right now."

My heart skipped a beat.

"And, if you're wondering about the dog, she was easy. Stupid bitch attacked me every time I passed the apartment. I did that as much for myself as I did it for you."

"I never asked you to kill the dog."

"And I didn't kill it. I just – how did you put it? – 'shut it up permanently.' Anyway, enough chitchat. It's time for you to do what you came to do." Softly rose from his chair and spread his arms apart. "Go ahead, Max. Shoot me."

I looked at Softly's sunken chest buried sadly beneath the thin layer of red jogging suit. He looked defenseless. Suddenly, I could barely breathe.

"Come on, Max," he said. He locked his gaze onto mine. "Not losing your nerve, are you?"

The gun grew heavier in my hand and the strength went out of my trigger finger. My mind said "pull" but the appendage hung there weakly, as I realized too late what Softly was doing. I felt his tug on my psyche like swollen fingers squeezing around my brain. I hadn't bargained for this, him wanting *my* essence. Perhaps that was what he had wanted all along. Perhaps that had been the object of the game right from the beginning. A game I had never really had a chance to win or even understand. My anger was receding, and I felt a strange kind of love growing for the man. It was as if I were unconsciously thanking him for setting me free, for unlocking me from the temper that had so often held me captive. *But he's not doing this for you,* I told myself, and I tried to lift the pistol to point it back at Mr. Softly's chest.

I couldn't do it. My arm remained limp at my side.

"You disappoint me again, Max," I heard Softly say. "I thought you would be a much tougher adversary. Perhaps your temper was more myth than fact."

A spike of hatred allowed me to lift the gun, and I heard Softly emit a low chuckle as I cocked the trigger. My mind swam in a blur of images. I was so confused. I saw Softly smiling at me, beckoning me to come to him, to hold him, as the gun grew heavy again. What was I doing? I asked myself. Why was I pointing a gun at this man. This man I loved...

"Much better, Max," I heard him say. "Let it go. It's always been your Achilles' heel, hasn't it? Got you an early retirement. 'Grumpy old Max' they called you. Let it go, Max. Let it go."

I was weakening. Only a small bit of anger remained, and of all places it seemed to be attached to my heart. I felt it fighting Mr. Softly, but finally it too conceded defeat. And then suddenly, there I stood, shocked and dismayed to find myself pointing a gun at my best friend.

"Thank you, Max," I heard Softly say through the haze of my mind. "Perhaps you'd like to put the gun down now and have another drink. Maybe play a friendly game of rummy."

"Yes," I heard myself say. I looked stupidly at the gun, but couldn't put it aside. Something was still wrong, but what? "A drink would be nice," I said. "Perhaps that would calm me down."

"Yes, Max," Softly said, his voice dreamy, soothing. "A drink would do you wonders. Now, please, hand me the gun. Our game's over."

I looked at the gun and then looked at Softly: this wonderful man who had done so much for me. So why couldn't I stop pointing a gun at him?

"Please, Max," Softly said, sounding a little more concerned now. "The gun."

I began to hand the gun to Softly. I can't say what I felt then. It wasn't really defeat or even submission. All I felt was confusion. I was just inches from placing the gun in his hand when I heard a loud gasp from behind.

"Max! Oh dear God! What are you doing?"

I whirled around to see Margaret standing in Softly's living-room. She had gone out despite my wishes, and must have stopped here to check on me on her way to Clara's. How sweet of her, always thinking of me. Had I been mad at her, too? It seemed perhaps I had, but not to worry. I would never be mad at her or anyone else ever again.

"Hello, Margaret," Softly said. He had released his hold on me and I saw him lock his eyes onto hers. Margaret seemed to weaken a bit, as if she might swoon. "Please join us, won't you? We were just having a drink."

"M-m-m-max, what is he doing to me?"

Softly's eyes turned bloodshot and the corners of his smile took on an evil cast. This was my friend? I asked myself.

"You are so sweet, Margaret," Softly said. Yes, I thought in agreement, Margaret must be the sweetest women on God's green earth. Who else could have put up with a cantankerous old fool like me for forty years? "So why don't you share some of that sweetness with me?" Softly said.

"Max, I feel funny," Margaret said. "I don't like this. Make him stop, Max. Please."

Margaret's face filled with pain. Why was Softly doing it? Why was he hurting her? Then I remembered our game, and I remembered about Mrs. Hawkins and Winky and Nurse Lusty, and I remembered the conversation Softly and I had had earlier that day, when he had told me how he wanted to settle the score. When he had told me he wanted Margaret. I looked at the gun that was still in my hand. I pointed it at Mr. Softly.

"You're not my friend," I said.

Softly's concentration broke off from Margaret. He looked over at me and the smile fell from his face.

"Now, Max," he said. "Please. You know I'm your friend. I've always been your friend."

"No, you're not," I said, taking aim. "You're not my friend at all."

The gun fired. Funny. It wasn't anger that pulled the trigger, but love. Love for Margaret. The first shot caught Softly in the chest and threw him back into his chair. I had expected to see blood, but perhaps it was blending in with the red of his jogging suit. The second shot hit him square in the forehead and caused Mr. Softly to glow. His body shook in spasms and his mouth flew open, releasing a tumult of voices. I thought I could hear Winky's familiar yap mixed in with the confusion of frightened human screaming, a lifetime of stolen personalities being purged from their plunderer. The sound disappeared quickly, as did Softly, who vanished in a haze of red mist right before our eyes. He was gone.

I had killed Mr. Softly.

It took a little while to get over what went on that night. At first there were a lot of questions about what had happened to Mr. Softly but, as it turned out, few people had cared much for the old man. Eventually, everyone just figured he'd skipped town leaving his rent unpaid. Margaret and I were lucky no one had heard the gun shots. One of the benefits of living in a retirement community, I suppose.

As for me and Margaret, we're doing just fine. She seems to like me more without my temper, though I must say she gets a bit frustrated at me when I don't stand up for myself, like when I suffer through a burnt steak at a restaurant instead of sending it back like I used to. Though I still love her dearly, I must say she's become a bit of a grouch. You should have seen her go off when she found that nudie tape of Nurse Lusty. Boy, did I hear it that day! Luckily there's still enough sweetness to outweigh the grumpiness.

And Mr. Softly? Occasionally I think about him. I suppose he unintentionally did us some good turns, but I shudder to think what might have happened if I hadn't, well, you know. Still, I can't help but smile when I pass by Winky's old place. Mrs. Atkinson has a new dog now, and I swear this one yaps louder than the last.

At least she has the good sense to keep this one on a leash.

New Writings in the Fantastic
Raise Your Hands
Gary McMahon

It starts again in a downtown nightclub.

Late Friday, early hours of Saturday morning, he can't be sure which: a boozy get-together with colleagues. The firm has just landed a multimillion-pound five-year contract to provide corporate literature, training brochures and videos for a huge City law firm. Tyler's boss took the entire team out for a celebratory dinner at some fancy French restaurant where you can't get in without a tie. Drinks after; then on to this seedy neon haze of a club.

Nobody deemed it necessary to mention the fact that it is also Tyler's birthday. His thirtieth year, a milestone. He has now officially spent the same number of years on the planet as his murdered father.

It's late, or it's early; he's forcing his way toward one of the four raised bars, desperate for a drink. Needing some form of respite from the bland, dead-eyed corporate faces that surround him every day in the office.

Somebody's elbow catches him a sharp one in the ribs. A drink is spilled down the back of his legs, drenching the brand new slacks he bought two days ago – a treat for his birthday weekend. A lazily thrown punch makes contact with the side of his face, just below the right eye.

Tyler spins around and tries to pinpoint the culprit in the dry-ice landscape. Not a glance is turned in his direction; he remains unnoticed, just another featureless blur in the swaying crowd.

Dizzy from the drink, the dry heat and the sudden blow, he decides to leave without saying goodbye. He doubts any of his so-called peer group will miss him anyway. As Tyler's on his way out the door, a narrow-eyed bouncer glares at him suspiciously, adjusting his posture: fighting stance. Tyler hurries outside into the light drizzle, turning up the collar of his blazer to lock out the cold.

There is a taxi idling at the kerb – an illegal minicab. Because of the weather, and the fact that he promised Janis he'd be home at a reasonable hour, he chances it.

The surly Turkish driver watches him all the way in the rearview mirror, a look of undisguised disdain etched into his swarthy face. For some reason that Tyler fails to comprehend, this man hates him. Loathes his suit and his money and his handsome benefits package.

Tyler tips the driver generously when he pays the fare, habitually assuaging some kind of nameless middle-class guilt. Just before the ungrateful bastard winds up the side window, Tyler cannot be certain the man doesn't swing a loose fist in his direction, aiming at the back of his head. When Tyler turns around, the car is pulling away from the kerb, belching fumes into the damp night air.

Inside the house he sits in the dark and listens to a CD of old blues standards. Muddy Waters and single malt; the glass quivering between his fingers as the aching music crackles through expensive speakers.

Janis is asleep upstairs; the baby monitor is placed in its usual spot near her head, positioned at just the right angle on the bedside cabinet on her side of the room. Little Jessie, all four gurgling months of her, snores crisply in the cot tucked into a corner of what will be the nursery when Tyler can find the time to decorate.

His family. His clan.

When the glass is drained he climbs the stairs to Jessie's room and looks in on her, his usual ritual before settling in for the night. She smiles in her sleep, shallow dimples creasing her papery cheeks. He walks softly to the side of the cot, bends down and offers a kiss to her downy fontanel. The baby stirs in her sleep, clenched little hands rising smoothly and swiftly to batter at his face.

He retreats onto the darkened landing, the skin beneath his eyes prickling.

What is this? What is going on? Tyler is beginning to feel bullied, abused, debased. Everyone, it seems, feels the need to strike him, to lash out as if he were their own personal demon.

He spends the remainder of the night in the guestroom, confused and alienated in his own home, his own life. And when sleep finally steals across him like a vast soft wave, he dreams of a narrow, stagnant canal and an empty warehouse. The feel of tight bonds cutting into the flesh of his wrists. The echo of distant screams.

Morning arrives with its own distinct combination of body shots: pain, white hot and searing, engulfs him. His head feels as if it has been dipped in molten metal and left to harden; he can barely lift it from the pillow.

He hears Jessie burbling to herself, and then Janis rising from their bed. Her feet drum a quick military tattoo across the bare boards, sounding more muffled after she puts them into the soft slippers she keeps by the door.

"Morning, baby!" she says, a smile in her voice. The infant coos and twitters in reply.

Despite Tyler's fervent prayers that she do otherwise, Janis pops her head around the doorframe, her eyes heavy, cheeks sallow. But she smiles at him, and it's all OK again. Everything is going to be fine.

"Good morning, hangover-boy," she says. "I'll feed this one, you get some rest. Enjoy your birthday night out?"

And she's gone before he fails to answer, clomping down the stairs wrapped in a heavy winter dressing gown.

But no matter how hard he tries he cannot go back to sleep; his skull is tight with repressed memories, and a bruise has developed on his cheekbone. It hurts when he attempts to lie on that side.

The aroma of frying bacon lures him down to the kitchen, where the kettle is boiling. Two cups – coffee granules, milk and sugar in each – sit on the draining board by the sink. Tyler fills them with piping hot water from the kettle, taking extra care not to scald his shaking hands.

He scoops the crispy bacon from under the grill, makes sandwiches for two, and carries breakfast through into the lounge.

Janis is sitting on the long sofa, feeding Jessie from a swollen, purple-veined breast. A weary smile hangs from her face, barely supported by the brittle structure of her bones. Tyler sits down beside her, eating his food in silence as the radio plays early morning banalities from its perch on the dining table.

When Janis hits him it is impossible to even fake surprise. A straight left: hard, fast and accurate. A boxer's punch. Tyler feels his body flop over onto its left side. The plate and partially eaten sandwich slide from his lap. He has time to register only the look of utter shock on his wife's tired face before he blacks out.

White light floods in, numbing him from the outside in and then back again. It takes a few minutes for the pain to announce itself, and when it does it is just the right side of bearable.

Janis stands over him, holding Jessie tightly against her chest. Her face is slack, ashen, as if the flesh has detached from the skull beneath. Tyler sees her as a huge death's head grinning down at him.

"I'm so sorry," she says, her voice bordering on hysteria. "I... I don't even know why the *fuck* I did that. My hands. They moved. On their own."

Tyler tries so hard to smile, but it hurts too much. Instead he sits upright, prodding at the tender areas of his burning face. So much pain, all the time.

"I think I'd better leave," he says. "Go for a walk."

He's out the door and on the street before she can even object, running, fleeing, from... from *what?*

Strangers hurl speculative punches as he passes by, not even aware of what they are doing. All Tyler sees is rapidly approaching white-knuckled fists, wide eyes, open mouths... the isolated elements of unknowing assailants perpetrating unconscious acts of aggression.

He has no idea how to protect himself; he has been a sworn pacifist since childhood, when his mother was sent to jail.

Since his seventh birthday; his father's last day on earth.

Now there's a thing. Is *that* what this is all about? Familial acts of abuse revisited by anyone whose path he crosses?

A woman slapping him in the face rouses him from his thoughts; her huge sovereign rings cut his cheek as she pulls back her wrinkled, bony hand. Haggard, she twists her lined mouth in shame and disbelief as she backs away, shaking her head in a useless gesture of rejection.

Warm blood runs down Tyler's face, mingling with the stinging tears. He retreats inside himself, chasing questions and answers like scraps of paper along a windy street.

Tyler's mother suffered years of beatings before she finally snapped. Then on that sultry and airless night she straightened out a wire coat hanger and inserted it into her drunken husband's ear as he slept. He died quickly, and without much fuss; after the act, Tyler's mother rolled over and went to sleep. She admitted later that it was the best, most peaceful and dreamless slumber she had ever experienced.

She turned herself in to the authorities early the following morning, swearing she did what she did to protect her son. She could handle the pain inflicted upon her own withered body, but, once the old man began to exhibit signs of starting on Tyler, she decided as a mother that enough was enough. She made a choice.

Tyler retains only dim memories of the attack that made up his mother's mind: his father's stubby-fingered hands at his throat, pinning him against the wall; the sensation of his tiny, dangling feet kicking against the skirting board; his mother screaming, her face crimson and bloated, like a ripe tomato.

Screaming... screams... *it always comes back to the screams.*

Battered and bloodied, Tyler makes his way to the park. It is empty at this hour but for the occasional dog walker. He sits on a wooden bench near the brackish pond and weeps into his rubbery fists, wishing he could raise them, fight back. But he can't; he never could. His mother knew that, and made her choice accordingly.

Tyler never went to see her in prison; she died alone and neglected. He didn't even answer her letters, the ones that begged him to acknowledge her existence. He excised her from his life like a malignant growth, a cancer. But the stain of violence remained, buried like a race memory, slowly metastasizing through his cells.

And years later that emotional tumor manifested itself in a way he still cannot recall for certain. The memory is hazy, dreamlike, as if viewed through heavy gauze. Like it happened to somebody else.

Three months later, wounds fully healed, Tyler is alone on a rundown cattle farm located deep in the Northumbrian wilds, renting the place until he can think of something better, something that might put an end to this madness.

The ramshackle outbuildings are all abandoned, disused; the smallholding ceased to be a working farm after the government culled its little dairy herd during the last BSE crisis. But Tyler knows all he needs to about mad cows. Now the farm is rented to disillusioned wage slaves who desire nothing more than to spend a long weekend recharging their batteries in the sticks. He has taken a longer-term lease than that.

It is dark outside, and wind rattles the windows in their rotting casings. He has the shutters pulled across the glass, but still feels exposed. Nobody has hit him since he came here; the nearest neighbor is five miles away, the closest town ten. All necessary provisions are delivered every two weeks, and left outside on the porch. Everything is paid for by credit card. Soon Tyler's funds will run out.

There is a sense of something finally coming to an end, of a circle closing. Somehow he knows a point has been reached, a conceptual boundary crossed.

The wind rises like a choir of lost souls, brushing its fingers against the rickety timber-frame building.

A strange sensation of sadness passes over Tyler's entire body, like a wave of gooseflesh, like the sun shimmering on cool waters. He stands, opens the door and stares out into the night, taking a mental snapshot of the thin crescent moon, the faraway pinheads of stars. This may well be his last glimpse of the world.

The old cowshed lies just across the yard. The door is wide open even though he is certain he locked it earlier in the week, after inspecting the compound and being oddly disturbed by the cold feelings of dread it evoked. There is fear in that shed, and horror. The shapeless crawling horror of sanctioned death. It reminds him of another vacant space, a screaming place that haunts the hallways of his heart like a hungry ghost.

Tyler crosses the dusty yard and approaches the shed, pausing only briefly outside the gaping door. He walks inside, feeling the chill as he steps across into pure shadow.

There is a wide earthen corridor running up the center of the room, with wooden stalls on either side. The low three-bar gates to these enclosures are closed, secured by heavy iron padlocks.

The darkness that has gathered in the stalls is syrupy, gelatinous. And hanging casually over the topmost bar of each gate is a naked, heavily muscled arm. Smooth, hairless, unlined flesh; bulging biceps, even at rest. The tops of these pale limbs disappear into that rich treacly blackness, and Tyler knows deep at his core that there is no trunk attached to each rounded shoulder.

There is only that terrible row of disembodied arms, and the gargantuan hands that dangle like weights from each one. A long line of random acts of brutality waiting patiently to be unleashed.

Tyler can tell without looking that the shed door has closed behind him, and the lock has slipped silently into place. He stares straight ahead, focusing on the unlocked double doors at the rear of the structure, trying to imagine what might lie beyond. Old bloodstains and deep, jagged gouges darken the wood, but in his mind's eye Tyler sees only a possible solution to the puzzle his life has become.

Without his mind telling it to do so, Tyler's body snaps into action. One foot eases in front of the other, and he begins to walk that pounding hundred yards, which seems like a mile.

At the periphery of his vision he is aware of the arms as they twitch spastically into life: long thick fingers flexing and curling up into huge square fists. The punches (*straight-armed, wild haymakers, tight little jabs, backfists, uppercuts*), when they come, are like hammer blows. The pain is immense, yet he welcomes it. Embracing its truth.

He carries on, no longer even trying to understand; merely moving as best he can at the command of some dark and masochistic instinct. The blows and punches rain down upon him like the fists of God Himself.

And still he is unable to raise his own hands in defense. They simply lie numb and inert at his sides, useless and unfeeling as slabs of dead meat.

The arms at the end of the row are small, dwarfish. Childlike. Tyler halts before them, feeling poised at the brink of revelation. His mind swells with the promise of knowledge, then cowers before what he might learn.

One of the tiny hands opens, palm upward. It offers him a small leather pouch tied with twine. Tyler reaches out, takes it from the cold and empty spot the hand has become. He opens the package, staring at its contents through swollen eyes; everything is tinged with a slight red hue.

Soil. The parcel contains a handful of dirty earth. As he rakes his fingers through it, spilling the gritty stuff onto the floor, he sees there is blood mixed in with the compost.

That is when he finally remembers what they did.

The children. The beatings, the sexual humiliation, the blood and the screams and the agony. But was Tyler the victim or the perpetrator? The abuser or the abused? Reality has fragmented so much that he cannot be entirely sure.

When the final blows fall he is no longer even there; his mind has been drawn back to the rough earthen floor of a derelict warehouse building on the crumbling banks of a disused canal, and he can do nothing but marvel at the horrors he finds there.

New Writings in the Fantastic
The Interference from Heaven
Peter Hagelslag

I: AT THE END OF MY ROPE

Is there rivalry in reverie? Can the abstract influence the real? I don't think so but David decidedly believes otherwise. He senses good or bad vibes about almost anything. No extrasensory perception or bright-coloured auras, but oblique patterns in the interstices of existence. You'd think a biology teacher would be more down to earth. He's even convinced that the conceptual is – at times – his direct opponent.

"There," he says. "You're doing it again." Breaking my train of thought. Although it wasn't going anywhere, I'm still annoyed.

"Can't you enjoy the silence for a minute?" I say, while pushing back an obstinate red lock.

"Jesus, Liona, I was talking to you."

Oops. Carried away again, just while the evening seemed to be going swell. Orange pekoe in my favorite café, some relaxation after a toiling day in the lab, and David offering me a bouquet of purple fuchsia. If only they played something else than these irritating Inuit rappers:

I'm contradictory, baby, fire and ice
  A different strain, the latent gene
  An impossible joint, incongruent splice
  Like a live M.C. Escher scene

"I'm sorry," I say. "And I'm tired."
"Aren't you always? I feel bad vibes coming up."
"You and your vibes. Stick to something real."
"Well, I sure wish our passion was more real."
"My work's eating me right now."
"Exactly. You're too obsessed. The greater the difficulties, the harder you try. As a result, you're neglecting me."

Ouch. Part of me knows he's right but is overruled by the proud bitch taking over. The music raps on as I take a breath.

I lead the parade of the impossible
  A master of misdirection, prankish paradox
  Axiomatic actor, creating the incredible
  Spectacular specter escaping reality's locks

"That's not true. We see each other every weekend, we go out, we talk, we sleep together."

"You said it: We sleep. Friday evenings you're too tired to go out and Saturday nights you want to go home early. And every time I'd like to make love you have a headache, you're not in the mood—"

"Not every time!"

"The times we do make love you're so distracted, going through the motions. A far cry from the lioness who drove me completely crazy."

"I'm very tired."

"And very obsessed. You twist and turn in bed; you take notes in the middle of the night. You won't let go of it."

In this rarest of moments, I shut up. Unfortunately, the fast-rhyming voices do not:

Catch me, baby, if you can
   Dualistic lover, imperfect man
   Spicier than the hottest spice
   Cooler than 50 types of ice

"Therefore I think it's better if we didn't see each other for a while," he says.

"Stop seeing each other? Just because I'm a little overworked?"

"It's more than that. You're pushing yourself too hard, trying to take on too much."

"I'm carrying the world on my shoulders and as a reward you leave me to it?"

Tears well up in my eyes. I throw the flowers in his face. Still he has the nerve to hold my hand and say soothing words.

"I think we both need some rest, some time to come to our senses. Give our relationship breathing space so it can heal."

He's so even-tempered, so understanding, so reasonable. Why doesn't he lose it, get angry with me, just for once? If only because I deserve it.

"That's why I'm going to the Buddhist retreat center tomorrow. I've wanted to do that for so long, and this seems the right time."

"Tomorrow? Why didn't you tell me earlier?"

"Because you'd talk me out of it. If you're set on getting your way you're extremely persuasive."

"So you made it an accomplished fact. I've always suspected you love your puny God more than me."

"Liona, this is ridiculous. This is not a competition."

"It is. You just told me my love for science is engaging me too much."

"That's not what I meant. I just think we need to get off each other's backs for a while."

"And that's exactly what I'm doing!" I shout as I walk out fuming, leaving him with the bill. Even so, he's walking next to me in no time, trying to argue. But I – temperamental, *moi*? – shrug him off and tell him I want to be on my own. So I go to bed alone and let my anger set fire to the cool night.

The next morning, I feel like hell. Disorder clouds my thoughts, each and every one of my countless freckles itches maddeningly and, as an added bonus, my period just started.

Chaos rules. Again and again I fight it, putting in much energy, hoping the system is still far from equilibrium and that our strange attraction will re-emerge.

Pain, dull pain in my abdomen. Only menstrual, of course, not because I miss him. I'll dedicate myself to the project even more.

Michael Holland – our scientific leader – baptized it the Quantum Parallel Processor project, supposedly a forerunner of a real quantum computer. At the moment, anyway, it isn't even processing. It's freezing, both literally and figuratively.

Nanotech can't manipulate individual atoms yet, so in order to make a prototype of a quantum parallel processor we need to use quantum objects that are big enough to handle. For this we cool great numbers of rubidium gas atoms (typically about 2000 of them) to form a Bose–Einstein condensate. Such a condensate behaves like a single quantum entity, exactly the basic component we need for our prototype.

We charge the condensates (*quantum dots* as we call them; when functioning they might become qubits), then keep them separated and suspended in a 3D-array of superconducting wire – easy enough since they have to be kept a few nanoKelvins above absolute zero anyway – which yours truly helped develop. Neatly arranged between the coils with supercooled helium shielding the array are the lasers that can excite the quantum dots into a superposition of states.

So far it looks like a cakewalk on easy street. However, the arrangement doesn't seem to work. Or it does, depending on your point of view, but we cannot extract results from it due to our observational interference. You see, when we program the lasers to let the quantum dots do some straightforward calculations, we can't see any results. Maybe our observation collapses the computing probability wave. Or maybe there hasn't been any quantum parallelism going on in the first place, meaning there are no parallel universes and the many-worlds interpretation is a dead end. This would devastate Mike, who is such a vocal proponent of that theory.

Whatever the cause: We send questions in and get noise out. Worse: We don't know why. I've checked and rechecked all the individual components but can find nothing wrong there. Personally, I think we are missing some principle here, but my intuition's so vague I can't put my finger on it. Once again, I try to leave it for *mañana*.

But my thoughts keep racing. Through them, this stupid song keeps playing in my head. Chilly voices through warm dubs, *a cappella* rap heating up the cold winds of conformity:

I come out from the cold
    Immersed in arctic bliss
    Wild ideas, concepts so bold
    Condensed from static hiss

Get me, baby, in the can
    A state of superposition
    Your flash in the pan
    An orgiastic supposition

Cause I'm order from chaos
    Better than your worst vice
    More exciting than Eros
    Cooler than 50 types of ice

– Aura Aurora, the Eskimo dubskid rap sensation, playing their megahit "50 Types of Ice"– my Total Sense System™ announces —If you had turned on sight, smell and sensation you would have appreciated this immeasurably more—

"Total immersion is for the brain-dead," I respond, "I don't need my imagination to be killed off like that."

Then it hits me: "Why are you playing this? I can't recall switching you on."

– Your emotional signs displayed confusion, so I played something appropriate—

"Appropriate? I hate that song!"

– Hate it? But you've been humming it all day—

"I do that subconsciously, because it has nestled there and I can't get rid of it."

– So if you're singing it, it doesn't mean you like it?—

"Sometimes it does and sometimes it doesn't. None of your business anyway."

– It is my business. I am an expert system that is self-learning and try to home in on your preferences—

"Well, I aim to keep you searching forever. Now, keep silent until my express command. I need to think."

The pros and cons of using the newest shit. The TSS™ is great for the 3D-component design I use for the QPP project. Sound and projection quality are superb, and when I'm making new designs the user interface is fantastic, almost like an ideal assistant. The downside is that the interface doesn't shut itself down when you use it for private things. Actually, it makes no distinction between work and free time: it just wants to interface with you all the time.

The next day, in the University's lab, it's business as usual: no progress. Nevertheless, everybody remains professional, hiding their frustrations. All except me, absentminded, clumsy at the controls, humming that stupid song again, ashamed, flushing and shining like a red beacon in the gloom. Even Mike, always so focused, cannot help but notice it.

"You're not your normal self today, Liona."

"Sorry, my personal problems shouldn't interfere with my work. Please excuse me."

"Don't take it so hard, your head's almost the colour of your hair. Overheated, if I might be so..."

Suddenly he's quiet. His eyes unfocus, gaze into infinity. We all hold our breaths, as not to disturb his thoughts. Just before we collectively suffocate he speaks:

"Thermal disturbance!"

"*¿Que?*" The ever eloquent me, the rapidity of my response equaling its profundity.

"Our lasers – they're pumping too much energy into the quantum dots. This excess heat is removed by our cooling array – that tries to maintain near absolute zero – in the process extracting our signals."

Enlightenment. Everybody talks at once.

"We must cool the lasers."

"You can't cool light."

"You'd only be absorbing photons."

"So what then?"

"We use lower-energy photons, a lower-frequency laser."

"Microwaves or even radio waves. But then we're losing probing accuracy. We still may not see anything."

"There might be an optimum; we can experiment with different wavelengths."

"This is so obvious, why didn't we see it before?"

"My mistake, dear friends. The frequency we use should be the theoretically best one. Sometimes you don't see the forest for the trees." The *mea culpa* from our big leader.

In the following days, we experiment. We use various ranges across the electromagnetic spectrum, looking for a discernable signal. Mostly we get nothing. Sometimes we get noise. Rarely, we get something in the noise that – if squinted at in the right way – might be interpreted as signal. We fine-tune in those ranges. In most, the randomness remains. But, in some, the signal to noise ratio is gaining.

We are getting answers to our questions. We ask again and again and try to show that what we are getting is not what we want to see. So we ask questions for which we do not know the answers in advance, calculations that still need to be done in the classical supercomputers. We note the QPP's answers. We compare them with the classically obtained ones. And, lo and behold: They match. We have the bloody thing working.

I'm at the zeppelin station, waiting for his return. He sent me a card, asking me if I wanted to pick him up. There he comes. He looks normal, he looks fine. Actually, he looks so good...

But I have to restrain myself. Keep cool. I haven't forgotten our little fight. I won't show him right away how much I've missed him. Let him suffer a bit.

"Well right, bitch," part of me protests, "that's why you've squirmed yourself into your tightest jeans and put on your most revealing top." *Shut up,* I tell it. *Let the bitch handle this.*

He sees me. He smiles, so warm, so inviting. I can't help but smile too. I walk toward him, slowly, languidly. Let him do the running, if he wants to. He is walking a bit faster, now. How did I ever fall for him? Is it his long, lean body and that head of cute, curly hair? Is it that warm smile, those glowing brown eyes? Mostly I fool myself by saying it's the dry humor and witty remarks that snared me in. After all, I'm supposed to go for intelligence, right?

He's walking fast now, arms outstretched and – BANG – I'm hanging around his neck and we kiss like crazy while swirling around like a mini-tornado.

"Liona, freckled goddess of my dreams, I missed you so. Did you miss me?"

Don't pout, don't forget not to pout. Because he thinks that's sooo charming. "Not really," I say while pouting madly. He laughs that warm, irresistible laugh, and before I know it our tongues are playing Gordian knot again.

"Yes, I missed you intensely," I admit as we disentangle and I tug him forward by his belt, "and we better get home *pronto* before I perform a public act of fellatio."

Forget about the bus, forget about the tram. Forget about any form of public transport. We take the nearest taxi and have to fight all the way to keep our clothes on. I just hope one of us paid the driver and closed the door before we made love in the hall. Somehow, we finally make it to the bedroom and, as the worst waves of desire are transformed in that deep, lingering afterglow, we start doing something rational like talking.

"I still don't understand why you went there."

"I went to find myself—"

"Yeah, right."

"– and to think about spirituality."

"Find God?"

"Liona, ease up. Let me finish my sentence."

(Me being quiet through an unprecedented act of self-control.)

"Good. I also went to see what would happen, to see if I could do it."

"You sound like a mountain climber mesmerized by some unattainable heights."

"A bit. It was quite different from what I expected, but I did find a kind of peace, a sort of restfulness deep within me."

"I don't get it. You go to this Buddhist retreat center, and for two weeks the only things you're allowed to do are eating, sleeping, meditating and being quiet?"

"Yes."

"You can't read?"

"No."

"You can't write?"

"No."

"Just smother in your own thoughts? Do absolutely nothing creative or constructive?"

"Meditate. Become at peace with yourself."

"It makes a normal prison sound like paradise. I'd go up the walls halfway through the third day."

"I don't think so."

"You don't? I–"

"You'd explode before the first day was over and walk off, telling everybody they're totally bonkers."

"You bet I would. Just thinking about it gives me the shakes. What it comes down to is that I just can't figure out why you're so obsessed with the godhead."

"Each to her own. Your preoccupation is called science."

"I know. But at least science, or the scientific method, doesn't pretend to hold all the answers. It just tries to obtain better explanations for observed phenomena."

"And make predictions based on those explanations. I know that. But it's not something really new, in the evolutionary sense."

"*¿Que?*" Ever so fluent, especially caught off-guard, that's me.

"The scientific method is nothing but an extension of monkey curiosity."

"So the discovery of DNA, quantum mechanics and relativity theory are just examples of excessive monkey curiosity?"

"Elaborate ones, admittedly, but basically the same thing. The same kind of curiosity that has reared its head in other species but not had enough survival value, not yet."

"Yo, mister biologist, so I'm just a speculative monkey. Now, before I show you my pink ass, could you tell me what is new in *Homo sapiens*?"

"Deity worship. Looking for God. Admitting that something bigger than ourselves might exist."

"Give me a break. That's just intellectual laziness: I can't figure out how this works so God did it."

"Consider this. You try to figure it out but, unable to do so with the limited knowledge available, you make an intuitional leap: Something higher did it. It's way above 'it just happens.'"

"That's throwing in the towel," I say. "Something higher did it and we can only humbly guess but never know its motivations. I can't help but sympathize with those who say, 'So it's more difficult than we thought, maybe so complicated we might never find the reason. It just happens but we're gonna try to find out why anyway, goddammit.'"

"So you do admit there are things we might never know?"

"Some things may be beyond our physical ability to probe, but they might be approached by the best theoretical explanation. A philosophical limit might be the greater barrier."

"A 'philosophical limit,' Liona? How interesting. And what would that be?"

"We – that is, our brains – might not have the right abilities to understand the ultimate physical laws."

"You mean, being rooted in our senses that receive only a thin slice of the real world."

I nod. "Possibly. On the other hand, receiving all possible information would overload us. So it's anybody's guess if we receive enough to make us think but not too much to distract us or drive us crazy."

"The roulette wheel of evolution. Now take a pure spiritual being. It would not be distracted by earthly worries, and so would obtain a deeper insight."

"So *that's* your metaphysical motivation, David? Cutting yourself off from all sources of information will give you the ultimate insight? I don't think so."

"That's because you're too deeply rooted in your earthly existence. Free yourself from your desires and you will be set free." He doesn't even try to hide his sarcasm here.

"So I'm too obsessed with my worldly pleasures, such as you?" I inquire, lick his earlobe and softly bite his neck.

"A one hundred percent pure, spiritual being will rise above the need for sex," he says while I tickle him *there*. "In the search for divine bliss it will leave pain and pleasure behind."

"And you are one such spiritual being?" I ask while I bend down and suck him so hard the sheet is crawling up his ass. His libido answers for him. He's still far from that kind of perfection, thank God.

II: ENTROPY, THE MAD FOE

The only way of discovering the limits of the possible is to venture a little way past them into the impossible.
– Arthur C. Clarke, Clarke's Second Law

In order to be able to draw a limit to thought, we should have to find both sides of the limit thinkable... we would have to be able to think what cannot be thought.
– Ludwig Wittgenstein

As our experiments with the QPP continue, everybody focuses on the working of the thing. Nobody cares how much energy it absorbs. Am I the only one noticing?

Because it's not using as much energy as it should. Maybe I'm wrong, maybe I'm crazy, but, apart from the energy required for the cooling, the superconducting and the lasers, the computing itself – I mean, the quantum parallel processing – should use energy. It doesn't seem to do so.

It's not right. Even handling information costs energy, should increase entropy in such an amount that the information gained against entropy is offset by a larger increase of entropy: the second law of thermodynamics holds.

In the beginning the calculations we made it do were so small – relatively speaking – that the energy required for them was below the measuring limit. But now we're factorizing such enormous numbers into two primes that the fastest classical computer existing would take longer than the current age of our universe to solve the same problem. So obviously this incredible number-crunching should *eat* energy.

I'm reluctant to bother Mike with this – I might be overlooking something so obvious – but I've checked and double-checked the energy expenditure of the set-up and, as far as I can see, it's still the same as in the beginning. So what's going on? Is a quantum computer a violation of the second law of thermodynamics? Does it "ride piggyback" on all those parallel universes, not only for the processing but using the energy of those universes to do so?

Come to think of it, we haven't even equipped the QPP with something to feed the necessary energy. So theoretically the QPP should come closer to absolute zero. But it doesn't: The supercooling does not need less energy. Neither do we need to increase the power of both inducing and observing lasers to get the results; they're loud and clear as ever.

The free lunch? The *perpetuum mobile*? I'm going to discuss this with Michael over lunch.

I'm not crazy, or at least not completely. Mike is taking my idea seriously, says I may be onto something. Cause for celebration. I take David out for tea in that nice vegetarian restaurant which has such excellent, rich food that even a carnivore like me doesn't miss the meat. They're a bit controversial, too, offering a choice between "pure Nature" and genemod dishes and even a teaser's selection, daring you to taste the difference between them.

After a romantic dinner we head for the Irish pub. Strongbow for me, Guinness for David, and a lot of happy banter with friends.

Then, at the oddest of moments, I become distracted. Either something strikes me or I brood about my latest obsession. While David is having lively discussions, I sit at the far corner of the bar, nursing my cider, while my thoughts enter esoteric realms.

I don't understand entropy. Suppose it's a statistical thing, like throwing dice, card games or, say, roulette. In roulette the bank always wins because there is this extra number, "0", added to the wheel. You might be lucky for a short time, but in the long run the bank always wins.

Now you play against entropy – *but there is no such extra number*. The basic rule says energy is conserved, there is no energy lost. Now, they theorize on and on that the usability of that energy gets lost, not the energy itself. But I don't see the "extra number" causing that. I see no fundamental rule underlying this. The second law of thermodynamics is the biggest axiom we have; almost everybody believes it to be true, but absolutely no one can prove (or disprove) it.

So how is it we still lose from entropy in the long run? To me it looks suspiciously like someone or something is stacking the deck or loading the dice.

Before I can think up any suspects, David embraces me from behind, kisses me on my neck and whispers in my ear: "Why don't we go to your place before – you know – one of us gets too drunk?"

Music to my ears. My considerate hunk anticipates my every need. I was drawing blanks anyway.

In my apartment, I give my TSS™ signal six so that in the background this soft, lingering intro starts building up, the prelude to a favorite song and an overture to intimate action. We snuggle up close, real close, and do all these things lovers have done since time immemorial. He's getting to the point too fast, so I slow him down (not too much, of course), as I want to enjoy the foreplay as much as the rest. It's the love tug-of-war we both enjoy intensely, perfecting each other's techniques.

Then, right when the going gets good, strange phenomena happen at the periphery of my senses. Things that are slightly off, not merging perfectly with my feelings. For one, what happened to the subtle crescendo of my favorite snuggle-song, building ever so progressively to its melodic climax? It's been replaced by eerie echoes, nauseating bass waves and twisting whooshes swirling around us.

I take my longing gaze – very reluctantly – off my lover and what do I see? Cobras, rattlesnakes and other poisonous reptiles are slithering over the carpet, oversized spiders with threatening fangs are slowly descending from the ceiling, huge rats are loudly gnawing on our couch. A sweeping wind is throwing sleets of rain against the roof and windows; ethereal forms slide through the air emanating a whiny howl, interrupted by the occasional burst of thunder and flash of lightning.

"TSS, what the hell do you think you're doing?"

– I put on the advancing nightmare menu, the one I'm perfecting to creep you out–

"Only when I'm reading horror stories. Not *now*!"

– It seemed perfect. You, the damsel in distress, seeking refuge in the arms of your champion David, knight of the order of–

"Guinness!" My champion shouts while surrendering to an enormous fit of laughter. Through his uncontrolled spasms of wheezing, hiccupping amusement I try to smite him to death with the nearest pillow. Luckily for him, my anger subsides at the same time as his Homeric laughter dies out. I merely look away haughtily as he holds me, caresses me and says: "Come on, Liona, give it a break."

"This overintrusive interface is ruining my love life and I should give it a break? I–"

"Our love life can take this in stride, easily."

"It broke up a perfect moment and–"

"I sympathize with it. It's also desperately trying to understand you."

"You sympathize with it? A user-friendly software program that's a bloody pain in the ass?"

"An expert system that tries to know you. But you enjoy being mysterious, unpredictable."

– Which does increase your predictability, but only a bit–

"While also making you that much more desirable."

"Finishing each other's sentences? Are you two in this together?"

– We do exchange information sometimes–

"Especially in the morning, while you're still having your beauty sleep."

"Analyze me while I sleep? You two are worse than a couple of old housewives."

– Housewives have a lot of life experience–

"And make sharp observations, too."

Actually, the idea of my lover gossiping with my expert system is so absurd as to make me smile. I barely contain myself as I cast a baleful look at David. He has to make this up, so will be just that much more motivated in bed later on. It has the desired effect: he binds in.

"Tess, stop intruding and play her favorite music."

"Tess? You've given it a name?"

"Well, long for TSS and short for tesseract. The instruction manual says its hardware configuration is based on a hypercube."

"You know it better than I do."

"Liona, we're both your slaves. Do you know that German saying: *waß sich nicht das liebt sich*? What is teasing you loves you?"

"What a way to show affection." I say as I push him off, slightly.

"Come on, it's the way we do things here. Your family's the same." Said with that lovely smile, his secret weapon.

"I'm a poor girl teased by everybody." Accompanied by my trademark pout, copyright Liona the Freckled, Inc.

"And loved by all."

"I just wish you said it more."

"I love you. But I prefer to show it."

We reconcile, and how. Little fights can be great foreplays. Tonight is one of our best.

Nevertheless, I remain a hopeless daydreamer. Even in the inevitable interludes between our love sessions, my mind drifts off.

I wonder what Heaven would be like. Suppose you had a perfect lover and making love was the best every time. Wouldn't it get boring? Wouldn't you need a change of menu every now and then? Or would you become a sex junkie craving for the next fix all the time?

It leads me to think that Heaven would not be very much unlike reality. We humans need interaction. A perfect wish-fulfillment lover is nothing but an extended form of masturbation. I believe we need the little imperfections to make it really click. Not too many, of course, but just enough to keep things interesting. After all, working toward perfection is better than achieving it. Because after perfection things can only get worse, not better.

In the afterglow of our passion play, I light one up and we both want to talk. Continuing our musings on human and artificial intelligence and the limits of thought.

"Strange how our mind seems capable of explaining the world around it."

"Our mind is an evolutionary artifact, David. It is not custom-made to understand the world."

"Well, I think it actually evolved just for that."

"OK, for understanding the world, but not the whole universe. Therefore our senses are much too limited."

"So our senses are limited, but maybe our brain is not. Possibly its overcapacity is a survival trait; instead of developing a whole new central nervous system it might be cheaper to develop a grossly oversized one and use only the features that come in handy."

"Then monkey curiosity is just a handy by-product?"

"Probably. Also our tendency to look for the immaterial might be such a by-product. There might be more in store for us."

"I don't think the plethora of our brain's possibilities is endless. Instead of a Pandora's box full of surprises, it may have only a limited bag of tricks."

"I don't know. Don't forget it's still evolving."

"Evolution is being outpaced by scientific progress right now. I suspect we'll run into the limits of thought sooner than we think."

"Like Wittgenstein said: To find the limits of thought, we need to think what cannot be thought."

"That's a self-contradictory statement, a logical loophole. You cannot think the unthinkable, so we never know where the limits of thought are."

"Humans alone, no. But we could create something that does this for us. An Artificial Intelligence that could think, extrapolate or whatchamacallit in ways we can't."

"An AI to explain the working of reality to us? Such an AI would actually be... like a divine oracle."

There's nothing I can add to that. So we kiss goodnight. David's asleep in no time, the satiated animal. As I snuggle up against my sleeping lover, my mind – too restless to sleep – drifts off again.

The thing with entropy: Can it have some kind of purpose? This may sound weird but consider the alternative: Without entropy we would have a constant free lunch. Everything would be a lot easier. No usable energy gone forever. No far-from-equilibrium states needed for order to arise. No disorder from which to develop, nothing to evolve away from.

Maybe we need entropy as a negative state from which to set ourselves off, an antithesis to fight against. This train of thought makes me wonder: Could we have evolved without entropy? Is entropy a prerequisite for the development of intelligence? Or of life?

III: THE INTERFERENCE FROM HEAVEN

Any sufficiently advanced technology will be indistinguishable from magic.
  – Arthur C. Clarke, Clarke's Third Law

Any sufficiently advanced ETI will be indistinguishable from God.
  – Michael Shermer, Shermer's Last Law
  (*Scientific American*, January 2001)

David is going on a field trip with his class. On a whim, I've decided to join him. That takes him by surprise all right.

"You want to come along? That's quite unusual."

"Is it forbidden by that school of yours?"

"No, but... don't they need you for the experiments?"

"The QPP is running fine. The mathematical theorems they're feeding it now are way over my head."

"City girl like you will be bored to death."

"I'll be with you, follow the excursions, daydream and relax."

"You'll starve. The menu's vegetarian rabbit food with the occasional soup cooked over a campfire."

"Good, I need to lose some pounds."

"It's primitive. We camp under starlight."

"How romantic. My blood quickens at the thought alone."

"That's the whole point – during lovemaking you make enough noise to raise an army."

"So that's your problem! Ashamed of your little lover?"

"No, no, not that. It's just that I'll be the talk of the school plaza for the rest of the semester."

"That's the price of love, baby. But don't you worry: I'll tone down my expressions of delight to a more civilized level."

"Well, OK. Or maybe we could, you know, refrain?"

"Have no sex for a whole week? Then everybody will think you're some kind of eunuch. Or, worse, they'll think you don't love me."

"Oh, Liona. Just try to be a bit more... quiet, OK?"

Arriving in these moorlands, David leads his class and points out rare plants and signs of animals. I see the autumnal marshes differently: I look for patterns.

I never realized Nature's chaos is so rich, elegant and multitudinous. Especially at this time, about halfway into the fall. Yellow, long-stemmed grass shooting through still-green leaves. Branches of beech and bare trees. Floating vegetation on a slow-flowing creek. Mushrooms and moss on a log.

The subtle shades of autumn enhance the intricacy of the self-iterative patterns. Waiting within the disorder of grasses strewn on the meadow or bleached leaves in a dark puddle are uncanny kinds of structure. Nature's fractals, another example of order out of chaos. As if it's reacting to some invisible vibe.

All this is boosting my imagination. In my mind, fallen leaves on water metamorphose into fractalized computer graphics, then fade into outer-shell electron clouds whose interactions form the basis of all chemistry, zoom further to the abstract mathematical representations of

Calabi-Yau shapes of M-theory.

Or, conversely, shiny surface discolourations in a mud pot expand into rings of planetary debris orbiting giant stars like hugging halos, then evolve into gaseous nebulas on the brink of star-formation and through a sudden burst of massive galaxy clusters explode into the hyper-inflated soap-bubble structure of an eternal expanding universe.

I'm so enthralled throughout the day that in the evening, after setting up camp, David wonders if I've lost it.

"Hello, alien. Why did you abduct my girlfriend?"

I tear my gaze from the starry sky and frown.

"You know, this woman called Liona used to talk so much my nodding along gave me neck cramps."

I lift one brow, smirk and hold my peace.

"Also, provoking her in the slightest would involve making up half the night."

"Only half? I must be getting old."

"Or growing up. What's the quiet?" he asks as he embraces me.

I nestle my head on his shoulder and say: "Enjoying myself. Surprises me as much as you."

This marshland is too peaceful for a fake fight. Give it to him, he settles into my serene mood without a glitch. Soundless, we watch the stars in this clear night. Unusually, he's the first to break the silence.

"Do you still donate Tess's spare capacity to SETI?"

"Yes."

"Any progress?"

"Not that I know. Believe me, you would be the first to hear."

Strange, how at such moments our thoughts center on the same subject. Telepathy (just kidding), chance, or a sign of getting to know each other better? Anyway, deep in my heart I've given up on SETI finding signals in radio waves. With the continuous increase in computing power analyzing more and more of the incoming noise from the skies, we should have found something already. Maybe I'm just too impatient. With mass-produced quantum computers we could analyze all those incoming waves real fast...

Wait: Our QPP works. Theoretically there's nothing against our developing a quantum computer. Actually, we – the human race, that is – should be able to make improved versions.

Now suppose there's an alien race in a parallel universe developing quantum computers way before us. That shouldn't be too far-fetched, probably there's more than one that did, maybe millions, perhaps countless of them.

If just one of those has a penchant for preparing themselves for a very long future, an almost infinitely long future, then sooner or later they have to face the ultimate enemy: entropy. *But a quantum computer is not affected by this.* So they can make software copies of themselves that will run virtually forever. The originals will eventually die, but immortality for the race is ensured.

Hell's bells, if they make the quantum computer large enough they can create almost any world, real, imaginary, surreal, honkers-bonkers, whatever they want. It won't be reality, but so closely based upon it that its inhabitants would hardly notice the difference. *They can create their own Heaven.*

It'd ride piggyback on all the parallel universes it interfaces with. So it uses their energy. But that's impossible: forbidden by the law of conservation of energy. So it doesn't use the energy but it uses the usability of the energy. It degrades energy in other universes. Oh, shit, this sounds exactly like entropy!

Make the connection. Entropy might be an effect, not a cause. Entropy might be caused by quantum computers running in parallel universes. But then...

SETI, the Search for Extra-Terrestrial Intelligence is looking in the wrong direction. Signs of alien interference have been going on for ages. We just didn't realize it. Entropy is the interference from heaven. From an infinite amount of heavens.

Lost in my thoughts, I haven't noticed all those mosquito bites until I undress in our tent. Desperately trying not to scratch, I kiss David hard. Maybe if I scratch this big itch I won't notice the dozens of tiny others.

Later, when our lovemaking becomes a bit too enthusiastic and I cannot keep my ecstatic moans to myself, David tries to put his hand over my mouth to silence me. This makes me laugh so hard that the whole camp is awakened anyway. It effectively ends our passion play. The rest of the night, every time he comes on to me again I start to giggle and he abandons his amorous intents. Poor David. I'll make it up in the quietness of my apartment, later.

I really should get some sleep but it's hopeless. Apart from my mosquito bites and my unquiet David, my mind is in overdrive; I need to work my loony hypothesis out. Because maybe I still haven't gone far enough. An alien race that can build a Universal Quantum Computer should be intelligent enough to foresee that entropy would arise in universes parallel to theirs. So why didn't they do anything about it? I cannot believe that such superintelligent beings would be uncaring. So either they can't help it, bound by the laws of physics, or maybe they decide *not* to stop it.

Like I speculated before: Entropy might serve as a booster, a kind of catalyst to initiate, aid or speed up the onset of life and intelligence. It might be part of a test: Can you overcome it? Then, congratulations, you're on your way to making your own Heaven. A soothing thought to put me to sleep.

The next morning, David is reluctant to join the group for breakfast. But I do everything short of physically pushing him out of the tent to get him there. It's priceless, the way he blushes when his students make suggestive remarks. Of course, they hope to kill two birds with one stone but – ashamed, *moi?* – I laugh along with them, even with the most casual comments. When some become too bold I ask what makes them such specialists, shutting them right up.

Eventually, we head for the moor once more. The weather is still very mild, almost warm this late in the season. After some false starts, David leads the class to point out things only his trained eyes seem to spot. When I see he's in control again, I veer off in my own direction. Although I still see examples of Nature's yin and yang of disarrayed structure, I'm less focused than the day before.

The restless night has made me a little giddy, shaking like I'm having good vibes. Now I almost sound like David. Odd how we found each other in a world of social interactions where randomness seems the rule. The weird couple: a spiritual biologist and an earthly scientist. One always aware of the interconnectedness of the whole, the other always looking for the working of the parts. A feel for *savoir-faire* balancing an air of *joie de vivre*.

Is it chance, a case of opposites attract, or some higher principle at work here, bringing us together? Strange attractors re-emerge in my mind. There is no law stating they should arise. That they do is as much an axiom as the second law of thermodynamics. Are they another side-effect of those parallel quantum computers generating ETI heavens? Or something else?

My rumbling stomach interrupts my musings. Lunchtime, and believe me my body needs it. After lunch David assigns his class certain tasks to perform in little groups of their own. As soon as they've set out, we head off in another direction to work on some unfinished business. We stop near the edge of the water where swaying sedge and lapping waves move to a syncopated rhythm. Under a sunny sky where majestic clouds present their fractal beauty we start making out. Still, David's a bit anxious.

"Suppose someone accidentally walks by?"

"That would give them a great practical lesson in sexual education. Aren't you supposed to teach them that as well?"

"But not like John Cleese in Monty Python's *The Meaning of Life*. Although you wouldn't mind, would you, my little exhibitionist?"

My smug smile is answer enough as I urge him on. Actually, the idea of being caught in the act makes it all the more exciting. So exciting, I'm

glowing in places I haven't glowed before. Glowing a bit too much...
"Stop!" I cry.
"What?"
"Stop it. Now!"
"Stop? But you're moving so enthusiastically, so wild."
"That's because my ass is in a stinging nettle, you idiot."

He stops, he bites his tongue, he stares up to the heavens but – God help him – he doesn't laugh. After this visible show of restraint, he lifts me up, takes me to a prickle-free place, turns me around and says: "I'm so sorry, Liona, let me kiss your ass," and then promptly does so. I'm thankful for it, so thankful that we end up doing it doggy-style. Last thing I want to hear is that I'm an ungrateful bitch.

What a moment. I'm so excited that all my senses are hypersensitive to the point of data overload. The rustle of wind through the reeds carrying birdcalls that are soon drowned out by my ecstatic moans. The swampy smell of the marsh, the moist fragrance of rotting leaves. The sour and salty taste of our intermingled sweat, the feeling of mud on my knees and hands, of David sticking to me like moss on a bog pool. All these impressions filtering aimlessly through the almost overwhelming mutual thrusts of our lust, as if they belong there, as if they contribute something too.

So, enormously advanced technologies are indistinguishable from magic. Well, this isn't far from it, either. Quite indistinguishable from Heaven, too. Right now I wouldn't care if David's whole class were filming it all. Hey, I'd ask for a copy afterwards. Fortunately for David, this doesn't happen. Our climax is coming, it's that "sum of the parts exceeding the whole"...

Afterwards, as we lie spent against each other, the hormonal surges recede from my mind and my thinking becomes sharp and clear.

Are the fundamental laws alone enough for the genesis of life from physical reality? Or is something extra needed?

Keywords: "emergent properties." Laws arising from a system irrespective of its basic components, like the laws of chaos. Yet there are other "emergent properties," such as chemistry, life and evolution. Might the interaction of elementary particles with their counterparts in parallel universes be the root cause for these "emergent properties"?

Take for example the number of possible permutations of an amino acid. It's mind-bending. The chance of the amino acids that exist today (forming the basis of most proteins and DNA) arising from earth's primordial oceans is astonishingly small. Then why did exactly those make the final cut? Chance? Evolution? Or were they helped along by some secret ingredients? Like entropy, if only for pointing the direction in which to develop? Like strange attractors? How about higher-dimensional geometry prescribing the lowest energy configurations?

So here we are: Is life the strange attractor arising from the primeval soup? Have beings in a parallel universe – evolved so far that we can only see them as Gods – found a method to tweak interactions of elementary particles between different cosmoses in such a way as strongly to favor the emergence of life?

My esoteric castle in the air collapses as David slaps my behind.

"Come, Liona, let's get dressed."

"Why?"

"You shameless bitch. I wonder why I stay with you."

"For the beauty of our interaction? Or for the transcendence of togetherness?"

His eyes look skyward, but there's nothing he can say to that.

New Writings in the Fantastic
Babble
Gavin Salisbury

Jason's living room was piled high with tape recorders, most of them ancient, some of them not even working. He had a talent for breathing life into mechanical things, but he couldn't save all of them. It seemed that every time I went round to see him he'd acquired a few more – from car boot sales, mostly. He would gradually dispose of those he could get no sound from, by which I mean he threw them in the back garden, to join the shopping trolleys hiding in the four-foot-high grass.

He lived in a one-bedroom ground-floor council flat in a nasty area of town, and had done ever since his first psychotic episode when he was eighteen. We were like brother and sister when we were little – we used to be next-door neighbors for a while – and I never gave up on him. OK, when I went to college I didn't see him for weeks or even a month at a time, but he knew I was at the end of a phone whenever it all got too much. I was the one who convinced him to stay on the medication, that his freedom depended on it.

But then freedom can be difficult to take. Most of us pare down our lives, deny ourselves options, just to stay on firm ground. For my part, I settled for someone I didn't really love, because he was dependable and decent. I was content to be needed, I suppose.

Jason generally shied away from relationships altogether. He even grew distant from his mum and dad, who had always doted on him, despite everything. Yet he accepted my visits, and I think he mostly enjoyed my company. I had the knack of making him laugh: maybe that was it.

"Why all the tape recorders?" I asked him early on, just after the first four or five appeared. "Is one not loud enough for you? Are you trying to piss off the neighbors by tuning into three different radio stations at once?"

Jason scratched his head with both hands, as he often did when excited, and smiled at the floor. "It's my new project, Di," he said with a chuckle, and glanced at me briefly before looking down again. "I'm trying to recreate the first language of mankind."

I was too used to his projects to smirk, and was grateful he seemed to have given up building strange battery-powered flying machines, which he used to launch off the multistory car park in the middle of the night. I used to be very worried he would get set upon by drunken yobs, or arrested. Piling up tape recorders was surely safe by comparison.

"I say it again," I replied. "What's with the tape recorders?"

"Let me explain, then!" Jason shouted. I raised my hand apologetically. I had missed the signs that he was in a dramatic pause.

"It's all about overlaying sounds, you see. If I can find tapes of all the major languages of the world, and can play them all at the same time, I'll be able to hear the common factors rising out of the babble. It's babble back to Babel!"

Jason was pleased with his non-joke, so I was too. But I still felt the need to push him. "But surely linguists all over the world have already classified languages as far back as they can go. You think you can do better just by listening to a few Linguaphone tapes?"

He liked this about me: that I didn't pussyfoot around him, or pretend he was made of glass. That didn't mean of course that I believed his answers always made sense.

"I have a special ear," he said. "The real language of God will rise out of the babble like music from an orchestra tuning up."

"Are you the conductor or the audience?" I asked, but this time he didn't answer.

Another day I went round, when this Babel thing had been going on for several months, it occurred to me I hadn't ever seen or heard any sign of any of the language tapes so necessary to this whole project.

Jason just laughed. "Details, Di – details!" He handed me a cup of tea, but the milk was off and had curdled in lumps and made me feel queasy. "You're always fretting about the little things!" Then he saw the look of disgust on my face and took the mug back off me. "Let's go for a walk and get some fresh milk while we're out," he said.

"You can be really sweet at times," I said. I meant it too, though he could be stupendously manipulative too. This was brought home to me again on the way to the park, when he said, "You're going to be in charge of the language collection, Di." He flashed me a huge grin, as if he was doing me the biggest favor the world had ever seen. "Isn't that great? You can be a part of my Babel project!"

I stopped walking, put a firm hand on Jason's arm, and turned him round to face me. "Jason, I'm very sorry, but I'm afraid I can't be a big part in your project." His look of disappointment was like a kick in the stomach. "You know I will always do everything I can for you, but I just don't have the time at the moment to hunt around charity shops and boot sales. I'm flat out at work, and you know I have to study at weekends for my exams."

Jason pulled his arm free and started to walk away from me. "Come back and visit soon, Di," he said, with a voice like a soul fading away.

"Jason!" I called after him, but he was determined not to look back. I recognized that set of his shoulders when he was sulking – it hadn't changed a bit since he was six, when I shouted at him for pulling the head off one of my dolls.

I didn't see him for a couple of months after that. It wasn't just the exams. Even when that particular hurdle was passed, somehow I kept putting off my next visit, without even knowing why. Now that it's all over, though, I know the reason was fear.

To show comradeship with his project, when I did eventually go round again I took round some tapes and CDs I had managed to harvest from friends. It's amazing how many people have once tried to learn an exotic language, when you press them about it. I was therefore able to offer a passable peace offering, which included Urdu, Arabic and Korean material, as well as more standard fare, such as Italian and French.

If I was expecting a grateful, enthusiastic welcome, I was disappointed. Jason was preoccupied and distant. When I could get him to talk, he said his progress was too slow.

"I hadn't realized there are so many languages," he said sadly. "There is much more splintering than I thought." He banged his fist on the side of his head angrily. "I would need many lifetimes to gather all the tapes I need. Some families are going to be impossible to represent, because there aren't even any recordings, so that whatever I come up with is going to be imperfect."

It was then that I decided I was going to help. To be in the gang again, like when we were kids. "Well," I said, "maybe we don't need perfection. Maybe close enough will do."

Jason looked at me questioningly, but with new hope in his eyes. I knew I had to produce some sort of argument to back this up.

Something in my brain shouted "logarithm," and I knew I had it. "Have you got a pen and paper?" I asked.

Jason looked at me as if were totally stupid. "Over there, Di. On my desk."

He showed no inclination to fetch them for me, so I went over myself, and drew this graph:

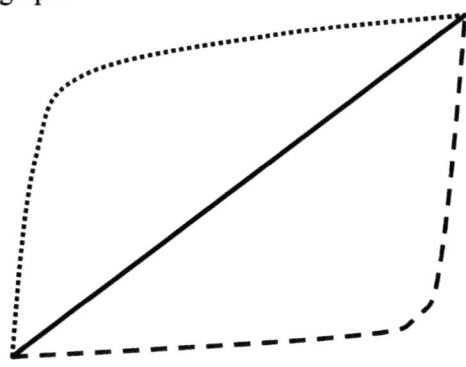

They weren't great curves, I knew, but they were good enough for my purposes.

I showed this graph to Jason. He looked baffled, but intrigued. "Imagine if the number of language families we include is directly proportional to the similarity we can achieve to pre-Babel language," I said. "In that case, we will have to include most language families to get a reasonable approximation. That's the straight line." Jason nodded dubiously. "The worst-case scenario is if we follow the dashed curve – that's an exponential increase in similarity depending on the number of language families we include. In that case, we would need virtually all families represented to get even remotely close." Jason looked suitably downcast. "I'm sure you're agreed that, if that's true, we can forget the whole project.

"What we have to hope for is that the dotted line represents the true scenario – the logarithmic increase. In that case, even if we have only about 60% of all language families represented, we can achieve over 90% similarity to the pre-Babel language. What we're relying on here is basic human nature – none of us like change if there's no very good reason for it. And I think it's the same with languages. The original mother of all languages is still there, bubbling just under the surface of all the others." I made a dramatic, sweeping gesture. "The development of all the world's languages has been a slow, logarithmic creeping away from the original, not a linear movement or an exponential leap."

"You know, Di," Jason said after a short pause and a sip of his coffee. "That makes a lot of sense!" We smiled and even hugged. That meant a lot to me, because Jason didn't normally like physical contact.

I almost had myself convinced.

Next came the intensive tape and CD collecting. Jason already had some stuff, but nothing unusual. So I took charge of things for him after all, and placed orders with obscure mail-order companies online all over the world. I even commissioned special recordings to be made in some cases. That went on for several months, and proved rather a drain on my savings, since some of the American and Asian languages were not at all easy to find a way into. Eventually, when the last tape we had ordered arrived from New Zealand, Jason couldn't be held back any longer, and he insisted it was time to try a Babel lesson.

The logical part of me rebelled strongly at this stage, now that the reality of the game I was playing finally hit me. What about all those thousands of extinct languages? What about the fact that the Tower of Babel is just a myth? What about the fact that all our tapes had different material on them, and were probably without even a single common phrase or sentence to play simultaneously, even forgetting synchronization problems?

But I had never been a killjoy when I was a child, and I didn't want to become one for Jason now. When this was over, we would just move onto something else – no harm done.

Jason took charge of the final preparations himself. He told me to go away and leave him to it, while he tested all the tape recorders, and made sure all the tapes played properly. When he rang me a couple of days later, his voice was calmer than I'd ever known it. His words lacked that edge which normally scraped against the world and made it fear him.

"How about this evening, Di?" he asked. "Can you make it?"

"I wouldn't miss it for anything," I said.

We agreed on eight o'clock, but I was rather late, as usual.

I let myself in, also as usual. I thought at first there was no one home, it was so dark in the little hallway. "Jason?" I called, though my voice almost died on me as I spoke. Telling myself not to be silly, I hung my coat up and opened the door to the living-room, more softly and carefully than I really meant to.

It was dark in the whole flat, I saw. Everything in the room was much as I remembered, except that Jason was lying on the sofa, perfectly still. Tape recorders hummed all around; voices issued from some of them, but most had reached the end of their material and were just hissing threateningly.

I rushed over to Jason and tried to see if he was breathing and feel for a pulse at the same time. He was warm. He was alive. But his breath was almost unnoticeable, it was so light.

Even in the gloom, though, I could see his eyes moving underneath their lids.

OK, Di, OK, I told myself. *He's just asleep.*

I took a couple of very deep breaths myself, partly in the illogical hope that it might encourage Jason to breathe properly. For some reason I decided it was the most important thing to do at that moment to switch off all the tape recorders – as if this would make everything normal again. I left all the lights off, except one small reading lamp, because I was afraid of waking him up suddenly. The strange thing was, just as I switched off the very last tape recorder, which had taken me some time to find because it was buried under others in a corner, Jason woke up of his own accord.

"Diane," he said, which was odd, because he never called me by my full name, "I'm so sorry, my angel. I couldn't wait to start the experiment." He smiled serenely in a way I found deeply disturbing. "You know I never *was* very patient!"

I returned his smile as best I could. We both stared at each other unmoving for several moments. It was as if neither of us *could* move.

His face was different somehow, I decided. There was a softness there I had never seen before. I asked the question I had to ask: "Jason, have you taken your medication today?"

I was expecting him to snap at me, but he just smiled benevolently. "I have no need of medication," he said. "I have God's language to guide me now."

I sighed, relaxing back into my comfortable mother-hen role. "Come on," I said sharply. "Don't give me that crap, please. I know you too well, and we've been over this too many times. Where are you keeping the pills these days? Still under the bed?" I moved to fetch them, but he stopped me dead just by raising his hand. I mean literally: I was powerless to move an inch.

"Sit down, Diane," he said kindly. "I want to tell you a story."

I sat down, although I had every intention to defy him and stay standing exactly where I was.

"You will follow me everywhere," he said. "Because you love me more than anything." My head nodded involuntarily, as if controlled by someone else.

Jason started speaking in words I didn't understand, and yet which I knew had been inside me all my life, waiting to be unlocked.

A new world sprang up around me, where everything was possible, where he and I could do *anything*. If only people would listen, rather than fear him.

And, even though I knew it was hopeless, because people are ruled by their fear of freedom, I knew that Jason was right. I would follow him everywhere: into the old world's light and darkness, and beyond.

New Writings in the Fantastic
Reality TV
John Bushore

"**P**ervert!" I heard someone shout as I followed my two bodyguards through the mob in front of the TV studio. It didn't bother me; I'd been hearing it for the past year.

My thin, beak-nosed face was well known, since I was one of the most popular performers ever on the series. I wasn't handsome, my hairline had long ago gone north, and I had a few extra pounds around my middle. But I was a star, thanks to reality TV.

Quite a few morality-watchdogs had come to protest today; this was the season climax of *The Mating Game* and it would be the last opportunity for them to foam at the mouth until next fall. The usual contingent of hard-liners carried placards with slogans like "Keep Smut off the Air." The media crews hadn't bothered to turn out, though. These demonstrations had become old news.

They weren't all protesters. Some of them were fans – mostly young women, smiling and waving at me. They hung back, though, afraid of being banged on the head by a sign-wielding matron if they tried to get my autograph.

We took the elevator to the top floor, where the procedure rooms were located. I went into the dressingroom, while the bodyguards stayed on duty outside. I doubted anybody could get past the studio's security, but I wasn't taking chances. Some of those demonstrators were real nutcases.

The usual inspector was inside, a little wrinkled old fellow. I ignored him and removed my clothing. He watched as I showered thoroughly. Then I cleaned beneath my finger- and toenails, brushed my teeth, and presented myself for inspection. He checked between my fingers and toes and in every body orifice. The price of fame, I told myself. When he was satisfied I wasn't sneaking something in, he handed me a sealed gown. I tore open the plastic wrapper and put it on.

The inspector escorted me down an inner hall, into the procedure room, and then left. Two observers were there to confirm everything was on the up and up. The producer would have liked cameras in the room, but government regulations had drawn the line here.

My assigned assistant was there also. I had never seen the woman before, which was one of the precautions against cheating. An attractive, green-eyed brunette with her lower face masked, she was also gowned. I knew she had been through a rigorous inspection, same as me. She had a clear, direct gaze, which I liked.

It was against the rules for me to perform the procedure myself, another precaution against cheating. The show's producers provided each contestant with an assistant hired by the studio.

An observer pointed out a digital clock on the wall. It read 00:00. The procedure had to be completed in 15 minutes, he reminded me. He recited a list of the network's regulations, satisfying the legal requirements, but I didn't pay attention. I had done this a couple of times before; I knew the drill. At the end of his speech, he asked me if I was ready.

I nodded.

"You may begin," he said, and my assistant moved closer to me. I felt her breast pressing against my arm through the thin gowns.

We were only a couple of minutes into the operation when I realized she had great hands, but I was the one who must actually "perform" as the network was limited to calling it. If they had actually named what we were doing, or showed it on the screen, the churches and women's groups would have forced the program off the air; there are limits to everything, even reality TV.

This was where a lot of wannabes failed. It was their big shot at fame and fortune, but, no matter how many times they had practiced, doing it in front of observers made it a lot harder. And that clock didn't help, even though they say it doesn't take long if you know what you're doing.

And my assistant knew what she was doing. With her help, I finished in half the time allowed. The observers left the room with a small container of my stab at the Grand Prize. They would keep it in a friendly, body-temperature environment until the program started.

I was free to go, so I went back for my clothes. Since I had half an hour before the show aired, I collected my bodyguards and wandered to the commissary for a cigarette and a cup of coffee.

The brunette came in while I was pouring cream into my coffee and she gave me a little wink and a smile. I answered with a thumbs-up signal. I would have liked to ask her to sit with me, but you've guessed it: against the rules.

The screening theater was nearly full when I arrived. It was divided into eight sections; fights had been known to break out between excited contestants in the past. Pride and fame weren't the only things at stake; there'd be a substantial cash prize for the winner.

Other than my bodyguards, I was the only one in my area. I ignored the other competitors, some with trainers, girlfriends or even wives and parents. Procedural assistants like the brunette were not allowed here; their jobs were done.

Everyone in the room turned to the big wall-screen as the lights dimmed. Young men and women were dancing to the theme song, "Stupid Cupid," on the familiar-to-the-viewing-public set of *The Mating Game*. Then Peter Sandrake, <<NOT Chippendale>> the program's smiling, white-toothed host, walked on camera and began the big build-up. This was after all, the season finale: the winners from past episodes of *The Mating Game* competing for the Grand Prize. I was here, however, as the Grand Prize winner from the previous season, coming off a year of talk show appearances and lucrative commercial endorsements.

Next Peter introduced the contestants, and we contenders appeared on the screen one by one. Some raised their hands over their heads like prizefighters; one man actually beat his chest. When they came to me, last because I was the defending champion, Peter gave a brief bio and added the details of my previous appearances on the program. I tried to appear aloof and confident, but still give the impression I was rarin' to go. But, as everyone knows, the proof is in the pudding. We wouldn't be judged on appearances, but on results.

Then they introduced the celebrity donor, the "starlet" Felicity Barnes, who was a household name because she was one of the Hollywood Squares. She was the average, run of the mill starlet – a girl every guy drooled over. She had doe eyes, pouting lips, soft blonde hair, a body that had been crafted by the finest technicians; what guy wouldn't fight for a chance to impregnate her? Especially since he'd be paid a hundred grand if he won!

And that's what we were here for. Felicity had donated an egg (well, *technically* donated – she had been paid big bucks) that each of the contestants' entries would have a chance of getting to first. Peter reminded the audience that the resulting fetus, if viable, would be put up for adoption on the network's affiliated program, *The Adoption Game*.

These two shows consistently topped the ratings, with *The Mating Game* at the pinnacle of the heap. As close to live sex as you could get on television, it was irresistible to the average beer-swilling, couch-potato male, especially since it was timed not to coincide with any major sporting event. There were office pools all over the country where men could bet on their favorite contestants.

The show took a break for commercials, and then returned for the main event. Felicity's egg appeared on the big screen, looking like a slightly deflated basketball in the middle of a misty, circular cloud. Equidistant along the edges were eight smaller clouds, packed tightly with squirming masses of snake-like threads, digitally altered on the screen to appear in different colours. An announcer told the viewers that the contest was being monitored by the firm of Price–Paterhouse and identified which colour represented each contestant. Labels with contestant names sprang up on the screen.

"And they're off!" Peter shouted. The smaller clouds were simultaneously absorbed into the larger mist and the tangled balls of long-tailed cells separated into streams of tail-whipping swimmers, heading toward the egg. Now it was a matter of whose sperm could beat the others.

Insets appeared around the main action as cameras showed each contestant's reactions; I was on the bottom. Some of the younger men and their flushed companions were urging their little stallions as they plunged on, but I tried to exude an aura of calm confidence, as befitted my status. Peter's voice was calling the race in excited tones and I could hear the studio audience cheering their favorites on. I tuned it out.

I wondered; did I want to win again? Sure, the past year of fame had been great, especially the "attention" of my female fans, something a guy like me could normally only dream of. It surely wasn't my looks; maybe it was those superior little swimmers of mine? Or, perhaps it was just the reflected fame of being with me? Did I care?

And then there was the infamy, which was hard to live with sometimes. My mother had quit attending church out of embarrassment after I'd first appeared on *The Mating Game*.

But, as my microscopic progeny thrust slightly into the lead, my apathy faded and I began to silently urge them on. Those little guys on the screen were *me*, dammit. I wasn't about to give up my championship to some up-and-coming young stud. I *loved* show business!

New Writings in the Fantastic
The Whole of the Law
Cyril Simsa

There were three of them at the bar: one Tall, one Short, and one Eagle-eyed. Just like that old Slavic fairytale with the three guys who go a-roving and have all kinds of adventures. Except, of course, that these three were girls, and the rover was me, and I only found out which was which later. Still, every story has to have a beginning, and this is mine.

If this were a proper fairytale, I suppose I would start by telling you what had possessed me to go to The Whole of the Law in the first place – what quest I was pursuing, whose hand I was seeking, which dragon I was meant to be slaying – but the truth is, I don't remember. The Law was never a club I liked very much, and that night it was not living up to its name, let alone its fast reputation. The girls sat in a row, all on their own, and I could see straight away they were bored. They loomed, silent as menhirs, picking at the meticulously shredded ruins of a whole packet of beer mats, and sipping improbable cocktails through straws which might have been lifted straight out of a Karelian folk circumcision ceremony by a rogue anthropologist. (You know the type, I'm sure: all those well meaning younger sons of Devonshire clergymen who traveled the world – Sir James Frazer in one hand and an industrial-strength package of thigh-hugging scout-masters' leather pants in the other – looking for indigenous peoples to rob. Kind of like Kurtz Junior with ribbons and jangles.)

Anyway, there they were: a trio of latter-day Norns at the bar – their faces split into shards by the fake patina of the mirror on the far side of the counter, their cheeks tinted blue by the light of the barman's touch-screen console. One Queen of Wands, one Queen of the Harvest, one High Priestess (Reformed Lunar Rite). One athletic blonde, one raven-haired Scythian, one redhead (probably dyed). Not necessarily in that order.

The Scythian was the closest of the three, but something about her seemed terribly distant. She leaned forward with her head in her hands, as if in intense concentration, her body so stiff that at first I wasn't even sure she was breathing. The blonde – the one who looked like a cross between a strapping young highwayman's moll and a silkie – was doing her best to put back together the pieces of cardboard she had pulled apart earlier, except that the geometry was giving her grief. Only the redhead seemed at all aware of her surroundings, her eyes watching their own reflection in the murky depths of the mirror, her strangely triangular face unfocused, like a pixie caught on the cusp of the Otherworld, undecided as yet whether to cross over.

None of them spoke. None of them danced. None of them so much as signaled to the barman. For tonight, at least, it seemed the club had decided to take the "wilt" of Uncle Aleister's famous commandment a little too literally – not so much doing nothing as nothing doing. And it seemed to have been left up to me to take the initiative.

So there I was with three exotic-looking women at the bar of a dodgy nightclub. Well, what would you have done? Apart from the obvious, of course, like running away?

I went up to order a drink, and the blonde spoke to me.

"Goodness, is it always this dull?"

Now I was closer, I could see her arms were stained with a complex web of tattoos, mostly lifesize representations of the foliage of the greenwood. Exuberant swathes of leaves swept up over her elbows like the suburban jungles of the Douanier Rousseau, only to vanish under the sleeves of her thick, mahogany blouse in a flourish of top-heavy ellipses. With her brown trunk and her foliage, she reminded me of nothing so much as Goethe's Green Woman, stretching thirsty tendrils up to the sky in her constant struggle to reach the source of the light. Not-so-idly I wondered how much further over her body the leaves extended.

"I can't imagine what we're doing here..." she continued.

"Oh fie, Magnolia," answered the redhead. "You know exactly why we came here. We saw it in a vision."

The Scythian came suddenly awake. "A prophecy..."

I thought she was kidding.

"And you are?"

She had a musical voice, with just a hint of that infinite tiredness which suggests a depth of experience far beyond the bounds of a single lifetime. Her cheeks, when she raised her head from her hands, were flushed and rosy – as if she had been running these past several centuries. Her eyes were such a deep shade of brown I could not tell their irises apart from their pupils. They were eyes for drowning in. And, as a stray light swung our way from the half-empty dance floor, I thought I caught a glimpse of strong brown nipples ghosting through the silk of her shirt, incongruous against pale white skin.

"Ermmm... Leon," I muttered, flustered by both the reaction the three girls were evoking and the laughing gaze of the redhead, who seemed well aware of my sudden discomfort.

"Maritsa," the Scythian said formally, bowing. I realized she spoke with just the faintest trace of an accent. "And this is Candace." She indicated the redhead.

"And you are Magnolia?" I asked the blonde awkwardly.

"Magnolia Banyan-Tree Asphodel," Candace cut in, suppressing a smile. "To give her her full Goddess-name."

Magnolia shrugged apologetically. "What can I say? Hippie parents. You know how it goes." Without warning, they both collapsed into a fit of giggles.

"Poor Leon..."

They spluttered.

"He looks so serious..."

They laughed some more.

"And so out of touch with his destiny..."

Maritsa watched the pair of them with an expression of strained indulgence, like an embarrassed parent, but they were so carried away by then that they seemed quite unaware of anything but their own hilarity.

"Well, we can soon fix that," Magnolia said cheerfully, her laughter finally subsiding into a series of snuffles. "Come on, let's get out of here."

Candace wiped the tears from her cheeks, and turned to look at me with eyes the colour of amber. "Leon – this place is terrible. How on earth did you choose it? I mean, we were sent here by a vision, but what's *your* excuse?"

As she got down off the barstool, I saw she was shorter than the other two, but very attractive for all that. Her black tank-top swelled over the contours of her body suggestively, nocturnal shadows on a rolling hillside, set off by a silver pendant which shone in the combe of her breasts like the moon over a witches' sabbat.

It was my turn to shrug apologetically. "I liked the name. But it seems that tonight they have an empty statute book..."

Maritsa swept back her hair with thickly painted, blunt red fingernails. "They're not the only ones," she said in that peculiarly world-weary voice of hers. "Sometimes I feel as if this whole messed-up world of ours went out to lunch somewhere roundabout 1970 and never came back, as if the spirits of our ancestors – not just my own, but yours and Thomas Jefferson's as well – have all gone running back to the Balkans (or wherever they came from), leaving only this empty exoskeleton of a civilization to struggle along on some kind of chitinous autopilot..."

The streets were wet outside, as if after a sudden downpour, but the sky was clear, and for a few seconds I was puzzled. Then I heard a distant clanking and I realized the Municipal Council had been sending out its water carts again to sluice down the heavy summer dust. How like those corporate drones to make a point of flushing away all the awkward residues that did not fit the squeaky-clean image of their sleek, new business district. There would be no riffraff here. Only dubious subterranean warehouses like The Whole of the Law to act as a kind of overly manicured id. I could feel the faint beat of its empty dance floor even here, echoing off the metallic blue windows and pink stone cladding of the empty office blocks. We must have been the only pedestrians for half a mile in any direction, and for all the life we could see around us, we might as well have been a group of Shelley's travelers from an antique land, staring at the truncated, postmodern portico of Ozymandias Corp. – or at least at the remains of their parking garage, poking up out of a drift of discarded computer components. Sand dunes and silicon chips – it all came down to the same thing after a few millennia. Hubris clobbered by bricolage.

But Maritsa evidently had other things on her mind. Silently, she led us out of the wilderness, and we followed, passing under the plexiglass tombs of the pharaohs with a kind of numb disaffection. Their cliffs towered above us as inscrutable as sphinxes; their potted palms no more than a mirage of an oasis. Then, before we quite knew it, we were back in the 19th century, surrounded by ragged fences and piles of litter, and the filthy black stone arches at the edge of the railway yards. Not quite the land of milk and honey, but certainly a relief after the desert.

Maritsa stopped by a four-door saloon parked under a single streetlamp by the water-stained brick of a dank, old railway bridge.

"You drive," she said, tossing the keys to Magnolia.

Magnolia smiled, catching the bundled metal with so little effort she barely seemed to move at all. This was clearly a role she was well used to.

"Here." She opened the near-side rear passenger door for me, and, as I stooped to avoid hitting my head, Candace slipped in beside me.

All of a sudden, I became acutely aware of her. Here I was in the back seat of a car, squashed up against this buxom, attractive woman I barely knew, close enough to feel her body heat. Even in the half-dark I could see the striking, triangular shape of her cheekbones, the elegant curve of her jawline, the omnipresent silver glow of her round lunar pendant, the warm, swelling blackness of her bosom... Her perfume filled my nostrils. And, even if I told myself it meant nothing, my body had other ideas. I was childishly embarrassed. Had I had to speak, I would have been selfconscious and tongue-tied. So I sat back in silence, letting the red, yellow and green lights of our journey flicker over me.

"Those chitin zombies," Magnolia was saying. "You know, those empty exoskeletons – do you think we could make some, too?"

Maritsa sighed, not unkindly. "Magnolia, my dear, it was only a metaphor."

"Pity. I rather liked them."

Candace laughed. "Maybe our Leon would like to demonstrate one for us."

And, just as inexplicably as it had arrived, the tension was gone.

I could see now that Magnolia was driving us up Loon Hill, the steep escarpment which rose like a basalt tsunami above the heart of the city.

Warehouses and faded Art Deco apartment blocks gave way abruptly to narrow tree-lined streets and ramshackle 18th-century townhouses – to parks and cemeteries. The railway lines were replaced by tiny, neglected cottages and ancient coaching inns with wooden gables. Without warning, we seemed to have gone back in time again. How much further, I wondered? Where would time have a stop tonight? Well, not here, not here – that, at least, seemed obvious.

Magnolia kept the lights of the city to her right as she wound block by block to the top of the hill. Soon we found ourselves in an area of substantial pseudo-Colonial mansions with extensive grounds and spectacular views out over the floodplain of the river. Even from the back seat of the car, I had to admit it was impressive. The networks of distant sodium lights seemed to embroider the darkness like ions in a cloud chamber, tracing secret lines of power with a muted glimmering, their outlines as inconstant as the speckled ears of a beast of the Otherworld. Or like the cat's-eyes of visitants.

And then we pulled up by the kerb outside an imposing redbrick manor house, set back from the road behind a well kept lawn and a hedge of carefully clipped yew trees. Several other cars were already parked in the driveway, and shadowy figures moved by the light of what seemed to be a storm lantern under the stark white colonnade of its Neoclassical porch.

"We're here," announced Candace in a waft of perfume.

I felt myself tense again.

"Where?" I asked stupidly.

"You'll see."

"At the party." Magnolia laughed.

"Come on." Candace must have sensed my discomfort, because she put her hand on my arm encouragingly. "We won't bite."

"At least not there," Magnolia smiled. Her words were innocent enough, I suppose, but all the same I couldn't help wondering what might lie hidden behind them.

Inside, we emerged into a wood-panelled entrance hall, with something that might originally have been a ballroom opening out to the left. The lighting was subdued, provided by old-fashioned overhead chandeliers, with real candles. They gave the whole scene a kind of well rounded, archaic glow, as if we had stepped back into a hand-tinted daguerreotype. The walls and the floors seemed to shine with their own inner radiance – all sepias and ebonies and warm chestnut browns – with only a few vases of faded roses and cornflowers to add highlights. There were no people, though. The figures we had seen on the porch seemed to have faded away into the background, leaving only a vague impression of recent activity – a whisper of movement in the shadows, the hint of a scent, the faintest suggestion of delicate footfalls on distant parqueting.

Gone elsewhere, an unwanted voice suggested, like the gravel-voiced prompter of some deep psychodrama – the compressed, oil-rich residue of a far memory, lost in the long-buried strata of my forgotten ancestry. *Back to wherever they came from. Otherwhere. Otherwhen.*

Then, looking around, I found that Candace and Maritsa had vanished, too, leaving me alone with Magnolia.

"Oh, don't worry about them," she tried to reassure me as I fought off a first wave of panic. "They have to get ready for the performance... And so do we."

She led me into the ballroom, which I now saw was almost entirely covered with mirrors, dark gaps looming only where a break in the walls gave way onto a side-chamber or an alcove. It was as we entered the nearest alcove that we finally met someone from the group which had earlier gone missing from the porch. A man emerged as we went in – at least I assumed it was man. Of his masculinity there could be no doubt, but he wore the mask of a pig on his head, and a long leather thong with a necklace of tusks around his neck. Apart from that, he was as naked as the day he was born, but rather hairier.

Magnolia nodded to him respectfully, and the pig's head nodded back. And then we were ourselves in the alcove, and Magnolia had started to unbutton her blouse, disconcertingly shadowed by half a dozen additional Magnolias in the mirrors' multiple reflections – the leaves on her arms and shoulders spreading around her like the coppiced hazel of a looking-glass forest.

"Oh, come on, don't say you're shy," she protested, catching my startled expression as it stretched out into an infinite regress on either side of her.

I was, but what could I do? I reached for my belt, and started to unbuckle my trousers.

"I'm Sister Cat," she added, reaching into her shoulder bag to pull out a mask which seemed to have been formed out of a tropical gourd by the skillful application of paint and fabric. The pointy ears suited her.

"You be Brother Fox." She pulled out another and passed it over.

Hesitantly I reached out and took it, and all of a sudden the mischievous face of a fox leered up at me from between my hands. The mask was surprisingly light, and attractively decorated with spirals of appliqued beechnuts. It had an elasticated strap at the back to hold it in place, and the inside had been padded to stop it chafing. It had obviously been a labor of love.

I pulled it up onto my face, still more than a little bemused by this latest turn of events, but to my surprise it fit perfectly. Almost as if made to measure.

"Yeah!" Magnolia approved, as she inspected the whole litter of fox spirits which had appeared as from nowhere in the mirrors behind her, her voice made deeper and echoey by her own cat face.

I took a good look in the mirror myself, and it was a most peculiar experience. To see my naked body transformed by so simple a device as a mask into something like a cross between an Ancient Egyptian god of the Underworld and an outtake from Reynard the Fox unnerved me more than I was willing to admit.

But Magnolia was in no mood for philosophizing. "Don't just stand there. It's not simply a mask, it's your identity. You have to try on your character for size. Be *foxy*..."

And it was true, I realized. As soon as I had put on the mask, I had started to feel a presence, as if I was no longer alone – as if I was sharing control of my mind and body with another being, a persona, a set of thoughts and movements and behaviors that belonged not to myself but to the role. It was like being inside the face of a fox, like losing track for a while of my human body – a kind of waking forgetfulness.

I had always assumed there had to be some kind of difference between religious ritual and dramatic performance – that the one was somehow more serious than the other. But perhaps it wasn't so. Perhaps they both contained an element of theatricality, with individual actions dictated more by the demands of one's part and one's costume than by the will. Don't actors always say they lose themselves in their characters? That the spirit of their role takes them over and plays them, displacing their own sense of identity, while revealing inner resources they scarce knew they had.

Where is the difference when a priest is possessed by the spirit?

All of a sudden it seemed to me there was no difference at all. Regardless of whether one was considering a naked animal-headed Goddess or a frock-coated parson in a chasuble, the principle was the same. The part dictated the actions. And, if the part truly clicked, their bodies would move by themselves, carried by a motive force that seemed to come from beyond, instinct taking over motor control from the intellect.

Ritual was like that. All ceremony...

"Erm, hello?" Magnolia tugged at my arm gently. "Meow? We have to go out now."

She led me back into the ballroom, and I saw that, while we'd been away, a congregation of about a dozen people had gathered – all of them naked, and all variously masked. There were horses and owls and magpies, rams, weasels and pigs, multiplied into a glowing candlelit infinity by the silvery walls. But, try as I might, I could not find anyone who looked as if they might be the masked Candace or Maritsa.

I turned to Magnolia, intending to ask what had become of them, but she put a finger to the tip of my snout and rolled her green cat's eyes, so I waited. And, as my senses acclimatized to my strange surroundings, I became aware of a keen edge of anticipation in the gathering tribe. Something was imminent, and many of them were so keyed up they could barely contain their excitement. They stood in a loose arc, twitching and twittering for all the world like a real menagerie, watching a darkened alcove at the far side of the chamber.

Then a familiar raven-haired figure entered, her face flushed, her nipples shockingly black against her pale body. But, instead of a mask, she wore a shiny metallic band on her head, topped with the twin silvery horns of the moon.

"Our Priestess," whispered Magnolia, her whiskers tickling my ear.

"But where's Candace?" I whispered back, acutely conscious that we were the only people speaking in the whole room.

"Our Maiden? She's next. Watch..."

And at that moment I saw her, being led out of another chamber by a man with the head of a stag. Her body was swathed from neck to ankle in a black leather bodysuit, stretched tight over the swelling curves of her body like the skin of a sea-lion. Her head had been partially shaved, exposing a bright band of skin on either side of her temples. Around her neck she wore what seemed to be a necklace of acorns. Most peculiar of all, though, she was blindfold.

I turned once again to Magnolia. "Why is she wearing clothes?"

"It's her second skin, the one she sheds when she's shapeshifting. It's so she can be transformed. Every well dressed shaman should have one."

"But..."

"Shh. Be patient. We're about to begin."

Looking away from the blunt nose of her enigmatic, feline profile, I realized the other animals were all watching Maritsa intently. Well, about as intently as those blank eyes in their masks of painted wood and papier-mâché could ever be said to watch anything.

"Brothers and Sisters," Maritsa intoned in that languid, imperious voice of hers, her left hand resting on what appeared to be an altar, draped in a deep blue cloth speckled with silver embroidered stars. "We are gathered here today to celebrate the rites of our Covenant in the presence of Artemis the Huntress, who is also called Diana of Ephesos, Great Mother and Mistress of Beasts...

"She, whose light shone over the wind-blown sands of ancient, canal-watered Khemennu, Egyptian Land of the Moon, and slipped through foliage to caress Her creatures in the cork groves of Tuscany. She, to whom the Amazons bared their throats in the swamps of the Danube delta, and the Witches their breasts on peat bog and mountain. Silver Egg

– Shining Mirror – Queen of the Tides, walking in brightness, by whose power we ride on the ever-cresting wave of dream and memory..."

She indicated a pair of crystal goblets that stood on one side of the altar.

"In Her name, we come together to celebrate the holy Mysteries. The Covenant of moonstone and mugwort, of white lead and bitter almond – the Covenant of the White Grail..."

She lifted her arms in an upraised curve, like the arc of the moon, and suddenly the animals started moving.

Magnolia kicked my leg from behind.

"This is where you dance," she whispered through clenched whiskers. "Just follow Sister Ferret in front of you."

She gave me the gentlest of shoves, so I was forced to take a tumbling step forward to avoid falling. Before I quite knew what was happening, I found myself being drawn into the circle of animals grunting and chirruping around the edge of the room, shadowed by the crazy spiral of their silent counterparts in the mirrors. Maritsa and Candace and the Stag Man remained in the middle, their images blurred by the swirling ebb and flow of the mad bacchanalia, like coracles at the heart of a storm. Candace, in her blindfold, held perfectly still, as if only peripherally aware of the chaos, her polished black leather torso as abstractly alluring as a statue. The Stag Man stood with his antlers bowed, as if listening to a distant sound with intense concentration; while Maritsa kept her arms aloft in their half-moon position, her eyes deep and sparkly as a tarn by starlight, and twice as mysterious.

I shivered with a sense of awakening, as I shook myself back to the present.

The dance was starting to pick up its pace, and pretty soon I found I was losing track of my own movements. All around me I could see only fragments of human bodies and the stylized faces of animals, ducking and diving in bizarre juxtapositions as they skimmed over the walls to come up for air on the far side of the mirrors. Horses suddenly seemed to grow antlers, stoats took wing, lecherous owls seemed to ogle the disembodied breasts of half a dozen fragmented young women from impossible angles, while boars chased behind to nibble their rumps. Sylph-like youths rode the backs of a whole flock of magpies. Sweat started to drip down my face, as my feet dodged the jabbing horns of ethereal billy goats...

All of a sudden Maritsa lowered her arms, and the moon shifted phases.

The effect was almost physical. Shadows seemed to scramble away into the corners of the mirror world to pick up their pieces, ghostly gray birds seemed to fly up to the ceiling. Impossibly, the candles grew dimmer. It was only when I ran into Magnolia's naked back that I realized the company had come to a halt, though strangely the room still had a strong sense of movement about it. There was still a vortex of lights and images which seemed to tug at my eyes each time I turned away, as if, when the rest of us stopped, the shadows had kept right on dancing, with some kind of inner force of their own.

Maritsa lowered her hands to lift one of the two crystal goblets on the altar, and turned to Candace.

"From the Cauldron of Light are we born, to the Cauldron we return," she intoned, as deadpan as ever. "In the Cauldron we find our destiny."

Candace, still unable to see, reached blindly in the direction of Maritsa's voice, and Maritsa placed the cup in her hands. With a ritualized gesture, Candace lifted the goblet and drank.

White liquid spilled down her chin, dripping onto the swelling curve of the black leather sheath over her breast. There was an audible intake of breath from the hollow mouths of the animals.

"What the...?" I mumbled, presumably not as silently as I had imagined, for Magnolia turned and purred in my ear.

"It's milk – the White Grail, remember?"

But, before I could really quite take this in, Candace handed the empty cup back to Maritsa, and the Stag Man stepped forward with a slight bow to face her. He took hold of the zipper on her bodysuit and, with a single, swift downward movement, unzipped her, exposing the pale curves of her bosom to the warm glow of the candlelight that filled the room. It was not until then, I think, that I fully realized how attractive I found her, how much I had been secretly longing for this moment, ever since I first saw her at the bar – was it only a few hours ago? I was trapped by the beam of her light like a rabbit entranced by the glow of the harvest moon. I was helpless as a sculptor's apprentice working on his first Greek statue...

She stepped out of the bodysuit, gleaming and radiant even by candlelight, accompanied by a great waft of that strange, rooty perfume I had noticed earlier. And, still blindfolded, she stepped over to an old-fashioned free-standing, dark-framed mirror which had been placed to the left of the altar.

She stood for a few seconds, for all the world as if admiring her reflection, though I knew that, blindfold, she couldn't be. And then, with a sureness that was almost shocking, she swung the mirror down on a pivot and stepped forward to crouch over it like a Sheila-na-Gig, casting multiple reflections of the maze of her labia into the already confusing play of shadows that swirled around the walls. She lowered her head as if staring into the depths of the folds which seemed at that moment to define the core of her being, and then raised her face, basking, it seemed, in the invisible light of the deity.

I was more than a little confused by now. "What's she doing?" I whispered to Magnolia.

"It's a form of oracle. She's reading our futures from the folds of her labia."

"But she can't see anything..."

"Oh, Leon! The oracle has to be blind."

"Shh," a warthog mask close behind us hissed incongruously.

Just then Candace spoke, and all our eyes moved back to give her our full attention.

"Our new brother, where is he?" she asked in a voice several notches deeper and growlier than usual.

"That's you." Magnolia pushed me forward. "Go up there and kneel."

I hesitated for a moment, overcome by a last-minute wave of embarrassment. Then the spirit of Brer Fox slipped out of the back of my mask to take me, and all of sudden my path stood before me, clear as a forest glade in the moonlight. I stepped forward, all bright-eyed and bushy-tailed – no, really, there was a moment there, when I would have sworn I could feel the Otherworldly fur of my speckled brush sweeping the leaves of the bramble bushes – and I bowed to my Lady with a mischievous flourish, like a fox, accompanied by the reflections of half a hundred fox-men in the mirrors.

When I raised my head, the Oracle reached out to touch me, and for a few seconds it seemed as if the mounds of her body had started to pucker with finely etched spirals of light – as if some ancient stonemason had belatedly decided to carve his serpentine traces on the tabula rasa of her marble. The lines wandered over her flesh like drunken fireflies.

And then, before I quite knew what was happening, the silvery lines leaped from her hands to play over the spirals of beechnuts that decorated the cheeks of my mask, and I felt the world slipping away from me...

See the power of moonlight on naked flesh, a voice that might have been Candace's whispered. *See the whiteness... The Moon and Her creatures caught up in the endless dance of Her tides, the eternal light of Her shining mirror. Her reflections are everywhere.*

And that was when I saw them – the slim, white body of Artemis, racing moonclouds through mighty thickets of oak, like one of her own brindled hounds, in the primeval old-growth forests of ancient Etruria... the round, white face of Isis, riding in majesty on the inky swell of the harbor at Cenchreae while ecstatic parties of donkey-boys cast bunches of roses in Her path to give thanks for Her blessing... the pale, white flesh of Epona the Horse Mother, swelling under the unruly scrub of the Downs, and brought up from below the turf by grizzled work-gangs of well disciplined tribal elders, who liked to cut sweeping pictograms direct into the naked chalk of the hills themselves...

But, above all, I saw the Grail. The two white marble Grails of the Goddess. Twin goblets overflowing with the bounty of the Goddess's warm milk. Bottomless paired cauldrons of moonlight.

This, then, was the eternity we men liked to spend our lives questing for, the source of our lunacy. And this was the attraction between spirit and mortal which was said by the Celts to open the gates of the Otherworld. As so often, it all came down to *Cherchez la femme*...

Goddess... Candace...

Candace... Goddess...

At that moment the lines seemed to be blurring... and the last thing I remember, before my mind passed out of consciousness, was Candace, her belly marbled and swirling, like the Mother of all protoplasm, her breasts swollen and gravid, plasma at the birth of a galaxy... Candace illuminated from within, resplendent and shining and ethereal with the true light of the Goddess...

Then there was only whiteness.

When I came to I was lying in one of the changing-rooms with a bundle of clothes under my head by way of a pillow. Candace was kneeling beside me, her face marred by an uncharacteristic frown of anxiety – I don't know whether from simple fright or uncertainty or a more complex form of detached, selfconscious bemusement. It was only later I realized she was wearing her tank-top again, and that the blindfold had gone. Come to that, my own mask had also vanished somewhere along the way.

The house was silent at last, and dark outside our small circle of candles, and for the first time that evening we were completely alone. Except for the omnipresent shadows and the infinite array of our other selves, which had somehow so mysteriously got trapped in the mirrors. But even they had at least stopped dancing.

"Well, your initiation is over," she said eventually, as if reluctant to break into the sudden sense of tranquillity. "You can go now."

But of course I didn't want to. Her transformation was still far too fresh in my memory. The very idea of leaving filled me with a horror like that of a man waiting to have his leg cut off – phantom limb-pain in advance.

"You've got to be kidding," I protested, peering up into the bright amber rings of her irises and admiring the way the light played with the stubble on either side of her head.

She gave me a strangely shocked, quizzical look, and I finally understood that she was just as nervous as I was.

She reached out to brush my forehead.

There were no fireworks this time, though I've always suspected that maybe she was blushing. It's hard to tell by candlelight.

"Well, at least get dressed, then. I don't want everyone to think I'm the sort of girl who goes to eternity with a guy on the first date." She smiled, though I could see her heart wasn't in it. "And for goodness' sake don't believe I'm a goddess outside the circle."

But she is. And this is how I met her.

The whole of my law.

I bowed with an imitation of gallantry. "For you, anywhere," I declared, not without a hint of irony, as she mutely watched me buckle my trousers. But I stopped when I saw her eyes filling with tears, as if the day's events had finally got too much for her.

"I mean it," I added urgently, my tone suddenly serious now, stepping forward to lay my hand with the utmost delicacy on her shoulder.

"It's eternity or bust for me... Eternity or bust..."

And then the rains came down.

New Writings in the Fantastic
Hot Cross Son
Steve Redwood

For most people, the name Ian Whiting simply recalls a somewhat gruesome Easter Day prank. For those of us who knew the full enormity of his crime, it was a little different. We were aware that we were facing the threat of the end of civilization as we knew it.

Yes, it really was that bad.

Here's what I was able to piece together from the local newspaper reports. The Reverend Ian Whiting was celebrating Mass in his small church in the Devon village of Ashleycombe as he had done for years now. Everything went fine up to the saying of the Lord's prayer. But then, instead of offering consecrated wafers and wine, he produced a small plastic bag from behind the altar and emptied its contents onto the table. Splosh! Out poured what looked like chunks of stewing steak.

"Bread and wine, me hearties!" said he, departing somewhat from the liturgy.

Even the most devout found it odd that the bread was bleeding.

"It's the latest style," announced the priest. "You get to eat the body and drink the blood all in one go. Saves problems with the chalice if any of you lot have got any poxy diseases!"

It is not for nothing that a church congregation is called a flock. Despite wondering looks, five pillars of the community meekly accepted the "host" until:

"But this is raw meat!" protested an old lady who had once shaken hands with Mrs. Thatcher, and so wasn't afraid to speak her mind.

"Isn't that what I just said? Come on, tuck in!"

But she staggered back, spitting the offering out of her mouth.

Her decisive action at last broke the sacrosanct spell. The communicants who had been obediently chewing away finally came to their senses, and followed the lady's example.

The priest became furious. "You fools! All these years you've been quite willing to be fobbed off with bread and wine, and now I offer you the real thing you don't want it! Bloody well eat it, you stupid cretins!"

And he leapt over the altar rail, picked up a bit of the "host" that had been spat out, and tried to force it into the mouth of the lady who had defied him.

Churchgoers are usually a placid lot, and loyal to their priests. As old Nietzsche said, Christianity is pretty much a slave morality. But this *was* Easter Sunday, and they *were* all wearing their best clothes: clothes which were now getting spattered with wine/blood and assorted retchings. This is the only way I can explain the ferocity of their attack on their pastor. A well wielded crutch put him into a coma which lasted a week.

There's a fascinating letter in the State Archives in Florence, dated July 24, 1567, from one Piero Gianfigliazzi in Pisa to Prince Francesco dei Medici:

On the 19th of the present month, while celebrating mass in the Cathedral of this city... the priest registered a most fetid taste and odor in the act of receiving the consecrated wine. However, he swallowed it down as best he could. Then, when he came to the purification, he wanted none of the wine that they wished to give him, saying that he didn't want any more of that piss [*non voleva più piscio*]. After expressing his displeasure to the choirmaster and the sacristan, he was brought another chalice and given good wine, which he was told he could purify. From all of this I deduce that he was given urine to consecrate in place of wine. Though the Vicar has not been able to uncover the truth regarding who is responsible for such an obscenity, he has put a priest named Giobbo in solitary confinement...

I never did find out whether they finally hung it on poor old Giobbo. I guess, with a name like that, suspicion was bound to fall on him.

I mention this little anecdote to show that this wasn't the first time the host and wine had been interfered with. The police were informed, but didn't find it important enough to investigate, or even to check just what meat it was. The deacon had already thrown it in the park for the local dogs, anyway.

But a contact of mine was so amazed by what the priest told her when he came out of his coma that she gave me a call. I was passing my Easter vacation in Torquay for sentimental reasons, revisiting the spot which had witnessed one of the most satisfying moments in my long tumultuous relationship with my darling Katie – the place where I had thrown her first lover off the cliffs. Well, he should have known better than to mention my accident.

I asked to be alone with the Reverend (my Ministry of Defence ID secured acquiescence) and he at once burst into an amazing diatribe.

"The Central Mystery of the Church! Poppycock! The only mystery is why people have swallowed it for so long! It's just word games. Transubstantiation: the bread and wine no longer exist, though there it is, sitting right in front of you. Consubstantiation: the bread and wine do at least exist, but they are *also* the body and blood of Christ. Impanation, Eucharist, host, elementals, accidentals, sacring bell, fraction, epiclesis, oblation, credence table, chalice, paten – words, words, words! Verbal foliage to hide the greatest con trick the world has ever known! Our version of the Emperor with no clothes!"

Strange stuff, coming from such a meek-looking priest, but in my profession we deal with all sorts.

"You're preaching to the perverted," I said. "But I don't see that making the congregation sick with raw meat is any solution, do you?"

"Flesh."

"What?"

"*Flesh*, not meat. You, you poor lost soul, indulge in the sins of the flesh, not the sins of the meat."

I was on holiday, so I didn't break his arm.

"You mean, that was *human* flesh you gave them?"

"Of course. A real Eucharist is the only way to save mankind! John 6:53-54: *Then Jesus said unto them, Verily, verily, I say unto you, Except ye eat the flesh of the Son of man, and drink His blood, ye have no life in you.*"

Well, you couldn't have put it much straighter than that!

"I've still got the rest of the body at home," he added, clearly concerned lest I doubt his word.

Well, I called in my contact, and we got him dressed and into his detached house faster than a premature orgasm. First the fridge. Contents: week-old skimmed milk, a few shivering veg, and a plastic bag containing maybe ten kilos of what looked liked diced stewing steak. Then the freezer. Contents: sundry innards, two arms, one leg, and a head attached to maybe half a torso.

I felt a new respect for this guy. Maybe we could recruit him later.

Only... that head. That head, I swear, was looking serenely up, with a warm forgiving smile on those frozen lips. Just looking at it, I felt this guy would have immediately understood why I'd arranged for my darling Katie's second lover to come into a terminal headlock with a bulldozer.

But that wasn't all. There were nasty-looking holes in the hands and the remaining foot.

You can't blame *everything* on junk food. I was starting to get a real bad feeling about this whole thing.

I kept my voice even.

"Who was this... gentleman?"

"Jesus, of course."

I'd expected that.

"No, I mean, who was he *really*?"

Whiting looked at me, puzzled.

I went on: "Yes, of course, *you* knew it was really Jesus paying a secret Return Visit, but who did other less discerning people think he was? How did he disguise his Divine Effulgence? What did he do? Where did he live?"

"He lived here, down in the cellar, of course. No one else ever saw him. That's not what I cloned him for."

Well, that one threw even me, and I'm trained for the unexpected. Yes, cloning's the in thing these days, but you still need something to clone *from*. That's why I still keep my darling Katie's little finger, just in case I go too far one day, though at the time I was cutting it off I admit I was doing it simply for pleasure: we were going through one of our transitory tiffs.

The good Reverend smiled indulgently.

"You're wondering where I got the DNA? Let me remind you, St. John again, chapter 20, 6-7: *Then cometh Simon Peter following him, and went into the sepulchre, and seeth the linen clothes lie, and the facecloth, that was about his head, not lying with the linen clothes, but wrapped together in a place by itself.*"

What did he think I was? Your average uncultured assassin?

"The Turin Shroud? That tatty old sheet that's supposed to have been wrapped round Jesus's body in the tomb, and seems to have got a negative photographic image of a crucified man on it? Don't come that old chestnut with me. That was carbon-14 dated ages ago and proved to be medieval, not first century."

"Hardly *proved*," muttered Whiting, for the first time looking a bit nettled, "since they only took tiny samples from the edge of the cloth, which could well have been contaminated by later accretions. But, yes, its authenticity is in doubt, and besides it would have been impossible to break into Turin Cathedral and steal it. Too well protected. Anyway, what I needed was *blood*. And there was much more chance of finding that on the Oviedo Sudarium."

Damn, he'd got me there. Sudarium? But, come on, my hobby is to break limbs, not read up on Fairy Tales for Religious Nutters.

He told me that the Cathedral of San Salvador in Oviedo in northern Spain is now really famous for one thing: It's the only cathedral in the world with just a single tower. This wasn't minimalist design, it was poverty. But it used to have a lot of prestige. El Cid himself had a quaff or two there in 1075. The reason was the silver chest in the Cámara Santa, which contained what was believed to be the Sudarium, or facecloth, which had been wrapped round Jesus's head on the Cross to mop up the blood and serum coming out of his nose, and which was taken out of Jerusalem at the time of the Persian invasion, reached Seville, and then moved north in stages before the Moorish advances. But times change, and very few have even heard of the Oviedo Sudarium, all the glory being stolen by the Turin Shroud. The Italians just have more razzmatazz than the Spanish; besides, the Pope lives there.

Whiting went on to explain how the Sudarium is brought out to be viewed only three times a year, twice on saints' days in September and then again on Good Friday, and how he had broken in and stolen it at the end of September, knowing it wouldn't be missed for six months.

He'd then cloned Jesus from the DNA he'd found there.

By now I was growing impatient. OK, so the guy was funny, and had a neat way of hacking off limbs, but was he trying to take me for a sucker? I know all about Dolly, Polly, Golly, and all the mice, cows, cats, cockroaches, and top models cloned since then. Cloning takes *time*. Not just six months.

"There speaks an abandoned soul!" Whiting said sadly. "You think a *god* isn't going to grow a bit quicker, you idiot?"

I saw he had a point, but I gave him a backhander anyway. Guess in my job it's a kind of reflex. Besides, my darling Katie's third lover had been a vicar.

Whiting turned the other cheek, bless him, so I smacked it, too, and then we went down to the cellar, and, yes, there sure enough was a pretty impressive-looking laboratory. (I learned later that Whiting wasn't the first priest to play around in labs. Apparently, Hoffmann's mad scientist in *Der Sandmann* was modelled on the Roman Catholic priest Lazzaro Spallanzani, who filled in his time blinding bats, decapitating snails, and resurrecting dried microscopic animals. It also turned out, would you believe it, that Whiting had once turned down a job in the Roslin Research Institute – you know, where they cloned Dolly – because Wilmut and the other researchers were "amateurs and charlatans" and had "a pathetically superficial knowledge of genetics"!)

In one corner of the lab was another freezer, its door hanging open and its shelves full of what looked like a lot of Easter eggs for undernourished Hobbits. But I only noted that subliminally. Because next to the freezer was a cross.

A used cross. Unoccupied now. But used.

Don't ask me. In my profession, you just *know*.

"But why the hell did you have to *crucify* him?" I asked the Reverend, who was tenderly releasing a fly trapped in a spider's web.

He looked at me pityingly. "Don't you know *anything*? A lot of good it would have done us if the Son of God had turned up the first time, taken a look round Palestine like Queen Elizabeth visiting Australia, and then just gone back to Heaven with unwanted gifts of Middle Eastern coffee pots and pictures of the Roman emperor! He had to die and be crucified to absolve us of our sins. The power lay in the *crucified* body, that was the whole point of it. The same with my new Jesus. Don't think I enjoyed it! Or that it was easy! Have you ever tried to lift a struggling man up onto a cross by yourself?"

Well, not entirely by myself. My darling Katie and myself had been close at that time. This was the guy who'd sliced off... but I don't want to think about that. Besides, *he'd* deserved it!

The Reverend was reminiscing. "And the names he called me! You could tell he had royal blood all right!" The gentle smile of the tolerant fanatic played about his lips.

I'd always thought the original Jesus must have done a bit of name-calling, too. "Forgive them, for they know not what they do" – my ass!

Well, we had a pretty gruesome murder on our hands. A benign-looking parish priest somehow breaks into a Spanish cathedral, steals one of its relics guarded behind an iron grille, impossibly clones a man from *old* DNA in the cloth, accelerates the growth so there's a full-grown man within a few months, crucifies him, chops him up into wafer-sized pieces, and offers the pieces to his congregation on Easter Day.

Pretty bad, eh?

Well, that wasn't the worst of it.

Those Easter eggs, you see.

The good Reverend suddenly noticed the open freezer, dashed across, and scrambled among the eggs – which I now saw were made of glass, not chocolate – with the ferocity of a tumescent but unprepared man searching for an unused condom. The eggs all had a spherical hole at one end.

"They've escaped!" he screamed.

The Reverend Ian Whiting was a true visionary, a man who cared deeply about the whole human race, who hadn't just wished to save the souls of his own small flock on this one Easter Day, but had planned to stamp out the Eucharistic fraud everywhere for a long time to come. A passing sheep had provided the uterus for his Jesus (no longer the Lamb of God, but the God of Lamb), but he had retained a hundred embryos which he had intended to later implant in other unwary passing sheep.

Now I admit I'm only guessing here. Very little research, it seems, has been done on divine chromosomes. A divine cell doesn't necessarily obey the same laws as a humble undivine one, as Whiting had found out with his accelerated Jesus. Certain faculties may be developed before the organs normally associated with them. The auditory sense, for instance, might precede the ear. Prayers not only have to reach as far as Heaven, which I'm told on *very* good authority is quite some distance away, but frequently aren't even uttered until one reaches one's death bed, by which time one's voice tends to be muted. Maybe straining to hear these deathbed prayers had preternaturally developed the Divine audition.

Now the good Reverend had crucified his Jesus just a few feet away from the embryos. What if they'd heard the nails going in, sensed what was in store for them, and, during the week the Reverend had been in a coma, done a bit of accelerated growing up by themselves, and then scarpered? Can't say I'd blame them really.

Of course, I had to report all this to Section Thirteen. And the instructions went out just as I'd expected.

Search and destroy.

The world is ruled by economic imperialism. But, judging from the antics of the original JC in the temple with the moneylenders, his clones wouldn't be likely to accept that. And some of those Commandments! No other gods: end of the pop music and film industry. No killing: end of the armaments industry. No bearing false witness: end of politics and international diplomacy. No coveting your neighbor's cow or wife: end of capitalism and good healthy competition.

In short, living by Christian precepts would rapidly bring the Christian world to its knees.

The next few days were tense. The Section's greatest stroke of luck was when the main body of jaycees got cornered in Portsmouth, remembered their old skills, and cockily walked across the Solent to the Isle of Wight, making rude signs as they went. Hubris. Next day the island was nuked. Pity about the local inhabitants, but Section Thirteen has to see the bigger picture.

After that, it was a case of mopping up. Three jaycees foolishly headed for the Vatican, and were brought down by the halberds of the Swiss Guard on the direct orders of the Pope himself, twitching furiously and mumbling incoherently on his balcony. Well, he stood to lose most, I suppose. Bit like King Lear: once you hand over your power, people don't want to give it back.

The Simon Wiesenthal Center used their expertise and accounted for half a dozen more jaycees. Quite a few were spotted because of their allergic reaction to the sight of a cross, and a fair number were nabbed in brothels; well, each generation does tend to rebel against the earlier one. One particularly cunning fugitive even set himself up as a pawnbroker, but gave himself away by offering fair prices for the articles pawned.

Oh, yes, Whiting's jaycees got up to all the tricks in the book, but Section Thirteen has branches in every country in the world. Soon we were pretty sure we'd bagged the lot.

Except one.

Like Woody Allen in *Zelig*, this one popped up everywhere. Tiananmen Square, the White House Lawn, Red Square in Moscow, Mecca, the banks of the River Ganges, Super Bowl stadiums – anywhere there was a crowd he would appear, stick his tongue out, blow raspberries, make dire threats, and somehow melt away just before our agents could get there.

Me, I bided my time. I knew he would become more and more human every passing day. I knew that in the end he would fall victim to that most elemental of weaknesses – the desire for vengeance. I knew that some day he would come back to settle the score with the Reverend Ian Whiting.

And he did.

And I was waiting with my Kalashnikov.

He's got plans. Big plans. Big horrible plans.

Losing ninety-nine brothers. That's a lot. Kind of hardens your character. Seeing as he got resurrected on Easter Day, he declared last night as we placidly drank daiquiris, he's going to wait till All Hallows! Samhain. And it won't be the *spirits* of the dead he'll be raising, but what's left of their bodies. They'll start with the World Bank. Chuckling, he said to me: *For as the Father raiseth up the dead, and quickeneth them; even so the Son quickeneth whom he will.* Check in St. John, chapter 5, if you don't believe me, you heathen!" He slapped me on the shoulder. "It's not just the Devil who quotes the scriptures, you know!"

Oh, come on! You think I was going to blow away a guy who could heal the sick? Raise Lazarus? The gun was just to show him I wasn't negotiating out of weakness. For a guy like that, my embarrassing problem was nothing. I don't limp any more, and it sure does feel good having my balls back again.

My darling Katie's back with me now, now that I'm complete again. I guess that was the root of our problem all along.

Of course, I had to give him the Reverend in exchange. And I did feel a bit sorry for the old guy, dying like that – upside down, too, and in such a public place as the Dome of St. Paul's! – but then he *had* planned to crucify another five score jaycees.

Yep, I really do believe I'm going to enjoy working for my new boss.

New Writings in the Fantastic
The Ballad of Universal Jack
Vera Nazarian

In the beginning was the word. At first, it meant jack. But then it issued past lips and out of a cosmic mouth. That changed it. It was now loaded. It formed semantic ripples in the fabric of the dark matter around it, and became a pattern. The pattern stretched itself into an immeasurable span of radiance, and became the universe.

Much later, another, lesser mouth opened – a mouth of carbon-based organic flesh and water – and out came human language.

"So, why are you telling me this?" said Reanne. "Is it because I am supposed to open my lips and utter pearls for your swine ears?"

She was speaking to herself, of course, looking in the mirror. There was no sound, since she made no actual effort to vocalize, but her lips moved lightly, folds of soft rose flesh, and steam coagulated on the glass surface.

Herself answered with more esoteric thoughts and nonsense syllables, and a long discourse ensued in the span of a millisecond – Reanne and the other, *deeper* Reanne – upon the nature of pearls and swine, while Reanne dried her long dark clumps of soggy hair and wrapped herself in old terrycloth.

She stepped outside beyond the steam, where Matt waited for her, and she let the robe fall open so he could see her, while she also could see him, that part of him, rising. Matt sat on the bedcovers, leaning back. She came forward, and put her face-of-the-moon-white hands on his dark-side-of-the-moon-dark shoulders, leaned into him full force.

She positioned herself just above him, and took a dancer's stance, loose at the knees, then engulfed him with her vagina, sinking into impalement, sliding loose and soft and inevitable like a snowflake against a lamppost in the dark grim winter.

His lips muttered something, words issued out of him, and he moved beneath her, cloaking her with the pattern of radiance, and he became immeasurable.

She sank and rose and fell, and words came spurting in her mind, words and litanies and forms of lace.

When it was all over – or, rather, when the rest of things commenced – Reanne disengaged herself, lay back on the bedcovers and stared up into the ceiling. She felt the moisture, the semantic load of waters cooling at her thighs.

While, in her mind, her other self continued uttering words upon words of esoteric wisdom that had no beginning and no end, no relevance to her, and hence meant nothing and would not yield their cargo.

A little while later, or maybe a lot, Reanne – now an old withered creature – lay in a place of whiteness and sterility while two women and a boy stared down at her fading self. The boy was a grandchild and one of the women was her daughter, the direct issue of that encounter in a room of pale steam. The other woman was the daughter's geno-clone and the boy's real mother. Or, at least, she had been there when the boy cried and when he needed someone to whom he could confess his sin dreams – certainly not the innermost ones, but those floating like cream upon the surface, those that could be disclosed without involvement.

The geno-clone was perfect, because when she spoke her lips hardly moved at all, so that it seemed the words came forth out of the air itself, were thrown by a ventriloquist. In fact, the geno-clone spoke very little at all, but listened, and let the boy talk mostly, let him move his mouth rapidly and passionately in the throes of young speech, swallowing all logic and most of the meaning.

Reanne's daughter, Mariah, was speaking now. She was sobbing, her lips quivering, swollen nose, discoloured brimming eyes. The issuing wetness made patterns upon her cheeks. Occasional drops came to fall upon Reanne's bed coverings. Mariah's geno-clone stood silent, holding the boy with her hands and absently stroking his forehead.

Reanne's own dry lips moved once with the effort of trying to say something, until Mariah motioned for a nurse to bring a device that would temporarily give Reanne the ability to speak despite her destroyed lungs.

The nurse attached the expensive device to Reanne's life support, and suddenly the room echoed with the strong voice of the old woman, issuing out of the air and walls. The boy, standing all this time with his lids closed, opened his eyes and started to listen, for it reminded him so much of the geno-clone's aerial manner of speaking – safe, familiar, and *real*.

"What do you all want?" said Reanne. "*I* want you to know that I have nothing to say. Nothing new, except that you are all swine, and I am casting pearls before you, and yet I love you as I love salt."

"Mother?" sobbed Mariah. "What do you mean, mother?"

"Like I said, swine," said the old woman, and motioned with her finger. "Take this thing away."

And then she was silent, and closed her eyes, and wouldn't speak again. They disconnected the device finally, since every moment it was attached was costing Mariah immeasurable credits.

A bit later, the old woman died.

The boy watched his grandmother, her final passing unmarked, and something started in his mind, words and syllables, and song, and his lips began to move, while the geno-clone continued gently to stroke his hair.

The boy blinked, and he was a man. His mother (or was it the geno-clone? He could never keep them straight any longer, ever since he decided to stop needing to feel maternal warmth) was an old woman herself, and he hardly went to see either one of them.

Instead, the man was tall and strong, and he worked with large machines in a brightly lit room, wearing a protective full-body suit of fine plastic-metal alloy. The room was not a room, exactly, but the loading dock of a space station, high above the earth's surface, nearer in fact to the moon's orbit.

In space, except for the radio-transmitted holo-vocals, there were hardly any words, only silence. All earth speech was delayed by the cosmic distances, and communication was a matter of gestures or light codes that would show up on the receiver panels of his suit at both his wrists.

When the man was done with his work shift, he would enter the inner dock and then the low-gravity outer ring of the station. Here he turned in his heavy gear and became just Jack Westrig. It was the name he had earned with his own efforts. The previous Jack Westrig had been exceptionally creative and hard to live up to. All of the Jacks have been like that – swift, logical, full of formative energy. It took an extraordinary man to become Jack.

This Jack Westrig had a secret. When he took off his work gear he also put on an alternate frame of mind which included an acute verbal sense of beauty. Jack was a poet, because he would walk through corridors of the station and words would tumble into his mind out of the air, from the walls of metal alloy.

Maybe these words came in like neutrino particles through the hull, through the walls, and simply entered him, being ancient messengers of distant galaxies, carrying with them primeval seeds of the subatomic birth of stars? Or maybe they were white noise in his cortex.

Jack's mind seethed, bouncing raw crystal-and-rubber images, dissonant in their own internal dichotomy, and forming into fractal patterns of perfect imperfection. Jack had secretly learned dozens of human earth languages, and he would mouth the roots of words, feel their shape, and then use combinations of those linguistic roots to describe new terms, new words from the alien forms that came to him from the stars.

In his room, a woman greeted Jack. She was young and full-bodied, and he had felt sexually and emotionally drawn to her for some time now, seeing her in the botanosphere of the station, yet had been unable to approach her.

But, because his need had been so great, he had written to her through the net.

And apparently the poetic idiocy of his confession rendered in electrons had had its desired effect, for here she was, whether out of curiosity, or pity, or perversity, he was not sure. Did it matter?

She smiled at him and came forward, and he saw she had drawn the throat of her suit open all the way to her waist, and inside she wore nothing else. Her body came bursting though, mauve nipples sharp like flower buds on round animal whiteness...

He took hold of her, moving in reflex, and drew her close, while sine waves of disconnected words and word roots began to race through his mind. After several moments of fumbling movement, intimate tactile exploration, alien wilderness, she suddenly pushed him away.

"You're just like all the rest of them, Jack," she said, wiping her lips, breathing fast, her breasts quivering as she stuffed them hurriedly back inside her outfit. "I thought you'd be different, with your pretty images and fractal thoughts, and your need for me."

"What?" he said in confusion, rendered verbally impotent by this unexpected turn.

"Just like a man. Now you have nothing to say to me. You are a pig, Jack," said the nameless woman, "and I don't need to cast my pearls before you."

"But..." he again started, unbelieving. "But you –"

You must love me like salt, he wanted to end.

She made him lose his pattern of words. Her accusation made no sense. She came to him, offered herself, and now this? And she expected him to understand what she had anticipated from him in return? The encounter degenerated into a reminder that there were no means to bridge the cosmic comprehension-void between male and female.

It was a wonder the species persisted, extended into the cosmic vacuum beyond earth. All these languages, nuances, and still no common ground, except through a blurred filter of demonstrated intent followed by feedback reinforcement. No common definitions for words and terms that seemed to be clone-similar yet obviously had to be residing in interlaced but separate dimensions.

The problem arose within Jack's mind, and in that instant he forgot the rejection, so taken was he with a creative possibility.

"Not just a pig, but a distracted idiot," said the woman as she left his room, the door sliding softly in her wake.

Unlike the door, with its functional motion sensors, he didn't even notice her leaving, because in that moment words came alive in a drift of snowflakes, and were swirling in his mind.

In the following weeks, Jack Westrig hummed a tune as he worked with the great mechanical monsters in the vacuum of the loading dock. He was doing the most delicate work of bio-electric repair on the machines, yet for some reason his poetry would not leave him as it normally did during his work shift.

A white sunlit space bird came sailing into the dock in perfect cosmic silence, a ship from the outer Solar System. He stared, watching its brilliant albedo against the vacuum of space in the background, and saw it as one great big Word.

We send parts of ourselves, these Words, forth into the outer space around us. They represent us as a species, they speak for us to anyone and anything that might be out there, waiting.

And yet, why couldn't humanity communicate perfectly within itself? Why was there a gap between sexes and ages and blood-bonds and generations, even between the self of childhood and the self of adulthood?

How could it then expect to reach out into the greater universe and make any damn' sense?

Thoughts and words and acts are not enough. Not enough to demonstrate one's love of salt by casting pearls before swine.

The moment passed and Jack continued his delicate techo-surgery, while a resolution was forming inside him. In hours, days, weeks, it would flower and bear fruit.

Jack was certain he had made a theoretical discovery of post-quantum linguo-physics, an absurdly easy missing link – not so much missing as misplaced. And he presented a part of it to a committee of the top scientists on the station.

He stood and spoke, and, as images entered him together with the oxygen, language poured out of him with the exhaled carbon dioxide, and shaped his breath and solidified into water vapor. Still, inside him, the essence of salt remained.

The panel listened, and one scientist, Miro Wastman, nodded slowly, and then stood up, and reached with his hand forward, palm upturned, and stood waiting for Jack to react to his hand.

"I know what you want me to do," said Jack. "But I will not do it just to demonstrate that my theory is valid."

"You're merely stalling and embellishing," said Miro.

Jack smiled. "Not at all. I am merely creating the future."

And so it was.

In the next earth year, the Westrig Theory of Formation was officially recorded in the annals of scientific knowledge, where it was promptly filed away and forgotten, as happens to all things most basic and as old as the species – things of naïveté or disguised subtlety.

The idea that words created the universe.

Jack Westrig had argued that, by organizing sensory incoming information into humanly recognizable patterns – thought – and then by externalizing those patterns into a symbolic form called language, human beings were able to perform actions based upon those thoughts. And sequences of actions formed the future.

And not just *Homo sapiens*, Jack had said, but any other form of sentience did this. We merely conceive something and then take steps to make it happen – tomorrow, the next year, the next millennium. Every single thing *now* is the result of someone's word *then*.

"And notice, I do not say *thought* but *word*. Why? Because a thought is private and internal, left to echo emptily against the inner boundaries of the mind. But a word – in its broadest meaning, an external symbol – is the first outward communication of one's intent.

"Also, I say a *word* and not an *action*," Jack continued. "Action is merely the interpretation. It is the going through the motions of one's intent without communicating it to others. It can and will be misconstrued, and will fall like a seed onto barren soil to be left to its own devices. Only an action directly accompanied by a word is going to cross the bridge between now and the future. Because it will be a thing shared, and hopefully understood – a goal given form and meaning.

"We open our lips and define the immediate shape that the universe takes around us, whether we offer – or withhold – a hand in greeting or a ship into the cosmic void."

And, saying that, he died. Because he'd been saying it for the last fifty earth years, and Jack Westrig had now become an old man.

But his word lived on beyond his lifespan and into the future. It was a minor commonsense thing, a forgettable theory, and yet it was the only and best offspring he had left. For the word shaped not only his future but that of others, as one day they venture into the farthest reaches by means of tools they themselves conceived in the distant past of today.

Indeed, words are the best offspring. They are the catalyst cause, with all else the effect. Even now, words from the distant past, originated by *someone*, race on ahead, slip deviously through us, through past, present, and future, ending universes and beginning new ones. In many cases they have devolved into proverbial clichés, but, Jack would tell you, never underestimate them.

Now, Jack is immortal. His DNA is dissolved into the universal soup but his little word has gone on ahead of him forever, spreading creative tentacles of meaning forward, hurtling through the nothingness between the stars.

If you miss a blink, you might even catch the word and hitch a circular ride on it that will swing you all the way to the beginning, and back again here, to the end.

You may even be doing it now, reading this.

Or, maybe not. There is more to the nature of words than simple meaning. Meaning is a charge, a positive load; not a constant, but a constant process.

And yet, as all immortals, Jack is a joker. He is like his grandmother, and the ones who came before them, in his love of salt and – unlike others – in his knowledge of its true value.

Like any joker, Jack is wary of confessing what is innermost, and has given us only the cream off the top. He has learned not to cast all his cliché pearls before swine, holding back just enough.

Jack may speak the word, and may even *be* the word. But a word alone is nothing, and means jack. And, even together, thoughts and words and acts and intentions are not enough.

In the beginning came the positive charge of original definition.

New Writings in the Fantastic
Song Cycle
Kate Riedel

1. TWO MAIDENS WENT MILKING ONE DAY

Once upon a time there were two cousins, Annie and Janet, born on the same day to two sisters.

Annie's father was a farmer, many years older than her mother. Janet's father was, at the time of her birth, an ambitious young corporate lawyer.

In the winter Annie walked down the long, snow-drifted driveway to catch the school bus into town, while Janet was driven to an exclusive girls' school which her parents, at first, really could not afford.

After school Annie helped her father in the barn, while her father moved with the milking machines between the cows, calling each by name – Daisy, Rose, Clover – whistling sometimes hymns, sometimes "My Darling Nellie Gray" or "The Rose of Tralee," but most often a nameless tune which was Annie's favorite, because it was her father's. After supper she did the dishes before settling down to her homework.

Janet, meanwhile, attended dance classes and took piano lessons.

Annie, if asked to describe her aunt and uncle from the city, would probably have said, "She has nice hair and he wears a suit all the time."

"Your father looks kind of like Old MacDonald, doesn't he?" Janet said once to Annie. It was the closest they ever came to a quarrel.

For Janet spent every summer on the farm, and the cousins were best friends then, sharing Annie's chores in house, barn and garden so they could have more time to play in the haymow, woods and pasture.

They would follow the path under the thornapple tree at the corner of the woods up to a willow that slanted across the creek just below where it emerged from an impenetrable tangle of woods and bog. There they sat, their feet in the cool brown water, and talked about what they had done in the winter: skating on the creek and cross-country skiing; downhill skiing and piano recitals; movies that Janet had seen in the city and were only now being shown in the small theater in town.

Annie pointed out the wild flowers that grew at the edge of the woods, and taught Janet to listen for the rolling song of meadow larks, the rattle of woodpeckers, and the sad notes of the woodthrush that sang deep in the heart of the thicket.

Janet in turn demonstrated dance steps she had learned, and Annie would try to follow, and then collapse, tripping over her own feet, although she was nimble enough walking the high beams in the haymow, or following the cows through rough pasture. "I guess I'm just not meant to dance," she said.

Sometimes they rode their mothers' old bikes to the Martin farm down the road, where they played anti-i-over and softball with the half-dozen Martin children, down the long summer evenings between milking and bedtime. What a pity, they agreed, that the Martin child their age had to be that boy Hank.

In bed together at night, they planned for the time when Annie would stay with Janet in the city, in winter, while they both attended college.

And at the end of August Janet would get on the train and go home, and they would resume their separate lives.

Indian print skirts, headbands and beads were in style the year Annie and Janet, just turned fourteen, took turns painfully stretching their fingers over the neck of Annie's new guitar as they sat at the foot of the willow. The F chord was difficult, but more difficult were E-flat, and the B-seventh of the E-minor progression that matched the simpler G progression.

These chords and more were all necessary for the book of English folk songs Annie had received for her birthday along with her guitar. "The Trees are Getting High" was simple enough, but "Early One Morning" required not only E-flat but B-flat-seventh.

"This one has only one chord," Janet said, strumming D-minor and singing "A bold young farmer courted me..." she broke off. "Who'd marry a farmer?"

"My mother," Annie answered in half-mock indignation. "Anyway, *I'm* not afraid of the F chord," and she proceeded to show she could also play C-seventh.

> *... Two maidens went milking one day,*
> *And the wind it did blow high,*
> *And the wind it did blow low,*
> *And it tossed their pails to and fro...*

Janet leaned over to join the second verse.

> *They met with a man they did know,*
> *And they said, have you the will,*
> *And they said, have you the skill*
> *For to catch us a small bird or two? Fa-la-la...*

Annie fumbled the last chord, and in the pause a voice from the woods took up the next verse.

> *If you'll come along with me,*

Under yonder flowering tree,
I might catch you a small bird or two...

"Hank Martin, you come right out of there!" Annie yelled. Because who else could it be? But Hank Martin did not put in an appearance. And they both knew that Hank was far more likely to be singing "One-eyed, One-horned, Flying Purple People Eater" than some folk song out of a book.

Or perhaps it had not been someone singing, but only the whistling wings of a startled mourning dove.

"That song..." Janet said that night as they prepared for bed in Annie's room upstairs.

Annie didn't need to ask which song. "Both of them?" she said, shivering, aroused by possibilities, although the details as yet might be unclear. They were only fourteen, but that was quite old enough for them to suspect the man in the song was not really talking about birds.

"Go to sleep, girls," Annie's mother called. "Haying tomorrow."

They turned out the light, but did not go to sleep.

"Look at the moon," Annie finally whispered. "It's bright as day. And it's so hot in here."

"I bet we'd sleep better if we took a walk," said Janet. "A moonlit walk..." Dreamily.

"With Hank Martin?" Annie whispered back, and Janet giggled and punched her cousin in the arm.

A few minutes later they were dressed and following the field road that led to the willow over the creek. But the moon gives tricksy light, and as they left the road they tripped over tufts of grass, stumbled into hollows they could not see.

Just as they reached the thornapple tree a tatter of clouds drifted across the moon, making the pattern of a grinning face.

"It looks like a skull!" Janet squeaked, clutching Annie's arm. The same arm she had earlier punched, perhaps harder than intended, and Annie thought she could feel a bruise forming where Janet's fingers pressed her flesh. "Let's go back."

"Scaredy cat!" Annie jeered. After that they had no choice but to go on, under the thornapple that marked the near corner of the woods, stumbling along the cowpath, giggling with relief as they climbed out along the willow.

The moon went under a cloud again, a real cloud this time, leaving the night so dark they had only the rough bark under their hands to inform them where they were, while the sound of the water below could have been the riffling of the familiar creek or the flow of a broad river deep in another world.

As they sat, each clutching the other with no thought now of pain, the sound of the river altered as if it parted to flow around an object thrust into it, then altered again to a musical trickle of droplets falling from something lifted from the stream, and then returned to its usual smooth purl.

Someone laughed.

"Hank Martin, you come right out of there!" Annie called, but her voice was not steady.

The cloud passed, leaving two moons, one in the sky and one in the water, and in the double light someone moved toward them, stepping along the willow trunk with the ease of a tightrope walker.

Afterwards, even if they had talked about it (and they never did), neither could have said for sure what he looked like – then – although his face would one day be familiar to both of them. At that instant they could only have said he was no longer a boy but not yet a man. Teenager would have been too common, too much like Hank Martin.

He held out the cup he had just filled and smiled at them.

Janet found her voice first.

"That's from the creek," she said. "Cows go in that creek. *I'm* not going to drink that."

"The cows only walk through it downstream," said Annie, as close to hating Janet as she had ever been since the time Janet made that remark about Old MacDonald. "That creek comes from the same place as our well water. Do you think my father would give us dirty water to drink?"

"Oh," said the boy-man, still laughing, "your father. We remember him. And of course this is the same water your mother uses to wash the dishes."

"What's so funny about that?" asked Annie.

He did not reply, but continued to hold out the cup of water. Annie took it from him. As her fingers touched his she thought, perhaps, she was just a little closer to knowing about those birds the man had offered to catch.

She could feel a pattern engraved on the cup, and, holding it up to the moonlight, saw a shadowy band of stars and leaves around the rim. She lowered the cup and drank, and when the water was all gone she wiped her mouth on her wrist and handed the cup back.

"Let me see that," said Janet, and took the cup from his hand. He let her. She turned it round in the moonlight, examining the pattern. And then she dropped it down the front of her blouse.

"That's not yours!" Annie gasped.

The boy-man said, "It is, now." At least that's what he might have said, but just then a cloud went over the moon once again, and once again the girls shrieked and clutched at each other. Annie could feel the rim of the cup cutting into her side from under the fabric of Janet's blouse. When the moon came out the boy-man was gone. The girls ran like rabbits back to the house.

The first wagonload of hay from the next day's haying was just in the barn when Annie's mother called Janet to the telephone. Annie and her father waited, then returned to the field without Janet. They had rounded the second corner when they were stopped by Janet dancing up and down in the windrows.

"We're moving to France!" Janet shouted over the roar of the tractor. "Can you believe it? To *France*!"

"I guess you're pretty lonesome," Annie's father said to her as they did the milking together, the night after seeing Janet off on the train.

"Sort of," said Annie. When she said no more, her father returned to whistling his favorite tune.

"Are there words to that?" Annie asked.

"Well, yes, there are."

"What are they?"

Her father thought a minute, but when he finally sang the words it was as if he had been singing them in his head for years.

Stay on the farm, boys, stay on the farm,
  Tho' profits come in rather slow,
  Stay on the farm, boys, stay on the farm,
  Don't be in a hurry to go.

Annie tried it out that night on her guitar.

The city has many attractions,
  But think of its vices and sins,
  And once in the vortex of fashion
  How swift your destruction begins.

So it's stay on the farm, boys...

The song fit nicely into the D progression.

At first, even before Labor Day and the beginning of the school year, there were a great many letters with foreign stamps arriving in the mailbox at the end of the long driveway.

At the Thanksgiving concert and talent contest, Annie and Hank Martin brought down the house with their rendition of "Purple People Eater", and Annie wrote Janet all about it. Janet wrote about how she missed celebrating Thanksgiving.

For Christmas Janet sent LPs – one of Scottish ballads, and one of Julian Bream. Annie played them on her portable hi-fi, along with the Joan Baez and Peter, Paul and Mary records she'd got from her mom and dad. The Scottish ballads seemed to be mostly yarns about romantic and ill fated love affairs with elves, false knights, and similar trash, as Annie's mother put it.

"Why anyone would give up a nice man with a steady job like a house carpenter for someone who brags about having been engaged to a princess—!" Annie's mother said after listening to the record, and Annie and her father laughed.

The day after Christmas, Annie went down to the creek for a solitary skate, but didn't stay long. Not because she was afraid, but because she wasn't. Sometimes, she thought, perhaps just sometimes, one really should be just a little afraid of *not* being afraid. She wondered, as she returned to the warmth and safety of the barn, what Janet had done with the cup.

Janet's mother decided that a summer in Europe instead of on the farm would broaden her daughter's horizons. The postcards continued: Vienna, Rome, London.

Annie's mother expanded her garden and rented a stall at the Saturday farmers' market. Annie tended the stall with the understanding that the money from it would go into a savings account for her college expenses. If her mother hoped for more than cash from this enterprise she said nothing, but she was always willing to let Annie go for coffee with some of the other young people from the market, after the stalls were packed up, and sometimes even stay in town with them for movies and pizza. There was this nice boy from the goat-cheese stand across the aisle...

Janet wrote about clothes from Carnaby Street.

"The vortex of fashion!" Annie wrote back, but Janet, of course, did not get the reference.

Janet wrote about a house party on the Riviera, where, she hinted, she had learned something about catching a small bird or two.

Annie fended off Hank Martin one night after they had been to a movie when, instead of going straight home, Hank had parked his father's pickup truck in a field road. To admire the moon, he'd said. After that Annie decided it wasn't worth the trouble just for admission to a movie or a date to a dance, when everyone laughed at the way she danced anyhow.

Besides, she really didn't have time for a social life. There was homework: market stall or not, she would still need that scholarship. And one day she looked at her father and saw, with the helpless fear that comes with the first intimations of mortality, how stooped he had become, his hands slowed by arthritis, and she began going to the barn earlier in order to have the heavy work done before her father came out for the milking.

"You never play your guitar any more," Annie's mother said.

The guitar had been a present from her father. Annie found a book on classical guitar on a dusty back shelf of the local music store, and made time to teach herself that. Folk music was hokey.

The letters and postcards were now only Christmas and birthday cards. Annie wondered if Janet would even remember her birthday had their birthdays not happened to fall on the same day.

In February, Annie's English class took up *Hamlet* and, thanks to inter-library loan, Annie earned extra credits by seeking out authentic 16th-century tunes to match Ophelia's songs. She brought her guitar to school and boldly stared down the snickering boys as she sang "Tomorrow is St. Valentine's Day."

Annie's mother declared Ophelia's taste in music depressing, so once the project was over, Annie returned to classical guitar.

She won her scholarship.

2. STAY ON THE FARM

Once upon a time there was a farmer who had only one child, a daughter who was, at least in his eyes, as beautiful as the moon. One midsummer day this farmer went out to his field, where, with the help of his daughter – who, as he would have told anyone who asked, was as good as she was beautiful – he brought in the first cutting of hay and stored it in his barn.

That night Annie's father fell asleep in his rocking chair and never woke up.

Janet sent a sympathy card, and Janet's mother sent a cheque. Annie's mother looked at the amount, read the accompanying note, pursed her lips, dropped the note in the wastebasket and set the cheque aside for deposit.

The house overflowed with cakes, casseroles, jello salads and the neighbors who brought them. Annie moved among them, automatically pouring coffee, offering cake, accepting condolences.

"Pity he didn't have any sons..." Annie winced. "Well, he waited so long to get married..." "Of course *she* was making the best of a bad situation..." "Of *course* she wasn't his. Neither of them could afford to be picky, after all..."

Annie's mother took the tilting plate from Annie's hands just before the cake could slide off.

That evening, when the last car had rolled down the driveway, the last plate had been washed, dried, and put away, Annie's mother took her daughter firmly by the shoulders and faced her toward the mirror on the dresser. Then she pointed to the framed photograph of the sober older man standing beside the slim young girl. No wedding dress, just both in their good clothes.

"What do *you* think?" Annie's mother asked.

Annie rubbed her nose, slightly too long, slightly but not unattractively crooked, exactly like the nose of the man in the photograph.

"We were married," her mother said, "Exactly ten months before you were born. Some people, unfortunately, enjoy a good story so much they forget whatever arithmetic they ever learned."

For the first time since haying, Annie laughed. Then sobered.

"Mom," she said, "Were you ever in love with someone besides Dad?"

"I might have been. But I wasn't."

"Was Dad ever in love with someone else?"

"Yes."

"You're kidding. Who?"

"This farm," her mother smiled.

"He was so much older than you. Why..."

"You know. I've told you."

"How you met Dad because you were trespassing, and you found a cow giving birth, a breech birth, and he asked you to call the vet while he looked after the cow. And when the vet came, you went back to the house and did the dishes. And that's when you decided to marry him. But that's *how*, not *why*. Dishes..." she added thoughtfully, trying to remember something. Somebody had once said something about her mother doing the dishes...

"By the time you were born," her mother went on, "the house was looking pretty much the way it does now. But before then all the money had been spent in the barn. The barn was snug and tight, whitewashed, automatic water for the cows, cream separator and Laval milking machines all shining in a row. But the house – half of it closed off, bare lightbulbs... at least there was electricity. Kitchen walls covered with soot from the wood stove, rusty sink full of dishes – oh, dear, *somebody* had to marry the man." Now Annie's mother brushed the tears away. "And, I don't know how, or why, but all of a sudden I knew I wanted it to be me. So I ran water in the sink and did the dishes right then and there. And I was never sorry."

"But you kept the wood stove, even when you got the electric one," said Annie.

"A fire's nice, in winter." Her mother wiped at tears again, then straightened and said, "We might as well get this over with. Jim Martin's expanding his dairy operation. He's made me an offer for the herd, and for the farm, if I want to sell. Or to rent the fields, if I don't want to sell. I've had a separate offer for the pasture; the town's expanding, you know, and the far side of the creek can't be cultivated."

"No," said Annie. "You mustn't sell that. Our water comes from there."

"I can't run the farm by myself, and you have to go to school."

"I've been to school."

"High school."

"I've graduated, I'm eighteen years old, and I know what probate is."

"Annie!"

"You sound as if I've just told you I know where babies come from."

"You'd better, by now," her mother said with a weak laugh. "But Annie, you're a *girl*."

"'Pity he didn't have any sons.'"

"So you heard that too."

"*He* didn't think so."

"No, he didn't."

"You know those people with the goat-cheese stand?" Annie said to her mother when she got back from the market.

"That nice young man?"

"Hector?"

"Ah, so he does have a name. Yes?"

"No, Mother, he hasn't asked me to marry him. I've made arrangements to work for them this winter, to learn the business. If Jim Martin buys the herd that will give us enough to take us through the winter, and Aunt Margaret's cheque" – she grinned at her mother – "will pay for remodeling the barn, and what I've earned from the market will pay for goat-proof fencing. And the goats. For a one-person operation, goats –"

"But there's no market!"

"You haven't noticed those people hurting, have you? People with allergies, health-food nuts, fancy restaurants. They have to *import* milk to meet the demand for chevre. They might just as well buy some of it from us. And if we rent the fields to the Martins for a share of the crops—"

"How long have you been thinking about this?"

"Maybe since Janet said Dad looked like Old MacDonald."

Despite her businesslike reference to "the herd," despite having seen many Daisys, Roses and Clovers come and go in her own lifetime, it hurt Annie to see the barn empty except for the barn cats, now making do on reconstituted powdered milk.

"I wonder how they'll like goat's milk?" Annie said to Hank

Martin, who was doing the renovations at bargain rates because it counted toward his carpentry apprenticeship out of the community college.

"If they don't, they'll have plenty of cow's milk," said Hank. "You know Dad's projecting a herd of five hundred in the next few years? You seen the automatic barn cleaning system he's just installed?"

"Five hundred! Dad never had more than two dozen."

"Those days are over."

Perhaps, Annie thought, part of the hurt was dread of the time when dairy cows would no longer be called by name.

Annie drove back and forth on snowy roads for her own apprenticeship, where she learned about feeding, fencing, shelter and pasture; how to milk goats, how to breed them and take them through birthing, how to decide which kids to keep, which to hand-raise, which to leave to their mothers.

Spring saw the first pretty Saanens installed in the newly remodelled barn, and soon responding to their names – Clover, Daisy, Rose...

The thornapple tree bloomed and then shed its petals, but Annie was too busy, days, to visit the willow over the stream, and nights the guitar remained in its case while she labored over account books, breeders' journals, and government pamphlets.

The first kids came, and Annie spent long nights in the barn, fell into bed exhausted, and rose again to do the milking.

"You remind me of your father in more than looks," said her mother. "You should get out more."

"Out where?" said Annie. "When?"

Haying came and went, and harvest, and winter.

But in May came a cream-coloured square envelope with another envelope inside, and inside that, a wedding invitation.

"Does she expect me to *attend*? What does she expect me to *wear*? My *overalls*?"

Annie threw the invitation aside and strode from the house.

Her mother watched her disappear from sight beyond the thornapple tree that overhung the path to the creek. *It's blooming early this year,* she thought as she picked up the discarded invitation. The groom's name was James Harris. From Edinburgh. As she thinned her tomato seedlings she wondered if the quilt on which she was working, the one made from the India-cotton skirts her daughter and niece had worn one summer (not that long ago, although it seemed suddenly like centuries), would be a suitable present for that niece on her marriage to a wealthy foreigner.

She looked at the clock and saw it was time to start supper.

She didn't start to worry until milking time.

She found Annie already in the barn, milking one goat and keeping

her eye on another that was restless in pre-birth in a separate pen.
"You could still go to college," said her mother.
"No," said Annie. "It's too late for that."

3. TOMORROW IS ST. VALENTINE'S DAY

Once upon a time there was a young girl who went down a path and under a thornapple tree to a willow aslant a stream, where she met –
Not Tam Lin. Not True Thomas. It might have been a demon lover, but wasn't. Whatever he was, she was sure of this.

"I'm yours, you know," he said as he put his arm around her against the early May chill, against her loneliness. "And I don't even expect you to do the dishes."

"No more," she said, "would I expect you to do the milking."

They laughed, and the creek seemed to laugh back.

Spring became summer, and summer autumn.

Annie no longer went anywhere except to the feed store and to deliver milk, not even to church, so she could not hear the small town rehashing how she had once sung dirty songs in school – right in English class! Or speculating on what she might have learned from that city cousin of hers.

Some pointed the finger at Hank Martin, and some at that pleasant young man with the unlikely name of Hector, son of the family who ran the goat-cheese factory. Both were rumored to have proposed to Annie after the fact, but who had done the deed and who was offering charity (if marriage to a young woman who owned a valuable piece of real estate could be called charity) remained up in the air. In any case, Annie turned down both of them.

Annie's mother didn't ask who, only when.

"St. Valentine's Day," Annie answered. "When you let in the maid that out a maid never departs more."

"Anyone less like Ophelia than you I cannot imagine," her mother said. "I just asked because I suppose we'll have to hire someone, at least temporarily."

"Maybe," said Annie. "Any mail?"

If she saw her mother hesitate before handing over the goat-breeder's journal, she knew of no reason to wonder about it.

It's for her own good, Annie's mother thought, re-reading, once Annie had gone to the barn, the letter she had not handed over. *It's for her own good. And it's not as if they're strangers, after all. At least not...*

She sat down to write a carefully worded response.

On a clear still night just days before Christmas, a night so brittle you expected it to shatter in the stillness – December twenty-first as a matter of fact – Annie hunched over the kitchen table by the wood stove, working on the accounts.

Snow crunched under tires. Annie raised her head. Headlights flashed across the frosted kitchen window, then died with the motor. Footsteps on snow; chill from an open door.

"Annie?"

A voice as musical as it had been when it joined in harmony on "Two Maidens Went Milking One Day."

Annie looked at the foxfur coat, the sleek and shiny hair and the perfect complexion above and the buttery leather boots below.

She looked down at her house dress stretched across her distended stomach, at her own rough-skinned hands.

She pulled away from Janet's kiss. Since when had Janet become the huggy-kissy type?

"We wanted to be here when the baby came," Janet said, stripping off her gloves. Annie's eyes fastened on the bracelet revealed; a broad silver band, like the rim of a cup, engraved with leaves and stars. "That way he will know us," Janet said.

"Why?" said Annie.

Janet and Annie's mother exchanged glances.

"Why, we're adopting him," said Janet.

For the first time Annie looked at the slim and well tailored young man standing behind Janet. That wool coat had to have cost as much as her pickup truck. Probably more; the pickup had been bought second-hand.

She knew him; he had once strode lightly along a slanted willow; had said to her on a chill May day, "I'm yours."

Or had he? That one had seemed more boy than man, although a boy who knew what it would mean to be a man. This was more man than boy, and what remained of the boy was the kind of child that other children avoid, although they might be hard-put for an answer if you were to ask them why.

A wind rose outside.

Frost melted from the kitchen window in a darkening circle, as if from someone's breath trying to make a space to see through. Annie stared at the dark glass, although it seemed to show only her own reflection. Then she turned to Janet's husband.

"Oh no, you're not," she said to him. She pushed past Janet and her husband and ran out, without bothering with coat or boots. The wind softened; the night returned to its brittle quiet.

Annie's mother ran after her, of course, and Janet followed. But the footsteps in the snow stopped at the willow; there were none further into the woods, or the pasture, or on the ice of the creek.

The official search organized the next morning found no more. The brown stream, ripped free of its ice, gave up no body.

"I'll stay with you, Aunt Ellen," Janet said to Annie's mother.

"Oh, no, my dear," said James Harris. "What could you do with those soft hands?"

"I've worked on this farm."

"But only in the summer, darling. Only played at it. And do you forget, my love, that your commitment is now elsewhere? Here is your coat, my dear."

If James Harris' grip on his wife's arm was perhaps a little overly forceful despite all his endearments, Annie's mother was too preoccupied with her own grief to notice, except, perhaps, to think to herself that that sort of husband would never expect his wife to ever do other than what he said.

Christmas came and went, and the search was abandoned.

Annie's mother milked the goats, and fed the goats and cats, delivered milk and brought back feed. The neighbors helped, but after the first few days she told them politely that she could carry on.

January turned to February. Annie's mother dozed over the milk records in a kitchen that, while not the smoke-browned, bare-bulbed room it had been the first time she had ever done dishes there, still showed those signs of neglect that creep in when there is only one person to run both farm and farmhouse. Dust in the corners, spatters on the stove, dishes in the sink...

Tomorrow is St. Valentine's Day...

Her head jerked up. Dreaming. She sat up, rubbed her eyes, bent over the papers.

It was at that moment that the bus from the city dropped off a single passenger at the station next to the feed store.

The driver of the town's lone taxi, who took that passenger as far as the end of the long country driveway, said later she paid very well, and that she remained standing at the end of the driveway, between the snow banks, until he could no longer see her in his rearview mirror.

No one saw where she went after the red tail-lights of the taxi had vanished over the hill.

Did she, perhaps, break her way across the crusted, moonlit snow down to the creek that ran between the woods and the pasture? Did she come to where the willow slanted across the stream, and where subsequent snowfall had covered the banks trampled by the search parties, where subzero temperatures had re-formed the ice except in the center where the water ran swiftest?

She did, it could be guessed, strip her glove from her ringless left hand and tug at something on her left wrist, something that left raw scrapes on her wrist as it came off. Those who have accepted such gifts only to regret them might know how the scrape stings.

It would have been about that time that Mrs. Martin heard a big car roar down the country road between the snow banks, saw it skid to a halt at the end of the driveway where Janet and the taxi driver had watched each other out of sight.

It must have been then that something – perhaps a silver bracelet with a pattern of stars and leaves – splashed into the brown water that purled between shelves of ice: splashed and sank to the rolling pebbles below.

It was exactly at the moment the bracelet hit the water that the big car reversed, turned, sped back toward the highway, and was never seen again.

Janet did not know this. For at the same moment her arm was seized and a familiar voice said, "Come, we need you."

Meanwhile, Annie's mother's head drooped once again over the milk records. *Tomorrow is St. Valentine's Day...*

The clock struck one.

Today is St. Valentine's Day. Something is supposed to happen today...

Her head jerked up as someone knocked loudly at the door.

Today is St. Valentine's Day.

Annie's mother rose so quickly she knocked over the chair, didn't bother to right it, but flung herself through the inner door and across the cold, barn-coat-smelling porch to the outer door.

"It was never locked! You should know that!" she gasped as she pulled it open.

Janet stumbled through, her foxfur coat clasped tightly to herself.

Annie's mother stepped back in disappointment.

Janet leaned against the closed door, and, without speaking, opened her foxfur coat.

4. JAMES HARRIS, OR THE HOUSE CARPENTER

Once upon a time there was a gently nurtured young woman who made a very wealthy marriage indeed. But upon discovering that her husband's connections had brought her into an intolerable and even dangerous situation, she had left him in order to raise her cousin's orphaned child on the farm with her Aunt Ellen.

At least, it was assumed the child, a little boy, was orphaned; there was never any doubt that he was Annie's. A search was made for the mother after Janet turned up early one February morning – Valentine's

Day – her cashmere sweater and the lining of her foxfur coat ruined with blood and afterbirth. But Janet would not or could not say where she had got the baby, and only Janet's footsteps were found, leading from the end of the driveway to where a willow slanted across a frozen creek, and from there to the house. The taxi driver was sure there had been no baby when he picked her up at the bus station.

The doctor who was called in that night pronounced the baby perfectly healthy, and was more concerned about the scrapes on Janet's left wrist.

"We'll have the baby baptized on Sunday," Aunt Ellen said. "What shall–? Does he have a name?"

"Hayward," said Janet. She pronounced it as two words, Hay Ward. "Annie named him Hayward Thomas."

"We can call him Tommy," Aunt Ellen said.

There was talk, of course. The most popular theory was that Annie had died in childbirth, and that Annie's mother and cousin had buried the body, or, rather, the earth being hard-frozen, had hidden it in the tangled woods; never mind that nobody had ever entered those woods and never mind the doctor's testimony.

The subsequent investigation by the state police turned up no more, and Janet and Annie's mother were left to raise Tommy in peace.

"You'll be selling the farm, of course," Janet said to her aunt.

"Of course not," said Aunt Ellen. "Annie worked hard to keep this farm. Besides, you know, her father died without a will, so legally the farm belongs to Annie, and legally she's just missing, and we can't assume death for, oh, years."

"How many?" asked Janet, examining the still-raw scrapes on her wrist and beginning to fear her husband might not be so easily got rid of as she had hoped.

"Oh... I don't know. Seven, maybe?"

Seven. Janet shivered, and a ballad learned from a record ran uninvited through her head.

Oh where have ye been, my long, long love,
 This seven long years and more?
 I've come to seek my former vows
 Ye granted me before...

Seven years. Well, much might be done in seven years.

"Then I'll stay and help. You can't run this place on your own, not and look after a baby as well."

"But you –" Aunt Ellen closed her mouth but her eyes were on Janet's hands, soft and smooth except for those raw patches on her wrist.

"Annie did it," said Janet. "I can learn to do it. I used to help out when

I visited in the summer, remember?"

"Yes, I do remember. It seems..." She paused to control her voice. "It seems as if those summers were the only times Annie ever really *played*."

"You know what? Those were the only times I ever really *worked*. I can do it, Aunt Ellen. Let me try."

"What about your parents?"

"They wanted me to marry James. I would prefer, by the way, not to be known as Mrs. Harris."

So Janet learned about feeding goats, and milking goats, and birthing kids. ("I took the St. John's Ambulance course," she joked to her aunt.) She learned to keep milk records and accounts, and she drove back and forth to the feed store and to deliver milk. She learned about muscles that dancing and tennis had never reached, and her hands were no longer soft and smooth. *This is what Annie was doing,* she thought as she cleaned the goat pens. *While I was attending private schools in Switzerland, and dancing, and playing tennis, and... bird-catching, Annie was doing this.*

But she still found time, in the evenings, to play Annie's old guitar, and her aunt remarked on her skill in the classical mode.

"I studied with Bream for a while," Janet confessed.

"Then what are you doing here?"

"I'm not *that* good. Anyway, I got married, remember?"

It had been James, Janet remembered, who had suggested adopting Annie's baby. Seven years... Her fears, being still unformed, were not to be shared with her aunt.

Sometimes Janet woke to a draft, as if someone had just left the room, and often at these times Tommy was wide awake. Although Tommy displayed no distress, Janet was glad when the phenomenon faded, and she finally consented to the child having his own room.

Her concern rose again as Tommy learned to walk, and wandered whither his infant whims took him.

"I found him halfway to the creek!" Janet had to shout to make herself heard, because the usually good-tempered Tommy was screaming and flailing at her with hard little fists and feet.

Tommy was mollified only when Hector, that pleasant young son of the owners of the cheese factory, stopped by that evening to check on some pasturage as a favor to Janet and her aunt, and took young Tommy along, riding on his shoulders.

"Aunt Ellen," Janet said after Hector had left, "have you ever reconsidered selling?"

"I can't, legally. You know that."

"Aunt Ellen, you know there's no profit to me in the sale – I'm just worried about you."

"Me? I've lived here most of my adult life."

"All right. I'm worried about Tommy."

"Annie followed her father around the whole farm from the time she could walk, and never came to any harm."

"Annie was born here."

"So was Tommy."

Janet sighed, and after a moment picked up the guitar and began to play a sonatina by Carulli. Halfway through she found herself switching to arpeggios, and then singing:

Oh, are you weeping for houses and land,
  Are you weeping for the shore?
  Or are you weeping for that house carpenter,
  Whose face you'll see never more?

"I remember," Aunt Ellen said, "I teased Annie about that song. A nice steady husband, and a baby, and what does she do?"

"She wrote me about that," said Janet. "She thought it was funny."

"It's been four years," Janet said as she set Tommy down to his lunch after dragging him back, once again, from the creek. "Aunt Ellen... Aunt Ellen, you can apply to have someone declared – at least assumed – dead after four years."

"But why?" asked Aunt Ellen.

Janet shrugged, finished her own lunch, and went out to clean the goat pens, trying not to cry.

For, the night before, she had crept down to the thornapple tree, and cautiously found her way to the willow aslant the stream. There had been a man sitting on the willow, tossing something into the air and catching it, and laughing, and when the moonlight glinted on the object it looked like a silver bracelet, and she had recognized the laugh.

She had fled back toward the house and met Tommy on the lawn, heading toward the south pasture where the fireflies danced in midair, like circles of stars...

"Janet?" Her aunt spoke from the door of the barn. "Janet, if you aren't happy here, you don't have to stay. I'm not telling you to go, I like having you here, but if you're not happy –"

"I am, Aunt Ellen. I want to stay here with you and Tommy. I don't mind the work, really, and I *am* happy here."

If one can be happy and afraid at the same time, she thought. *I was always afraid of James. That's what made him so sexy...*

She remembered the feeling of smug triumph when she had accepted James Harris's proposal, cold triumph, like that cup against her skin when she had dropped it inside her blouse. James had suggested the bracelet, and she had thought it charming. He had taken the cup to a jeweller's to have the bowl cut away, leaving only the rim for the bracelet that had been so hard to take off...

"If you don't want to sell the farm, then what about that south pasture? We don't really need it, and part of it's not used at all."

"That's where our water comes from."

Tommy turned six, and would be going to school in the fall.

"Don't you think, Aunt Ellen, that it would be easier for Tommy to go to school if he were in town? We could rent an apartment for you, and I could stay out here –"

"And who would do the dishes?" laughed Aunt Ellen, looking around at the kitchen, once again clean, neat and cozy, with firewood collected with Tommy's help stacked by the woodstove in preparation for the first cold evenings.

"Oh, Aunt Ellen..."

"Annie rode the bus into town, and there were no problems."

So Tommy also rode the bus into town once the school year started.

"I'd like to do something special for Tommy's seventh birthday," said Janet.

"That's not until February," said his grandmother. "But no reason we can't start thinking about it now. A combined birthday and Valentine's Party, maybe?"

"I was thinking," said Janet, "more of a trip to Florida."

"You've got to be kidding," said his grandmother.

"He's smart enough to miss a couple of weeks of school. And it wouldn't be expensive – Mom and Dad have a house on the Keys. You could come along..."

Janet had to admit to herself it sounded pretty lame. She let it drop, but was determined that, when Tommy turned seven, he was going to be off that farm if she had to face kidnaping charges. *There are more things in Heaven and Hell than are dreamt of in your philosophy, Aunt Ellen,* she thought.

5. STAY ON THE FARM: REPRISE

Once upon a time there was an orphan boy named Tommy, who lived with his Grandma and his Aunt Janet on a farm where his grandmother kept the house and garden and his aunt raised goats.

In the normal way of stories of this kind, one would expect Tommy to be mistreated, ragged, and miserable. But, although he was expected to do his share, within his abilities, around the garden and the farm from a very early age, he was not only not mistreated but dearly loved by both his grandmother and his aunt. Indeed, the only point upon which his aunt was unreasonably strict was regarding the south pasture and the creek that ran through it.

"You must *not* play there," his aunt told him many, many times, but Tommy disobeyed her at every opportunity. It was the only point on which he did regularly disobey her, his aunt had to admit.

When Tommy started first grade in town, his good nature recommended him to the other children, and his readiness to learn recommended him to his teacher. His teacher's only worry about Tommy was his imagination, for he insisted that his mother danced and sang and played all day. It was common knowledge among those who remembered her that Tommy's mother was a good singer (a talent which Tommy inherited), but when it came to dancing she had had two left feet, and, as for playing, there had been little enough of that in her short life, poor thing. One hardly knew where she'd found the time to get pregnant.

September became October, and October November, and then it was December, and Tommy had a solo in the Christmas concert.

Tommy's grandmother and his Aunt Janet sat on folding chairs in the school auditorium, through the kindergarten singing "Jingle Bells" and the first grade singing a medley of carols accompanied by triangles, tambourines, blocks and bird whistles. Then Tommy walked out on the stage with a confidence his grandmother thought must be an echo of that displayed by Annie when she had sung Ophelia's songs to her English class. The teacher sounded the key on a pitch-pipe and Tommy began to sing in a clear, true, soprano, his childish voice unhurried and articulating every word.

> *Stay on the farm, boys, stay on the farm,*
>   *Tho' profits come in mighty slow.*
> *Stay on the farm, boys, stay on the farm,*
>   *Don't be in a hurry to go.*
>
> *They talk of the mines of Australia,*
>   *And fortunes are found there, no doubt;*
> *And yet there is gold in the farm, boys,*
>   *If only you'll shovel it out...*

The largely country audience chuckled appreciatively at that, and applauded loudly as Tommy finished.

Please, no encores about St. Valentine's Day, his grandmother prayed silently, and sagged in relief as the concert proceeded through the second, third, fourth and fifth grades' series of skits and medleys to the sixth grade's nativity pageant with no further side-trips into rural morality tales.

"He was supposed to sing this nice Norwegian carol," his teacher explained in some embarrassment after the concert, "but he said he was going to sing his mother's favorite song, and by the time I realized what he was doing..."

"It was certainly his grandfather's," his grandmother said.

"Where did you learn that song?" she asked Tommy on the ride home. But Tommy, after all the excitement, had fallen asleep.

Janet maintained grim silence, but furtively touched the linen handkerchief she had tied over the bandage on her wrist, and remembered a St. Valentine's Day nearly seven years ago. She had never known the words to that song, but she knew the tune, although she hadn't heard it since she'd gone to France. She was determined now to book those plane reservations for Florida as soon as Christmas was over.

Tommy woke when the car stopped in front of the farmhouse. The full moon was so bright the snow crystals sparkled as if from their own inner light, and the crisp snow squeaked underfoot as they walked from the car to the house.

Tommy perched on a chair next to the wood stove while Grandma lit the fire she'd left laid in it and Aunt Janet prepared to heat milk for hot chocolate on the electric stove.

Tires crunched in the driveway, and a minute later Hank Martin knocked on the door and entered.

"Hi, Hank," said Tommy. He liked Hank. Hank sometimes built things for Aunt Janet and let Tommy help. It was nice to have him here tonight.

"That was quite a performance you gave at the concert, young man," said Hank. "Where did you learn that?"

"My mother," said Tommy, but already he knew enough not to expect more than a sympathetic smile at that statement, and a quick change of subject, as now.

"Mom sent over some of her Dundee cake," Hank said.

"It will go well with the hot chocolate," said Janet. "Stay and have some with us."

"Cow's or goat's milk?"

"Cow's. Goat's milk is too valuable to use in hot chocolate."

She poured more milk into the pan, and Hank stood at her shoulder, while Tommy's grandmother sliced the Dundee cake.

Janet was just reaching into the cupboard for the cocoa when once again tires crunched in the driveway, there was another knock on the door, footsteps across the outer porch, and Hector opened the door.

That was good, too, Tommy thought. He liked Hector as well, and so did his mother.

"It's snowing out," said Hector, as if the flakes caught in his toque and on the shoulders of his pea jacket weren't proof enough. He took off his boots and hung his jacket on the porch, and closed the door behind him. "That came up fast – clear as day only half an hour ago. You aren't making that from cow's milk, are you, Janet?"

"She says goat's milk is too good for me," said Hank.

"Well, it is," said Hector.

"We have to help keep the Martins in business," said Janet.

Tommy's grandmother may have wished it was her daughter exchanging frivolities with the two young men rather than her niece, but she did not say so.

Tommy sat up, then stood on the chair so he could see better out the hole that was appearing in the frost on the kitchen window, a dark spot, as if from someone's breath, but the grown-ups were too busy with their banter to notice.

Hector presented a bottle of brandy. "And some of my mother's baklava," he added.

"I knew I should have brought whiskey along with the Dundee cake," Hank grumbled.

Janet reached down the mugs.

Dad's here, thought Tommy.

"You ever had baklava, Tommy?" Hector said, turning toward the wood stove.

The chair beside it was empty.

"Oh, my God," said Janet.

"He's probably just gone upstairs to bed," said his grandmother, even as a draft blew the porch door open.

Snow drifted across the porch floor from the open outside door. The glow of the yard light revealed boy-sized tracks leading away toward where the thornapple tree was just visible through the falling snow. The tracks were already half-covered.

"Seven years," Janet whispered. "Not seven years come St. Valentine's day. It was seven years tonight. December twenty-first! Seven years tonight!"

She ran bare-headed, coatless, to follow the swiftly disappearing tracks. The others pushed through the door and down the steps, where they nearly bumped into Janet.

The snow was now so thick they could barely see the last remains of Tommy's tracks. The various vehicles – Aunt Ellen's car, Hank's pickup truck, Hector's four-wheel drive – loomed dimly a few feet away, the only indication of where the driveway was. Beyond that they could see only curtain after curtain of snow sweeping down from the sky.

They huddled together in the quiet of the night – so quiet they could hear the snow fall – staring into the white.

Out of the snow came Tommy, running like an excited puppy, but before they could grab him, or even yell to him, he vanished again into the white.

Then he was back, grabbing his grandmother's and Aunt Janet's hands, trying to pull them out into the snow even as they tried to haul him up the steps and into the house.

At last he broke away and ran down the drifted lawn, leaving the four adults huddled close together, and, if Hank's arm crept around Janet's shoulders, it may have been just because there was nowhere else for it to go.

As they watched, from out of the snow walked Annie. She wore only the house dress she had worn when she had run from the house seven years ago, but she walked in the swirling snow as if it were a summer breeze.

She looks young, her mother thought. *Younger than I've ever seen her, and that's stupid because she was my baby, you can't get any younger than that, but she looks so young...*

Look at her, Janet thought. *She walks as if she's dancing...*

And Annie walked toward them through the falling snow, with every hair on her head, every thread in her dress, as clearly defined as if the sun shone on them, and she laughed at Tommy dancing around her.

"Annie!" shrieked her mother as summer enveloped them all, and she ran to embrace her daughter.

Then everyone laughed, and cried, and embraced, and only when Annie said, "Don't you think we should get Tommy inside before he catches cold?" did they all realize they were standing outside in a snowstorm, and all were most inadequately dressed.

CODA

And did they all live happily ever after?

"I can dance!" Annie laughed as she sat beside the wood stove, drinking hot chocolate and eating Dundee cake and baklava.

"How did you do that?" asked Janet. "Not learn to dance, I mean. How did you... stay warm?"

"How do you think we all stayed warm, that Valentine's night?"

"I don't know. I guess I was afraid it was Hellfire," said Janet.

"No," said Annie. "It might have been, but not any more. Look."

She undid the handkerchief from around Janet's wrist. There were only clean scars under it. Tommy leaned over and whispered something to his Aunt Janet, who looked at Annie.

"Truly?" she said. "It's been mended?"

"It could always be mended, you know, as long as there was still water to fill it."

"My Dad mended it," said Tommy. "So I could drink from it."

"Annie," said Janet hesitantly, quietly, so the others couldn't hear. "Who is Tommy's father?" But the others did hear, and fell silent as they waited for the answer.

"This farm," said Annie, and they all had to be satisfied with that.

Well," she went on, hugging Tommy, but speaking to Janet. "I'm here. So what do you want to do now?"

"Maybe I'll find another guitar teacher," said Janet. "It's not too late."

"But not until this spring, surely," said Hank, and blushed.

So *did* they live happily ever after?

It's happened before.

New Writings in the Fantastic
Two Double Beds in a Comfort Hotel
Donna Gagnon

The stars have hidden
their fires
Light sees not her black
and deep desires.

Kimmy Beach
Alarum Within

* * * *

This Comes...
three days too late

horoscope, Toronto Star, Monday, November 29, 2004:

Cancer (June 22–July 22)
  Within moments of meeting someone, you find yourself silently, intuitively empathizing. Your inner sensors reach for the best way to echo or mirror the other person. Try your best not to go beyond the call of duty right now. There is a danger of creating an imbalance.

* * * *

Wanting cannot make it so...
this is how it really began -

we arrange to meet inside Theater Books
5:30 Friday night

I was early.
I smiled and said hello to the sales clerk.

I was early.

You were late.

this is how I imagined it would begin -

I enter and walk to my left. Stand in front of a shelf filled with

Canadian plays.

I know that in five minutes a man will push open the door of Theater Books.

He will stand for a moment, look around, get his bearings.

He will not greet the sales clerk

His hooded gray eyes will settle on my back, forming two soft circles of heat on the shoulders of my red wool coat.

The man will walk towards me – I will hear this but will not turn to face him.

I will wait until I feel his breath separate the hairs on the top of my head, I will wait for his hands to circle me from behind.

I will wait for his voice.

Hey...

One lovely rumbling word from his throat that will vibrate into my heart.

The man will bend and touch my neck with his lips.
Only then will I turn and embrace him and lift my face for a kiss
and our two nights and two days will begin.

and this is more of how it really began –

I have placed three candles, a bottle of blackberry Merlot and two wine glasses on a round wooden table in Room 512 at the Comfort Hotel on Charles St. E. The table stands before a wall of windows. I have opened the sheer curtains and allowed thousands of city lights to rain into the room. A nest.

In the drawer between the two double beds, I have placed four condoms.

* * * *

Because you said you wanted to talk

I take you to a bar

I've been here before with my son who's at university

the paint on the walls
begins a pale brown, grows darker, to purple, then to black
as you and I climb three flights of stairs, carrying our little plastic bags of scripts
from Theater Books

we can smoke up here, on the enclosed, heated patio
soon these spaces will be illegal
someone will come and tear away the blue tarp walls, rip out boards, toss detritus into large metal dumpsters in the alleyway below
but tonight there are people and smoke and soft lights and a cute young waiter who smiles and swings his pony tail as he serves us Coors Light in the bottle

I concentrate on the menu
you put your feet up on an empty chair, lean back and light a Number 7, suck on your beer

we talk and you look around and say things like

"You know, I really have a thing for Asian women."

and

"It has to be special... the right place, the right time...

[pause]

I hope the room you've booked has double beds."

I ordered rosie ravioli and more Coors Light. The food was good.
I asked –
"So, why are you here?"
You stared at me and answered –
"Because... you said you wanted to talk."
Stupid.

* * * *

Interlude #1

we got so drunk
three different bars, too much beer

then
I wanted to taste the green olives as you slipped them out of your martini
but you never offered so I watched you bite them off a plastic stick and chew them
and when you swallowed I wanted to kick the plastic chair right out from underneath you
but I remained still and drank more beer

we finally went up to the hotel room and I lit the candles, opened the Merlot, poured and drank some more and I served black pepper pâté on flatbread that was awfully dry and
all we did was talk
until 2am
until I said it was late and blew out the candles you somehow thought had come with the room

I woke at 4am wondering who all the people were in my bed, marveled at the whispering and prodding and thumping that was happening in and around my body, why were my pajamas so itchy, what was cinched so tightly around my belly, who was pounding on my chest making my heart feel like exploding???

You were snoring.

I went for a pee. Went back to bed and cried into my pillow. You were lying on your left side, your shoulders and naked back uncovered, staring me in the face as I lay in my bed across the room. I stared at your skin in the early morning city darkness and thought about wanting something I could not have because I was afraid to move.

In doing nothing things remain...
not correct
but safe.

To get what I want requires action but I do not act 'cause I know the actions to achieve the required result would not be welcomed. The wanting does not stop even though I know that I cannot get what I want because of fear. So, I fall back to sleep after inventing a voice that tells me to stop wanting... or stop being afraid.

* * * *

4:30am Saturday

think about loving him

dream about murder

I could kill him as he sleeps – light a candle and touch it to the sheets –
exit the room as flames lift and grow and crack
and his snoring stops

I could walk through the misty early morning streets of Toronto in November

I could look for a reason
for all of this

* * * *

Driving

we're hung over and
we're late...

traffic heading south on Bay is slow – I turn and turn again and try University
but it's slow, still slow,
it's slow and annoying and there are too many goddamn red brake lights and stop lights and where do all these people come from anyway?

it's Saturday night
curtain's at eight
and we're gonna be late
absolutely no latecomers will be seated

you sit in the pushed-back passenger seat
lost in your silence.
you do not comment on my excessive speed
or my voice as I insert a CD and sing along with Josh Groban

yet I somehow believe you know what I'm thinking

those words I'm too afraid to say

while I speed on the QEW
are inside of you, somewhere

what I don't know
is what the hell you're doing with my words

when they have been swallowed
and digested
then what?

* * * *

Secrets

now the secret's out
you said

someone we both know
has seen us together
in the theater

and I tell you
that there is no secret.
what anyone else thinks
about us together
will most likely be incorrect
anyway
and who cares?

I could tell you
that, having none, I do not believe
in the existence
or the value
of secrets

I would be lying, of course

the truth is
I wish what you and I have done together this weekend
had enough guts within it
to be worthy of being held tight and deep within
someone's breast
guarded zealously with sharp swords and

holy darkness

if only our time together
held something so precious
as a secret...

* * * *

Never Lovers

you don't say it
but I hear this
as we drink Starbucks coffee
on Sunday morning at Yonge & Charles –

we can be friends
yes... that... but
lovers? no, never lovers

I lick eggnog latte foam
out of the corner of my mouth
and talk about the endless
list
of things that must be done
when I get home

oil change and snow tires, appointment with the hairdresser, work on the high-school musical that opens in ten days...

you say
stop making lists
and
finish your coffee

we stare out the window

before we leave
you tell me to go home
and relax

* * * *

Interlude #2

I will write you

throw words onto the page
spit all of this out
get it down, hard ink
denting layers and layers of ruled paper
filling up all of this space
this empty, wasted space
that screams to be filled with
you
and words

until nothing more will fit

until I am worn out, slitty-eyed and covered with sweat

and you are no longer here
no longer real or warm or desirable

just
a
word

one
word

Love

New Writings in the Fantastic
About the Authors

Naomi Alderman was born in London in 1974. She has a BA in Philosophy from Oxford University and an MA in Creative Writing from the University of East Anglia, where she won the David Higham Award. Other awards include the Asham Award and the Writers' Bureau Short Story Prize. In 2004 she was Writer in Residence at the University of Arizona. Her first novel, *Disobedience*, won the Orange Broadband Award for New Writers in 2006 and the *Sunday Times* Young Writer of the Year Award in 2007.

Paul L Bates lives a life of astounding adventure, flies without the use of a cape, and is lord to a host of fearsome clawed and fanged beings that remain docile as kittens around him. He is, however, plagued by the recurring nightmare that he is a construction estimator, spending long tedious hours in a small office counting all manner of things of which most people remain blessedly unaware. His novel *Imprint* is available wherever good books are sold, and his short fiction has appeared in such venues as *Beyond the Last Star*, *City Slab*, *Underworlds*, *Here & Now*, *Zahir* and *Fantasque*. *Dreamer*, the companion/sequel to *Imprint*, is scheduled to appear in 2008.

Greg Beatty has a PhD in English from the University of Iowa, where he wrote a dissertation on serial-killer novels. He attended Clarion West 2000, and any rumors you've heard about his time there are, unfortunately, probably true. He publishes everything from poetry about stars to reviews of books that don't exist.

Bryan Berg was born and raised in Erie, PA. He worked briefly as a telephone-directory proofreader where the most exciting moment came when he caught the misspelling of the word "cemetery." He currently lives in Las Vegas and travels the American Southwest in search of historical sites and ghost towns. His fiction has appeared in *Zodiac Fantastic*, *Pirate Writings*, *Embraces* and other books and magazines. He can found at www.bryanberg.us.

Scott Emerson Bull scribbles his dark tales in the rural charms of Carroll County, Maryland. He's been published in various magazines and anthologies, and his story "Mr. Sly Stops for a Cup of Joe" was selected for 2004's *The Year's Best Fantasy & Horror*. He lives with his wife Deb, his stepkids Kristina and Brennan, and their cat and puppy. They all fear for his sanity. You can reach Scott at his website www.scottemersonbull.com.

John Bushore's genre poetry and short stories have appeared in many magazines and anthologies, both print and internet. He is a two-time winner of the James Award, and was voted one of the top ten internet authors of 2004 in the annual Preditors and Editors Poll. As "MonkeyJohn" he runs a web-page magazine (MonkeyJohn-dot-Banana) where kids can get their work published. His "SpaceMonkey" serial appears in the print magazine *Beyond Centauri*. He has published a children's fantasy poetry book, *What's Under the Bed?*, and a themed anthology of time-travel stories for older kids will be coming out in 2005.

Harry R. Campion was born, raised, lived, works and will some day perish in Michigan; he has lived in Harper Woods for the past eleven years. He discovered his ambition to be a writer thanks to his father's collection of Larry Niven paperbacks and almost decided there was no point in it after reading J.R.R. Tolkien. He has taught high school English at Grosse Pointe South. His writing has won awards from Southwest Writers, The Maryland Writer's Association, The Florida First Coast Writer's Festival, CrossTime and WriteTight.

Paul Finch works primarily in TV and film, but he's no stranger to short-story markets. His first collection, *After Shocks*, won the British Fantasy Award for Best Collection of 2001, and he has had stories in such recent anthologies as *Children of Cthulhu, Quietly Now, Shadows over Baker Street, A Walk on the Darkside* and *Daikaiju (Giant Monster Tales)*. He is a regular contributor to horror and fantasy magazines like *All Hallows, Paradox* and *Supernatural Tales*. The British-made horror movie *Spirit Trap*, which he co-wrote, is due for cinematic release later in 2005.

A retired professional student, **Toiya Kristen Finley** received her PhD in Literature and Creative Writing from Binghamton University in 2003. She now finds herself back in her native wilds of Nashville working as a freelancer of various stuffs. Her fiction and nonfiction have appeared in or are forthcoming in encyclopedias of popular contemporary authors and of science fiction and fantasy, and in *Citizen Culture, The Elastic Book of Numbers, Tales of the Unanticipated, Fortean Bureau, Full Unit Hookup, The Nine Muses, H.P. Lovecraft's Magazine of Horror* and *Under Her Skin: How Girls Experience Race in America*. She is the founding and former managing/fiction editor of *Harpur Palate*. She enjoys watching animated series, movies and sports, and wishes she had more time to play video games.

Donna Gagnon lives in the gorgeous countryside of northeastern Ontario, Canada. Her fiction has appeared in *SmokeLong Quarterly*, Gatto Publishing's *StoriEs* e-anthology and at mystericale.com and is showcased at bewrite.net. Her one-act drama *Deception* appeared at the 2005 Toronto Fringe Festival and the Bancroft Arts Festival. She works with Alex Keegan's Boot Camp, and is currently writing a second one-act drama and an erotic novel.

Derek J. Goodman was born in Wisconsin in 1979. He attended school at the Colourado Institute of Art for a year and a half before leaving to pursue writing. Living once more in Wisconsin, he has had stories published in the magazines *Cthulhu Sex* and *Seasons in the Night*. His short-story collection is *The Voices in My Head Don't Like You*.

Liza Granville was born in Worcestershire and brought up in rural Gloucestershire. She declared herself a writer at the age of six, but life got in the way. She's been a farmer, a builder, a maker of patchwork quilts and a painter; she has bred Persian cats and rare-breed poultry, made cheese, run a wholefood restaurant and catering business, taught English to foreign students, and done innumerable unrewarding jobs to keep body and writing spark together.

In 1998 she graduated from Dartington College of Arts. Subsequently she got an MA in Creative Writing from Plymouth University, and is now halfheartedly tackling a PhD. Her novel *Curing the Pig* is published by Flame Books, and other work has appeared in many magazine and anthologies.

J. Todd Gwinn was born and lives in Spartanburg, South Carolina, where he works in the field of social work with individuals having developmental disabilities. With a background in psychology, he has always been interested in and explored human motivations and perceptions, particularly in regards to the evil men do to each other and why. He has published various stories in e-zines and on websites. "Channel 18" was written about eight years ago and revised countless times: "I'm thrilled and eternally grateful that this 'orphan child' has finally find a home. It never actually fit in with my other psychological horror stories and poetry. I didn't quite intend to make a political statement on the death penalty with it, but rather pose some questions on the role of the media in societal violence and atrocity."

Peter Hagelslag is a sailor who, after traveling around the world on merchant vessels, now works for an offshore company in the Black Sea. A few years ago, he started committing some of his musings to paper. To his utter surprise (English is not his native language; he picked it up on his travels and subsequent reading of tons of paperbacks), he found a couple of US magazines were willing to publish his stories. Look for them in *Intracities: The Journal of Pulse-Pounding Narratives, volume 2* and the Summer 2005 issue of *Apex Science Fiction & Horror Digest*.

Holden Herbert is a creative artist in many fields: sculpture, blues rock and the written word – see www.powerverbs.com/gallery. He's been resolute for many years, as demonstrated by his MFA from UC Berkeley. Oakland, California, has been his home for the last twenty years, during which time he has had careers as a medical researcher, graphic designer and teacher. Currently, he's working on his second novel in the horror genre. He welcomes all inquiries and donations to holden94@sbcglobal.net.

Andrew Hook has had over sixty short stories published over the last ten years, some of which were collected as *The Virtual Menagerie* (Elastic Press, 2002), which was shortlisted for a British Fantasy Society Award. A new collection of stories, *Beyond Each Blue Horizon* is available from Crowswing Books. He is also the author of the novel *Moon Beaver* and other sundry bits of fiction looking to find a home. He lives in Norwich, UK, with his daughter.

Stuart Jaffe's stories have appeared in a variety of print and online magazines as well as in the anthology *Strange Pleasures #3*. In addition, he writes book reviews for *Infinity Plus*. He resides in North Carolina with his wife, son, ten fish, two frogs, three aquatic turtles, three snails, two geckoes and two cats. Despite his best efforts, this list of creatures keeps growing.

Mark Justice lives with his wife and cats in Kentucky, where he hosts a morning radio program. In his rare free time he writes stories, which have appeared (or will soon appear) in *Dark Discoveries, Bare Bone, Damned Nation, Mythos Collector, In Laymon's Terms, Gothic.Net, Horror Carousel* and *Dark Krypt*, among others. He also reviews fiction for *Hellnotes* and edits the Story Station children's fiction site at www.viatouch.com.

Stephen Kilpatrick was born in the North of England in 1971. As well as writing, he has worked as a guitarist and composer since his teens. From 2001 to 2005 he lived in Hungary studying Hungarian music and spent time travelling around Transylvania. The landscape as well as the literary and folktale tradition of these areas have proved to be a valuable source of inspiration in his writing and his music. He is currently teaching music at the University of Salford and working on the first of a series of historical/fantasy/horror novels set in Hungary's dark prehistory.

M.F. Korn has written twelve novels and has published over 235 stories in magazines worldwide. His new paperback, *Swamp Witch Piquante and Scream Queen Bisque*, was released in 2005. Currently available are two paperback collections, *Confessions of a Ghoul and Other Stories* and *Aliens, Minibikes and Other Staples of Suburbia*, and two novels, *Skimming the Gumbo Nuclear* and *Rachmaninoff's Ghost*, as well as a collection of four sf novels, *All the Mutant Trash in All the Galaxies*. He resides in Louisiana as a programmer, and has a daughter, Savannah, who is eight years old. One of his degrees is in Piano Performance. Mike enjoys playing Rachmaninoff, Gershwin, Chopin and ragtime, and listening to requiems. His web page is www.geocities.com/rachmaninoff_70815.

Andrew Magowan lives in Durham, North Carolina, with his wife Abby. When he's not writing he plays eerie soundtrack music with Malt Swagger and brainiac pop music with The Sleepies. When he's not doing any of those things he works as a professional chef in order to pay the bills.

Geoffrey Maloney lives in Brisbane, Australia, with his wife and three young daughters. Since the early 1990s, his short stories have regularly appeared in Australia's leading speculative fiction magazines, as well as in the occasional US and UK publication. He has had over sixty stories published, and his work has been nominated for six Aurealis Awards and regularly appears in the various Year's Best "honorable mention" lists compiled in the US. His "The World According to Kipling" won the Aurealis Award for best fantasy short story in 2001. A mainly retrospective collection of his stories, *Tales from the Crypto-System*, was released by Prime Books in the US in December 2003.

As assistant editor, Geoffrey has just completed work on a new anthology, *The Devil in Brisbane*, with the internationally acclaimed Serbian writer, Zoran Zivkovic.

Thomas Marcinko's stories have appeared in *Interzone*, *Science Fiction Age* and *Rosebud*, on Ellen Datlow's eventhorizon.com, and elsewhere. He has contributed essays to *Creative Screenwriting* and *Asian Cult Cinema*. A graduate of Clarion West, he now lives in Arizona, and is very sorry it turned out to be a red state. His random comments about science, fiction, media, politics, and our current pressing need to establish twin outposts – "foundations," if you will, at opposite ends of Blue America – appear in the blog *Tomorrow's Ancient History Today*.

Gary McMahon lives with his wife and son in West Yorkshire. He has placed stories in magazines such as *Midnight Street*, *Fusing Horizons*,

Bare Bone, Supernatural Tales, All Hallows, Lighthouse, Dark Corners and *Nemonymous*; anthology appearances include *Poe's Progeny, Dark Highways, Dark Sins & Desires Unveiled, Maelstrom Vol I, U-nrestrained K-reations* and *Acquainted With the Night*. His story from *Nemonymous 4*, "My Burglar," received an Honorable Mention in the 2005 edition of the Datlow/Link/Grant *Year's Best Fantasy & Horror*.

Vera Nazarian left the former Soviet Union at the height of the Cold War as an eight-year-old refugee, and arrived in the US a month before her 10th birthday by way of Lebanon, Greece and Italy. As soon as she figured out the English language, she started to write in it, selling her first short story at the age of 17. She has since published numerous works of short fiction in anthologies and magazines such as the *Sword and Sorceress* and *Darkover* series edited by the late Marion Zimmer Bradley, *MZBFM, Talebones, Outside the Box, On-Spec, The Age of Reason, Fictionwise.com, Beyond the Last Star, Strange Pleasures #2* and *Lords of Swords*, and has seen her work on Preliminary Nebula Awards Ballots, honorably mentioned in Year's Best volumes, and translated into seven languages. She made her debut as a novelist with the critically acclaimed *Dreams of the Compass Rose*, which was followed by the epic fantasy *Lords of Rainbow*. Her novella *The Clock King and the Queen of the Hourglass*, with an introduction by Charles de Lint, made the *Locus* Recommended List for 2005. Her latest work includes *The Duke in his Castle*, a lush dark fairytale novella in the vein of the early *contes des fées*, and her first story collection, *Salt of the Air*, with an introduction by Gene Wolfe. In addition to being a writer, Vera is also the owner and publisher of the new independent press Norilana Books (www.norilana.com).

Barbara Nickless sold her first short story to *Pulphouse*, and has since appeared regularly in other magazines and anthologies. She holds a BA in English, with additional degree work in physics, physical anthropology and educational technology. Her interest in other cultures can be seen in her novel *To Each Man an Island*, which won the Colourado Gold Writing Contest for mystery. A classically trained pianist who also teaches, she is currently working on mastering the Hungarian Rhapsody No. 2 by Liszt. During her free time, she likes to read, hike, stargaze and cave. She lives in Colourado with her husband and two children.

Mike Philbin is the man behind the surrealist writing entity Hertzan Chimera R.I.P., who gave us *Szmonhfu* (novel), *United States* (novel), *Animal Instincts* (collection), *Spidered Web* (nonfiction interviews), *Chim+Her* (collaborations), *Chim+Him* (collaborations), the annual

World anthology and website Weird Space's *F*ck Star* series (co-written with M.F. Korn and Alex Severin). He is now relaunching his writing career with a fresh style of writing. Mike will continue to edit future *World* editions. His new novel *Yôroppa* is due in early 2006. See www.mikephilbin.com and mikephilbin.blogspot.com.

Paul Pinn lives in England and is employed in the field of psychiatric healthcare. He has published over 120 short stories in various magazines and anthologies. He has published two novels – *The Pariah* and *The Horizontal Split* – and three story collections: *Idiopathic Condition Red*, *Scattered Remains* and *Black God Fever and Other Sicknesses*. In addition, he has published two poetry collections – *Static Ataxia* and *Anthrax* – and co-wrote *A Rogue's Guide to Psychology*. In 1991 he was an Ian St James Award finalist, and between 1995 and 2001 he received no fewer than 13 Honorable Mentions in the *The Year's Best Fantasy & Horror* anthologies.

Roberto Quaglia is an Italian surrealist-humorist SF writer who divides his life surrealistically between Genoa in Italy and Bucharest in Romania, commuting between the two in a big white Mercedes. His double novel *Bread, Butter and Paradoxine* is available in English, with an introduction by Robert Sheckley, from Delos Books of Milan (www.delos.fantascienza.com). A former bartender, photographer, comic book creator, cultural organizer and surrealist Councillor of the city of Genoa, he is currently Vice-President of the European SF Association. "The Colonoscopy of My Beloved" is one of a series of conceptually linked stories he has co-written with Ian Watson; others have appeared in *Lust for Life*, *Weird Tales*, *Helix* and *Clarkesworld*, and the completed volume – called *The Beloved of the Beloved* – now seeks a brave and demented publisher. His website, "Astounding Quagliaspace: The Strange World of Roberto Quaglia," is at www.robertoquaglia.com.

Steve Redwood was born in the UK, a country he left in his mid-twenties; much of his life since has been misspent pretending to teach in Turkey, Saudi Arabia, and Spain. His humorous fantasy novel *Fisher of Devils* was nominated for the British Fantasy Society's 2003 Best Novel Award, much to the annoyance of his chapbook of short stories, *The Heisenberg Mutation and Other Transfigurations*, which hasn't yet been nominated for anything. A second SF novel, *Who Needs Cleopatra?*, was published in 2005.

He has shared a consulting room with some extremely dubious doctors in the Hugo and World Fantasy Award runner-up *Thackery T. Lambshead Pocket Guide to Eccentric and Discredited Diseases*, cracked a joke or two with assorted pranksters in *The Mammoth Book of New Comic Fantasy*, and trembled fearfully with various frightening creatures in *Darkness Rising 2005*. In addition, about fifty of his short stories have been published in various magazines.

Kate Riedel was born and raised in Minnesota, but has been a card-carrying Canadian for years and years, and now lives in Toronto, Ontario. Previous publication credits include *Not One of Us*, *On Spec*, *Realms of Fantasy* and *Weird Tales*. There are different versions of "Stay on the Farm." The one used here is from the performance of Toronto banjoist Arnie Naiman and his wife Kathy Reid. Arnie was kind enough to confirm to her that the song is in the public domain.

Gavin Salisbury has published stories and poems in a variety of magazines over the last few years. His first novel, *Fade-Out*, will be available from Pendragon Press. His most recent solo publications include *Foreign Parts*, a chapbook of short stories, and *Virtual Landmarks*, a collection of poems.

Vincent L. Scarsella has been an attorney for over twenty-five years, licensed in New York. After a tour in the Navy Judge Advocate General Corps, he prosecuted organized and white-collar crime in the Erie County District Attorney's Office. For the past fifteen years of his legal career, he has been Deputy Chief Counsel in charge of the Attorney Grievance Committee in Buffalo, New York, which investigates complaints of professional and ethical misconduct filed against attorneys practicing in Western New York. Married for twenty-five years, he has three children.

His short story "The Cards of Unknown Players," published in the Fall 2000–Spring 2001 edition of *Aethlon: The Journal of Sports Literature*, was nominated by that journal's editor for the Pushcart Prize. His other baseball-oriented speculative fiction short story, "The Last Natural," was published in the April 2004 edition of *The Leading Edge*. He has published further short stories with the speculative-fiction webzine *Aphelion* (www.aphelion-webzine.com).

E. Sedia lives in Southern New Jersey, in the company of the best spouse in the world, two emotionally distant cats, two leopard geckoes, one paddletail newt and an indeterminate number of fish. To date she has survived drowning in the White Sea, standing in front of a moving tank, and graduate school. Her first novel, *According to Crow*, was published in May 2005, and her short stories have sold to *Analog*, *Lenox Avenue*, *Aeon Magazine* and *Poe's Progeny*, among others. "Alphabet Angels", a story she co-wrote with David Bartell, won *Analog Science Fiction & Fact*'s AnLab Award in 2006.

Craig Sernotti has had poetry appear in *Illumen*, *Poe Little Thing* and *Decompositions*. Fiction has appeared in *The Dream People* and is scheduled to appear in *Mind Scraps*, edited by Nancy Jackson. He is the editor of *Crown of Bones*, an e-anthology of flash fiction. His body resides in New Jersey, but his mind, he says, is "elsewhere, always elsewhere."

A former journalist, **Jamie Shanks** discovered the joys of reading at a very early age. Over the years he has brooded with Achilles in his tent, piloted rockets with the boldest of Bradbury's uniformed space captains, regressed with an amnesiac Tarzan after a plot-advancing crack on the melon, taken a punch with the Continental Op, and battled giant squid upon the hull of the *Nautilus*. Currently he is working on a novella based on a story published serially in the science e-zine *HMS Beagle* in 2001–2. He lives in Saskatchewan with his wife and two young children.

Kim Sheard has a degree in chemistry and works as a technical writer. Her fiction has previously appeared in two of Pocket Books' *Strange New Worlds* anthologies as well as in *Star Trek Voyager: Distant Shores*. Her nonfiction has appeared in *A Cup of Comfort Devotional* and the magazine *Today's Christian*. She lives in Fairfax, Virginia with her husband, Henry, and two dogs.

Lisa Silverthorne has published nearly fifty short stories. She dreams of becoming a novelist, and writes to discover the magic in ordinary things. Much of her inspiration is drawn from the Pacific Northwest and Puget Sound, where she journeys every year to greet the returning Orca whales. Her first short fiction collection, *The Sound of Angels*, will appear this summer from Wildside Press. Her website is at www.drewes.org.

Cyril Simsa was born and brought up in London, has a degree in zoology, and has worked as a librarian, as a museum curator, and as the map editor of the new centenary facsimile of *Domesday Book*. Since 1992 he has lived in Prague, where he runs student exchange programs for Charles University. He has contributed reviews and articles to a wide variety of genre publications (*Foundation*, *Locus*, *The Encyclopedia of Fantasy* and others). His stories have appeared in *Weird Tales*, *Darkness Rising*, *Here & Now*, *Ideomancer*, *Fantasy Tales* and *Central Europe Review*. He has also published translations of works by Czech writers.

Hugh Spencer has lived in Toronto since 1982. His work includes the short stories "Why I Hunt Flying Saucers," "The Progressive Apparatus" and "... And the Retrograde Mentor," all of which have been subsequently dramatized by Shoestring Radio Theatre for the Satellite Network of National Public Radio. His original miniseries *Amazing Struggles, Astonishing Failures and Disappointing Success* was also performed by SRT. His latest radio play, *21st Century Scientific Romance*, is scheduled for broadcast in 2005.

Hailing from Hollywood, now in North Hollywood, **Greg Story** is a well traveled writer whose works may be found in such publications as *Agony in Black, Black October, Hadrosaur Tales, Penumbric, Permutations: The Journal of Unsettling Fiction, Scared Naked, These Thirteen* and *Zahir*. Postings of his stories also occasionally appear at Horrorfind.com, WildChild.com, TavernWench.com and Bloodlust-UK.com.

Edd Vick's short stories have been published by *Asimov's SF, Electric Velocipede* and *Antipodean SF*, as well as in the anthologies *Distant Planes* and *Fundamentally Challenged*. He is the publisher of MU Press and its imprint AEON, producing volumes of work by Donna Barr, Matt Howarth, and many others since 1989. He is a 2002 graduate of the Clarion SF writing workshop, and works for an adoption agency by day.

Ian Watson taught in universities in Tanzania, Japan and Birmingham, UK, before becoming a full-time SF writer three years after the publication of his award-winning first novel *The Embedding* in 1973. To date he has published thirty novels – most recently *Mockymen* (2003); his 10th story collection, *Butterflies of Memory*, appeared in Fall 2005 from PS Publishing. By now he has written about 150 short stories. From 1990 to 1991 he worked eyeball to eyeball with Stanley Kubrick on *A.I.: Artificial Intelligence*, subsequently directed by Steven Spielberg, for which he has screen credit for screen story. His first collection of poetry, *The Lexicographer's Love Song*, appeared in 2001 from DNA Publications; he has won a Rhysling Award for his SF poetry. His books have been translated into about 16 languages. He lives in a little village in South Northamptonshire, England, with his black cat Poppy. His website (with fun photos!) is at www.ianwatson.info.

New Writings in the Fantastic
Other Books Available from
www.pendragonpress.co.uk
(or your local bookshop by quoting the ISBN)

Nasty Snips edited by Christopher C Teague
(0 9536833 0 3; £5.99)

Shenanigans by Noel K Hannan
(0 9538598 0 0; £6.99)

The Ice Maiden by Steve Lockley & Paul Lewis
(0 9538598 1 9; £4.99)

The Extremist and Other Tales of Conflict by Paul Finch
(0 9538598 2 7; £4.99)

The Mask Behind the Face by Stuart Young
(0 9538598 3 5; £4.99)

Double Negative by Robin Gilbert
(0 9538598 4 3; £7.99)

In the Rain with the Dead by Mark West
(0 9538598 5 1; £7.99)

An Occupation of Angels by Lavie Tidhar
(0 9538598 6 X; £4.99)

Triquorum One
(0 9538598 7 8; £5.99)

At the Molehills of Madness by Rhys Hughes
(0 9538598 8 6; £7.99)

Rough Cut by Gary McMahon
(0 9538598 9 4; £6.99)

Dalton Quayle Rides Out by Paul Kane
(978 0 9554452 2 4; £5.99)

New Writings in the Fantastic

Coming Soon

No-Man and Other Tales
by
Tony Richards

The Reef
by
Mark Charan Newton

Kingston to Cable
by
Gary Greenwood

New Writings in the Fantastic

The British Fantasy Society exists to promote and enjoy the genres of fantasy, science fiction and horror in all its forms. We are well supported by the publishing industry and have many well known authors among our members, not least our president, Ramsey Campbell, who says: "This is an invitation to you to join the community of the fantastic. Many years ago, when I was a struggling writer and a vociferous fan, I tried to convince people that we admirers of fantasy needed a society to bring us together for fun and for sharing our ideas, and I don't know of a better such organisation than the British Fantasy Society..."

We hold regular Open Nights which are open to all, not just our members, and these are listed on our website, http://www.britishfantasysociety.org.uk, as well as in our bi-monthly news magazine, *Prism*. We also publish a bi-annual fiction magazine, *Dark Horizons*. Once a year, we hold our main convention, FantasyCon, an event that is always well attended by known and unknown alike. Recent Guests of Honour include Clive Barker, Neil Gaiman, Raymond E. Feist, Juliet E. McKenna, Robert Holdstock, Steven Erikson, not to mention our president, Ramsey Campbell.

Subscriptions: £25 (UK), £30 (Europe), £45 (Rest of World) p.a. Membership entitles you to six free issues of Prism, two of Dark Horizons, and free copies of all BFS Special Publications, also discounted attendance at BFS events. Cheques should be made payable to: British Fantasy Society, The British Fantasy Society, 36 Town End, Cheadle, STAFFS, ST10 1PF England. Or you can join online at the BFS Cyberstore: http://www.britishfantasysociety.org.uk/shop/info.htm